Arab-Israeli Military/Political Relations

(Pergamon Policy Studies—25)

Pergamon Policy Studies on International Politics

PERGAMON
POLICY
STUDIES
ON INTERNATIONAL POLITICS

Arab-Israeli Military/Political Relations
Arab Perceptions and the Politics of Escalation

John W. Amos II

Pergamon Press

NEW YORK • OXFORD • TORONTO • SYDNEY • FRANKFURT • PARIS

Pergamon Press Offices:

U.S.A.   Pergamon Press Inc., Maxwell House, Fairview Park, Elmsford, New York 10523, U.S.A.

U.K.   Pergamon Press Ltd., Headington Hill Hall, Oxford OX3 0BW, England

CANADA   Pergamon of Canada, Ltd., 150 Consumers Road, Willowdale, Ontario M2J, 1P9, Canada

AUSTRALIA   Pergamon Press (Aust) Pty. Ltd., P O Box 544, Potts Point, NSW 2011, Australia

FRANCE   Pergamon Press SARL, 24 rue des Ecoles, 75240 Paris, Cedex 05, France

FEDERAL REPUBLIC Pergamon Press GmbH, 6242 Kronberg/Taunus,
OF GERMANY   Pferdstrasse 1, Federal Republic of Germany

Library of Congress Cataloging in Publication Data

Amos, John W   1936-
     Arab-Israeli political/military relations.

     (Pergamon policy studies)
     Includes index.
     1.   Jewish-Arab relations—1967-1973.   2.   Israel-Arab
War, 1967—Influence and results.   3.   Israel-Arab War,
1973—Influence and results.   4.   Arab countries—
Politics and government.   5.   Arabs—Psychology.
I.   Title.
DS119.7.A665   1979   327.5694'017'4927   78-31869
ISBN 0-08-023865-3

This work was completed with a number of colleagues and students from the Naval Postgraduate School. Many of the ideas herein were clarified with their intellectual insight and criticism. It follows of course that any errors or shortcomings are solely the author's. In addition, it should be made clear that the views expressed are those of the author and do not in any way represent the opinion or policy of either the Naval Postgraduate School or the U.S. Navy.

To my wife, who does not approve of wars

Contents

Note on Transliteration

NOTE ON TRANSLITERATION

Normally the rendering of Arab words follows their actual written nomenclature. There are, however, a number of exceptions to this practice because of the multiplicity of sources used:

(a)   Names of persons or places that occur in translations are spelled as they occur in the original source. For example, "Nasir" is usually rendered "Nasser" in Western sources.

(b)   The names of authors footnoted are spelled as they are set down in the title of the book or article. This may differ from their spelling in the text.

(c)   Place names that have generally accepted spelling in the West are so rendered. For example, Golan instead of al-Jawlan.

(d)   Certain Arab proper names that have been anglicized are so spelled.

(e)   Some Arabic names or terms which have doubled consonants have been shortened because the doubling of these consonants confuses the Western eye: al-Qadhafi, for example, rather than al-Qadhdhafi.

(f)   Although Arabic does not utilize capital letters, proper nouns have generally been capitalized in conformity with English usage.

(g)   The silent "h" on some nouns has not been transliterated: al-sa'iqa, for example, rather than al-Sa'iqah.

List of Abbreviations

ALF	Arab Liberation Front (Iraq)
al-Sa'iqa	Shock Forces (Egypt)
al-Sa'iqa	The Thunderbolt: Vanguards of the Popular War of Liberation (Syria)
ASU	Arab Socialist Union (Egypt)
Ba'th	Arab Socialist Renaissance Party (Syria and Iraq)
BSO	Black September Organization
Fatah	Palestine National Liberation Movement
Frolinat	Front for the Liberation of Chad
IDF	Israeli Defense Forces
OAU	Organization of African Unity
PDF	Popular Democratic Front for the Liberation of Palestine
PDRY	People's Democratic Republic of Yemen (South Yemen)
PFLOAG	Popular Front for the Liberation of Oman and the Arabian Gulf

PFLP   Popular Front for the Liberation of Palestine

PLA   Palestine Liberation Army

PLO   Palestine Liberation Organization

Polisario   Popular Front for the Liberation of Sequia
                        el-Hamra and Wadi al-Dhahab

RCC   Revolutionary Command Council (Egypt)

UAE   United Arab Emirates

UAR   United Arab Republic (Syria and Egypt,
                        1958-1961, but usually refers to Egypt
                        alone)

UNEF   UN Emergency Force

UNDOF   UN Disengagement Observer Force

The Israeli Army defeated militarily the Arab armies in 1967. If the enemy withdrew without a fight, this constitutes, in my opinion, the greatest insult to Arab militarism, because the enemy who stripped us of our land by force, insulted our pride....and desecrated our shrines, should not, under any condition, get out without punishment....

> Mustafa Talas Armed Struggle Facing the Israeli Challenge 1972

So let us together regain the glory of Arabism and prove to the whole world that we are men of war, who either live proudly or die honorably....

> Sa'ad al-Din Shadhili Address to Arab Chiefs of Staff Conference November 1971

You should know that we are facing an enemy that is beginning to set little store by us, thinking we are not capable of fighting, which makes him rampage in the region without fear of being repelled or punished....

> Ahmad Isma'il 'Ali Directive to the Egyptian Armed Forces October 1972

It doesn't matter if the Israelis eventually counterattack and drive us back. What matters is that the world will no longer laugh at us when we threaten to fight. No longer will it dismiss our threats as a lot of bluff and bluster. It will have to take us seriously.

> Arab Journalist October 1973

1

A Perspective
on October 1973:
Arabs, Israelis,
and War

This is a study of the escalatory patterns of Arab-Israeli relations. As such it is concerned with the preconditions, conditions and ultimate precipitants of wars (conflicts characterized by increasing intensity and scope) which have broken out with some repetitiveness in the Middle East. In addition, it is concerned with the impact of the latest of these wars, the October 1973 War, on the United States interests in the Middle East.

The October War, known as the Yom Kippur War, or the War of the Day of Judgment (1) in the West, and the Ramadan War in Arab countries, contained in its brief duration a good many surprises. The armed forces of Egypt and Syria were able to organize and execute an attack which achieved near complete strategic and tactical surprise. These forces then conducted themselves during the conflict with an unexpectedly high degree of discipline and determination. Throughout the war Arab governments inaugurated and carried out a coordinated diplomatic and economic policy vis-a-vis Western nations; a policy whose sophistication in concept and implementation was likewise completely unexpected.

The 1973 War will no doubt be studied for years to come and its various aspects analyzed from different perspectives. Studies of the war have multiplied and range from highly technical accounts of the military aspects to emotional assessments of the war's political impact. (2) However, even granting the existence of this literature, some attempt should be made to put it in historical and political perspective. This war marks a significant alteration, even a reversal, from commonly accepted ideas of Arab political/military behavior in the following respects.

Arab governments initiated large-scale military action against Israeli forces. In all previous wars (1948, 1956, and 1967) Arab forces responded (unsuccessfully) to Israeli initiatives. In 1956 and 1967 especially, Arab forces were in defensive positions, dug into static emplacements with few units deployed for offensive purposes. In each

1

case these forces were overwhelmed by Israeli units utilizing the tactics of surprise and mobility.

In 1973 the governments of Egypt and Syria coordinated an attack, forcing the Israelis to fight a two-front war. In all previous conflicts Arab countries operated without any apparent cooperation. This allowed the Israelis to defeat them on a sequential basis, and permitted the Israelis to exploit their interior lines by rapidly mobilizing and sequentially concentrating forces against selected Arab units.

In 1973, Egypt and Syria managed to conceal their true purpose in building up forces along Israeli borders. Their attack was launched swiftly and with preponderant advantage in forces deployed along the ceasefire lines. In previous engagements, especially in 1967, Arab communications security was remarkably ineffective. The Israelis were able to gather extremely accurate intelligence concerning the deployment and probable missions of Arab forces. This gave them sufficient warning and time to mobilize their reserves and to attack under conditions of advantage.

In 1973, Arab forces aggressively attacked Israeli units, in many cases voluntarily taking heavy casualties, and maintained a surprisingly high level of discipline. In all previous conflicts Arab military units (with some exceptions, notably Jordan's Arab Legion) broke off contact with Israeli units after relatively brief exchanges of fire. During the 1967 War, in particular, some Egyptian and Syrian units either retreated or surrendered to Israeli forces without offering significant resistance.

In 1973, a considerable degree of political/diplomatic coordination between Arab governments, combatant and noncombatant, was effected. A coordination that was all the more impressive because of the obvious disarray of Western governments against whom it was directed. The heretofore dominant pattern had been that of each Arab government seeking its own interests without seeming to concern itself with the problems of its allies. Until the 1973 oil embargo, Arab oil stoppages had been both short lived and piecemeal, broken as the interests of each Arab government dictated. (3)

During the course of the 1973 conflict, Arab reportage of military actions was remarkable (relative to earlier war reportage) for its accuracy and low keyed approach. Instead, the Israelis produced the bombast with early statements by high officials to the effect that the Israeli forces were going to "crush the bones" of Arab armies, or that Arab forces were retreating everywhere, etc., etc. In the three earlier wars the Arab media was noted for its semihysterical threats and anti-Western statements, its incredible inaccuracies, and its general lack of touch with reality. (4)

In sum, then, the 1973 War presents a change from previous Arab behavior, both military and political. It is thus a difficult problem for Western analysts. How did numbers of Arabs, elite and mass, manage to alter their behavior to an unexpected, even incredible extent? What are the implications of this newfound ability to control heretofore semi-anarchic behavior? What are the longterm consequences of the 1973 War? Does it represent a permanent shift in Arab-Israeli, intra-Arab, and Arab-Western power relationships? Or is it an aberration on an existing pattern of relations? What about Soviet-United States strategic considerations in the Middle East: does the 1973 War open or foreclose opportunities for the United States to move into the Middle East and blunt a trend of Soviet penetration? This work will address itself to these considerations within the framework of three specific issues:

a) What factors led Egyptian and Syrian leaders to decide to attack, and what were their strategic and tactical goals?

b) How were Arab military operations conducted during the course of the war, and, more importantly, what was the Arab assessment of these operations?

c) What are the wider political and military implications of the war with specific reference to super power interests?

SCOPE OF RESEARCH

The original intent was to focus as closely as possible on the events of October and November 1973, and within this time to limit investigation to:

a) Those Arab states actually involved in the war, especially Egypt and Syria.

b) Those Arab states having geographical access to either the Mediterranean or Indian Oceans, including the oil producing states.

Almost at once, however, it became apparent that any assessment of the 1973 War would require some coverage of prior years. In particular, events in Egypt and Syria would need examination from 1971 onward - especially if the complex factors which led to the decision to risk an attack on Israeli forces were to be understood. Moreover, in reading Egyptian commentary concerning the conduct and assessment of the 1973 War it became rapidly clear that the Egyptians were self consciously contrasting their behavior in 1973 with that of 1967. Therefore, some attention had to be paid to the June 1967 War, especially as this war seemed to be the source of those perceptions which influenced Arab strategy in 1973.

Although the October War is the critical event, what has emerged is a much broader study, one focused on recurring patterns of escalation rather than being exclusively concerned with a single war. In this context, a number of themes have emerged and been touched on in varying degrees. First and foremost, it would appear that the periodic escalation of Arab-Israeli tensions into full scale conflict is the product of a complex interaction pattern: a pattern in which local conflicts are linked with external intra Arab conflicts, linkages which are in turn embedded in a system of perceptions oriented around images of self and others as being locked in continuous conflict of varying levels of intensity. Second, this Arab interaction pattern is characterized by a discontinuousness, a lack of predictability that seems to invite, almost require, ultra sensitivity to threats on the part of local decision makers. Perhaps more than anything else the combination of systematic unpredictability and perceptual sensitivity to threats provides an independent factor in contributing to periodic escalations. Third, there is an emerging Arab ability to analyze and then learn from past mistakes. An ability which extends to the assessment of Western perceptions and expectations concerning Arab behavior, and then to the development of strategies designed to play into these misperceptions for Arab advantage. An ability that adds even more uncertainty to the Middle Eastern escalatory equation because it limits the applicability of analyses of Arab behavior based on assumptions concerning its repetitiveness, hence the problems connected with the so-called "intelligence failure." (5) Finally, although goals, strategies, tactics and even personnel may change, these larger escalatory configurations seem to have remained relatively permanent.

A NOTE ON ARABIC SOURCE MATERIAL

Major portions of the data utilized in this study were drawn from Arabic sources, either directly or in various translations. Since one of the major concerns is that of the nature of Arab perceptions of events, this source material is invaluable. And it should be stressed, that the "reality" with which this study deals is that of the perceptions themselves. Whether Arab accounts, images or interpretations of events are objectively "true" or not is beside the question here. The perception is the reality. Therefore some of the Arab reportage of the October War which is clearly at variance with Western reportage is used as an indicator of Arab imagery, not of what actually may have happened. The advantage, therefore, of using Arabic source materials lies in this fact. And to the extent that this media presentation coincides with actual perceptions and views of Arab decision makers, it provides additional insight into the Arab decision making process.

However, the utilization of Arabic source material presents a number of problems. The most obvious one is that of adequate translation. The Arabic language is remarkably developed in its ability to project nuances of behavior and subtleties of meaning - subtleties which can be expressed either by vocabularly or by grammatical construction. Fortunately, a political dialogue is not carried on in rarified terminology or classical linguistic usage. Newspaper Arabic is a simplified version of the classical language, and radio and television dialogues are carried on (with the exception of Qur'anic broadcasts) in local dialects which also are relatively straightforward in vocabulary and grammar. Nevertheless, technical problems posed by translation remain.

A more basic problem than that posed by the mechanical difficulties of translation, however, is that of determining the concrete meaning that lies behind the idiosyncracies of Arab political discourse. Arab techniques of handling information have an inner logic of their own which is alien to Western minds. (6)   To the Westerner, Arab communication patterns seem overloaded with histrionics, unnecessary invective, and a conspiratorial world view.   They have an emotive quality which appears out of keeping with the actual subject matter, and a resort to ad hominem attack that would bring a torrent of libel suits in the West.   For instance, during the latter part of 1976 the Egyptian press referred to Libya's al-Qadhafi as the "lunatic" or "madman" of Libya. Libyan media responded by describing Al-Sadat as the "hashish eater of Cairo." Take these exchanges from the Egyptian press, for example, one directed at al-Qadhafi, the other aimed at Syria's al-Asad:

> What does Libya's lunatic and idiotic Colonel want. He must have lost his mind when he sent a man to Cairo with two explosive charges to plant them into the water closets of an administrative building which resulted in the injury of innocent peaceful citizens. (7)

> The merchants of political prostitution in Damascus are claiming in their official statements that they are the protectors of the Palestinian people and the guardians of the Palestinian resistance, while at the same time the resistance leaders are declaring to the whole world that the Syrian crime of liquidating the resistance continues .... So what are the merchants of political prostitution in Damascus saying? .... (8)

In addition, Arab political rhetoric is constantly full of references to war (harb) or crisis ('azama). These terms occur regularly in speech or print. So regularly in fact that they lose their original ominous meaning with over exposure.   For this reason, if no other, it is extremely difficult to calculate the real intent of the communicator, or to judge the seriousness with which any given bellicose statement should be viewed. Therefore, a considerable debate has arisen over the credibility to be attached to Arab utterances (some of this debate is summarized in the following chapter). As if this were not enough, when a carefully orchestrated disinformation strategy is added, it becomes next to impossible to identify any indicators of intent. (9)   The problem of picking up relevant "signals" under these conditions is mind-boggling.
A critical case in point is the assessment of Egyptian President al-Sadat's repeated threats to undertake some military action in the Sinai. These threats were made in almost all of his public statements and in a series of interviews - most notably with <u>Newsweek</u> editor Arnaud de Borchgrave - as well.   They were echoed by various Egyptian commentators and military figures. They began with the declaration that 1971 was to be the year of decision. This declaration was repeated so often, with no effect, that it eventually led to a standing joke in Egypt that since al-Sadat couldn't make a decision, he extended the

year instead. (10) President al-Sadat's goals in making, or authorizing, these threats were probably some combination of:

a) An attempt to play for time at home by giving the appearance of doing something about the Israeli occupation of the Sinai, and thus countering an escalating domestic unrest.

b) A parallel move to draw Western attention to the gravity of the situation in the hope that the U.S. in particular would be moved to pressure to withdraw.

c) An effort to retain Egyptian leadership in the Arab world in the face of mounting pressure from both the Libyans and radical Palestinians.

d) To prepare public opinion within Egypt for some resumption of fighting, if all else should fail.

However, in a postwar address delivered in Alexandria on April 3, 1974, al-Sadat stated that the initial decision to go to war was made in the previous April. (11)   Yet Egyptian media continued to grind out roughly the same hard line throughout the rest of 1973; that some major military confrontation was inevitable unless something was done about the Israeli occupation; that the Egyptians were determined to act; that Western interests would inevitably suffer. By continuing these threats al-Sadat must have been aware of the dangers involved. Israelis tend to take such utterances seriously and to respond accordingly. If al-Sadat were really intent on launching some sort of surprise attack, it would hardly behoove him to warn the Israelis in advance. Moreover, he had the unhappy experience of the 1967 War before him: a war in which the Egyptians isolated themselves from world opinion by just such a series of threats, and provided the Israelis with sufficient excuses to justify a preemptive attack. In al-Sadat's mind, the benefits, both domestic and foreign, of this policy must have outweighed its potential cost of alerting the Israelis.

Nevertheless, after April 1973, al-Sadat's statement predicting an Egyptian military move became an actual statement of intent.   The astonishing fact is that al-Sadat and other Egyptian officials kept pronouncing this intention to move militarily almost to the very week of the attack.   On September 1, 1973, 'abd al-Quddus, the principal editorial spokesman for al-Sadat, argues in an Akhbar al-Yawm editorial that some form of military initiative was necessary to preempt a Kissinger sponsored Israeli attack. (12)   On September 21, 1973, al-Nahar carried a report that Egypt had informed Palestinian groups that some military action across the canal was forthcoming.   (13) On September 28, al-Sadat, himself, in an address to the Arab Socialist Union Central Committee made this oblique pronouncement:

When we want to open the Suez Canal, I need not ask for permission of Israel or the United States to open the Suez Canal. The Suez Canal existed before Israel existed and it will remain Egyptian, in Egyptian land, and by Egyptian will...(applause). (14)

This behavior raises a series of questions. Were these statements part of a sophisticated disinformation strategy - continuing business as usual so that no change in behavior would be noticed? Were they a last ditch attempt to get Western intervention and thus avoid the necessity for going to war? Were they entirely unconnected with upcoming military action, the result of simply not informing highly placed Egyptian media personnel? Or was this verbal behavior inertial, a habitual and ingrained pattern of rhetoric, or a phenomenon of the linguistic idiosyncracies of the Arabic language?

In addition to the problems of interpreting, in both a literal and figurative sense, the verbiage of the Arab media, there are a number of other issues. Arab media tend to be problematic because of several localized factors:

a) With the partial exception of the Lebanese press, the various Arab medias are subject to relatively stringent censorship, or as it is sometimes termed, "guidance". Arab governments, especially since the 1967 debacle, have been extremely concerned with image projection. Information deemed unfavorable to this desired self image, or to that of some preferred intra-Arab political environment is ruthlessly excised. The result is a sort of "non-news" wherein local or international trivia is covered in detail, but where reportage of significant political development is either missing or is so vague in particulars as to be useless. Because of this emphasis on image projection, elite intentions are usually masked behind more or less standard ideological stances: pan-Arabist-Socialist in the case of Egypt, Syria and Iraq; Islamic-Conservative in that of Saudi Arabia, Jordan, and Kuwayt. (15)

b) Even where ubiquitous censorship is not an issue, standards of reportage vary from the responsible to the mischievous. Many "news" items are produced clearly for effect, rather than for information. Moreover, the Arab media have a highly developed conspiratorial outlook, and this tendency is particularly acute in respect to reportage of rumors concerning political upheavals. Where it is not censored or otherwise manipulated, Arab journalistic practice is preeminently in the yellow journalism tradition (with some notable exceptions).

c) Arab media are embedded in, and project, a complex sociocultural system. For a variety of historical, political, and religious reasons the Middle East is a mosaic of ethnic, sectarian, and linguistic groups - not to mention political divisions. These communal groupings provide the substructure of Arab politics, and their viewpoints are represented in the Arab press. This is particularly the case of the Lebanese press.

d) In addition, most, if not all, of the media have pronounced political leanings, and these are given full sway on otherwise ordinary news reportage. Lebanon until the imposition of censorship by Syrian forces in 1976 and 1977 has had the maximum press freedom. With the exception of the Syrian insistence on restricting news commentary, there has been no official press censorship, aside from ad hoc military censorship. And even in the case of military restrictions, usually applied in the context of intense domestic crisis, censorship has met with vigorous objection, and has not been especially effective. (16) In the aftermath of the Syrian occupation in 1976, however, many Lebanese papers and periodicals closed down. Others, however, moved their editorial staffs elsewhere, France or Cyprus for example, and continued printing, albeit on a reduced scale.

Politically, Lebanese media are restrained from publishing derogatory material concerning the heads of Arab governments by an ordinance, known as the "Law of Kings and Presidents." This law was designed to spare the Lebanese government any diplomatic repercussions of exuberant Lebanese press treatment of political issues in the Arab world. This exuberance bordered at times upon anarchy since almost every illegal party, splinter group, sectarian organization, or disaffected intellectual published in Beirut. (17)

In addition, regular Arab governments have established working relations with various Lebanese publications, and utilize them either to defend their own policies or attack those of opponents. (18) For this reason alone, the source of information in the Lebanese press, whether right or left wing, is critical. The appendix to this study contains a rough classification of Lebanese sources according to their political and other orientations.

Syria, Iraq, and Egypt have tightly controlled media, as might be expected. The Syrian and Iraqi media faithfully reflect the official line of the dominant Ba'th party faction in each state. Egyptian media are more complex. All publications are subject to censorship by the Ministry of Culture and Information, and news of domestic unrest is not reported until it becomes too difficult to conceal. However, within the general political and ideological framework imposed by the government, differences of opinion are expressed. These differences have their origin in the organizational division of Egyptian media among several large publishing houses, each with its own staff tradition of reportage. (19) Intra elite criticism can be expressed within limits: Muhammad Hassanayn Haykal was dismissed as editor of al-Ahram in 1974 following al-Ahram's publication of a series of attacks on al-Sadat's conduct of the war, and his acceptance of a cease-fire. (20) But this was done only after considerable provocation.

Jordan, Saudi Arabia, and Kuwayt likewise control their respective press establishments, although the Kuwayt press is relatively open in comparison to that of the former states. Each has a Press Law which enables the government in question to shut down offensive media. In Jordan and Saudi Arabia, additional control is ensured by the use of joint stock companies with governmental participation: government representatives sit on the various boards of directors, and the editorship of newspapers is subject to governmental control (much like the Egyptian system). (21)

LEVELS OF ANALYSIS: WAR, THEORY AND HISTORIOGRAPHY

Donna Devine in her brief summary of literature on the October War suggests that explanations of the War fell into one of four categories:

a) Theories which focus on the cultural antecedents; psychological theories that stress the role of honor in driving Arab leaders to a decision for war. Indeed, as will be seen, Arab concern to regain what was perceived as a lost honor did play a significant place in the decision making process.

b) Theories which analyze the decision for war as the product of systemic forces, forces flowing from intra Arab and even international power constellations which constrained Arab leaders to the point where war became the only option. Likewise, these systemic factors can be and are in fact demonstrated by the material which follows.

c) Theories which stress super power influence, in this case, that of the USSR. Here again, it is possible to make an argument that the USSR by original arms transfers prior to October and by its resupply efforts during October did provide the capability for the Arab attack. (22)

d) To the foregoing, Devine then adds her own analysis which focuses on the domestic component. She argues, using Graham Allison's models of decision making, (23) that the Egyptian decision for war was the product of a combination of rational calculation, interest accommodation and bureaucratic or organizational politics.

The data seem to bear any and all of these interpretations out. The October War has thus been analyzed on three levels: at the most generalized, the level of Arab/Islamic culture (a); at a less generalized, level, that of the international or intraArab system (b and c); and at the lowest level, that of local Arab politics (d). (24)

Theoretically speaking, these levels provide a structure for the analysis of Arab politics or Arab-Israeli relations, but they do not necessarily supply a theory of the dynamics of Arab decision making behavior. To supply these dynamics two other variables have been added: images and strategy. Image analysis seeks to delineate the perceptual environment in which Arab decision makers operate. (25) Its theoretical rationale is the notion that a decision maker's image of his environment is the cognitive operationalization of that environment; and that these images or perceptions are the ultimate determinant of decisions. In this sense, the image provides the linkage between the constraints identified in terms of other levels of analysis.

The concern with statements of Arab strategy carries image analysis one step further by focusing on articulated responses to images and environment. A strategy is merely a self conscious pattern of decision making, an identification of environmental constraints, a statement of policy goals, and a set of decision making paradigms for matching goals with constraints. Here the more abstract and conceptual models of Arab decision making are brought down to very concrete historical and geographical concerns: the Egyptian strategy for a limited war, and the apparently excessive caution of Egyptian generals make sense if one

takes into account the fact that these same generals had seen an
Egyptian army destroyed in the Sinai seven years earlier.   These
generals were well aware of the shortcomings of their troops and
armament and they were careful to tailor their military strategy to
take these shortcomings into account.   Moreover, the givens of the
military environment were permanently set by the geography and
topology of the battlefield: there are only three major routes across
the Sinai, and there are only a couple of access points to the Golan
Heights.   Actual warfare in the Middle East follows land routes which
have been used for centuries; all three wars in the twentieth century
have been fought over roughly the same terrain.   Strategy, then,
whether political or military, or a blend of both, is concerned with
generating and applying valuable resources within this concretely
defined compass. (26)

The concern with strategy leads, however, to another issue: the role
of historiography.   In the context of Arab-Israeli relations, historiography has taken on an enormous political and military significance.
The way history is written, the style of explanation used, the "lesson"
drawn from each major confrontation becomes a critical factor in
shaping future patterns of response.   Historiography is used in a number
of ways, and in a very sophisticated fashion by all sides to the Arab-
Israeli conflict.   At the simplest level, historiography is merely a
technique for writing, or rewriting, history to defend one's past
decisions or actions.   In the Arab world, for example, the history of the
1967 war is completely different from that which appears in Western
sources.   The reason for this is that the Arab leaderships caught up in
this overwhelming defeat had, of necessity, to find some interpretation
which would allow them to maintain themselves in power.

Beyond this overtly apologetic usage, historiography serves two
other functions: first as a technique to discover, and as a statement of
the actual conclusions deduced from past wars; second as an exercise in
disinformation, a statement of the lessons that one wants an opponent
to think one has learned, lessons which, when analyzed by the opponent
and internalized into his strategy, will lead him to the wrong response.
An illustration of this is the "lesson" drawn by Arab military strategists
concerning the supposed necessity for air superiority: A lesson which
was correct enough at the outset, and one picked up by Israeli
strategists, and in turn, worked into what was called the "conception," a
theory that Arabs would not attack unless they were somehow assured
of air superiority. (27) In fact, Arab strategists actually turned this
lesson around and came to the conclusion that an air defense system
capable of seriously interfering with Israeli low level tactical air
bombardment was sufficient for a limited war.

Even beyond this, the resort to historiography complicates the task
of analyzing future Arab-Israeli scenarios.   The Arab sources and the
Egyptians in particular, have put a great deal of energy into promoting
an interpretation of the events leading up to the October War as the
unfolding of a superbly calculated and rational plan for altering the
existing Arab-Israeli stalemate.   It is natural that they should do this,
the canal crossing operation clearly ranks as one of the major military

feats of the twentieth century.   The political accompaniament and follow-up was an incredibly bold and imaginative diplomatic initiative. But to characterize this, as contemporary Egyptian interpretations do, as the smooth unrolling of a gigantically conceived strategy is an overstatement.   Such an interpretation misleads by its emphasis on rationality and control: future Arab-Israeli escalations are as much a product of spasm response to gut feelings as they are to the rational calculation of deterrence theories.   To reduce or eliminate this unplanned emotionalism as a major factor is to distort seriously the realities of Arab-Israeli relations.

2

The Perceptual Context of Arab Politics: Image, Uncertainty, and Conflict

Political decisions in the Arab world appear to be the product of ad hoc considerations, almost spontaneous political reactions. The dramatic events of contemporary Arab politics have burst upon the world with little, or no, forewarning. Consider the following: Nasir's nationalization of the Suez Canal in July 1956, the sudden build up and war of June 1967, the joint Egyptian-Syrian surprise attack of October 1973, and President Sadat's unexpected visit to Israel in November 1977. Although each of these events is related to the Arab-Israeli confronta-tion, each, when analyzed in detail, is the consequence of a microcosm of cross cutting conflicts. Each is, thus, at once unique and also part of a major conflict pattern.

Yet even if the centrality of the Arab-Israeli theme is recognized as the link between major upheavals in the Arab world, the impression of discontinuity and of abrupt escalation remains. Clearly there must be some more general pattern which shapes Arab decision making: one grounded in relatively larger and more stable social and cultural factors. Here the concept of the 'image' may prove to be useful to integrate the complex factors which influence Arab decision making. The term 'image' can be used in a number of different senses; here it refers to the totality of cognitive, affective and evaluative perceptions that decision makers have concerning themselves and their environ-ment. (1) The apparent contradictions of Arab politics, the unexplained reversals of policy, the emphasis on verbal overreaction, may make some sense then if they are analyzed as products of a pervasive image system. One builds up layers of images of various levels of generality which functions to provide Arab decision makers with perceptual maps of their environment: As K.J. Holsti notes:

> Any delineation of objectives, choice among courses of action, or responses to a situation in the environment may be explained partly in terms of policy makers' perceptions of reality. Man acts and reacts according to his 'images' of the environment. In policy

making the state of the environment does not matter so much as what governmental officials believe that state to be. By 'image' we mean an individual's perception of an object, fact, or condition his 'evaluation' of that object, fact, or condition in terms of its goodness or badness, friendliness or hostility, or value, and the 'meaning' ascribed to, or deduced from, that fact, object, or condition. (2)

Images obviously do not exist in a vacuum. On the one hand they are products of ongoing social and cultural systems; on the other hand they are a response to the flow of political events. (3)   The social and cultural bases of Arab image systems are analyzed in this chapter. Arab imagery in response to political events is analyzed in subsequent chapters. But before going further, this point must be made, that the term Arab as used here is probably a misnomer. Images with which this work is concerned are basically those of Egyptian and Syrian elites, with some supporting material on other Arab decision makers.

These images are permeated with an element of "threat." This sense of threat stems from a number of sources, among them: (a) pervasive local or domestic conflicts, some   the legacy of Middle Eastern demographic history, some the result of social change, which contribute to what might be called an "escalatory perception of events." (b) Large scale and relatively permanent patterns of intra-Arab politics and political style which add their own impetus to escalatory behavior and perception. (c) An apparently stable system of perceptions revolving around images of the self and others as being locked in continuous conflict. In short, both the content of Arab imagery and the structural relationships between images form a conceptual model of the decision maker's universe, a model which has given its operative assumptions a logical and cognitive consistency that shapes decision makers' perceptions of events and predispose decision makers toward interpretations of other actors' conduct as being hostile. (4)

EXCURSUS INTO PROPAGANDA ANALYSIS

In the case of Arab decision makers, the process of image formation is dominated by the linguistic and symbolic medium of the Arab language, (5) a medium that is reinforced by Arab/Muslim cultural patterns.   Because of linguistic/cultural emphasis on both expressive and theoretical "closure" (in psychological terms, on gestalt formation), these images appear to have more emotional power and more autonomy from day to day events than images in the West. (6) As a consequence, there is considerable debate concerning the credence to be accorded the verbalization of these images, i.e., Arab, political, utterances.   The starting point is usually an assertion that Arab verbal behavior is the product of a cultural system in which thought and action, wish and reality, are either confused or substituted for one another.   For example, anthropologist Rapheal Patai argues as follows:

Arab thought processes are relatively autonomous, that is, more dependent on reality than the thought processes typical of Western man.   Nor is Arab verbal formulation influenced by reality to the degree which it is in the West...Arab speech likewise tends to express ideal thoughts, and to represent what is desired or hoped for as if it were an actual fact in evidence, rather than cleave to the limitations of the real. There is thus among the Arabs a relatively greater discrepancy between thought and speech on the one hand and action on the other. (7)

From here, alternative theories (both highly politicized in the sense that one is basically an Arab apologetic and the other a defense of Israeli policy) are presented as bases for interpreting Arab communications. Palestinian spokesman Hisham Sharabi argues that the characteristic approach of Arab commentators to information is to distort it so as to serve their own advantage. Information, even when it is accurate, therefore, has to be weighed against the putative motives of its source. Arab spokesmen tend to adjust reality willy-nilly to make it coincide with the preferred state of affairs: (thus President Nasir's declarations that the Straits of Tiran had been mined, for example, when, in truth, few if any mines seem to have been laid.) Moreover, there is a tendency for Arab officials to tell their audiences that which the audiences wish to hear. Fact and fiction are merged; reality and wish become one, a tendency which is heightened by the linguistic characteristics of the language.   Therefore, Arab verbal behavior, especially threats, should be seen as part of a cultural pattern wherein words are substituted for actions, and discounted as such. (8)

Alternatively, Y. Harkabi, former head of Israeli Intelligence, holds that Arab rhetoric should be taken with great seriousness. While it may not be possible to infer intent from any single set of statements by an Arab leader, these statements do operate to create a set of expectations concerning courses of action.   When repeated often enough, they indicate a fundamental mind set. Therefore, the thesis that there is a significant gap between Arab speech and action is misleading because speech or ideology conditions actions. "From this point of view ideology is a reservoir of institutionalized aspirations which pass through the filter of reason before they are carried out in practice." (9) Arab statements may express a wish, but the gap between wish and reality is only a function of the lack of ability to act. (10)

Stated in the above terms, there can be no truly satisfactory answer to questions concerning the reliability of Arab statements as indicators of subsequent behavior.   However, if, instead of dealing with such statements on a discrete basis, the focus of analysis is directed toward interpreting them as expressions of a coherent and internalized cognitive model, then some prediction becomes possible. Certainly this would be so if the properties of the model can be set forth, and if it can be shown that Arab decision makers have, in the past, behaved in conformity with these properties.

This cognitive model or image system defines the politically relevant environment: relationships between the Arab/Muslim world and the larger international system; relationships within the Arab world itself; domestic political patterns, and ultimately, the parameters of the individual decision maker's role itself. It shapes and limits policy makers' options in several ways. At the level of Arab elites (plus these elites' perception of mass opinion) it sets the context within which otherwise rational calculations of risk/benefit are made. At the level of the man in the street, it determines public tolerance for governmental policies, or for the very government itself. For both Arab elite and mass, it shapes the pattern of political communication.

A PERCEPTUAL MODEL: CONFLICT AS AN ORDERING PRINCIPLE

If it can be said that the image, the "ideal" in a platonic sense, seems to have an independence of its own in Arab decision making behavior, what sorts of properties can an Arab image system be said to possess? Here it can be argued that the generalized structure of Arab cognitions approximates, in thematic content and organizational format, that of a conflict model of behavior.

As both an image system and a theory of human interaction, a conflict model is one that stresses conflict as the basic datum of individual and social existence. Conflict theories usually start from the same assumption, stated or unstated, about human nature: that man is essentially an aggressive self interested entity, and that he is driven by a variety of impulses, learned or instinctive, to expand his wants at the expense of others. (11) Conflict is then a ubiquitous phenomenon; it is the ultimate social fact from which any theory of actions should start. (12) The consequence, as Thomas Hobbes once put it, is that human life tends to be "nasty, brutish, and short."

However, contemporary social science theories of conflict do not stop with this picturesque statement. Conflict is analyzed as being the product of either culture or social structure, or both, and the institutions and patterns of social or political orders are conceived as products of conflict. Conflict is "a struggle over values and claims to scarce status, power and resources in which the aims of the opponents are to neutralize, injure or eliminate rivals." (13) This clash of values is then articulated in terms of group formation, of individuals combining together to attack or defend. (14) The awareness of this clash and of the pervasiveness of conflict shapes the individuals' perceptions of their environment. "Conflict may be defined as a situation of competition in which parties are aware of the incompatibility of potential future positions, and in which, each party wishes to occupy a position that is incompatible with the wishes of the other." (15) Opponents then develop and engage in various strategies of conflict, rational calculations of their goals and of the probable outcomes of their actions. (16)

Taken together, the propositions of conflict theory form a complete model of behavior. There is a substantive content which demonstrates the pervasiveness of conflict, a formal structure which specifies the articulation of conflict patterns, and a theory of process which introduces an action dynamic. The problem, then, becomes one of translating this body of theory into the terms of image analysis. Here it can be argued that a conflict model "image" system should contain a content which is demonstrably oriented around conflict themes, and a structure of images organized in terms of discrete conceptions of related conflicts.

In terms of content, these images would be composed of perceptions, values, and meanings, or evaluative standards, which flow from a basic belief in the "giveness" of conflict: Perceptions or cognitions which would view the world as being essentially a jungle, an environment characterized by both scarcity and intense competition, a source of continuous threat. A conflict oriented value system would stress the incessant need to prove one's superiority, to master or dominate one's social environment, and alternatively, to protect one's identity, however defined, from some form of dishonor, loss of esteem and ability to dominate. Finally, standards of judgment, the meaning attached to actions, would be premised on assumptions about the ubiquity of aggressive drives and their articulation in terms of calculated and cynical policy decisions. Insofar as the image system is concerned, this content supplies both an organizing principle with which to order discrete images of the environment and an explanatory theory. The relations between other actors in the environment can be understood as products of calculated strategies of conflict.

The structural format of the image system can take any shape. For example, Michael Brecher found that Israeli decision makers tended to perceive their environment as a series of concentric circles of states: an Arab core, an Arab periphery, and a larger international circle. Israeli policy alternatives were then focused on strategies to deal with any given circle. (17) Alternatively, Kenneth Waltz suggests that the organization is hierarchical. The decision maker's world is divided into levels of images, each level complete with its own situational definition, its panoply of friends and enemies, its theories of the origins and nature of conflict and its prescriptions for action. (18) According to Waltz, these levels are that of the international system itself, that of the structure of politics within given states, and that of the nature of interpersonal relations. (19)

CULTURAL SOURCES OF ARAB IMAGES:
THE THEME OF UBIQUITOUS CONFLICT

Robert Jervis, (20) summarizing some of the findings of decision making theories, suggests that the sources of perceptions, the stimuli, so to speak, can be divided into two broad categories: external and internal. External, or situational factors, are the concrete "givens" of the situation in which Arab decision makers operate geography, resources, and demography, and stable political relationships are built upon them. These combine with political and organizational patterns unique to each Arab regime to set the parameters within which long or short term policy options can be dealt with. While these "givens" are such that an outside observer might set them down as objective limits on policy, their conversion into actual decisions by Arab leaders is a matter of subjective and selective interpretation by the leaders concerned. Arab decision making in this sense is a combination of more or less calculated responses to an objective environment whose structure is filtered through various subjective "definitions of the situation." (21) These subjective definitions are, in turn, the product of Arab historiography, theology, and ideology.

However, the basic source of decision makers' images is internal, i.e., Arab/Muslim culture: a system of values, symbols, and behavioral explanations which provides guidance for one's own behavior and for the interpretation of that of others. (22) This cultural system supplies Arab decision makers with sets of generalized images concerning the basic source and nature of conflict in the Arab world: images of human nature, of man's innate propensity toward good or evil; images of correct interpersonal behavior, of the nature of loyalty and hostility; images of larger political relationships, of the basic nature of the world, whether it is benign or threatening. These images, in turn, produce basic attitudes of trust or mistrust of others and of the environment in general.

Sociologist Morroe Berger notes that the dominant characteristic of Arab life is intense suspicion of one's surroundings. This suspicion, says Berger, has several sources. In cultural terms, it is the product of a blend of bedouin original behavioral traits: the stress on exaggerated manliness, on the one hand, and the exaggerated conformity to the mores of the clan or tribal unit, on the other. Both individual egotism and clan-group solidarity are functional attitudes in a society faced with adaptation to desert conditions. Nevertheless, their byproduct is individual behavior characterized by intense rivalries and hatreds, by feuds, and by a sharp perceptual division of the world into friends and enemies. To be defined as a friend was to receive elaborate hospitality; to be defined as an enemy was to be the recipient of intense hostility. (23)

A second source stemmed from the dynamics of Arab history. In this case, a history which was dominated by wars, dynastic upheavals, and conquests by waves of invaders. The legacy of these cumulative historical experiences is a distrust of any individual or any institution whose intentions cannot be ascertained, whose status cannot be vouched for by friendly kinsmen. Here, governments in particular came to be perceived as entities which could not be trusted, as objects of collective avoidance behavior extending over centuries of Arab history. Consequently, it is extremely difficult for contemporary Arab governments to collect any demographic information, or elicit positive cooperation from their populations. (24)

Thirdly, the heretofore predominant Arab marriage and child raising patterns contribute to this pervasive insecurity. Arab marriage patterns are predominately endogamous, the preferred marriage partners being cousins. The long term consequence of this pattern has been the development of a social order divided among tightly knit extended families. This has the advantage of providing maximum group solidarity against a hostile environment, but the disadvantage of reinforcing existing cultural tendencies, a pervasive in group/out group mentality. (25)

According to some sources, Arab parents apparently do not regularly deal with their children on a predictable basis. During early childhood, the child is given only enough attention to assure his physical survival. He is neither loved, nor disciplined. At the age of seven or so, there is an abrupt and, one may assume, traumatic transition to rigid and arbitrary discipline.   Authoritarian responses are socialized into the child's behavior. (26)   In psychological terms, the consequence of this bifurcated child rearing practice is the production of individuals with orientations toward either authoritarian dominance or authoritarian submission. (27)

While these factors alone probably are enough to produce a culture which alternates between the expression of conflict and the quest for security, they are also reinforced by Islam. Islam, as a value system, incorporates many of the preexisting tribal and clan practices of Arab society. But it does so within the special context of controlling man's behavior in this world in order that he may gain salvation in the next one. Like Christianity, Islam defines the problem of control in terms of the nature of man. Human nature is seen as being inherently depraved. If left to his own devices, man would live in a perpetual state of anarchy, of a "war of all against all," in Hobbesian terms. This state of uncontrolled conflict, the "jahiliyya," is contrasted sharply with the ordered community of Islam, the umma. (28)

Islam, as a behavioral system, provides an answer to this problem of personal and group security.   It does so both in terms of an all embracing code of interpersonal relations, the shari'a law, and in terms of a theological insistence of the necessity of order at all costs. Muslims are enjoined to obey whatever government that can maintain order in the streets. The slogan "one day of anarchy is worse than sixty years of tyranny," was attributed to the eleventh century theologian/ philosopher al-Ghazali, and is symbolic of this stress on the control at all costs.

Islam, as a philosophical system, contributes yet another element to Arab imagery: a style of historical explanation. For a variety of reasons connected with the theological issue of man's Free Will versus God's Determination, Muslim theologians developed what might be called the "particle theory" of event analysis. Originally propounded by the tenth century theologian al-Ash'ari, this theory held that, although the ultimate relationship between events was determined by God, man could choose of his own will to respond to each event. (29) In sum, therefore, history was composed of a series of discrete event quanta whose causal relationship was unknowable, but to which man had to react.   The temporal relationship between events, their chronological distribution, became the focus of explanation. Chronology rather than cause and effect analysis became the dominant style of Muslim historiography.

In addition, a second form of intellectualizing about events came from Islamic jurisprudence. The extensive use of analogy (qiyas), the application of human reason in a limited fashion to compare contemporary situations with similar situations adjudicated in the Qur'an and Sunna, became the common juridical practice. (30) This practice finds its counterpart in the extensive use of analogies from the Arab/Muslim past which are then applied to present day situations.

Thus, cultural, historical and intellectual factors have combined over centuries to produce security oriented behavior. The institutions of Arab/Muslim culture add up to what psychologist Abram Kardiner calls a basic security system:

> The important thing to note about different types of effective reality supplied by different institutional systems is that each demands different types of adaptation to guarantee the individual security within his own environment. Another consequence is that each type of effective reality creates its own conceptual systems...The security system of the individual can be defined as that system of adaptations which insures the individual acceptance, approval, support when necessary, esteem, and maintenance of status. It demands impulse control and development of resources along specific lines.

> The security system of the group can be defined as the activities or attitudes expected of each individual which safeguard the group against dangers coming both from without the group and from within. In the first group belong such different activities as warfare and religion. The dangers from within the group are the disrupting influences of individuals or groups within the society. The security systems vary widely, but, generally, sanctions, compensations, and force are the chief methods of dealing with these disrupting influences which come from within. (31)

These security systems supply the behavioral dynamics of Arab responses to the environment. Each level of imagery is tied together by common culturally induced patterns of response. The Arab tendency to personify the world, to perceive it in essentially kinship or personalized terms is a phenomenon of this cultural pattern. So, also, is the tendency to adopt exaggerated political positions and to stress ideological rigidity at the expense of other political considerations. The Palestinian guerrilla organizations, for example, have never been able to effectively coordinate their efforts because of ideological differences. Yet the advantages of such coordination would appear to be obvious. (32)

LEVELS OF IMAGES: A HIERARCHY OF CONFLICT

In addition to the general thematic concern with the pervasiveness of conflict, Arab imagery is structurally organized in the form of a hierarchy of conflicts. This image structure consists of levels of conflict perceptions, from area wide, or culture wide conflicts, to localized, domestic conflict patterns. (33)

At the most general level, the Arab image of the international environment is dominated by the perception of a permanent conflict between the Arab/Muslim world and the Christian West. (34) Differences between the U.S. and Europe, and the Soviet bloc, as well as those between individual states are perceived, but they are of secondary importance. This conflict has two distinct perceptual manifestations, religious or political, depending on the relative secularization of the individuals involved. However, these tend to blend in practice into a sort of subliminal hostility, a disposition to mistrust Western intentions, and a gut feeling that Westerners, in general, are up to no good. (35)

In religious terms the West is seen as a monolithic religious system, an ever present theological opponent, a threat to Islamic values. Theologically, this view has its source in the mirrorlike dogmatic structure of Christiantiy and Islam, both claiming to be sole vehicles of divine revelation. (36) This claim was conceptualized by Muslim theologians as a basic division of the world between believer and unbeliever, between the sphere of Islam (dar al-Islam) and the sphere of war (dar al-harb), between the Arabs as God's chosen people and all others.

In contemporary behavior this sense of religious antagonism takes various forms: the banning of mini skirts as Western inventions designed to subvert Muslim youth; the existence of a number of fundamentalist organizations whose goals are the defense of Islam in the face of Western/Christian threats to its values. The largest of these, the Muslim Brethren, operates with a quite explicit theory of a Christian conspiracy (headed by the Pope, with Israel as its military component) to destroy Islam. As an even more exotic example, the Dirkawa Brotherhood of Morocco and the Spanish Sahara is said to have been very pro-German in the 1930s, not for specific political reasons, but because the Germans had started a conflict in which many thousands of Christians would die, and thus helped the ultimate triumph of Islam. (37) Or, on a personal level, King Faysal's otherwise curious equation of Zionism and Communism makes sense if one assumes, as did Faysal, a monolithic West.

Normally this religious image is latent. However, in times of crises it can surface dramatically. In the days immediately preceding the 1967 War, observers in Cairo noted a peculiar pattern of behavior on the part of many Egyptians. Having taken limited civil defense measures, notably painting headlights and windows a bright blue and piling sandbags in front of doors, Egyptians then appeared in the streets reading copies of Sahih al-Bukhari. Al-Bukhari is a collection of hadith, a compendium of the Prophet's behavior; literally, a manual of religiously correct behavior for a variety of situations. When it appeared obvious that a major war was about to begin, the Egyptians chose a religious response. Some six years later, Haykal observed the Qur'ans appeared on the desks of Egyptian officers as the date set for the October attack approached. (38)

Politically, the West is perceived as an overwhelmingly powerful opponent; an opponent that must be confronted periodically; an opponent whose technology and culture are impressive, but which nevertheless is dangerous. (39) The contemporary Arab image of Israel (up to October 1973) as the possessor of overwhelming military might is only an extension of this general view. (40)   The standard Arab propaganda line concerning the unity of the U.S. and Israel is, in part, a deliberate oversimplification of a complex relationship. But it is, in part, also a reflection of this image of a unified West.

This image of Western power is often articulated in terms of the impact and devastation of the Crusades; and an analogy is usually drawn between the existence of the state of Israel and that of the Latin kingdom of Jerusalem in eleventh and twelfth centuries. As 'abd al-Nasir put it:

> If the Crusades were the beginning of the Renaissance in Europe, they were the beginning of the dark ages in our country. Our people alone bore most of the sufferings of the Crusades, out of which they emerged poor, destitute and exhausted. In their exhaustion they were simultaneously destined by circumstances to submit to and to suffer further indignity under the hoofs of the Mongol and Caucasian tyrants. (41)

Symbolically enough one of the contemporary Egyptian colloquial terms for Westerner is "farangi" - Frank or Crusader. Moreover, this image of Crusader destructiveness is usually contrasted, either implicitly or explicitly, with an image of past Arab political glory, with the determination on the part of most Arab leaders to reverse the present situation of Arab weakness - just as their ancestors drove out the Crusaders.

Here again, a whole series of behavioral manifestations illustrate this determination: the title of the Ba'th party, "The Arab Socialist Resurrection Party". Or consider the imagery and role of Salah al-Din adopted by 'abd al-Nasir: the Egyptian national emblem is Salah al-Din's shield device. Or 'abd al-Nasir's conception of a role in search of a hero, a role which he interpreted as being that of tilting against the West:

> I do not know why I recall, whenever I reach this point in my recollections as I meditate alone in my room, a famous tale by a great Italian poet, Luigi Pirandello - "Six Characters in Search of an Author." The pages of history are full of heroes who created for themselves roles of glorious valor which they played at decisive moments: Likewise the pages of history are full of heroic and glorious roles which never found heroes to perform them. (42)

Or consider al-Qadhafi's notion of an Islamic revival, a notion operationalized as a foreign policy of supporting groups perceived as anti-western almost at random in the Arab world, Indonesia, the Philippines, or Northern Ireland. (43)

The consequence of this negative image of the West is to limit Arab decision makers' options vis-a-vis Western countries, particularly the United States. Under normal circumstances these leaders cannot afford to become too identified with a pro-Western policy, even if they judge it to be in their own national interests. To do so in public is to lay oneself open to both domestic and intra-Arab attack. President al-Sadat is currently isolated in the Arab world because of his movement toward the United States. He faces growing domestic opposition from both his own military and local fundamentalist Islamic groups, and hostility from Libya, Syria, Iraq, and to some extent, Saudi Arabia, abroad.

In crises situations, these options become even more limited. King Husayn faced the difficult problem in October 1973 of balancing between the realities of an unfavorable military situation and the passions of his population. On the one hand, there was no air cover to protect his forces from Israeli air strikes should he join in the war. On the other hand, it was politically impossible to remain aloof from the battle all the more so as it appeared that Arab forces might win. His dispatch of the 40th regiment to Syria was a minimum risk response calculated to satisfy both contingencies.

Interacting with this generalized Islamic/Western image is a second level imagery, that of the intra-Arab environment. Here the dominant theme is that of endemic territorial revisionism. (44) Most, if not all of the boundaries of the area were drawn by Western powers. They cross cut existing demographic and historical divisions of the area, and provide the basis for persistent territorial claims. Because these boundaries were imposed by the West, they are perceived illegitimate and do not, therefore, inhibit Arab elites from interfering in each other's domestic affairs. Syrian activities in both Jordan and Lebanon, ostensibly on behalf of the Palestinian cause, are but one such example. Nor do these boundaries operate to separate the intrastate policies of the area: domestic upheavals in one state have an exaggerated impact on surrounding states, hence the domino effect of military coups on the Arab world.

The imagery of intra-Arab politics is that of relatively permanent conflict between sets of contending Arab elites. Each elite possesses, in varying degree, the capacity to threaten the stability of all other elites, and each is similarly vulnerable to outside threat. A very common practice of intra-Arab conflict is to plant stories concerning the rumored overthrow of an opponent in the Beirut press. These stories often then become self fulfilling prophecies, triggering the very coup that was rumored. Aside from boundary issues, there are a multitude of other sources of conflict:

(a) Strategic conflicts revolving around control of land/sea access routes. These are of very ancient origin and have been relatively stable in their configuration since pharaonic antiquity. They have two principal foci: Egyptian versus Mesopotamian power struggles over control of the Levant; Egyptian or Mesopotamian states versus South Arabian states over domination of the Red Sea and Arabian Gulf.

(b) Economic conflicts over scarce resources between oil rich states and their poorer neighbors. These have resulted in the creation of two loose coalitions, Saudi Arabia, Kuwayt, and the Trucial Shaykhdoms in one group; Egypt, Syria and Iraq in the other. The territorial focal point of this confrontation is the control of the oil rich areas of the Arabian Peninsula: Egyptian/Saudi activities in the two Yemens are an example.

(c) Ideological conflicts over the definition of political community and the pace of modernization. These pit Egypt, Syria, Iraq, and marginally Libya, against Jordan, Kuwayt, and Saudi Arabia. They are linked with the conflict over resources in the sense that the radical states are also the resource poor states, while the conservatives are resource rich.

(d) Dynastic and tribal rivalries. The oldest of these are the legacy of tribal warfare, the wars of the Ridda, which occurred in the 7th century following the death of the Prophet. More contemporary in origin are dynastic conflicts between the Sa'uds and the Hashemites, between ex-Ottoman "great families" in the Levant, or between Palestinian clans in the West Bank.

(e) Interpersonal rivalries. The latest of these is the now intense dislike between al-Sadat and al-Qadhafi. This animosity had been building up before the October War, mostly because of al-Qadhafi's egregious habit of lecturing his fellow Arab leaders (and their wives) on correct Muslim moral and political behavior, including the joys of sobriety and the proper role of women. This behavior ultimately triggered a whole series of calculated Egyptian snubs: plans, drafted in 1969, for an Egyptian/Libyan federation were scuttled by the Egyptians. Later, al-Qadhafi was not informed of the October 1973 attack, which made him look the fool. After that War, ex-King Idris was invited to the wedding of al-Sadat's daughter, while al-Qadhafi was not (a subtle comment on al-Qadhafi's political stability within Libya). The upshot of all this interpersonal hostility was at least one Libyan sponsored attempt on al-Sadat's life, extensive sabotage activity, and verbal fireworks on all sides. Ultimately Egyptian/Libyan relations deteriorated to the point where a short lived border war was fought in July 1977. (45)

(f) Cultural and sectarian antagonisms. Most of these have their sources in the various religious schisms, both Islamic and Christian, which have rocked the area. Over a period of time these religious differences have taken on political and psychological dimensions. Because of the geography of the area and the traditional techniques of decentralized territorial administration, these minority groups have remained largely unassimilated, and still resist submergence into larger national communities.

In addition, cutting across sectarian cleavage is an age-old conflict between nomadic and settled populations, between the "badu" and the "hadar," between groups who perceive themselves as carriers of "Arab" culture and others. The most obvious example here is the intense hatred between bedouin and Palestinian populations in Jordan. Each feels that the other is slightly less than human, and the savagery of the 1970 civil war bears witness to this feeling. On a more subtle level, there are other tensions. The urbane and polished Egyptian leadership is slightly uneasy in the company of Arabian Peninsula leaders; while men brought up in nomadic tradition look upon their city brethren in Egypt, Syria, and Iraq as not quite up to snuff, not quite "real" Arabs, merely imitations. Old line Sunni families in Damascus can remember when the 'Alawis, who currently run the government, were the chief source of domestic servants. Palestinians question the Arabness of Egyptians whose Sudanic physical characteristics are contrasted with the Palestinians' Semitic features.

As a consequence of this image of intra-Arab relations, perceived policy options are limited, especially in terms of coalition politics. Alliances are difficult to maintain, since each partner is most suspicious of his allies' territorial intentions. Military alliances involving the movement of troops through each other's territory are especially difficult because of the possibility that these same troops might be used against their host government. Relations with outside powers are inevitably suspect because they are perceived almost solely in terms of their potential impact on intra-Arab politics. Such area wide cooperation that has occurred, Arab summit agreements for example, has been basically negative in nature; agreements to refrain from taking action, rather than positive policy. (46)

Domestically, each Arab elite faces a multiplicity of mutually suspicious, contentious groups. Arab states' internal politics are structured by the relative size and status of these groups. Arab society, as noted above, is characterized by a pervasive tendency toward in group/out group divisions which revolve around foci of language, religion, and kinship. These differences are symbolized by a whole series of minute idiosyncracies of dress and behavior that Westerners find hard to distinguish. (47) Relations between these groups are basically those of controlled antagonism. Much of Arab interpersonal and inter group behavior revolves around techniques for avoiding or muting the outbreak of overt conflict. The famous Arab hospitality of politeness is, in fact, a mechanism for stabilizing otherwise unpredictable relationships. (48)

This in group/out group social pattern is projected into Arab leaders' images of their domestic environment - an environment which is perceived as being both marginally anarchic in its politics and at the same time teeming with actual or potential enemies. Again, 'abd al-Nasir described this image succinctly:

Every man we questioned had nothing to recommend except to kill someone else. Every idea we listened to was nothing but an attack on some other idea. If we had gone along with everything we heard, we would have killed off all the people and torn down every idea and there would have been nothing left for us to do but sit down among the corpses and ruins, bewailing our evil fortune and cursing our wretched fate.

We were deluged with petitions and complaints by the thousands and hundreds of thousands, and had these complaints and petitions dealt with cases demanding justice or grievances calling for redress, this motive would have been understandable and logical. But most of the cases referred to us were no more or less than demands for revenge, as though the revolution had taken place in order to become a weapon in the hand of hatred and vindictiveness. (49)

As Michael Hudson points out, Arab governments in general lack legitimacy, a disposition on the part of their citizens to support governments and to obey governmental edicts without being physically compelled to do so. (50) This lack of legitimacy is a phenomenon of the change from a traditional political order to a "modern" political order. (51) In any event, it adds a political dimension to existing social and cultural conflicts. Each Arab government is acutely sensitive, therefore, to the possibility of internal subversion. The threshold of tolerance for threat perception is very low. At times this sensitivity borders on paranoia: the government of Iraq reportedly went so far as to disarm its own garrison in Baghdad out of fear of a possible coup.

Politically, these conflict ridden societies present Arab leaders with the necessity of continuously balancing off group demands. Or, if lack of resources forecloses this option, of either repressing these demands by force and then censoring news reports, or of diverting domestic discontent outward onto other Arab world or international targets. Hence the combination of vagueness in describing domestic problems, so as not to offend any given group, and excessive aggressiveness toward outsiders that characterizes Arab political rhetoric.

Finally, at the level of the individual decision maker is the image of the self - or rather that of the idealized self. Here the overriding concern is with honor (sharaf) or, in its existential form, with wajh (face). The world is perceived as being the source of continual threat to this image. (52) The response to this continual threat is an exaggerated emphasis on virility in much the same sense as the Latin American term "machismo" - bravado, unpredictability, and extreme aggressiveness. In Arab cultural usage this manliness is a very fragile quality, one that is destroyed by the very smallest of dishonors; hence the sensitivity to the slightest insult - real or imagined. Any injury done this image of wajh must be revenged, traditionally in a literal sense of physical violence, more often now in a verbal sense. Behavioral instances of this wajh mentality are legion.

For example, a whole panoply of practices surround the seclusion of women. Women are perceived as a constant source of dishonor, and perpetual vigilance is necessary to prevent indiscrete female behavior. While Arab men boast of their own virility, they must be ever careful not to fall victim, through their women, to the virility of other men. (53) These practices and attitudes in regard to women are of very ancient origin, but they show no signs of being mitigated by social change in the Middle East. Western educated Arabs appear on the outside to be as modern and swinging as their European counterparts -

except where it comes to their womenfolk. In Lebanon, there were perhaps as many female victims of the traditional but large scale feuding between various Lebanese factions that ultimately escalated into civil war in the fall of 1975. Where the deaths of men were openly admitted by all sides, the deaths of women were not. To do so would have been to admit that one's womenfolk had been harmed and one's family or clan therefore dishonored. Elsewhere a survey of some of the 1967 Palestinian refugees turned up the finding that a significant number fled to avoid the possibility of Israeli molestation of their women. (54)

Perhaps the most famous example of the political consequences of the wajh mentality is that of 'abd al-Nasir's furious reaction to the insulting withdrawal of United States financing for the Aswan Dam. However there were others. Arabs in general were humiliated by the Israeli use of women to guard Arab prisoners of war. Later, Palestinian insurgents became a force in the Arab world politics following the battle of al-Karama in March 1968. The Palestinian mystique gained from this encounter (where they lost a battle according to Western standards of judgment) stemmed from the fact that they fought honorably, fought "with white weapons" as the news broadcasts described it. This honorable and warrior-like behavior was then contrasted by Palestinian media with the dishonor that had occurred in 1967, and the comparison was skillfully used by the Palestinian leadership as a basis for demands on Arab governments. The subsequent conciliatory approach toward Palestinian demands taken by the Jordanian government triggered a counter response by Jordanian Bedouins who identified themselves and their honor with the fortunes of the regime. Symbolically, some Jordanian Bedouin army units tied brassieres on the antennas of their vehicles in the Fall of 1970. This was said to express their collective dishonor, their feeling that Husayn's conciliatory approach to the Palestinians had dishonored them and made them into women.

IMAGES AND POLICY:
THE CONFLICT MODEL OF POLITICS

The combination of a cultural focus on conflict as the norm of interpersonal and intergroup action and the structure of cognitions in terms of layers of conflicts adds up, therefore, to a conflict model of politics. (55) The parameters of this model and its apparent internalization in the cognitions of Arab decision makers function to shape Arab responses to their political environment. It produces the fluidity and factionalism which characterize Arab politics and builds in the escalatory dynamics which appears to dominate Arab interactions.

In practice the conflict model operates to produce an extremely complex and subtle politics. Levels of imagery and their behavioral manifestations tend to cross cut one another and to produce a convoluted pattern of political alignments. For example, the Lebanese crisis of 1958 involved group conflict within Lebanon over governmental economic policies, pro and anti Nasir intra Arab conflicts, and conflicts over Lebanon's relationship to the West. The crisis of 1975/76 was even more complex, involving additional factions based on pro or anti Palestinian, pro or anti Syrian alignments as well as linkages between some groups and the Israelis.

Arab standards of political action are based in pragmatic assumptions about the limits and stability of coalition behavior. The key operative principle is that of flexibility; both conflicts and coalitions are carefully defined in scope on the theory both friends and enemies may, at a moment's notice, shift sides. Allies are chosen for their immediate policy value without apparent consideration of long range implications. As an Arab saying puts it, "The friend of my friend is my friend; the enemy of my enemy is my enemy." Arab decision makers are evaluated in terms of their ability to adjust to changing situations without seeming regard for the content of their policies. The behavioral result is a fluid political environment characterized by ever shifting coalitions, coalitions which are the result of narrowly based pragmatic considerations, coalitions which are ever prone to dissolution because of mutual mistrust. (56)

Arab political behavior then, subjectively speaking, is dominated by a quest for security. This quest takes place within an image framework which is organized in a conflict model, perceptions of various levels of conflict - the Arab world versus the West, Arab versus Arab, domestic faction versus domestic faction. The quality and character of response to this environment is in large part culturally determined, the product of culturally defined security systems of behavior. In its existential dimension, Arab political behavior is a compound of intense verbal hostility and pragmatic action. Since the intentions of others can never be really known, Arab leaders can trust no one. In this situation of mutual mistrust, there is a natural tendency to over react to threats, real or imagined. There is thus a built in escalatory potential to Arab politics, Arab leaders reacting and over reacting to the reactions of other Arab leaders, ad infinitum.

3

The Structure
of Escalation:
Personality, System,
Media—1967

In this, and the following chapters, the wars of 1967 and 1973 are treated as case studies of Arab-Israeli military relations; as examples of the impact of Arab conflict imagery on an inherently escalatory situation. The geographical and political parameters of the Arab-Israeli conflict, along with the configurations, specifically of Arab conflicts, form a background to these images. This background provided the necessary, but not the sufficient causes for war. (1) The ultimate determinant of the series of decisions that led to war lay elsewhere - in Arab image systems.

The projection of conflict imagery onto the environment, however, is not a simple one to one phenomenon. The impact of decision makers' imagery is limited in two ways: (a) by the degree of actual stability of the external environment; and (b) by the level of bureaucratic institutionalization of the decision makers' international environment. Leaving aside, for a moment, the external environment, one of the propositions about politics in situations of social changes is that there is an inverse relationship between the degree of institutionalization and the pace of change. (2) The corollary to this is that where institutionalization, i.e., the extent of bureaucratic routine associated with decision making, is low, the impact of personality and personal perception is accentuated. (3) In the case of Arab decision makers, the combination of rapid social change, combined with existing cultural traditions of highly personalized and autocratic decision making, facilitates the projection of individual idiosyncracies.

Equally, the lack of external stability, itself partially a consequence of idiosyncratic decision making, adds an additional element of uncertainty. The result is that, unlike some Western conflict systems where opponents have created relatively stable threat systems (4) (the relationship between the United States and USSR is such a system), Middle Eastern conflicts tend to be relatively unstructured. To borrow a term popularized by Emile Durkheim, Middle Eastern conflicts are anomic; they are characterized by either an absence of rules, or by very weakly developed rules. Hence, for example, when Palestinian groups attack Israeli settlements, there is substantial fear of a reprisal on the part of all surrounding Arab governments because none of them really know where the Israelis will retaliate.

In the case at hand - Syrian and Egyptian conflict imagery - while defined in general by similar external and internal environments, differs in its source. Syrian imagery is very much the consequence of a minority group outlook, an outlook that is the product of hundreds of years of group dynamics in the Levant, whose existing conflict imagery has been intensified by its contemporary articulation in terms of Ba'th Socialist ideology. Egyptian imagery, by contrast, is more closely tied to the personality of a single decision maker, originally that of 'abd al-Nasir, now President al-Sadat.

In many ways the October 1973 War is a replay of the earlier June War. In their assessment of the events leading up to October, of the consequences of the attack, and its aftermath, Arab spokesmen consistently refer to the 1967 situation. When tension in the Golan Heights escalated into a series of ground and air battles between Israeli and Syrian forces in November/December 1972, all sides - Syrian, Egyptian, and Israeli - likened the situation to that of the Spring of 1967.

Egyptian Foreign Minister Muhammad al-Zayyat at the time stated that, "We are nearing a situation similar to that of 1967." A Syrian spokesman made a parallel comparison in reference to Israeli air strikes,

> The Israelis come here, they attack what they say are Palestinian bases, they attack Syrian army bases...Do you expect us to just sit and watch? Don't worry: we will not be lured into a battle with Israel the timing, of which, is not decided by us.

Referring to a message sent to the Egyptians through UN sources, an Israeli official declared,

> We do not want Egypt to err and (as the consequence of Israeli reprisals against Palestinian bases following the Munich massacre in September) allow itself to be drawn in by the Syrians - as it was in 1967. (5)

The parallel between events in the months leading to the 1967 war and those transpiring in 1973 continued to impress itself on Arab observers. It came more and more to dominate the perceptions and interpretations of those concerned, especially of Egyptian and Syrian decision makers. In retrospect, the resemblance between 1967 and 1973 is startling: a series of small scale, unconventional, Palestinian operations against Israeli personnel and installations followed by large scale conventional Israeli reprisals against villages in neighboring Arab states - against Jordanian settlements in 1966/67 and against Lebanese in 1972/73. (6)

The analogy became uncannily complete on September 13, 1973 when Syrian and Israeli aircraft clashed over Tarsus. In the ensuing combat, thirteen Syrian MIG-21s and one Israeli Mirage were downed. To those concerned, this must have appeared as an instant replay of an air battle over Damascus on April 7, 1967 in which seven Syrian aircraft were destroyed.

The Israeli reaction was almost identical in both 1967 and 1973. Prime Minister Meir declared, much as her predecessor Levi Eshkol had done, that:

> This battle was one of the results of the reinforcement of IDF power, and not just in the air, since the ceasefire three years ago. (7)

Radio Cairo followed a day later with commentary similarly harking back to the official Egyptian view in 1967:

> The results of the air battles initiated by Israel on the Syrian front, Thursday, indicate that Israel failed to achieve the objectives of this large scale attack on Syria. The attack definitely had major objectives and was very carefully planned over a period of time. It is also definite that the United States took part in this operation in one way or another through joint planning and coordination between Washington and Tel Aviv... (8)

(It was after this confrontation that al-Sadat and al-Asad finally came to an agreement on the immediate necessity of a preemptive attack.) (9)

The June 1967 War was, in the terminology of escalation, an unintended war: (10) A war which was the consequence of an escalatory process in which each of several sides, Arab and Israeli, responded ad hoc to specific, short term crisis situations as they perceived them. The combined result of their activities was an escalation and combination of conflicts into a relatively large scale war. (11) As Israeli historian Walter Laqueur was to describe the outbreak of the war a year later:

> War broke out in June as the result of a series of events that had started three weeks earlier. It was a textbook case of escalation; one event led to another with almost iron consequence. Yet calculation looms larger in retrospect than it was, improvisation and accident played a great role. There is so often a temptation to read too much purpose and premeditation and far reaching planning into the course of events. (12)

This escalatory process had its historical source in the tensions deriving from the establishment of the state of Israel in 1948: The creation of a large refugee population which was located principally in Jordan and the Gaza Strip, but with sizable numbers in Lebanon, Syria, and the Arabian Gulf sheykdoms; a population which was also unabsorbable by host countries for a variety of political, economic, and cultural reasons. (13) The existence of this refugee problem and the traumatic (the war of

1948 is known in the Arab world as al-nakba - the disaster or catastrophe) (14) events of its creation, set the style of subsequent Arab politics. No Arab leaders could afford to be branded as being "soft on Israel," or to be accused of selling out to the Palestinians.

But these same Palestinians represented a threat to the security of these host countries because of their espousal of radical, anti establishment causes, and their penchant for launching small scale border crossing expeditions into Israel. Given the fact that all Arab governments were officially dedicated to the "sacred cause of Palestine," any attempt to crack down on Palestinian activities per se was an extremely touchy business. The consequence was a verbal one-up-manship on the Palestine issue, with each Arab leader trying to out do his fellows in hawkishness. This was combined with sub rosa efforts to control the border crossing activities of Palestinian groups. After a period of uncontrolled activity in the early 1950s, Palestinian incursions into Israel were tightly controlled by the Arab governments concerned. The frequency of these attacks was the outcome of domestic and intra-Arab politics. (15)

In addition to the refugee problem, there were a series of conflicts over boundaries, particularly over the Syrian-Israeli boundary. (16) The armistice lines of 1948-49 had left the Syrian-Israeli borders demarcated with a hodge podge of demilitarized zones and territorial no man's lands. The patterns of land holding and usufruct were interspersed between Syrians and Israelis in a checkerboard fashion. The Israelis espoused the doctrine that these areas were under Israeli sovereignty and consistently attempted to farm them. The Syrians replied to these attempts by firing on Israeli farmers. The Israelis then countered by sporadic, but relatively large scale, "massive retaliations," raids against either Syrian or Jordanian villages. The United Nations forces which were supposed to prevent this sort of border exchange were not especially effective. (17)

Another factor was added to the border problems in 1963. In that year the Israelis began work on a series of pipelines to divert the Jordan waters from Lake Tiberias to the Negev Desert. The amount of water ultimately to be diverted was based upon the division embodied in the Johnston Plan of 1955, and therefore seemed to be a reasonable (to United States opinion at least) utilization of the Jordan's waters. It was vehemently rejected by bordering Arab states. They argued that such a diversion would lower the water table significantly and thus increase the saline content of the remaining waters, rendering them useless for irrigation and other purposes. Nevertheless, the Israelis moved ahead with the waterwork construction while their Arab neighbors fumed.

But as Laqueur again so aptly put it:

In May 1967 all the ingredients existed for a major flare up in the Middle East; the arms race had continued for twelve years. Arab guerilla activities against Israel had reached a new climax in the past few months; there was more tension than ever before between Israel and the Arab countries. But these ingredients had existed all along, and yet war had not broken out on past occasions. (18)

In the middle 1950s, these ever present ingredients began to cycle together: worsened domestic conflicts in one or more Arab states, particularly Syria and Egypt; intensified intra-Arab rivalries leading to a pattern of "overbidding" on the issue of the Israeli water diversion - including Syrian sponsored raids by Fatah on Israeli installations; and increased Russian influence in both Egypt and Syria. In short, two levels of conflicts, domestic and intra-Arab international were involved. But these cycled together in the context of a third level of cultural conflicts, and of images drawn from earlier Arab-Israeli clashes. Images which took the form of a series of self fulfilling prophecies; perceptions of contemporaneous events sharply colored by interpretations drawn from conflict model imagery; in particular, "lessons" drawn from the Suez crisis of 1956 and the experiences of years of border exchanges. These lessons were in turn worked into the general perceptual framework of Arab politics. This was particularly the case in Syria where a recently installed neo-Ba'th leadership was becoming increasingly worried about its chances for survival, and in Egypt where President 'abd al-Nasir found himself increasingly isolated both domestically and within the Arab world.

SYRIA: THE PROJECTION OF PRIMORDIAL CONFLICT

Since the middle fifties Syrian politics have revolved around the attempts of various governments to legitimate themselves. This became especially true after February 23, 1966. On that date a radical faction of the Ba'th party had overthrown the original Ba'th leadership which had ruled since 1963. This new group (nicknamed the neo-Ba'th to distinguish it from its predecessor) was of younger officers and provincial politicians. Sociologically speaking it represented a less well educated, rural elite in contrast to the sophisticated, Western educated, urban (especially Damascene) old line Ba'th elite. (19)

This regime was dominated by a military/civilian coalition in which schismatic Shi'a Muslim sects were heavily over represented; in particular Shi'as belonging to the 'Alawi sect. Both the Minister of Defense and Commander of the Air Force, Lt. General Hafiz al-Asad and the Assistant Secretary General of the Ba'th Party, Major General Salah Jadid, were 'Alawis. The 'Alawis along with two other groups, the Isma'ilis and Druzes, had been recruited into both the Syrian officer corps and the membership of the Ba'th. (20) They had moved into the military because this was one of the few avenues of upward mobility open to minorities in Syria. By contrast, orthodox Sunni Muslim families did not encourage their sons to go into the military, nor were Sunni attracted by the secularist doctrines of the Ba'th.

The net effect of this sectarian recruitment pattern was to focus existing primordial tensions on the Syrian government. With the advent of Ba'th rule, one set of sectarian groups, the Shi'as, dominate the government, another larger sectarian community, the Sunnis, is, in turn, dominated by this government. The consequence, as Clifford Geertz has argued, (21) was the creation of a situation of primordial conflict: a conflict pattern in which two or more primordial groups contend for control of the apparatus of the state. The issues of the conflict are those of the "honor" of each community; the feeling on the part of each that it is superior to the others because of some primordial "givens" - in this case superiority deriving from religious confession, and consequently the belief that to be ruled by a government controlled by a rival primordial group meant collective dishonor to one's own group. Normally, this type of conflict would present an extremely explosive situation by itself (the civil war between Hindus and Muslims in India in the 1940s, which led to partition between India and Pakistan is an example), but the Syrian situation was made more complex by the dislocations caused by rapid social change.

In any event, Shi'as of various sects were systematically recruited into the Syrian government, and consequently found their communal status bound up with its existence and policies. Some Shi'a sects were more closely involved than others. The 'Alawi community in particular developed a proprietary interest in, and a collective identification with both the Ba'th and the air force. (22) This primordial identification of the 'Alawis with the Ba'th and the air force became a critical factor in Syrian politics after 1966; as went the fortunes of either the Ba'th or the Air Force, so went the collective honor of the 'Alawis.

What is important here, in addition to the web of domestic conflicts within Syria itself, is the conjunction of two well developed sets of conflict images: Shi'a Islam and Ba'th Socialist ideology. The Shi'a branch of Islam emerged in the 7th century A.D. as the consequence of a struggle within the Muslim elite over not only the proper personnel to succeed the Prophet, but also over the appropriate principle of succession. In brief, the majority of Sunni Muslims opted for three subsequent heirs to the Prophet's political and administrative role, Abu Bakr, 'Umar and 'Uthman. The Shi'as on the contrary believed that only the Prophet's son-in-law, 'Ali, was fit to take over leadership of the Islamic community. In addition, the Sunnis accepted an elective theory of succession, while the Shi'as adopted a charismatic theory, holding that only those decendants of 'Ali were possessed of a grace which would make them worthy to lead the Muslims. These contending viewpoints met in a major civil war which split the Islamic community toward the end of the seventh century. The Shi'as were defeated, 'Ali and his immediate descendants slain, and the survivors took refuge in mountainous areas in the Levant and Mesopotamia.

From then to present, Sunni-Shi'a hostility formed a backdrop to Islamic politics. Shi'as were more or less continuously persecuted by agents of Sunni governments. Shi'a governments, where they were established, engaged in overt and covert attacks on Sunni establishments, operating either with armies in the field or through clandestine networks of propagandists who fomented uprisings. Chronicles of Levantine history during the Middle Ages, for example, are full of cycles of uprising and persecutions. Whatever the historical outcomes, the Shi'a perceptual system that emerged is that of a persecuted

minority: the whole world was seen as being hostile. This sense of
overwhelming outside threat was, in turn, formalized into a theological
doctrine. Under the doctrine of "taqiya" (concealment), Shi'a Muslims
were allowed to pass themselves off as practicing Sunnis to avoid
persecution. (23)

Thus even in the absence of political considerations, Shi'as in Syria
had a well developed conflict orientation. However, there were
political considerations, and these were supplied by the additional
factor of nationalism, or rather nationalist ideology. As a political
response to their minority social status, Shi'as (along with Christians)
became adherents of versions of Arab nationalism which emphasized
Arab cultural elements as the common core of a nationalist
identity. (24) According to Sylvia Haim, one of the earliest proponents
of what became Ba'th socialism was an 'Alawi. (25) Alternatively,
Michel Aflaq the premier ideologist of the Ba'th is Greek Orthodox. In
any event this ideology attempted to bypass or at least reduce, in
theory, the importance of Islam as a definition of Arabism, thus
avoiding emphasis on religious differences with majority/minority
connotations. (26)

Originally, Ba'thist ideology was drawn from a composite of
Western, especially Germanic, nationalist writings and Arab intellectual
sources. As such, it is an interesting study in the process of cultural
selection, since the European concepts that were used mirror existing
Arab political notions. Syncretism aside, Ba'thism as a nation building
ideology was uniquely adapted to the discontinuities of social change in
post-World War II Syria. French colonial policies designed to secure
French control and to Frenchify Syria had accelerated the social
mobilization of the middle strata of Syrian society. The upshot of this
mobilization process was that by the 1940s, these strata had become
both politicized and alienated. In the immediate post independence
period an entrenched, land owning elite of conservative nationalists
found themselves increasingly opposed by a growing "new Middle class,"
a younger generation of Syrians; a generation which was sociologically
outside of traditional society, but not capable of moving upward into
the nationalist elite.

In psychoanalytic terms, this generation was in the throes of an
identity crisis, both generational and individual, on a massive scale.
Lerner's 1951 United States Information Agency (USIA) survey data
documents the extent of this crisis, its individual protocols indicate the
depth of frustration, bitterness, and desire for extreme solutions on the
part of respondents:

The only way I can do something is to become a dictator. A
large enlightened minority must take hold of the situation by force...

I would blow up all the government and have a new one that
would respect the people and fear God...I would act as a dictator and
educate the people to work for their good...

I would have a sword and kill all those in the big chairs in the government now...Once I have done that I could set up a dictatorship and strike with an iron hand at all who dare move... (27)

In this situation of intense intra communal and intra generation hostility, Ba'th socialism offered a solution. In almost Freudian terms, Ba'th ideologists spelled out a program for ministering to the psyches of these dislocated young Syrians. Endemic conflict within Syria was to be ended; religious cleavages were to be submerged in a secular definition of political community. Group and individual anomie were to be ended by an emotional commitment to the mystical ideal of the Arab nation. Alienation and apathy were to be cured by the solidarity of the mission of the Arab nation. A world of conflict was to be replaced by a world of love:

> The Arabs are one nation. This nation has the natural right to live in a single state and to be free to direct its own destiny. The Party of the Arab Ba'th therefore believes that: (1) The Arab fatherland constitutes an indivisible political and economic unity. No Arab country can live apart from the others. (2) The Arab nation constitutes a cultural unity. Any differences existing among its sons are accidental and unimportant. They will disappear with the awakening of the Arab consciousness....Art. 7. The Arab fatherland is that part of the globe inhabited by the Arab nation which stretches from the Taurus Mountain, the Pocht-i-Kouh Mountains, the Gulf of Basra, the Arab Ocean, the Ethiopian Mountains, the Sahara, the Atlantic Ocean, and the Mediterranean. Art. 10. An Arab is he whose language is Arabic, who has lived on Arab soil, or who, after having been assimilated to Arab life, has faith in his belonging to the Arab nation... Constitution of the Arab Ba'th Party

> The nationalism for which we call is love before anything else. It is the very feeling that binds the individual to his family, because the fatherland is only a large household, and the nation is a large family. Nationalism, like every kind of love, fills the heart with joy and spreads hope in the soul; he who feels it, would wish to share with all people this joy which raises him above narrow egoism, draws him nearer to goodness and perfection....and as love is always linked to sacrifice, so is nationalism. Sacrifice for the sake of nationalism leads to heroism, for he who sacrifices everything for his people in defense of its past glory and future welfare, is more elevated in spirit and richer in life than he who makes a sacrifice for the sake of one person...Nationalism is Love Before Anything Else. (28)

But, in spite of the language of love, Syrian Ba'thists in practice pursued extremely aggressive policies against their opponents, real or imagined. Here the preexisting Shi'a and Ba'th conflict model image systems combined with a calculous of policy; a policy designed to preserve group cohesion. By defining its environment in terms of threats to be met at all costs, the Ba'th elite clearly hoped to maintain control over its own schismatic rank and file. Minorities within the party were to be kept loyal by accentuating religious cleavages, thus removing any minority option to identify with neo-Ba'this Sunni organizations. Individuals likewise were to be controlled by the insistence on party discipline in the face of a clear and present danger. (29)

In addition, this deliberate intensification of conflict had psychological overtones: the frustrations of the Ba'this elite could be projected onto selected targets, thus lowering the level of intra elite conflict. The frustration of the young Syrians, whose upward mobility had heretofore been blocked, was translated into a theory of radical social change when in power. The sense of powerlessness and the persecution complex of the Shi'as was transformed into a policy of thorough going secularization. Religious differences, with all the obliguity they implied for Shi'as , were to be eradicated. The conflict thus generated would function as a safety valve, an outlet for hostilities which might otherwise tear the Ba'th party and elite apart. (30)

But as a consequence, the Sunni majority, already hostile to the Ba'th because of its Shi'a connection, greatly intensified. In December 1963 a student at a Homs high school stabbed his teacher after the teacher had torn up a Qur'an. In April 1964 a group of Sunni 'ulama' barricaded themselves in several mosques in Hama and declared themselves in revolt against the godless regime. The government unwisely countered this by shelling the mosques. The revolt was crushed, but Sunni sensibilities were shocked. In December 1964 the leaders of a Sunni organization, Kata'ib Muhammad (Muhammad's Battalions), were arrested after they preached a series of sermons denouncing the Ba'th as godless. This time the government responded by using an armed workers militia to restore order, but this tactic only produced further problems, since the head of the militia was an Isma'ili. (31) Following these Sunni disturbances, the government decreed a number of restrictive measures against Druze, Kurdish, and Christian communities. These were apparently designed to mollify Sunni feelings, but they merely served to antagonize still other sectarian groups. (32)

Alternatively, and partly to diffuse tensions generated by their secularist orientation, the Ba'th opted for an extremely hard line against Israel. Here the safety valve technique was applied to Syrian society as a whole. When domestic tensions reached an unacceptable level, the Ba'thists could raise the salience of the ongoing border conflict with Israel and thus divert hostility outward. As a target, Israel was ideal. Arab ideology had for years been promulgating the image of a hostile and expansionist Israel; this image had been more or less completely internalized into the cognitions of Arabs, both elite and mass. Moreover, the image had a sufficient reality behind it. The Syrian/Israeli border had for years been the scene of tit for tat exchanges and fire fights. Israeli leaders had equally been openly bellicose in their utterances on the subject of these exchanges. In this case, both the old and neo-Ba'th advocated an immediate, and extensive, war of popular liberation against Israel. In line with this goal, the Ba'thists sponsored and organized a number of Palestinian groups, the most well known of which was Fatah. Fatah raids, in turn, led to Israeli reprisals.

Even though the Ba'th conceived of itself as being surrounded on all sides by enemies, this threat from outside was not sufficiently salient to repress intra elite conflicts:

a) In the 'Alawi community itself, Generals al-Asad and Jadid were rivals for control of the state, a rivalry that had both personal and familial components as well. Jadid's supporters dominated the Ba'th party organization and Syrian intelligence. Al-Asad's group controlled most of the ground forces, which were held for him by his Sunni supporter, Major General Mustafa Talas, and the Air Force. (33)

Ideologically speaking, Jadid wanted a radical restructuring of the Syrian economy along Marxist, or even Maoist, lines, and a foreign policy of unmitigated hostility to all less radical Arab states. By utilizing his position within the Ba'th party, he had managed to orient Syrian policies in this direction in 1966. Al-Asad and Talas opposed this radicalism in favor of a more pragmatic approach; less emphasis on ideology and more on training in the military, less stringent economic and social programs, and less isolationism in the Arab world. Al-Asad and Jadid, however, papered over their differences sufficiently to cooperate in order to preserve 'Alawi control over the military.

This conflict remained internal to the regime and party throughout the sixties, but burst into the open in September 1970. Jadid's faction had consistently pushed for a very aggressive Syrian support for the Palestinian cause. In particular they had attempted to dominate al-Sa'iqa, the Syrian organized Palestinian unit, and utilize it to accelerate attacks on Israel In addition, they had also managed to convince commanders of Syrian regular units to engage in a more active confrontation with Israeli forces, along with al-Sa'iqa units.

In September, Syrian regular armored units operating with PLA/al-Sa'iqa units moved into Jordan to aid embattled Palestinian insurgents. Al-Asad and his colleagues refused to permit Syrian aircraft (there was, of course, considerable outside pressure on the Syrian government to limit its involvement, anyway) to give air support to these units. In the aftermath of the inglorious Syrian military performance in Jordan, the al-Asad faction launched a coup within a coup and took power in November 1970. (34)

b) Between the 'Alawi and the Druze communities. For a variety of reasons relations between the two communal groups began to deteriorate rapidly in the middle sixties. The Druzes appear to have been particularly incensed by government/'Alawi measures designed to reduce Druze autonomy, and by 'Alawi domination of senior officer ranks. Bitter jokes circulated through the Druze population to the effect that things were so bad that 'Alawi women could order Druze men about at will.

The consequence of this Druze unrest was a September 8, 1966 attempted coup led by Major Salim Hatum (a key figure in the February 1966 coup), and a number of Druze officers, with both Jordanian and exiled Ba'thist support. (35) Purges in the army and air force followed; many of the best pilots in the air force were exiled to Saudi Arabia (where they became, it is said, school teachers), with the consequence that the efficiency of the Syrian military was seriously weakened. (36) In response to the purges, the Druzes of the al-Suwayda district revolted under the leadership of Sultan al-'Atrash. Syrian Druze opposition to the government was supported by Lebanese Druzes. (37)

c) There were further conflicts with the Isma'ili community. The Isma'ilis, especially the al-Jundi family, had entrenched themselves in Syrian intelligence and paramilitary workers' units, headed by Lt. Colonel 'abd al-Karim al-Jundi and Khalid al-Jundi respectively.   As such they had become a threat to both al-Asad and Jadid. Khalid al-Jundi was forced to resign his position in July and then was arrested in December; 'abd al-Karim's supporters in intelligence were systematically purged during 1967 and he, himself, forced out in 1968.

Thus, the conflict oriented tactics had not paid off internally, and had generated intense opposition externally. The Ba'thist government was unpopular among wide sections of the Syrian populace. Among Sunnis, it was derogatorily referred to as the 'adas (lentil bean) regime, the term 'adas being an acronym of words 'Alawi, Druze and Isma'ili. (38) It was opposed by economic interests which cross cut Sunni/non-Sunni identifications: urban capitalists and merchants were hostile to Ba'th socialism; rural landowners physically opposed Ba'th land reform programs. (39) Ba'th attempts to create a Maoist style cultural revolution alienated all sectarian groups.

In addition, Ba'thist foreign policies had produced a ring of hostile surrounding states. Israel was incensed by periodic Syrian shelling of border settlements, and by Syrian aid to Fatah. Jordan's conservative regime opposed the Syrians on two counts; because of the radical implications of Ba'th ideology operationalized in repeated Syrian interference in Jordanian politics, and because of long standing Syrian claims to Northern Jordan itself. The government of Iraq was outraged by Syrian pipe cutting tactics as part of a dispute over IPC transit revenues on pipelines crossing Syrian territory. The Egyptians saw the Syrians as their chief ideological rivals to leadership of the Arab nationalist movement and were more than a little concerned over the escalatory possibilities inherent in the Syrian doctrine, and practice of a popular war of liberation against Israel.   Last but not least, the remnants of the ousted Ba'th pan-Arab command were aggressively exploiting every opportunity to bring the neo-Ba'th regime down.

In this tense situation, an article appeared in al-Jaysh al-Sha'b (The People's Army), the official magazine of the Syrian army.   Its publication date, April 25, 1967, is significant, in fact it is probably a monument to bad timing, because it was published less than two weeks after the Israeli rout of the Syrian air force. (40) This defeat had significance out of proportion to the numbers of aircraft involved for two reasons: first, the Syrian air force was identified with the 'Alawi community. A loss by the air force was a blow to 'Alawi honor, and other groups in the Ba'th coalition were quick to draw implication concerning unfitness to head the regime. Second, the air force was itself the symbol of the neo-Ba'thist revolution; if the air force were ineffective, clearly the Ba'th was also.

The article itself called for a complete rejection of everything Islamic. Islam, the author argued, had been the chief enemy of progress in Syria. As such, Islam should be replaced by a secular belief system, one in which traditional Islamic fatalism would be superseded by a belief in man's ability to master his environment. This meant, said the author, that the Syrian government should dedicate itself to the creation of a society of "new Arab men," a society organized along Marxist or even Maoist lines.

This attack on Islam triggered an unexpectedly virulent wave of protests. All through April and into May, the 'ulama' preached revolt in their Friday sermons. Mass demonstrations and rioting followed, particularly in the Homs, Hama areas. Bazaar merchants joined the demonstrations and called for a general shutdown of the economy. The government responded by sentencing the article's author to death, but to no avail. The situation was further aggravated by Jordanian and Saudi propaganda broadcasts which called upon the populace to revolt in the name of God. (41) Due to divisions between Druzes and 'Alawis within the military, the government decided not to risk using regular troops. Again the Isma'ilis were called upon to bear the brunt of the fighting, and also the brunt of any subsequent Sunni retaliation. (42) Armed militia and worker units quelled the disturbances, but the prospect of a major Sunni uprising remained. (43)

The regime therefore found itself faced with a potential revolutionary situation: opposition from a majority of its population; division within its own security forces; the possibility of a major confrontation with its neighbors, and the ignominious defeat of its most prized symbol. The reality of conflict had suddenly become overwhelming; at this juncture, the Ba'thist image. system took over. Syrian decision makers appear to have been operating in a state of near hysteria. The Syrian press, if this is an indication of the regime's outlook, outdid itself in proclaiming that the riots were the work of Jordanian intelligence, the CIA, the Muslim Brethren, and a whole host of conspirators. (44)

EGYPT: ERIKSONIAN HERO IN SEARCH OF A ROLE

If Syrian politics prior to the June War were dominated by the efforts of the neo-Ba'th to legitimatize their rule, Egyptian politics were equally dominated by the personality of one man - Jamal 'abd al-Nasir. Although Nasir's role in shaping Arab events is now subject of some debate in the Arab world, it must not be forgotten that his personality has stamped itself on Arab politics. To those who had dealings with him, 'abd al-Nasir was an impressive and unpredictable figure. Miles Copeland, the self-proclaimed CIA man in Cairo, once described 'abd al-Nasir was "one of the most courageous, most incorruptible, most unprincipled, and, in his way, most humanitarian of all the nationalistic leaders it has been my pleasure to meet." (45) In any event, the concern here is not to attack or defend 'abd al-Nasir, but to examine the impact of his personality on the escalation and war of June 1967.

'Abd al-Nasir emerged from a behind-the-scenes organizer of a military coup in 1952 into a public figure, a personality who evolved from a somewhat boring orator who could not hold the attention of an unruly Egyptian audience, to a spell binder on the order of Daniel Webster (or more colloquially, a personality that came across as an Egyptian John Wayne). While this public metamorphosis was taking place, 'abd al-Nasir was consolidating his actual power by reducing his domestic opponents to temporary impotence by a strategy of selective attack: first Nationalistic parties, primarily the Wafd, then Egyptian communists, then the Muslim Brethren and General Muhammad Najib (as Eisenhower-like figure now restored to honor), and finally all other opponents, real or imagined. Details aside, what impressed the observer was 'abd al-Nasir's instinct for the opponent's jugular, his ability to isolate and then (literally in some cases) destroy an enemy; an ability that Machiavelli himself would have admired and probably incorporated into The Prince, for 'abd al-Nasir was indeed a modern condottiere.

But there is considerably more involved in connection with the rise to power of 'abd al-Nasir than the chronology of yet another Middle Eastern dictator. Hrair Dekmejian has analyzed 'abd al-Nasir's rule in terms of Max Weber's concept of charisma. Charisma as Weber defines it is:

> a certain quality of an individual personality by virtue of which he is set apart from ordinary men and treated as though endowed with supernatural and superhuman, or at least specifically exceptional powers or qualities. These are such as are not accessible to the ordinary person, but are regarded as of divine origin or as exemplary and on the basis of them the individual concerned is treated as a leader. (46)

As Dekmejian points out, 'abd al-Nasir rose to power in a time of great social upheaval in both Egypt and the Arab world. 'Abd al-Nasir's charisma, therefore, was the product of the interaction of his personality and the psychological needs of the masses of Egyptians (the same situation as existed in Syria):

(1) It appears that the incidence of charisma is tied to the interaction of a variety of complex factors...A situation of acute social crisis characterized by the pathological response of society to a break-down of the existing mechanisms of conflict resolution. In such times, irrational, schizophrenia-like disorientations occur creating a

deep sense of psychological dependence and heightened expectation. At the political level a crisis in legitimacy engulfs the system...The prevailing milieu of mass alienation, social atomization, and identity crisis renders the populace vulnerable to mass appeals.

(2) The appearance of an exemplary personage without whom the charismatic relationship will not begin... And vice versa, the process cannot be initiated without circumstance of turmoil, regardless of a leader's charismatic potential...The intervening variables which appear during the self revelation are performance message, personal qualities and the opportunity to propagate...The leader reveals himself through his heroic performance and a messianic message. These two components are mutually reinforcing; the leader's performance may represent the unfolding of his message, or the message may contain his program for heroic activity... (47)

In more concrete terms, post-World War I Egyptian society was fragmenting under the impact of change induced by that war. Conflicts inherent in Egyptian culture and society were heightened by this change. (48) At the same time, the normal mechanisms of dealing with conflict, Kardiner's "security systems," were very largely inadequate to cope with this new situation. Symptomatic of the increase of widespread psychological alienation and loss of community was the appearance of quasi totalitarian parties: Misr al-Fatat (young Egypt), a proto-fascist party, the Egyptian Communist Party, and the Muslim Brethren, an Islamic fundamentalist party. Although these parties had little in common by way of ideology, they shared the same psychological and social function: to provide new identities for their members, and new sources of communal security (exactly like the later Ba'th in Syria).

The key to 'abd al-Nasir's ability to identify with and articulate the emotions and fears of his fellow Egyptians lay in the fact that 'abd al-Nasir, himself, felt the same emotions. In this sense, 'abd al-Nasir was very much like Martin Luther who, as Erik Erikson described him, worked out his ego problems and in the process created a new theology. (49) Here it is well to requote the passage rendered earlier; this time in the context of 'abd al-Nasir's expression of his own role search:

> I do not know why I recall, whenever I reach this point in my recollections as I meditate alone in my room, a famous tale by a great Italian poet, Luigi Pirandello - "Six Characters in Search of an Author." The pages of history are full of heroes who created for themselves roles of glorious valor which they played at decisive moments. Likewise the pages of history are also full of heroic and glorious roles which never found heroes to perform them. (50)

This yearning to play the role of a hero appears to be very much an expression of 'abd al-Nasir's own sense of personal insecurity, or marginality, of inchoate expectations. A number of biographers have pointed out that, as a young man, 'abd al-Nasir was extremely moody and withdrawn. Dekmejian summarizes some details of 'abd al-Nasir's childhood which shed a little light on this moodiness:

> Reliable and detailed information concerning Nasir's early years is unavailable, beyond the fact that his family life was generally unstable. This was characterized by strained relations between young Nasir and his father especially after the death of his mother. After his father's remarriage, it appears that Nasir's home life became particularly unhappy as he was sent away to live with relatives.   Thus from the beginning one can discern the crisis conditions that fostered alienation in Nasir's person. As he stepped from his family crisis situation into the larger, Egyptian crisis milieu of the 1920s and 1930s, his alienation deepened and intensified. Born to a father of Sa'idi peasant stock from Upper Egypt, one might safely consider Nasir a marginal in terms of Egypt's urban, middle class - the status to which the family aspired. (51)

Al-Sadat himself testifies to the combination of tension, alienation and withdrawal that characterized 'abd al-Nasir's relations with members of the RCC:

> ....'abd al-Nasir was one of those people who always live on their nerves. His life was like a tight cord 24 hours a day. As a matter of fact, 'abd al-Nasir did not create this tense atmosphere in order to surround the regime with the necessary awe. This was his nature before and after the revolution, after he planned the revolution, after he became a member and then chairman of the Revolution Council, and after he became president. This tenseness was a basic feature of his personality from the time he was 20. He could not overcome it, and the burdens and responsibilities of power seemed to increase it...This tense nature made any attempt to approach him an uneasy matter, contrary to what one might think. This electrified atmosphere created a stiff barrier between him and others. Therefore, 'abd al-Nasir did not have friends in the simple meaning of the term.... (52)

'Abd al-Nasir himself precisely articulated the psychic crisis that Egypt (and the Arab world) was going through:

> All people go through two revolutions - a political one that helps them recover their right to self-government from the hands of a despot...; and a social revolution - a class conflict that ultimately ends realizing social justice for all inhabitants of the country...

> The disintegration of values, disruption of principles, dissension and discord among both class and individuals, and the domination of corruption, suspicion, perversion of egoism, for the foundation of a social upheaval...

> And between these two milestones we find ourselves today destined to go through two revolutions - one calling for unity, solidarity, self

sacrifice, and devotion to sacred duty, while the other imposes on us, against our will, nothing but envy, hatred, vindictiveness and egoism... (53)

And then, he set about curing both, and, in doing so, created a charismatic bond between himself, and the Egyptians and Arabs in general. Again al-Sadat:

> ...I explained that it was impossible for me to pose as another 'abd al-Nasir. What Egypt had accepted from 'abd al-Nasir it could not accept from me. 'Abd al-Nasir had established a tremendous relationship with the people through liberation battles and other victories represented by the nationalization of the Suez Canal and his defiance of imperialism and the major powers. He had triumphed. Every pulse of his had an echo among the people, who entrusted him with all of their affairs. Therefore, it was natural for them to accept everything from him as a result of trust... (54)

In a larger sense 'abd al-Nasir was responding to the same set of facts as Ba'th ideologists. But there is a difference, where the Syrians expressed their crises in terms of a loss of individual identity, Nasir spoke in terms of a loss of collective dignity, a loss of authority necessary to restore the Arabs to their rightful place in the world. The subsequent Ba'thist solution was Freudian, a therapeutic community of love designed to support anomic individuals. Nasir's alternative was organization, the creation of a community based on "Unity, Discipline, Work," the slogans of the regime. Where the Ba'th operated in categories largely drawn from the West, 'abd al-Nasir harked back to older, Islamic concepts of social order, concepts originally developed to create order out of tribal anarchy:

> I had imagined our role to be a commando advance guard lasting only a few hours, after which the Holy March of the whole nation, advancing in close orderly ranks to the Great Goal would follow. I felt I could even hear the terrific and tremendous uproar caused by these great masses advancing steadily in close orderly ranks to the Great Goal...
> (But) We were in need of discipline, but found nothing but anarchy...We were in need of unity, but found nothing but disunity...We were in need of work, but found nothing but indolence and inactivity.... Hence the motto of the Revolution - Discipline, Unity and Work.... (55)

Like Luther, Nasir's own ego development was bound up with the process of creating this order. And the intensity and uncertainty of the emotions involved in this process found expression in the ideological attitude of the regime. As Malcolm Kerr once noted, conflict in model politics was the feature of Nasir's political style:

> If Nasir's leadership has stamped the Egyptian revolution with one identifiable goal, it is to advance Egyptian prestige. Both Nasir's

championship of pan-Arabism and his undoubted desire to raise domestic living standards should be seen as subordinate to this aim. Once acquired, prestige may be a psychological and political reality, but it cannot be measured out in negotiated quantities. For yesterday's underdog, and especially for the revolutionary, prestige must be seized from others at their expense.

This helps to account for certain qualities of style of Egyptian revolutionary policies. One such quality is the constant inculcation of the spirit of struggle and the state of war mentality, whereby every success of the regime, however mundane, and even some of its failures, tend to be depicted as advances on the battlefield against the allied forces of imperialism and reaction.

Another stylistic quality is the regime's compulsion to keep the initiative in the eyes of its public, and to play up the succession of crises by which enthusiasm can be fostered. This creates a stake in a certain level of friction with one or another of the Western Powers, and usually with some other Arab state. But to what strategic end? No one can really say. Like other movements, Nasirism's first property is motion. Goals tend to emerge from what tactical situations produce, rather than tactics serving a long-range vision of concrete needs. This is not to say that Nasirism is devoid of a sense of purpose, but simply that it is equally a restless state of mind. (56)

Where Syrian conflict imagery drew heavily on Shi'a attitudes and historical experience, Nasir's model was more closely related to existing Arab, in addition to Sunni, Islamic values. In this case, these values, already described above, which relate to honor and the vindication of dishonor. Here the constant stress on struggle, the insistence that prestige be seized from others, the restless quality that characterized Nasirism is a projection not only of Nasir's inner turmoil but also that of the Arab male ego writ large. Patai's description of Arab machismo syndrome echoes Kerr's description of Nasirist politics:

Arab ethics revolve around a single focal point, that of self-esteem or self-respect...Since karama (dignity) depends on the respect accorded to a man by others, if a man is insulted, his karama is damaged. To restore it, one must put up a great show of reaction. By hurling back a greater insult than one sustained, one shows that one does acquiesce in the insult...The man who has self respect does not allow anybody to insult him with impunity. (57)

CHARISMA AND ITS CONSTRAINTS: INTERPLAY OF LOCAL AND SYSTEMATIC POLITICS

In summation, both the Syrian and Egyptian leadership had resorted to legitimizing techniques which rested on an ability to project discontent outward.   Local Syrian and Egyptian instabilities were, therefore, reflected in inherently escalatory foreign policies. However, there was a difference in the potential impact of these foreign policies. Where the Syrians were relatively limited by a lack of capabilities, military and otherwise, the Egyptians were not. This is so because 'abd al-Nasir was able to compensate for his limited ability to project Egyptian power directly by, instead, resorting to the media appeals. By using the media to amplify his charismatic appeal, 'abd al-Nasir linked the vagaries of local Egyptian politics with a much wider circle of intra-Arab conflicts.

Because of a series of historical accidents, e.g., the Czech arms agreement of 1955 and the Suez crisis and war of 1956, 'abd al-Nasir's political fortunes had become tied to his ability to project the image of an Arab hero doing battle against the West, and its allies in the Arab world. Indeed, one of the critical factors that enabled 'abd al-Nasir to stay in power had been his genius for using conflict imagery to divert domestic discontent away from his person and regime and onto external targets. His technique was strategically like that of the Syrian Ba'th, but tactically far more sophisticated and successful. Where the Ba'th suffered from a certain lack of glamour, Nasir radiated charisma.

Nevertheless, the resort to charismatic politics carried with it considerable danger. As Weber pointed out, the charismatic leaders of necessity had to continually work miracles. (58) In Nasir's case, the miracles were achieved by constantly switching targets.   As a consequence, Egyptian foreign and domestic policy looked like a sine wave: When domestic strategems aimed at elevating Egyptian standards of living failed (as they usually did, since the Egyptian birthrate outran all attempts to increase food and energy supplies), 'abd al-Nasir would resort to some spectacular foreign adventure. When these foreign extravaganzas lost their drama, he would return to some form of domestic development. (59)

But by the middle sixties 'abd al-Nasir's ability to maneuver in this fashion was seriously hampered by a number of factors:

a) A series of development plans had failed to live up to popular expectations conjured up by Egyptian media. By 1964 the Egyptians were forced to rely heavily on foreign credits to finance development projects. By 1965 the government was forced to introduce stringent restrictions on imports to conserve its dwindling foreign exchange. (60) The increasing foreign indebtedness coincided with local economic dislocations due to the operations of successive plans:

The expansion of employment and earnings, combined with the priority given to capital goods over consumer goods in both imports and home investment, led to inflation, shortages, and rising prices. Home agricultural production was not rising fast enough to meet the increased demand for food, and other consumer goods, such as clothing, were in short supply. The government attempts to control supply and prices through cooperatives led to a parallel black market and shortages of goods at official prices. (61)

Urban economic discontent was paralleled by rural unrest. In April 1966 the regime launched a drive to break the power of the 'umdas, a class of rural landowners that had grown up during the preceding century. This new attempt at land redistribution produced very active 'umda opposition which culminated in the murder of a local official. The "feudalists" were ultimately dispatched, but at the cost of dislocating rural Egyptian society. (62)

The Arab Socialist Union, which was created in 1962 as a vehicle to provide ersatz popular participation, and thus draw off popular resentment, had failed. (63) Designed to link all segments of Egyptian society together in a one party framework, (64) it had, instead, been captured by a combination of party officials and old line, anti-Nasir politicians. These "power centers," as they were later styled, came to be a threat themselves to the regime." (65)

As a consequence of these domestic policies and the Yemen war

Discontent was felt among the working class at the rising cost of living, and among some of the professional class and businessmen who had been affected by the nationalizations. The emergence of a new privileged group of army officers holding influential jobs in the expanding bureaucracy (sic: They staffed most of the local government positions) and the strengthening of the army's position through the Yemen war, also aroused resentment among the middle class and the intelligensia. Then there were, of course, the former rich (sic: The Mehmet 'Ali elite) who had lost at least part of their wealth and all their political influence. (66)

These discontents exploded in September 1965 during the course of a funeral for the Wafdist leader, Mustafa Nahas. The cortege was followed by enormous crowds which chanted anti regime slogans. (67)

b) At the same time, 'abd al-Nasir's ability to create grand coalitions of Arabs to move against enemies, real or imagined, of the Arab cause was seriously weakened. (68) The so-called radical camp of Egypt, Syria, and Iraq was bitterly divided among itself. The UAR had broken up in 1961 over substantial Egyptian/Syrian differences; the Tripartite Egyptian, Syrian, Iraqi Talks of 1963 had collapsed in acrimony. (69) Egypt found its leadership of the radical camp increasingly opposed by neo-Ba'th militants in Syria: Militants who were increasingly willing to utilize the Palestinian question for their own ends, regardless of the risk of confrontation with the Israelis, a risk which 'abd al-Nasir did not wish to chance. (70)

'Abd al-Nasir's response was to temporize. He called for a series of Summits of Kings and Presidents in 1964. During these, 'abd al-Nasir and the Syrians collided over the issue of Israel. The Syrians argued that some form of action against Israel and the diversion project must be undertaken at once; if not an all out conventional war, then at least a "war of popular liberation," using Palestinian irregulars. 'Abd al-Nasir replied by pointing out that any sort of conflict with Israel would require a massive strengthening of Arab military capabilities. This would necessitate a thorough going modernization of Arab societies, preferably by an Egyptian style revolution. Until this was accomplished the Arabs would neither be united enough nor strong enough to wage war. Therefore it was necessary to wait and, more importantly, to avoid provoking a premature confrontation, until such time as the Arabs were ready. (71)

'Abd al-Nasir managed to prevail on the assembly, but at a cost. As part of the interim strategy Jordan and Lebanon were to start their own diversionary projects. The Egyptians were forced to agree to provide the Jordanians with air cover for these irrigation works in case of Israeli attacks. Further, the Palestinians were to be given their own organization, the Palestine Liberation Organization (PLO) which was to be financed by the oil producing states. (72) In addition, Russia for its own reasons (mostly to both bolster and restrain Syrian leadership) pressed the Egyptians to negotiate a defense agreement with the Syrians - an agreement concluded on November 4, 1966.

According to Kerr, 'abd al-Nasir's own goals in opting for this strategy were fourfold:

(1) to propose the possibility of military confrontation with Israel into the indefinite future, thus avoiding a threat to Egypt's security;

(2) to reduce Egypt's unilateral responsibility for protecting Arab diversion projections;

(3) to hold his position as leader of the Arab world by appearing to be doing something about the Israelis; and

(4) by drawing the Syrians into a military treaty, to provide Egypt with some leverage to limit Syrian activities against Israel. (73)

The thrust of this strategy, in toto, was to reduce foreign policy risks while at the same time maintaining the benefits which accrued from the charismatic role assumed by 'abd al-Nasir.

However, the unforeseen consequences of this strategy were to appear with surprising speed. Decisions taken at the Arab summits had the effect of making 'abd al-Nasir personally responsible for the defense of Jordan, for all practical purposes. To borrow a notion from the law of torts, 'abd al-Nasir's charismatic foreign policy strategy had extended the zone of his political liability to events he could neither foresee, nor control. The fact that 'abd al-Nasir had been, for so long, the symbolic leader of the Arabs, a role constantly emphasized by Egyptian media, had produced a set of popular expectations about his role in protecting Jordan. Moreover, the Jordanian government itself chose to manipulate these expectations and utilize the attitudinal legacy of Egyptian propaganda for its own (anti-Nasir) purposes. (74) In a curious and unplanned way, 'abd al-Nasir had become the prisoner of his own propaganda, of his own media, of his own conflict imagery.

c) In any event, this temporizing strategy did not reduce intra-Arab attacks on 'abd al-Nasir. From 1965 onward he was increasingly under a sustained propaganda and diplomatic attack from Saudi Arabia. As a response to Egyptian involvement in the North Yemeni civil war - which King Faysal correctly interpreted as an Egyptian attempt to create a springboard from which to move into the Arabian Peninsula - Faysal had launched a drive to isolate 'abd al-Nasir in the Arab world. His strategy was to resurrect Muslim solidarity and forge an alliance of conservative forces throughout the area. (75)   What emerged from the conflict between 'abd al-Nasir and Faysal was literally a battle of the Titans: 'abd al-Nasir representing the forces of militant pan-Arab Nationalism pitted against Faysal, the Shaykh/Imam, the symbolic focal point of pan-Islam. 'Abd al-Nasir was the master of the media, the charismatic product of Sawt al-Arab, the "new Arab man" himself; Faysal was the archetype of the traditional Arab leader, the expert in harem politics. The battle was initially fought in the media. Saudi radios called upon the faithful to overthrow the Godless 'abd al-Nasir and his cohorts. The Voice of the Arabs replied by dwelling on the sins of Faisal, and scheduled early evening broadcasts so that the Saudi faithful could meditate on these sins while at prayer. (76)

The Islamic alliance provoked semi-hysterical Egyptian press and radio reaction; all the more so since it coincided with an upsurge of Muslim Brethren activity within Egypt.   In September 1965, the Lebanese press carried reports of arrests totalling approximately 1,000 persons, and of the discovery of large caches of arms in the Bulaq suburb of Cairo. (77) Arrests of Brethren continued for the better part of two years, until some 6,000 had been imprisoned. (78) The Brethren were charged with plotting to assassinate the Ambassadors of the United States, Russia, Britain, and France and with planning to assassinate 'abd al-Nasir himself, by either blowing up his speaker's rostrum, blowing up his train, or by killing him while he was on the way home. (79)

The Brethren had reorganized since their debacle in 1954, creating a clandestine unit known as the "Secret Organization." (80) The mission of this unit was to kill 'abd al-Nasir and overthrow his regime, and replace it with one dedicated to theocratic principles, an Islamic society:

Where the rules of the Qur'an would be strictly applied. Among these is to leave the ruling authority to God and not to human beings. Any human ruler or authority would be competing with the authority of God. (81)

Accordingly, they also planned to kill TV and movie stars to prevent the spread of corruption and vice. (82)

Brethren were also active in Syria, Jordan, Lebanon, and the Sudan, and had organizational ties with other fundamentalist groups in Turkey, Iran, Pakistan, and North Africa. (83) But the most prominent Brethren leaders had fled to Saudi Arabia in the 1950s, where they worked within Faysal's pan-Islamic framework. Most of the financing for the Egyptian "Secret Organization" had come from Brethren in Saudi Arabia. (84)

Thus, the Islamic Alliance presented the Egyptian government with the prospect of a return to the situation of the early 1950s when the Brethren had almost assassinated 'abd al-Nasir and overthrown his regime.

The Saudi campaign was joined by King Husayn and other Jordanian officials with a series of blistering attacks on 'abd al-Nasir and his policies. These became especially intense from October 1966 onward, and reached a crescendo following a major Israeli raid on the Jordanian village of al-Samu' on November 13 which left scores dead and wounded; and triggered anti-Husayn riots in West Bank cities. Jordanian Prime Minister Wasfi al-Tal accused the Egyptians of being either unwilling or unable to provide effective air cover for Jordan. This charge was later broadened to accusations that Egypt was hiding behind UNEF. In short, that 'abd al-Nasir was a coward: a devastating charge given the "machismo" orientation of Arab culture. (85)

For a variety of reasons, 'abd al-Nasir could not let these accusations go unchallenged. The basis of his charismatic strategy at home and abroad rested on his ability to project the image of the ever victorious hero. Policy calculations aside, there were personal reasons as well. According to al-Sadat, 'abd al-Nasir had come to believe that he was, indeed, a great hero. (86) Moreover, his own rural (baladi) origins had stamped him with a tremendous sensitivity to insults, either to himself or to any member of his family. Culture, therefore, combined with personality and politics to assure a response: 'Abd al-Nasir's sense of wahj (face), his identification with the collective honor (sharaf) of the Egyptians, and his calculous of intra-Arab politics all made a response imperative. (87)

CRISIS: PERSONALITY, EVENT, AND IMAGE

While these Arab attacks mounted in severity and scope, there was still another threat that 'abd al-Nasir perceived - this time, from outside the Arab world, in the form of a United States attempt to overthrow him. Here, the source of 'abd al-Nasir's increasing preoccupation with the notion that the United States was moving to end his regime appears to lie in his own personality. Or, more precisely, it stems from 'abd al-Nasir's tendency to be extremely suspicious of his surroundings, a generalized suspicion that, at times, apparently bordered on paranoia. Al-Sadat comments repeatedly on this suspicion:

I have said that Nasser was known to be suspicious by nature, especially when it came to his personal security. His pathological view of personal security was perhaps responsible for all the emergency measures taken at that time (sic: after the June war) on an interim basis but later established and magnified into the rule rather than the exception... (88)

What is important here is not only the documentation of 'abd al-Nasir's heightened sensitivity to perceived threat, but also that of the decision making situation which facilitated the projection of this sensitivity onto policy. Egyptian decision making lacked institutional constraint and continuity for at least three reasons: (89)

(a) 'Abd al-Nasir's charismatic legitimizing strategy was, by definition, a strategy based on emotion, rather than rational calculous of interest. Lucian Pye notes that charismatic leaders tend to prevail in societies undergoing rapid change, societies in which there is confusion over values. In these situations, the charismatic leader tends to operate in terms of emotions, since the communication of emotions bypasses problems of politically educating the populace. (90) In the Egyptian case, 'abd al-Nasir not only communicated in terms of emotions, but made policy as a result of emotional responses to the communications of others:

> Nasser's policies were much influenced by his own emotional reactions. Realizing this, his men could make him do exactly what they wanted. They would provide him with a certain piece of information at a time calculated to produce, in him, a strong reaction designed to have vast international repercussions.... (91)

(b) Egyptian decision making was carried out in the context of an aggravated intra elite conflict. By the 1960s, the originally homogeneous RCC had broken up into a number of factions, the two most powerful of which were cliqued around the figures of 'abd al-Hakim 'Amir, 'abd al-Nasir's brother-in-law and best friend, and Sha'rawi Jum'a, Minister of Interior, along with Sami Sharaf, Chief of the Cabinet. These coalitions played bureaucratic politics, using their positions within the Egyptian bureaucracy to further their personal interests. (92) The consequence was decision making in a context where bureaucratic roles were not defined, and standards of administration were lacking, an institutionally unregulated struggle for power at the top.

(c) 'Abd al-Nasir apparently lacked regular and reliable information about his policy making environment. Although he attempted to compensate by requiring two and three reports, to cross check information, he still was operating with limited knowledge:

> ... His vision would be blurred, and he would lose both insight and foresight, above all because he was so greatly influenced by the reports his entourage submitted to him. His men were not honest in giving advice; all they were interested in was magnifying Nasser's self-image in his own eyes and so maintaining their own posts and power... (93)

In any event, by the middle 1960s, as Haykal states, (94) 'abd al-Nasir had become persuaded that the United States was hostile, that it was in the process of creating a US/Israeli/Saudi coalition which would either destroy Egyptian forces in Yemen or attack Egypt itself. Haykal personally had been arguing for some time that the United States was leading a global counter revolution aimed at the overthrow of radical Third World leaders: Sukarno, Nkrumah and Ben Bellah. Moreover, the United States had overtly intervened in the Congo, the Dominican Republic, and Viet Nam. Now, according to Haykal, it was to be Egypt's turn. (95)   What seems astonishing to Westerners at least is the unchallenged assumption that the United States had virtually limitless powers. As Safran summarized Haykal's thesis:

> Haykal depicted the United States as having, somehow, a hand in the travails of the Egyptian army in Yemen, the economic difficulties in Egypt, the exploitation of the relaxed intra-Arab atmosphere of the summit meetings by Saudi Arabia and Jordan to launch the Islamic Alliance, the plotting by the Muslim Brethren to overthrow the regime in Egypt, as well as the intensified arming of Israel. Pulling these wires, taking advantage of the internal difficulties in Syria, Iraq, and Algeria, and capitalizing on the gall of Khrushchev, the Sino-Soviet conflict, and the counterrevolution it had unleashed in Africa and Asia, the United States was prepared to deal Egypt the coup de grace. (96)

This theory was projected in Egyptian media. In October 1966 Cairo newspapers carried front page stories claiming that Faysal and LBJ had made a deal to establish a pro-Saudi regime in Yemen in exchange for United States base rights in Saudi Arabia. (97) Other media consistently hammered away on an anti-United States line, equating the United States and Israel as collaborators in an anti-Egyptian plot. (98) Haykal expressed 'abd al-Nasir's perception of the situation thus:

> Anti-Egyptian Western propaganda, backed by the Arab reactionary elements, continued to attack Egypt fiercely. The attack went to the length of spreading the belief that the entire Egyptian Army had perished in Yemen, had been scattered into aimless groups, and that the remainder had been killed, wounded or captured. Similarly it was said that the Egyptian economy was collapsing and could not stand on its feet, let alone bear the weight of any bold venture, and carry on with it. But Egypt knew the truth and was confident that the truth would appear to the entire Arab nation one day when the time was ripe for serious action. (99)

This image of a hostile United States in collusion with Israel, had its concrete source in a whole series of frictions and misunderstandings between 'abd al-Nasir, and the United States, especially over the United States cancellation of wheat shipments which 'abd al-Nasir interpreted as an attempt to starve him out. (100) It was further strengthened by Egyptian intelligence analysis of classified United States documents obtained from A.I.D. Headquarters in Ta'iz in April 1967. (101) Whatever the realities of its source, however, 'abd al-Nasir seems to have begun interpreting events more and more in terms of the classic perception of Muslim/Christian relations, and of his own imagery of the West as Crusaders out to destroy Egypt. According to Badeau, 'abd al-Nasir also began to perceive the situation in late 1966-early 1967 as a replay of the Suez Crisis. The analogy (qiyas) between the generalized images of the two situations overwhelmed their objective differences. (102)

As the crisis intensified, 'abd al-Nasir operated more and more on the basis of this double imagery, and on a secondary set of impressions drawn from the 1956 crisis: Namely, that Israel would attack Egypt again, if a suitable opportunity presented itself and that, never again, could Egypt be caught with its armed forces unmobilized as it was in 1956. This mobilization itself would be less risky than doing nothing (103) and, if a crisis arose, he might be able to win a political victory (even after a limited military defeat) as he did in 1956. Thus 'abd al-Nasir was already predisposed to a certain course of action in advance of events, and was psychologically prepared to perceive every United States and Israeli move as a threat.

What seems crucial to the escalation of 1967 is this linkage between a sequence of events and Arab decision makers' preexisting perceptual frameworks. The temporal relation of events itself became a critical psychological factor. The logic of the perceived connection seems to have run like this: In Syria an increase in border warfare with Israel escalates into a major symbolic defeat for the regime. This defeat is followed within two weeks by a localized rebellion. To Syrian leadership the conclusion may have been obvious: An anti regime plot of considerable magnitude. The connection between these events may seem slight to a Western observer (other than to say that the Syrian government was antagonizing both its neighbors and its own population), but to the Syrians, they seem to have been clearly related.

No Westerner will ever know for certain what actually went through the minds of the Syrian leadership but one analyst has offered a theory that might explain Syrian behavior. Harkabi argues that Arab egoism translates itself into a political parochialism, the feeling that non-Arab governments have nothing better to do than meddle in Arab politics. (104) This sense of being the target for all kinds of Western plots combines with two other factors: the already low tolerance for any kind of perceived threat, and a cultural preference for conspiracy theories. (105) The consequence is that events which seem unrelated to each other or to the Arab world are seen by Arab leaders as having ominous implications.

When Syrian propaganda denounced the CIA, the Muslim Brethren, the Jordanian government, the Nassirists, the Israelis, and the U.S. (a quite unlikely combination of allies on the surface at least) - the Syrian leaders very probably believed it. To be sure, there was method in their madness, it was a desperate attempt to divert domestic hostility elsewhere. But the idea of such a coalition of enemies had to have some basis in belief. If not a belief on their part that such a conspiracy was in effect, then a belief that the audience for this propaganda line would find it believable.

Likewise, for the Egyptians, the notion of a gigantic United States conspiracy was proven by events. The events in Syria coincided with a conservative coup in Greece on April 21. Clearly United States/Israeli pressure on Syria (now connected with Egypt because of the November 1966 defense treaty) and U.S. attempts to make Jordan into an American satellite were now to be joined by a new anti-Egyptian front in Greece. (106) From the Egyptian view, this looked like a replay of the Western attempts to isolate Egypt in 1954/55 by creating the Baghdad Pact.

In a May 2 speech 'abd al-Nasir accused the United States of trying to exert economic pressure on the UAR, and of waging a psychological war against Egypt in other Arab countries. (107) In his May 22 speech to Egyptian air force units in the Sinai he repeated the charge:

> Therefore, it is clear that an alliance exists between the Western powers, chiefly represented by the United States and Great Britain, and Israel. There is a political alliance. This political alliance prompts Western powers to give military equipment to Israel....We all know that the Islamic Alliance is now represented by three states: the Kingdom of Saudi Arabia, the Kingdom of Jordan, and Iran...Who is supplying Israel with oil? The Islamic Alliance - Iran, an Islamic Alliance State...Such is the Islamic Alliance. It is an imperialist alliance, and this means it sides with Zionism because Zionism is the main ally of imperialism...There is currently a propaganda campaign, a psychological campaign, and a campaign of doubt against us. We leave all these behind and follow the course of duty and victory... (108)

Some writers have suggested that this anti-American, anti-Western barrage was merely for propaganda purposes, a big lie, in short. It would be a mistake to ascribe this behavior to some clear-cut propaganda strategy, or to some calculated, Machiavellian plan. This is to apply Western conceptions of behavior to a non-Western area. Moreover, there are three considerations which complicate such a straightforward explanation:

a) The fact that similar propaganda themes are repeated consistently by Arab leaders indicates that a substratum of belief lies behind these assertions. As Harkabi put it:

> The declarations of the leaders are not a reliable measure of what they intend to do, but their statements have much to teach us about the Arabs and their conduct, as well as emphasizing their "verbal behavior." The fact that they repeatedly emphasize the same ideas entitles us to assume that these ideas contain something fundamental to them, something important for the understanding of the Arabs and their attitude, even if we do not always see a direct connection between it and their actions. Even if we say that all this is nothing but phraseology, the fact that they use these phrases and not others is significant... (109)

b) Whether or not Arab leaders originally believed in the accuracy of their own slogans, these slogans have been repeated so often that they have become an article of faith. Again Harkabi:

> Sincerity may not be a primary datum, but the outcome of development. Let us assume that Arab leaders express opinions about Israel (sic: or the West) in which they do not believe at all. The result then would be the creation of a gap or dissonance between their words and their opinions or beliefs. Such a gap makes people feel uncomfortable, and they would therefore like to narrow it down...As the result of this process, the authors of the declarations tend to believe in their own statements... (110)

c) If they are used to legitimate Arab leaders in the eyes of their populations, these slogans eventually create a climate of popular expectations which, in turn, limits policy options. Using the earlier example of al-Sadat's prewar statements, his repeated declarations about his determination to go to war seem to have produced precisely this effect. In a very real sense, he was forced by Egyptian popular opinion to carry out his threats.

In May, the linkages, real and perceived, between events became even more pronounced. The incipient Egyptian-Saudi military confrontation in Yemen escalated. The Saudis, it was said, were building up Yemeni Royalist forces for a new summer offensive. Egyptian aircraft began a series of raids on Saudi positions, the port of Qizan and the oasis of Najran, which the Egyptians regarded as the key staging areas. In addition, Egyptian aircraft bombed a Saudi air defense complex at Khamis Mushayt. (111) These actions took place amid a series of unconfirmed reports from Beirut that the Egyptians had begun dropping arms to anti-Faysal tribes in the Western Hijaz, and that 'abd al-Nasir intended to restore deposed King Saud, who was conveniently exiled in Cairo. (112)

Tension along the Syrian/Israeli border also escalated at the same time. The Syrians had begun a series of harrassing tactics after the Spring air exchange, encouraging Arab herdsmen and flocks to move into the demilitarized zones, and escalating pin prick attacks on Israeli settlements in Northern Galilee. (113) These activities were accompanied by a stream of increasingly bellicose utterances by the Syrians.

The Israelis responded by warnings of the possibility of a blow against Syria. These were repeated in various contexts by Eshkol, General Rabin, and others. (114) Most of these speeches seemed designed for domestic consumption, but their interpretation in the Arab world was that the Israelis were, indeed, planning a major operation against Syria. Moreover, these warnings were underscored by a New York Times report that some Israeli officials had already decided on a punitive expedition into Syria. (115) This story was given special credence in the Arab world because it repeated, in effect, an earlier story in al-Muharrir on September 21, 1966. In the al-Muharrir version Prime Minister Eshkol had finally been won over to the viewpoint of

Israeli army officers who advocated preventive war against Syria. Therefore the Israelis were planning to make a conclusive strike against the Syrian border to:

(a)   suspend once and for all diversion works in Syria

(b)   stop any development of the slogan of popular liberation war advocated in Syria

(c)   stop any military coordination between Syria and other Arab countries

(d)   continue on to Damascus, if need be, and overthrow the regime

(e)   give forces hostile to the Syrian regime a chance to strike. (116)

The Israeli blow which followed within a month of the al-Muharrir story was aimed at the Jordanian village of al-Samu'. But in the Syrian mind it could just as easily (and more logically) have been aimed at Syria. Indeed, given the Israeli policy of "massive retaliation," any Israeli warning would have to be taken with utmost seriousness, especially so when it came within the context of apparent escalation. By May 1967, the situation seemed more explosive than it had at the time of the al-Samu' raid.

For a variety of reasons 'abd al-Nasir chose to respond by a dramatic mobilization and movement into the Sinai: partially because of the "lessons of 1956"; partially because the Soviets, supplied with intelligence to the effect that the Israelis had moved two brigades (not the 11-13 brigades which 'abd al-Nasir was later to claim publicly) to the Syrian frontier and were planning an immediate attack. (117) Given this information, which was also apparently duplicated by Syrian and Lebanese intelligence sources, (118) and the political consequences of inaction in the face of another Israeli move, no matter how small, 'abd al-Nasir moved. (If there was any doubt about Israeli intentions, it was removed by the absence of armor from the Israeli May 15th Independence Day Parade.) (119)

In his calculations of the risk involved, 'abd al-Nasir had the example of a previous situation in February/March 1960 where a similar Egyptian movement in the Sinai had deterred Israeli action. (120) As he declared later:

All of us know how the crisis started in the Middle East. At the beginning of last May, there was an enemy plan for the invasion of Syria, and the statements by his politicians and all his military leaders openly said so. There was plenty of evidence concerning the plan. Sources of our Syrian brothers were categorical on this, and our own reliable information confirmed it. Add to this fact that our friends in the Soviet Union warned the parliamentary delegation, which was on a visit to Moscow at the beginning of last month, that there was a premeditated plan against Syria. We considered it our

duty not to accept this silently. This was the duty of Arab
brotherhood, it was also the duty of national security. Whoever
starts with Syria will finish with Egypt. (121)

And:

On 13th May we received accurate information that Israel was
concentrating on the Syrian border huge armed forces of about 11
to 13 brigades. These forces were divided into two fronts, one south
of Lake Tiberias and the other north of the Lake. The decision made
by Israel at this time was to carry out an attack against Syria
starting on 17th May. On 14th May we took action, discussed the
matter and contacted our Syrian brothers. The Syrians also had this
information. (122)

On May 14 Egyptian Chief of Staff Muhammad Fawzi flew to Syria
to coordinate military action. (123)   On the same day, Deputy
Commander-in-Chief 'abd al-Hakim 'Amir ordered a full alert. (124) In
addition, the first of two waves of Egyptian armor began a spectacular
daylight movement through Cairo, past the United States Embassy, out
along the Cornishe and across the Nile into the Sinai. This dramatic and
highly publicized show of force was accompanied by warnings in al-
Ahram that Egypt intended to stand fast with Syria against the Israeli
threat. (125)
These initial actions were supplemented by an increasing mobilization for the rest of May. Civil defense plans were put into effect;
police leaves were cancelled; emergency measures were instituted in
hospitals, a plan to utilize schools and hotels as emergency hospitals
was announced; a state of emergency was proclaimed in industrial
plants; food supplies were distributed; popular resistance forces were
set up. (126)   This continued and extensive mobilization became a
critical factor in the assessment of Egyptian intentions. A movement
of troops may, or may not, indicate much more than a bluff, a symbolic
warning, a ploy in the strategy of deterrence, but an extensive
mobilization signals a much more serious possibility that the mobilizing
state intends to go to war.
Indeed, initial Israeli intelligence assessments of this spectacular
show of force were that it was just that: a psychological and military
move designed to get 'abd al-Nasir out of a difficult intra-Arab
predicament. But, as Egyptian mobilization measures continued, the
Israelis were forced to alter their judgment. By the third week in May,
Israeli intelligence was actively predicting an Egyptian attack; and
communicating this fear to United States officials. (127) Parenthetically, according to Quandt, United States intelligence sources did not
agree with the revised Israeli estimates; a disagreement which seems to
have created a minor credibility gap between the United States and
Israel. (128)
Whatever the accuracy of either of these estimates, events quickly
made them moot. The escalatory process could have either been slowed
down sufficient for outsiders to intervene, or perhaps even stopped
altogether, but for an incredible breakdown in the UN peacekeeping

mechanism. Since 1956, UN forces had been stationed on the Egyptian side of the Egyptian/Israeli border in the Sinai. These forces had functioned as a buffer, making this particular border the quietest of all Israel's borders. But on May 16, the Commander of UNEF was given what amounted to an ultimatum (in United Nations eyes at least) by General Muhammad al-Fawzi concerning a movement of Egyptian troops into forward positions. Western and Egyptian texts differ considerably on the wording of this communication, (129) and there is some confusion as to whether 'abd al-Nasir intended to have UNEF forces wholly removed (there were also reports that Egyptian units actually opened artillery fire on some United Nations positions.) (130) In any event U Thant decided to withdraw the United Nations buffer force, thus putting Egyptian and Israeli units face to face. (131)

ESCALATION AND INTRA-ARAB CONFLICT PATTERNS

The removal, accidental or calculated, of United Nations forces along Egyptian-Israeli boundaries altered the situation dramatically. What had heretofore been a series of localized conflicts involving Egypt, Syria, and Israel now, however, became directly linked to other Arab conflicts via the activity of the Arab media. These intertwined conflicts, in turn, began to cycle together, building up a dynamism of their own. As historian C. Ernest Dawn was later to point out there was a critical relationship between the Arab propaganda campaign that ensued and the subsequent pattern of escalation:

> The Arab propaganda campaign,...Haykal was later to write, played a major part in limiting Arab success in the international arena. He was undoubtedly right. What he did not say was that the propaganda campaign was the consequence of the remilitarization of the Sinai. This action was in the first place an instrument in intra-Arab politics, and as such it was meaningless unless accompanied by a battle of rhetoric. (132)

Within Egypt, and elsewhere in the Arab world, mass demonstrations in favor of 'abd al-Nasir's action became a daily occurrence. These put tremendous political and psychological pressure on all Arab leaders, and their response was to declare their support for the Egyptian move. Most of these actions were initially designed to satisfy local audiences by giving the impression that Arab leadership was, indeed, doing something. However, their combined effect was to create the impression that the "Arab Nation" was at last marching off to war as an overwhelmingly powerful unit. This feeling seems to have fed upon itself, affecting the calculations of the very leaders who started the process.

Throughout the rest of May and into early June, the Arab media continued to dwell on the imminence of war and the prospects for the destruction of Israel. The shame of 1948 was to be wiped out. The

Arabs were to return to their rightful role as a proud and valorous people. The ignominy of western domination was, at last, to be wiped out. Honor and wajh were at last to be restored to the Arabs. (133) Popular expectations were whipped up into an incredible pitch. 'Abd al-Nasir's status as leader of the Arab cause was restored; few of his erstwhile opponents dared challenge his popularity.

In this extraordinary atmosphere, 'abd al-Nasir's Arab colleagues were faced with a very difficult political situation. On one hand, they could not afford to let 'abd al-Nasir get away with an easy political victory by outbluffing the Israelis. Such a victory could be more devastating to Arab regimes than to the Israelis. In the curious logic of intra-Arab politics, an Israeli military victory was, in some ways, preferable to an Egyptian political success. An 'abd al-Nasir who successfully outbluffed the Israelis would be in an overwhelming position to overthrow any Arab government that dared oppose him. (134) On the other hand, they could not afford to openly challenge 'abd al-Nasir, nor even criticize his moves, because of the intensely pro-Nasir sentiments of their own populations. Their options were, in short, limited to:

a) Attempt to match 'abd al-Nasir in anti-Israeli utterances, and thereby share credit for a political victory.

b) Outbid him by continually raising the stakes of the confrontation, and thereby make his actions appear less bold.

c) Contrive to utilize the situation to settle old scores with either conservative or radical Arab opponents.

Symptomatic of the constraints on Arab governments by this surge in 'abd al-Nasir's popularity, and the infighting that grew out of it, was the complete reversal of Jordanian policy. On May 30, King Husayn flew to Cairo to sign a defense agreement with his bitter enemy. Husayn had every reason to stay out of a war with Israel. Yet as his cousin, Zayd bin Shakir noted, political conditions in Jordan were such that, had Husayn not acted, there would have been a civil war. (135) Husayn, himself, accounted for his trip thusly:

The fact is that my trip was forced on me by the obvious superiority of the forces opposing us. All my meetings with my officers were based on the certainty that hostilities were imminent....From now on we would have to improvise according to Israeli maneuvers. Unlike Israel, the Arabs were without a unified operational plan. We Jordanians tried to pull our weight as a diversion, thus minimizing the damage when war came. We had no real hope of winning. (136)

To begin with, in June, we were all bound by the Pan-Arab defense pact signed in Cairo during the first summit conference....But even without this agreement, should war break out, it would involve us all....In 1956, the Israelis opened hostilities against Egypt under the pretext that they were being harassed by terrorists coming from

Jordan....In 1966, the Israelis complained this time that the terrorists operated out of Syria, and so it was we, in Jordan, who took the brunt of the "punitive expeditions"....The conclusion was obvious....To the Israelis we were all alike.... (137)

My second reason was a moral one....I could, under no pretext, behave toward them (sic: his Arab allies) as I had accused them of behaving toward me. So there was no question of my breaking away from the Arab camp and standing aside from the conflict that threatened us all. Especially since I thought our unity was essential to our mutual security.... (138)

The option chosen by Arab leaders, for the most part, was to out bid Nasir. Each Egyptian escalatory move was thus greeted with the demand on the part of other Arab governments for still more escalation. Ironically enough, the Syrians, in whose behalf 'abd al-Nasir had originally acted, were the leaders in this outbidding. On May 16 Radio Damascus reiterated the Syrian demand for a war of national liberation. A series of strident appeals were made to the "Arab Masses" to join in such a war, and to overthrow any conservative regime which held back:

We shall stand fast before any aggression, we shall strike with an iron hand against all plots, and we shall be victorious in Palestine. Organization and solidarity to the utmost, O Arab countrymen, and let there be armed struggle; the war of national liberation is our weapon. (139)

Acting thus both embarrassed 'abd al-Nasir, and at the same time, attacked the Syrians' Jordanian and Saudi foes. (The Syrians punctuated this verbal attack with a carload of explosives designed to go off in Amman. Instead it exploded at the Jordanian border on May 21.)

The conservative camp replied in kind. Radio Amman noted that Jordan had been the first to demand a UNEF withdrawal and to call for a blockage of the Straits of Tiran, implying that 'abd al-Nasir was still not committing himself to anything new. Saudi (and oddly enough, even Tunisian) spokesmen joined in by claiming that the Egyptians had no intention of doing anything beyond their mobilization in the Sinai. (140)

This mounting intra-Arab pressure resulted in an Egyptian reassessment of the risks of the situation. The initial low keyed Israeli response to Egyptian moves (141) was apparently interpreted by 'abd al-Nasir as an indication that the Israelis were not prepared to match Egyptian escalation. The lack of any significant Western response solidified this feeling. (142) From this, he apparently drew two conclusions:

a) That the possibility of war was not very great. (143)

b) That if war did occur, Egyptian forces were sufficiently strong to at least hold off the Israelis until international pressures forced a ceasefire, along the lines of 1956. (144)

As late as May 15, 'abd-al-Nasir had been insisting that Egyptian forces could not cope with the Israelis. By the following week, he seems to have reversed this position. A number of factors entered into this reversal. Both 'Amir and Egyptian intelligence assured him that UAR forces could hold their own if attacked. (145) Additionally, the sight of the enormous quantities of men and armor in the desert appears to have convinced him that the Egyptian army could fight effectively. (146) As Haykal was to note wistfully later:

> Some of us were dazzled by the spectacle of the force we moved to Sinai. (147)

Indeed, his commanders pressed him to authorize a preemptive attack while the Israelis were still not fully mobilized. Apparently, 'Amir and Air Force Commander, General Sidqi Mahmud, were especially insistent on the necessity of a first strike. (148) On at least two occasions, May 26 (149) and June 4, (150) a tentative decision to attack appears to have been made, only to be called off at the last moment. (151)

Instead of reducing his risks, 'abd al-Nasir therefore chose to escalate the conflict. He declared on May 22 that the Straits of Tiran were closed to Israeli shipping; that the remaining vestiges of the Israeli aggression of 1956 were to be removed; that the governments of Jordan and Saudi Arabi were served notice that their access to the Red Sea was subject to Egyptian dictum. (In most of his speeches concerning the developing crisis, 'abd al-Nasir spent as much time attacking his Arab tormentors as he did in discussing the Israelis.) Thus, with one tactical stroke, he seemed to have dispatched both the Israelis and his Arab opponents.

The out-bidding process continued, however. On May 22, Syrian President Nur al-Din al-Atasi announced that:

> After today, threats and provocations will have no influence. Let Israel know that the fedayeen columns will not cease and their advance will continue until they have liberated their fatherland and cleansed its soil. (152)

Iraqi President 'abd al-Rahman 'Arif repeated the Syrian rhetoric on May 27:

> The armies of the Arab states are eager to eliminate the existence of Israel and return the million expelled Arabs to their homeland. (153)

On May 26 'abd al-Nasir announced that the original goal of deterring Israeli aggression was now to be superseded by a new one. This time the goal was to be that of solving the Palestine question:

> The problem today is not just Israel, but those behind it. If Israel embarks on aggression against Syria or Egypt, the battle against Israel will be a general one and our basic objective will be to destroy Israel....We will not relinquish the rights of the People of Pales-

tine....During the crusader's occupation, the Arabs waited 70 years before a suitable opportunity arose and they drove away the crusaders....we are determined that the Palestine question will not be liquidated or forgotten.... (154)

At the same time, he and other Egyptian officials reaffirmed their commitment to a second strike posture, clearly an attempt to win a political victory. Therefore, one gets a sense that 'abd al-Nasir himself was all too aware of the difficulties of his position. While he escalated the political crisis, he, and other officials, repeatedly declared their unwillingness to resort to force. In this case, Egyptian spokesmen continually reiterated their commitment to a second strike strategy: either an attempt to win a political victory without risking a war; or an attempt to forestall Israeli preemption and leave Egyptian military options open. For example, General 'abd al-Muhsin Kamal Murtaja, the commander of the Egyptian forces in the Sinai, declared that it would take a large Israeli attack to trigger an Egyptian response. (155) Haykal reiterated this in al-Ahram:

As from now, we must expect the enemy to deal us the first blow in the battle. But as we wait for that first blow, we should try to minimize its effect as much as possible. The second blow will then follow. But this will be the blow we will deliver against the enemy in retaliation and deterrence. Is this, then, the end of the matter? I would answer that I have explained - or rather tried to explain... in this inquiry that the problem has not ended - it, rather, has hardly begun. This is because I am confident that for many reasons, chiefly the psychological, Israel cannot accept or remain indifferent to what has taken place. In my opinion it simply cannot do so. This means, and that is what I intend to say in the second observation of this inquiry, that the next move is up to Israel. Israel has to reply now. It has to deal a blow. We have to be ready for it, as I said, to minimize its effect as much as possible. Then it will be our turn to deal the second blow, which we will deliver with the utmost possible effectiveness.

In short, Egypt has exercised its power and achieved the objectives of this stage without resorting to arms so far. But Israel has no alternative but to use arms if it wants to exercise power. This means that the logic of the fearful confrontation now taking place between Egypt, which is fortified by the might of the masses of the Arab nation, and Israel, which is fortified by the illusion of American might, dictates that Egypt, after all it has now succeeded in achieving, must wait, even though it has to wait for a blow. This is necessitated also by the sound conduct of the battle, particularly from the international point of view. Let Israel begin. Let our second blow then be ready. Let it be a knockout. (156)

'Abd al-Nasir, himself, assured British MP Christopher Mayhew in a June 2 interview that Egypt would not attack:

Mayhew: ...I mean a few days ago you said that if Israel attacks, it will be completely destroyed. Some Arab leaders actually say that their aim is the elimination of Israel without qualifications. What does this really mean?

'abd al-Nasir: If somebody attacks you, what would your reaction be? If somebody attacks us we will react. To react in war means destruction.

Mayhew: And if they don't attack, will you let them alone?

'abd al-Nasir: Yes, we will leave them alone. We have no intention of attacking Israel. (157)

Likewise, Egyptian units in the Sinai were deployed in a configuration designed apparently to absorb an Israeli attack and then mount a rapid counterattack. The bulk of the Egyptian ground forces were initially committed to this defense in depth deployment. (158)

In the context of this enormous propaganda campaign, this cycle of bidding and outbidding, it should not be astonishing that Arab media did not carry accurate accounts of the war. Beginning with reportage of the first Israeli air strikes at 0845/0900 Cairo time, through the disaster in the Mitla Pass, the Arab media carried stories of a series of Arab victories until the obvious could not longer be concealed. Radio Cairo, for example, broadcast a series of spurious reports about Egyptian victories and Israeli casualties. These were alternated with martial music and slogans: "We are today fighting the battle of honor. We shall eliminate the shame of Zionism in Palestine." (159)

4 The June War: Its Consequences and Its Lessons

The war, which started with this superbly planned and executed Israeli air strike, was a watershed in Arab/Israeli relations. Latent Israeli military superiority (only incompletely demonstrated in the War of 1956 because of British and French intervention) was translated into a crushing victory over Arab forces hastily and chaotically thrown into battle. At the war's end, Israeli strategists were confronted (if that is the right word) with an optimal situation. Israeli border difficulties had been largely erased by the victory; all of the indefensible positions, and the lack of strategic depth had been altered in Israel's favor. Most of the ancient territory of Biblical Israel, including the holy city of Jerusalem, was under Israeli control. Arab opponents were in political and military disarray, and not expected to be able to reorganize for the better part of a decade. In short, the entire balance of power in the Middle East had been altered in Israel's favor:

> The Six-Day War did affect the power balance in two respects. Israel acquired control over territory more than three times the size of the state when the war began and, with it, a marked improvement in defensible frontiers - the Jordan River, the Canal, and the Syrian (Golan) Heights. Secondly, as in 1948 and 1956, victory enhanced the sense of security of Israeli society as a whole. Indeed, Israel was clearly now the preeminent power... (1)

As a consequence, Israeli strategists had the luxury of utilizing time, in this case by withholding any territorial concessions until Arab states were willing to come to the negotiating table. The logic here was simple. Arab leaderships would find themselves under increasing domestic pressure to regain their lost territories; the longer they delayed, the more Israel would create "new facts" by settling into these territories. Therefore, Arab leaderships would eventually come to realize that negotiations were preferable to continued conflict. (2) Moreover, since Israel had overwhelming military superiority, Israel

Would define the framework within which these negotiations would take place. The parameters of this framework would be defined by two policy positions: (a) that any new Arab-Israeli relationships be based on "defensible borders"; and (b) that these relations be the product of "direct negotiations." (3)

However, if the June War presented one set of consequences for Israelis, it presented quite a different set for the Arabs. Indeed, on a number of levels, the June War is a complex and (for Arabs) traumatic event. Its long term effects are still not fully apparent; and in retrospect, the June War may be of more historical significance than the subsequent October War. In brief, some of the more obvious consequences of June 1967 can be identified:

(a) Psychologically speaking, the war intensified the existing Arab identity crisis: feelings of personal or group insecurity, alienation or inability to cope with a changing environment, which could be projected onto the Israeli target, now were turned inward. Psychic energies and discontents which could be displaced by legitimatizing strategies utilizing scapegoating ideologies were now blocked. Both emotional catharsis and political displacement, then, could not now be directed at the Israelis with impunity. The Israelis were not a weak and inferior (but periodically dangerous) opponent; they were clearly more powerful than the Arabs. The whole panoply of Arab conflict strategies, domestic and intra-Arab, and complementary media behavior was now obviously dysfunctional as a technique for dealing with the emotional consequences of social change. (4)

(b) Culturally - to the extent that a cultural response can be isolated from a psychological reaction - Arab culture (one might even say, civilization) was dishonored. Arab forces attempted to engage an enemy in Western style combat; these forces proved seemingly unable to do so successfully. The inferences were also clear: Arab culture and manhood as a whole were demonstrably inferior to those of a small, Westernized nation. Arab forces were unable to master Western cultural (in this case military) artifacts. The sense of cultural decline, of somehow having lost a past greatness, engendered by the original colonial penetration of the Arab world, was exacerbated anew by the defeat. (5)

(c) Politically, a new generation of Arabs was socialized into political awareness by the trauma of the defeat. This generation suffered from an authority crisis even more acutely than did their predecessors. Not only had contemporary Arab leadership failed to regain a lost glory, but this failure was the fault of the very leaders who presented themselves as the new Arab men, the men who were dedicated to regaining Arab honor and dignity. The consequence here was a further weakening of the legitimacy of Arab governments. (6)

In the June 1967 War, Israeli forces were able to carry out a rapid and decisive war of annihilation. The Israeli strategic goal was to attack and destroy each of several Arab armies - Egyptian, Jordanian, and Syrian - piecemeal. Thus they would avoid a relatively prolonged war in which attrition rates would soar.   The tactical problem was, therefore, to enable numerically inferior forces to attack and destroy several stronger enemies.   Their solution was to utilize the advantages of surprise and extreme mobility, to plan an offensive against Arab forces which called for a high degree of exactness and aggressiveness in execution: An offensive which would take advantage of Arab weaknesses in strategic coordination, training, and operational control. (7)

The cataclysmic defeat which resulted served as a catalyst for a remarkably wide ranging, self critique on the part of Arab thinkers, both civilian and military.   Out of this self critique emerged the strategy that led to the October 1973 attack by Egypt and Syria.   Of crucial importance here are two factors: (a) That Arab leaders devise a strategy to overcome them.   A critique that was all the more impressive and, in a sense, unexpected, because it represented a dramatic reversal of Arab attitudes toward the West.   Heretofore, intellectual inquiries into the Arab inability to withstand Western military power had been confined (with some exceptions, notably Mehmet 'Ali in Egypt and selected Ottoman sultans who were concerned with Ottoman, rather than Arab values) to introspective analysis of Arab culture and values.   In the wake of 1967, however, Arab analysts turned their attentions to the West (and Israel) and developed a coherent strategy to deal with Western power.   This focus on acquiring accurate knowledge (especially accurate intelligence) of the West, this self conscious avoidance of the uniformed emotionalism that led to 1967, is perhaps the greater surprise of 1973.

(b) Even granted the amount of calculation that went into Arab post 1967 analyses and planning, the image of 1967 - in the gestalt sense of a configuration of perceptions - dominated the cognitions of Arab planners and decision makers at critical moments.   It was built into Arab plans for a limited war; and when the opportunity presented itself to the Egyptians to break out into the Sinai, it led to the decision not to move.   Ironically enough, both the Egyptians and Syrians were well aware of this imagery.   Al-Sadat and Ahmad Isma'il, for example, devoted considerable efforts to debunking what they styled the "Israeli psychological warfare."   (Parenthetically, the Israelis had their own gestalt. The planning strategy behind the Bar-Lev line was based on the image of Egyptian forces as being relatively slow moving, being unable to move in strength across the Canal in much less than 48 hours.) (8)

The Air War

Israeli aircraft were able to achieve a maximum of surprise; Egyptian forces, in particular, were in a stand down posture. Air force commanders were airborne at the time of the attack; many of the senior officers were still hung over, recovering from the effects of a late night party of the night before.   Most Egyptian aircraft were caught on the ground, usually on the taxi strips. In the first days' air strikes Israeli aircraft destroyed 286 Egyptian aircraft, and decimated the Syrian and Jordanian air forces. (9)

Such Egyptian aircraft that did get airborne were easily disposed of by Israeli fighters. Trained in Soviet tactics, these Arab pilots were both relatively unfamiliar with their aircraft (due to lack of sufficient flying time), and trained in only three/four basic offensive tactics. When these were exhausted, they attempted to break off engagements, and became easy prey to Israeli pilots. Syrian pilots were of little better caliber.

Iraqi and Jordanian pilots were quite different. These retained the legacy of British air to air techniques. Iraqi pilots, in particular, behaved like their British counterparts. Jordanian airmen, in aging Hawker-Hunters, gave a more than adequate account of themselves, and were dispatched, ultimately, on the ground during turn arounds. (10)

The Ground War

Egyptian forces totalling 7 divisions (approximately 120,000 men) were committed to the Sinai. These were organized into two armored divisions, the 4th, and a special Task Force under General Sa'ad al-Din Shadhili; four infantry divisions, the 2nd, 3rd, 6th, and 7th; and a Palestinian division in the Gaza Strip. These were deployed in three major fortified positions: a forward line from Rafah, Umm Katif, and al-Qusayma; an intermediate line from al-'Arish to Jabal Libni, and a rear line from Bir Jifjafa to Bir Thamada. Infantry divisions manned the forward lines, armored divisions were placed at the rear. Most of the armor was dug into fixed positions, thus depriving it of mobility. (11)

This arrangement reflected the Egyptian view that the key to control of the Sinai was control of al-'Arish:

... In the Sinai campaign, in fact, what happened in 1956 and 1967 was not a brilliant move on the part of the Jews. From the military viewpoint, as we have learned and as all the military men know, any Sinai campaign has rules which must be followed by any would be conqueror...During history all the invasions across Sinai took the same form despite the developments in the instruments of warfare....In 1956 the Israeli forces used what is militarily called the plan of the fan. There is a base which revolves like a fan. The fighting moves from the north and sweeps the Sinai. We used to carry out this operation during our maneuvers in Sinai at the military staff college... (12)

During the war, additional reserves were also committed. The subsequent Israeli defeat of Egyptian forces, therefore, destroyed most of the army; many of these units were trapped in the Sinai, and forced to attempt to retreat through Israeli air bombardment with especially heavy losses.

IDF objectives were three-fold: To destroy the Egyptian army, to capture Sharm al-Shaykh, and to occupy the Sinai peninsula. (13) Israeli strategy called for a three phase operation: First, a breakthrough of the forward Egyptian line in two sectors, Rafah-al'Arish and Umm Katif-Abu Agayla; second, the overrunning of the Egyptian second line and the destruction of armored reserves; third, destruction of retreating Egyptian units. (14) All of these operations were successfully completed; Israeli ground forces were able to exploit the gaps between Egyptian positions, to bypass heavily defended areas, and to encircle these units.   The Egyptian army lost approximately 80% of its equipment, and about 17,000 were killed or wounded. (15)

Egyptian communications broke down early in the war, partially through Israeli electronic warfare techniques, and partially through Egyptian internal disorganization. Egyptian forward units began to send incorrect information back to HQs. The resulting confusion rendered any sort of organized control over troop movements impossible. (16)

Egyptian units in particular were unable to improvise; while many of them fought well in static situations, Israeli abilities to move and confront them with continually changing environments proved too much. (17)

The Egyptian High Command panicked on June 6 and ordered a general retreat, over the strenuous objections of its own planning staff. According to the staff's evaluation of the first day's fighting, the IDF had made only small advances into the Sinai, but had suffered considerable losses in so doing. Israeli air superiority had caused UAR forces losses along the front, but these had so far been relatively light due to the protection afforded troops by trenches and fortifications. The staff, therefore, recommended determined resistance along the second line of defense.   But the High Command, "suffering from paralysis," insisted on the retreat. (18) According to Haykal, most of the UAR losses occurred on the fourth day of fighting, during the "fearful nightmarish atmosphere that followed the order to withdraw." (19)

Ten of the eleven Jordanian brigades were concentrated in the West Bank. These were positioned defensively; eight infantry brigades spread out over the length of the front from Janin to al-Samu', with two armored brigades at Jericho, and the Damya Bridge available to reinforce any area of the front. (20)

The Israeli objectives here were to: Move Jordanian troops back in the Janin region thus putting Israeli settlements out of range of Jordanian artillery; to capture the Latrun salient; establish a corridor to Mt. Scopus, and ultimately take over Jerusalem and the West Bank. (21) Their tactics were to cut through Jordanian lines and encircle isolated units.

Jordanian troops fought well. But deprived of any sort of air cover, their armor was particularly vulnerable to Israeli air strikes. Syrian aircraft which were supposed to provide air defense and support were never committed to the Jordanian front. (22)

The majority of Syrian forces were positioned in fortified bunkers along the Western edge of the Golan Heights. These were organized into three parallel lines of defense with overlapping fields of fire, and deeply dug in communications trenches roofed with steel and concrete slabs. The overlapping fields of fire were so arranged that artillery fire could be directed on the forward positions, in case of their capture. The entire system was manned by 3 infantry brigades with supporting armor, and a combination of 5 armored and mechanized brigades were held in reserve. (23)

The Israelis breeched this system at the Qunaytira junction and attempted to encircle Syrian forces entrenched on the Heights. However, Syrian forces abandoned their positions and retreated toward Damascus. (24)

At the field level, all Arab units, except the Jordanians, seemed to prefer set piece battles, operating from dug in positions, and static defense lines. As such, they were easily routed by Israeli forces which emphasized attack, maneuverability, and flexibility. (25)

Arab leadership was lacking. Units did not trust their officers; and in many cases the officers in question either refused to advance when ordered, or themselves ordered retreats which were unjustified by the immediate tactical situation. Syrian units, in particular, lacked the morale to defend superior positions on the Golan Heights. They retreated with little utilization of their advantages in fields of fire. (26)

Arab logistics were bad; many tanks and other vehicles had to be abandoned because of lack of fuel or ammunition. Other armored vehicles were simply in bad repair, and were abandoned as an alternative to carrying out minor repairs. As with the 1956 encounter, Soviet equipment was generally unsuited to desert warfare; vehicles were equipped with heaters, but with no provision for air conditioning. Many were not even given suitable desert camouflage. (27)

At a strategic level, communication between political leaders and their military was lacking. 'Abd al-Nasir was not informed of the extent of Egyptian losses until the night of the sixth. (28) King Husayn was initially told by the Egyptians that they were attacking successfully in the Sinai. It was not until the sixth, that he realized the extent of the Egyptian defeat. (29)

Intra-Arab military cooperation was almost nonexistent. The Syrians, in particular, refused to commit any forces to aid the Jordanians, despite repeated requests. Iraqi forces were sent to the Jordanian front, but in insufficient numbers. Other Arab governments sent only token forces, or none at all. These forces usually arrived so late in the war as to be useless, and their commitment was clearly for political purposes.

The Semantics of Defeat

The June defeat left the Israelis in possession of even more Arab lands: the Sinai, the West Bank, and the Golan Heights. Another exodus of refugees occurred. Some 200,000 Palestinians fled from the West Bank to Eastern Jordan; between 80,000 and 100,000 Syrians left the Golan Heights area; and about 55,000 Egyptians and Palestinians were displaced from the Gaza Strip and Sinai. (30) Old Jerusalem and the

Muslim holy places were in Israeli hands. The economy of Jordan was shattered, and the UAR lost both the canal and its revenues. All the Arab misfortunes of the 1948 war, (known as the "disaster," in the sense of a traumatic blow to Arab culture and manhood)   were   repeated in magnified form.

The emotional and political impact of this crushing defeat was enormous since it struck at the very heart of Arab values and Arab self image. As already noted, Arab values revolve around the maintenance of honor, dignity (karama), and face. (31) Arab nationalism itself is, in some aspects, a political expression of this insistence on honor or face. (32) Arab linguistic behavior is marked by a conspicuous verbal self glorification. (33) Therefore, the stark contrast between this collectively preferred and promulgated self image of a glorious and warlike people, and the fact of an outrageously quick defeat at the hands of the Israelis was too much to accept. The immediate Arab reaction to the June 1967 defeat was to deny that it ever happened. This denial took a number of forms: diplomatic, linguistic, ideological.

The Arab summit conference at Khartoum, August 29 to September 1, laid down the joint Arab political stand.   Article Three of the Conference's public resolutions stated the Arab position:

> The Arab heads of state have agreed to unite their political efforts at the international and diplomatic level to eliminate the effects of the aggression and to ensure the withdrawal of the aggressive Israeli forces from the Arab lands which have been occupied since the aggression of June 5. This will be done within the framework of the main principles by which the Arab states abide, namely no peace with Israel, no recognition of Israel, no negotiations with it, and insistence on the rights of the Palestinian people within their own country. (34)

This resolution thus created a very odd situation (to Western minds at least) where the losers of a war refused to recognize the existence of their conqueror.

Linguistically this uncompromising political attitude was paralleled by descriptions of the defeat. It was officially styled al-naksa (the setback or the degeneration). (35) The term hazima (defeat) was used only sparingly to portray what had happened. Israeli occupation of Arab territory was likewise euphemistically termed, the "consequences of the aggression."

Ideologically, great stress was placed on the arguments that explained away the defeat:

(a) It was the result of United States intervention on the side of Israel, and therefore, Arab forces could not have been expected to win. 'Abd al-Nasir advanced this thesis in his June 9 resignation speech:

> Precise calculation of the enemy strength showed us that our armed forces, with their level of equipment and training they had reached, would be able to repulse him, and deter him....On the morning of last

Monday, June 5th, the enemy blow came. If we say now it was stronger than we had anticipated we must say at the same time, and with definite assurance, that it was much stronger than his resources....It also became clear from the very first instance that there were other forces behind the enemy which came to settle their accounts with the Arab nationalist movement....The indications are clear of the existence of an imperialist collusion with him, which seeks to benefit from the lesson of the former overt collusion of 1956, this time covering itself cunningly and yet it is established now that American and British aircraft carriers were near to the coast of the enemy helping his war effort.... (36)

(b) Israeli military success did not constitute a "real" victory since her war aims - the destruction of Arab radical regimes - had not been accomplished. Nor had the Arabs been, in fact, defeated. As King Husayn put it:

We are not defeated. A defeated man is one whose morale has been broken. Our morale has not been weakened. (37)

Moreover, Israel's military victory could not, by itself, impose a dictated peace upon the Arabs. In fact the Israelis would find themselves trapped in their new territorial boundaries. The editor of al-Musawwar, Ahmad Baha al-Din, argued that Israel had found herself in the trap of illegality (sic: the occupation of Arab lands) which fact the Arabs should exploit both diplomatically and propagandistically:

Escalation of action against Israeli occupation from within is what exposes the illegality of Israel's position, making the time element not in her favor. This makes the cards Israel holds in her hands now an instrument of pressure not against us but in our favor.... True, Israel now occupies (sic: several) Arab areas, following a quick military victory, but the Arabs have not yet awakened exactly from the impact of the blow. But let's look at the other side of the situation. Israel is in the trap....True, the door of the trap is not tightly shut. However, closing it tight is possible, and this depends on the Arab action.... (38)

(c) The battle against Israel had not been lost, it had only entered another stage. Arab strength would inevitably prevail in time, just as it had in other encounters with occupying powers. As al-Asad argued on April 16, 1973, the anniversary of Evacuation Day, making an analogy between the French and Israeli occupation of Syria:

Thanks to the heroism of the fighters in the battles against the forces of colonialism, thanks to the heroic confrontations by our masses against the weapons of the colonialists, thanks to the heroism of our martyrs, our people stood fast and triumphed. There followed the evacuation of the colonial forces and independence. Every resolute people who make sacrifices triumph. Past and recent history confirms this fact. (39)

COMMUNICATIONS AND POLITICS: A MEDIA WAR

The impact of the 1967 defeat was magnified, both sociologically and psychologically, by two long term trends in the region: The movement of large populations of Arabs out of traditional, isolated social units; and the spread of mass communications, especially radio. In the language of political science, these Arab numbers had become socially mobilized; become available available for new patterns of social and political behavior. (40) This large-scale social change also took place in a political situation of intense pan-Arab propaganda; especially propaganda about the nature of the 1948 war, and the Zionist menace to Arab unity.   By 1967, therefore, multitudes of Arabs were highly politicized and shared a feeling of "Arabness."

The June War was a media war (as Viet Nam was for the United States) in the sense that Arab populations as a whole experienced it vividly through the media. Arabs far removed from the actual scene of battle were emotionally involved. (41) To cite one individual example, Mu'ammar al-Qadhafi was profoundly affected by the June debacle, even though Libya was geographically well removed from the war. (42) The "slow motion" build up to the outbreak of fighting contributed to this sense of immediate involvement by raising expectations concerning the triumph of Arab arms. These heightened expectations were brought crashing down with the news of the defeat. As Haykal metaphorically described it:

> There was a big difference between the sky in which we flew (prior to the war) and the ground on which we dropped (after the Israeli victory). (43)

The defeat was thus extraordinarily moving for many who saw it as a humiliation, a loss of face, for their people as a whole. The sharp contrast between the heights of confidence and the depths of defeat produced a sense of alienation and hopelessness. A feeling that all was lost, that life was no longer worth living, a feeling that was ultimately styled al-qalaq (the anguish). (44) Intellectually and emotionally, this sense of malaise was expressed by a literature of despair, dwelling on the themes of the emptiness and pointlessness of man's existence, and of the necessity to engage in some sort of profound spiritual resurrection.   In Egypt this view was particularly articulated by the eminent novelist and playwright, Najib Mahfuz, in a series of bitter short stories; in Lebanon by American University of Beirut sociologist Halim Barakat, and by the late PFLP spokesman, Ghassan Kanafani. (45)

This feeling of humiliation was intensified among intellectuals with a Western language capability, who read and heard Western media presentations of the Arabs as being bumblers and cowards. Western jokes about Arabs were bitterly repeated in the Arab world:

> "How do you make a chicken sandwich? Put Nasir between two slices of bread!"

Arab academics spent time and effort doing content analyses of Western media to prove that the Arabs were getting very unfavorable treatment. (46) A number of these intellectuals preferred to leave the Arab world rather than face conditons there.   This problem became particularly acute with respect to Arab students sent to Western countries who refused to return home. The "brain drain" was especially problematic for the Egyptians who were faced with the loss of much of their scientific and technical community. (47)

The Credibility Gap

The credibility gap became a central issue for both intellectuals and governments.   The Arab media was completely mistrusted by wide segments of the population. (48)   Most propaganda apparatuses were overhauled in the wake of the war; propaganda directors' heads rolled in every direction. A barrage of articles and editorials called for changes in Arab media strategy vis a vis both Arab and Western audiences. An al-Ra'y al-'Amm article observed:

> Looking back now, we can see clearly that the Arab information policy was one of the main elements of the setback. Within our information policy lie the seeds of the danger which has led to the big setback. We lived twenty years enjoying songs about a return to Palestine, as if this return would be fulfilled by song and music writers. For twenty years, Arab radio stations were devoted to destroying the psychology of Arab unity of ranks....Treason was the simplest adjective which Arab radios used to bestow on this or that Arab leader....Charges of treason and subservience to imperialism became the salt of radio and press work in Arab countries; hardly any state or ruler escaped accusation. These campaigns of suspicion have borne their fruit, the Arabs reaped the thorns when the hour of war came, the Arabs, all the Arabs fell in the fire....
>
> Arab destiny can no longer stand any clowning....Let Arab radios remain silent for years, before they open their mouths to speak about treason. The Arab people are tired of what they have been hearing, and now they want to hear talk that would establish confidence in Arab leadership and their ability to undertake concerted efforts. We have lived with the truce with the enemy for nineteen years - and we have just seen the results. Therefore let there be truce among us that we may crush the enemy before he jumps over the life of all of us.... (49)

Other writers attacked Arab treatment of the conflict with Israel. al-Dustur noted:

> Arab information media looked on the Arab citizen as nothing more than a bundle of emotions....Consequently, we failed to equip the Arab individual with the necessary education, knowledge, construc-

tive logic and facts....Arab information media concentrated on posing Israeli as 'the little state' whose destruction needed only the mobilization of Arab emotion.... (50)

Moreover, Arab information media supplied the Israelis with valuable intelligence:

When Arabs buy a tank, they would splash its photos, taken from all sides and angles, on the front page. But when an Israeli buys a tank, they would bring it in unassembled, and even say that what was imported was agricultural equipment needed for development....At the same time, broadcast of cables sent to Arab leaders from commanders of Arab military units are enough to give Israel a picture in every Arab district....Furthermore, the lessening of the strength of Israel by Arab information media, and the simultaneous exaggeration of strength of the Arab people and their ability to destroy Israel, gave the latter justification to demand more arms.... (51)

al-Hawadith commented on the anti-Israeli slogans carried in Arab media:

Most of the (anti-Israel) songs were written for quick consumption; when I (sic: a Lebanese singer) hear them, I get the impression that their words had not been read by any responsible person. Zionists used to set up loudspeakers in the streets of Paris to broadcast textual translations of Arab songs which said, 'destroy, crush, kill, drink their blood.' The Zionists would comment on these songs: This is what the Arabs want to do with two million helpless Jews. The French, knowing nothing about the Palestine question, would then feel that there was a giant beast seeking the massacre of a small child. As a result there were mass demonstrations marching through the streets of Paris supporting Israel against the Arabs.... (52)

The slogan of the "destruction of Israel" came in for special criticism in the context of a more general analysis of the shortcomings of Arab propaganda by Egyptian editor Baha al-Din:

Let's take the example of 'destroying Israel.' This slogan cannot be fulfilled during the present stage due to the well known international, economic and imperialist reasons. But just the same we raise this slogan and talk about it as if it could be fulfilled tomorrow....

But this made us pay a dear price in the form of opposition in world opinion....The present stage is one for strengthening, grouping and developing the potential of the Arab world....It is a stage for exposing the truth about Israel as a military, racial, and aggressive state tied with imperialism. It is a stage for isolating Israel from the progressing forces in the world, and for using international interests connected with the Arabs to serve the Arabs....

No one in the world - be they friends, enemies or neutrals - would agree to obliteration of Israel. All of them have a wrong historical comprehension of the situation....Therefore this is not the point of departure. Raising the slogan made Israel win the first propaganda battle against us, even before we fired one shot. The world needs time to wake up to the fact that Israel was an arsenal of arms, that it was the one which initiated the aggression.... (53)

In 1968, Lebanese writer and ideologist Klufis Maqsud proposed an information strategy which he claimed would turn this state of affairs around. He argued that, contrary to accepted Arab belief, United States opinion was not impervious to Arab arguments. The problem for Arab media was to alter the equation set up by Israeli propaganda efforts: Israel presents herself as a cultural extension of the West in contrast to the Arabs who are seen as opposing the West. Moreover, Israel plays on Western guilt complexes about the persecution of Jews, and takes the position that Israel represents all Jews, and can absolve the West if the West does not ask what Israel is doing in the Middle East. Thus, at once, Israel appeals to liberals with a sense of guilt, and to imperialists with a desire to dominate the Third World. What Arab media should try to do is to counter Israeli efforts by appealing to several target audiences:

(1) Those who desire some sort of coexistence with Russia, and a reduction of Cold War tensions.

(2) Anti-war youth movements pressing for a revision of United States international commitments as a result of Viet Nam.

(3) Minority groups, especially blacks and the poor, who are natural allies with the Arabs on the issues of social justice, and are on the same wave length as the Palestinian Resistance.

(4) Specialists and others who are acquainted with the United States Middle East policy and have doubts concerning it.

(5) That section of United States Jewry which is more and more coming to realize that Zionism is a threat to their American sense of belonging. (54)

A series of Information Conferences were organized under the auspices of the Arab League. These were designed to coordinate Arab media efforts abroad. Among the alternatives considered were increased efforts to get texts of important communications translated and made immediately available to Western news sources; starting dialogues between Arab and Western intellectuals; and allowing Western correspondents access to Arab countries. (55)

Alienation: Political and Religious

The defeat of 1948 had affected only small groups of educated Arabs, mostly officers. These officers felt that the Arab governments of the day had, in effect, "stabbed the military in the back" by providing poor quality arms and poor leadership. The consequence was the generation of a series of localized coups in Syria and Egypt. The Suez war likewise had a relatively limited impact, mostly because of the surprise nature of the Israeli attack and the war's short duration. The consequences here was the production of even more coups in Syria, Iraq, Sudan, and Yemen, civil disturbances in Jordan and Lebanon, and an increased radicalization of sections of Arab public opinion.

The defeat of 1967, however, came as an abrupt reversal of over two weeks of boasting about Arab might in the best Bedouin tradition. Where the targets of popular wrath in 1948 and 1956 had been limited to relatively conservative, old line nationalist regimes, the targets of post 1967 were the newer generation of radical leaders as well. This wave of anti government alienation took on two distinct aspects: A political rejection of Arab leadership that was especially pronounced among a younger generation of students and officers, and a turning back to religion as an alternative to political involvement that seemed to cut across both generational and class lines.

While the governments of Egypt, Syria, and Jordan were the most violently affected, all Arab governments were threatened with domestic instability. Coups or attempted coups occurred in Egypt, Iraq, Libya, Saudi Arabia, Sudan, Syria, and North and South Yemen. (56) In addition, large scale student demonstrations rocked Egypt, and Lebanon, and a civil war broke out in Jordan. (57)

The wave of religiosity, which swept the area, affected both Christian and Muslim populations; (58) and presented Arab governments with the prospect of increased communal tensions. Symptomatic of heightened Christian feeling was a bizarre occurrence in the Cairo suburb of Heliopolis. The Coptic community there suddenly became convinced that the Virgin Mary was making nightly visitations to the local church in April/May 1968. This manifestation excited considerable Christian and Muslim attention throughout Egypt for a number of weeks. Several times during the vigils that preceded the Virgin's appearance the crowds of onlookers became so large and so packed together that a number of people were crushed. The Egyptian government was relatively powerless to interfere.

"After all," as one al-Ahram editor remarked, "We have enough trouble with the Israelis as it is, without taking on the Virgin Mary!"

Several similar appearances occurred at later dates in Nile delta towns.

Muslim revivalism was acerbated by a general sense of outrage at Israeli occupation of Islamic holy places, al-Haram and al-Sharif. This feeling was continually inflamed by reports of Israeli desecration of the holy places. Miniskirted tourists tripped through mosques (women are not allowed in certain parts of mosques), Westerners carved their names on the walls of Muslim shrines, and Israeli archeologists began digging at the foundations of The Dome of the Rock, the mosque from which the Prophet is said to have ascended to heaven. (59) King Faysal, as the official protector of these holy places, was exceptionally outraged. Saudi media reflected this feeling with an extremely hard line, calling for a jihad against Israel. (60)

The ultimate outrage, however, occurred on August 21, 1969 when a Christian, Michael Rohan, set fire to al-Aqsa. According to Rohan, God had ordered him to destroy the works of the false prophet, Muhammad. (61) The fire caused an immediate worldwide uproar among Muslims. (62) King Faysal called for a jihad on the spot:

> Now that all peaceful methods have been exhausted, I appeal to you to declare a jihad. (63)

The relative inability of regular Arab governments to do anything about Israeli occupation of Arab lands permitted two other actors to play a role in Arab politics out of proportion to their actual power resources: The Palestinian Liberation Movement, and the newly installed government of Libya. The Palestinians were urban and nationalistic, representing the antiestablishment trend. The Libyans were rural and Islamic, representing the Islamic revivalism. (64) Both were like the jinns of classical Muslim mythology, they were anarchic and unpredictable in their behavior. Neither had any stake in the existing intra-Arab power structure.

The Palestinian Resistance grew from a satellite of Arab states bordering Israel to a major force following the battle of al-Karama on March 21, 1968. (65) Trading on the reputation for bravery acquired at al-Karama, the Palestinian leadership utilized prevailing anti government sentiment in the Arab world to exact concessions from Arab governments. Don Peretz described the new Palestinian image:

> Increasingly, "Palestinian" is identified with the guerrilla warrior rather than with the downtrodden displaced person. This is evident among Arab students, intellectuals, professionals, and the man in the street, from Casablanca to Kuwait. While much guerrilla activity is exaggerated if not entirely fictitious, there is sufficient substance to their achievements to have created a guerrilla mystique. The daily radio bulletins and pronouncements by guerrilla leaders; and the Arabic press - all have created in the Arab consciousness the image of a new Palestinian who, unlike the traditional, and now aging military leadership, is young, vigorous, intelligent, self sacrificing, intensely patriotic, and single mindedly dedicated to the reestablishment of Arab Palestine. This image pervades even the thinking of guerrilla critics such as Lebanese and Jordanian officials.... (66)

Recruits and money flooded in. From groups numbering a few hundred, the Palestinian organizations grew in size and number. (67) By 1970 there were at least 10 major Palestinian groups in operation; their total

numbers ranged from 15,000 to 25,000; (68) their financial infrastructure covered the Middle East, Europe, and Latin America. (69)   They
rapidly developed organizational ties with a variety of other insurgent
groups, and began to recruit small numbers of non-Arab adherents. (70)
    The Palestinian Movement also quickly exhibited two tendencies
which made it increasingly dangerous to Arab governments:

    (a) An organizational tendency toward the fragmentation and pro-
liferation of competing groups; (71) groups whose leaders attempted to
outbid each other in both ideological militancy, and operational
"spectaculars" against Israel.   Intra-Palestinian rivalries, a microcosm
of intra-Arab conflict patterns, resulted in extremely unstable relations
between the Palestinians and Arab governments.   The conflict of two
organizations, Fatah and the PFLP, was a major factor in the escalation
of the fida'iyin government conflict in Jordan into a civil war in
September 1970.

    (b) A parallel ideological tendency to become increasingly hostile to
all established Arab governments. Partly, this hostility was the product
of infighting; a process whereby conservative leaders were forced to
take increasingly militant stands, or lose their adherents.   Partly too,
however, it was the inevitable growth of local Palestinian, as contrasted
with pan-Arab, nationalism. (72)
    The growing conflict of interests between Arab establishments who
wanted some sort of favorable territorial settlement and the
Palestinians who wanted the disestablishment of the state of Israel was
too profound to be papered over. In their own assessment of the post
1948 situation, the Palestinians, irrespective of other divisions, had all
reached the same conclusion: The Palestinians must control their own
destinies; non-Palestinian Arab governments had consistently failed to
improve the situation of the Palestinians in any way. Indeed, since the
debacle of 1967, the plight of the Palestinians was objectively worse.
    Fatah spokesmen analysed the situation in terms of a struggle
between competing Israeli and Palestinian nationalisms. In the course
of time this original nationalist conflict had been absorbed and distorted
by its insertion into the complex world of the intra-Arab politics. What
was necessary was that:

> We have to confirm the Palestinian identity of our struggle or else
> the world will not accept our movement as a national liberation
> movement. (73)

Other Arab states must no longer be allowed to control Palestinian
destiny.
    The PFLP put the same line of reasoning into the terminology of
Marxist class analysis.   The leadership of the national liberation
movement was usurped by:

> feudalists and large bourgeois aristocratic families represented by
> Hajj Amin al-Husayni... Shukri al-Kuwatli and the national party in
> Syria and similar leaderships in other Arab countries.... (74)

Subsequently these regimes were overthrown by national military and political organizations whose members came largely from the small bourgeoisie. But the main interest of these new Arab nationalist regimes was to retain their own privileges. Therefore they rejected any forms of war of popular liberation in Palestine because:

> Such a war of popular liberation would require that this class should abandon its privileges and start to live in the same manner as the commandos today are living.... (75)

Therefore both Arab conservative (feudal and large bourgeois) and radical (small bourgeois) regimes, were to be rejected by the Palestinians.

The fida'iyin mystique took hold of two key social groups in particular, the students and the intellectuals. In Lebanon, university students demonstrated in favor of the fida'iyin, and Lebanese artists collaborated in producing fida'iyin posters. The resistance leadership was well aware of its appeal to such groups and went out of its way to exploit it. The educational level of the Palestinians, and the concentration of numbers of them among the Arab intelligentsia, gave them a certain advantage in molding popular opinion. The progressive alienation, under the aegis of fida'iyin propaganda, of the younger educated generation from existing regimes raised the possibility of long term consequences quite apart from the Palestinian issue per se. (76)

The September 1, 1969 coup in Libya was carried out by a relatively young (between 20 and 30 years of age) group of officers and civilians. Their organization and subsequent "revolution" were patterned after the Egyptian Free Officers. Their leader, Mu'ammar al-Qadhafi, modeled himself along the lines of the youthful 'abd al-Nasir. (77) This takeover was the fourth of a series of coups that rocked Arab establishments. As such, it was part of the general antiestablishment trend after June 1967. From an Arab perspective, however, the Libyan coup was considerably more important than its predecessors for two reasons. First, it altered the radical conservative balance in the Arab world. Heretofore the conservatives - Saudi Arabia, Kuwait, Jordan, Tunisia, Morocco, Lebanon, and Libya - had equaled the radicals - Egypt, Syria, Iraq, Sudan, North and South Yemen, and Algeria. The shift of Libya from the conservative to the radical side was an event of major importance in the intra-Arab balance of power. (78) Second, King Idris' government was the first traditional state to be overthrown since the Yemeni coup of September 1962. Before this, the only conservative regimes to be deposed had been Egypt in 1952 and Iraq in 1958. (79)

Al-Qadhafi quite early developed a visionary ideology of an Islamic regeneration. Here, his historical role models appear to be either 'Umar, second successor to the Prophet, or Salah al-Din, the hero of the anti-Crusades. In a post war situation which clearly demonstrated the tremendous gap between Arab rhetoric and Arab action, al-Qadhafi espoused an existential philosophy: pragmatic action was to be the key, not politics or principles:

> We are not politicians! We are revolutionaries! (80)

The ideological sources of al-Qadhafi's theory of an Islamic revival are two-fold: Nasirism, which stems from the fact that he literally grew up listening to <u>Radio Cairo</u> (he was expelled from secondary school for demonstrating against the break up of the UAR - and he now claims to be the embodiment of the ideals and principles of Nasirism); (81) and Islam, which flows from his desert unbringing. Born in a tent near Sirta and brought up in Bedouin society, al-Qadhafi developed both an intense puritanism, influenced by Sannsi ethics, and an equally intense rejection of the lifestyles of Muslim urban and commercial classes. At one point, nine of the twelve leaders of the Libyan Revolutionary Command Council were still living in traditional mud houses or tents. (82)

This convergence of Nasirist confrontation politics and Islamic fundamentalism produced the strategy of a pan-Islamic revival. In this, al-Qadhafi took as a strategic starting point 'abd al-Nasir's conception of Egypt's geopolitical location in terms of three concentric circles:

> We cannot look stupidly at a map of the world not realizing our place therein, and the role assigned to us by that position. Neither can we ignore that there is an Arab Circle surrounding us and that this circle is as much a part of us as we are a part of it....Can we ignore that there is a continent of Africa in which fate has placed us and which is destined today to witness a terrible struggle for its future?... Can we ignore that there is a Moslem World to which we are tied by bonds forged not only by religious faith but also by a fact of history?... (83)

But in al-Qadhafi's usage the ordering of these foreign policy priorities was altered to become Islamic, Arab and African. (84)

In his own assessment of the June War, al-Qadhafi came to the conclusion that the defeat was a symptom of the Arab world's debility, a debility caused by a falling away from Islam; a substitution of Western secular notions for the true faith. What was necessary, therefore, was the regeneration of a united Arab world based upon Islamic principles. Islam would pay the key role in this regeneration:

> Islam becomes a regenerative force for the whole world, not just for Muslims. The Koran is an 'unchangeable truth' rendering the theories of Galileo and Darwin obscure. It combines all the holy books, and the Prophet Muhammed is a prophet not only for the Arabs, but for humanity at large. (85)

Such a regeneration, however, would require a revolution - in al-Qadhafi's terms, a jihad - to eliminate Western influences, imperialism and communism. (86)

In line with this reasoning, al-Qadhafi began a relentless attack on everything Western or Christian, first within Libya itself, then in the Arab world, then in Africa, and finally in the rest of the world. His slogans, obviously drawn from 'abd al-Nasir's policies, were:

1. Complete evacuation of foreign bases (and influence) in Libya.

2. Absolute "positive neutrality."

3. We shall be hostile to our enemies and friends of all those who wish to have our friendship. We shall also fight all those who wish to fight us.

4. National unity is a step on the road towards comprehensive Arab unity.

5. No parties after today. (87)

The consequence of this militant pan-Islam was that, like the Palestinians, the Libyans rapidly became a threat to other Arab regimes, conservative and radical alike. The conservative regimes like Morocco, Tunisia, and Jordan were attacked for two reasons: Their lack of commitment to the Arab Cause, and their ties with the West. All three were the targets of coup attempts in which there was evidence of Libyan involvement. (88)

The oil producers - Saudi Arabia, Kuwayt, and the Trucial Shaykh-doms - found themselves faced with a different kind of threat. Al-Qadhafi utilized both the low sulphur content of Libyan oil, and its relative cheapness, to bargain with Western oil firms. By imposing production cutbacks, and forcing independent producers to negotiate prices on a company by company basis, al-Qadhafi succeeded in driving up the posted price of oil. (89) For other Arab producers, however, these moves presented the uneasy prospect of a destabilized pricing and marketing system. On one hand, they were forced by a variety of factors, not the least of which was domestic nationalist pressure, to increase their own prices. On the other hand, they ran the risk of Western counter moves, either a reduction in purchasing (as happened to Musadiq in 1950-1951), or a shift to alternative, principally Iranian, sources.

Egypt and Syria also were endangered. Al-Qadhafi's pan-Islam was a direct challenge to Shi'a rule in Syria, and there is some evidence that Libyan money was channeled to Sunni Muslim opponents of the regime. (90) To the Egyptians, al-Qadhafi was yet another military rival trying to outbid them on the issue of Arab leadership. But where the Egyptians were vulnerable to the military consequences of anti-Israeli acts, the Libyans were not. Only 'abd al-Nasir's political skills and young al-Qadhafi's great admiration for him prevented open conflict. After his death, however, both Anwar al-Sadat and al-Qadhafi found themselves vying for 'abd al-Nasir's position as leader of the Arabs. (91)

THE LESSONS OF 1967

Almost immediately after the war, the Arabs began to analyze the reasons for their defeat. First the Jordanians, and later the Egyptians, produced various assessments. Understandably enough, the Syrians were silent for the most part. These assessments ranged from the strictly military mistakes to wideranging criticisms of Arab society and culture as a whole. The strictly military analyses concentrated on the effect of the surprise air attack, the lack of sufficient planning and military coordination, faulty intelligence estimates, and general misconduct of operations.

Most Arab commentators considered the Israeli air strike to be the key factor in the defeat. The late Egyptian Chief of Staff, Lt. General 'abd al-Mun'im Riyad summed up the effects of the air strike in the course of a report prepared in late June 1967:

> There was absolutely no equity in this battle from the point of view of operations on the Jordanian front. It was impossible for the battle to end in a way other than the way it did. For one thing, the surprise by which the UAR air forces were taken gave the enemy general control in the air from the first few hours of operations. Consequently the Syrian air force suffered considerable losses as a result of which it was forced out of the battle. This created a battlefield on the Jordanian front that was deprived of assistance and air cover. As for the Iraqi air forces, their range was limited and there were no airports on the Jordanian front to allow Iraqi fighter planes to operate and give cover for the Jordanian land forces. Therefore, the battle was, from beginning to end, an air battle where the enemy managed to get control of the air from the very beginning. (92)

As a result of its failure to check the Israelis, the Egyptian Air Force was purged from its commander, General Mahmud, on down. Many of these officers were put on trial in October 1967 for misconduct. The chief charge was that they had been forewarned by 'abd al-Nasir to expect the June 5 attack, and had failed to take adequate preparations. (93) Instead, it was charged that General Mahmud had given a party the night of the 4th which had lasted well into the morning of the 5th. (94) Curiously enough, Israeli Air Force Commander, General Hod, at one point proposed to go to Cairo and defend Mahmud on the grounds that he had done everything a commander should have in the circumstances. (95) By 1969, the Egyptian Air Force command structure had been reorganized three times as a consequence of 'abd al-Nasir's intense dissatisfaction with its performance. (96)

Lack of planning was also considered a major factor. Early in the crisis, 'abd al-Nasir and Haykal took note of the fact that the Egyptians had not prepared any plan for a Sinai confrontation:

> News agencies reported yesterday that these military movements must have been the result of a previously well laid plan. I say that the sequence of events determined the plan. We had no plan prior to May 13th because we believed that Israel would not have dared to make such an impertinent statement. (97)

Haykal repeated this assessment somewhat obliquely:

It was this Israeli threat to Syria and information confirming it concerning intentions and plans that precipitated the emergency situation to which Egypt had to react immediately even though it came as a surprise to it. There was preparation and mobilization of the effective Egyptian forces. There was national consciousness and abidance by its principles. There was creative leadership. What I mean to say is that Egypt was not prepared for this specific contingency but was prepared for all contingencies including such a one. (98)

The accuracy of these statements is, in part, attested to by the confusion in Egyptian troop movements prior to the war. The first wave of troops and armor moved smoothly out into the Sinai and into prepared positions. But the subsequent waves seemed confused; units jockeyed about as though their commanders were uncertain of their missions, positions, or both. Al-Sadat at one point recounted his conversation with the wounded commander (subsequently appointed Defense Minister in 1978) of an Egyptian tank brigade to drive this argument home:

Kamal told me: ...I will tell you the story of what has happened. From June 5 to 7 I was in the Sinai with the brigade under my command, going and coming in the Sinai, covering hundreds of kilometers. Wherever I went I found an order telling me to go to another place, and there I found a new order telling me to go to the previous place. Thus we covered hundreds of kilometers going and coming in the Sinai. The brigade had 100 tanks, going and coming on treads...

What happened in 1967 (sic: by contrast with 1973) was different. The tanks were coming and going on their treads for three days - from June 5 to 7.   Orders were given to cover hundreds of kilometers on the treads. This is militarily wrong. It is a kind of ignorance and madness. Let us now return to Kamal Hasan 'Ali's story. His tanks were dug-in at one of the positions ready for battle after these tanks had been sent to and fro in the Sinai by conflicting and senseless orders...Kamal Hasan 'Ali was suddenly attacked by a battalion of Israeli tanks. He had no orders at that moment, but like any other excellent commander, gave orders to his soldiers and officers who assumed the battle order... (99)

So that while, in actuality, they did have an operation plan, it was never really put into effect. Troops and commanders were not trained in its execution. As al-Sadat later summed up the failings of Egyptian planning in 1967:

What happened to the brigade of Kamal Hasan 'Ali in 1967 applied to all the Egyptian Army units and branches of the other armed forces.

In 1967 no orders were issued to the Egyptian army. When they were issued, they were foolish and contradictory. No one knew what was going on around him in the entire arena. As a result of this situation, defeat was inevitable. But when Kamal Hasan 'Ali and our sons, the officers and troops, launched a counteroffensive against the Jews, and used the arms they had in a sound manner, they managed to hit eight Israeli tanks and the Jews ran from them. But for Israel's air supremacy, the result would have been quite different and Kamal Hasan 'Ali would have been able to launch his offensive and to sustain it under air cover.

Thus we can say that our armed forces in 1967 were placed in Sinai without a command or a plan....By contrast, in 1973, we won every battle we entered against the Jews and specifically the tank battles. This was because the plan was complete and every person knew his role and duty. The orders were clear to all. Everything went in a sound military manner.... (100)

Events in Egypt after the war, 'abd al-Nasir's forced resignation, and the attempted coup led by Field Marshal 'Amir after dramatic restoration, are further indications of the gap that developed within the Egyptian military leadership, and the crises of confidence that followed. On one hand, 'abd al-Nasir felt that the army had let him down; on the other hand, 'Amir and his colleagues felt that they had been plunged into a war without any change for adequate preparation. In any event, most of the High Command was purged, and replaced with younger officers loyal to 'abd al-Nasir. (101)

Arab, particularly Egyptian, intelligence came in for heavy criticism. This was especially directed at the incorrect net evaluation of Egyptian versus Israeli air capabilities. According to Haykal, one of the "fatal mistakes" that the Egyptians made was to exaggerate the strength of their own forces, while minimizing that of the Israelis. (102) The main calculation that was at fault was that the Egyptian Air Force outnumbered the IAF by a factor of three to one:

The case was just the contrary, if we consider the airworthiness of (UAR) fighter planes and the number of military pilots who had the right standard of efficient training. (103)

Poor leadership, and failure of nerve at every echelon of command, was also savagely derided. Haykal accused the Egyptian High Command of a "paralysis" of nerve after the first Israeli air strikes. The High Command, he argued, had begun to think in terms of 1956, when the Egyptian Air Force was hit by French and British bombers. It then panicked and ordered a general withdrawal along the lines of 1956. This order, noted Haykal, may have been justified in 1956, but not in 1967. During the first three days of fighting, UAR forces in the Sinai had suffered only 250 casualities, but the rest of the heavy casualities were suffered during the withdrawal. (104)

Al-Sadat broadened this charge to an accusation that high ranking

Egyptian officers had been totally negligent, not only in their conduct
of the war, but also in the preplanning and coordination. Not only that,
but Egyptian military procedure was carried out with such unvarying
regularity that it was easy for the Israelis to attack when the Egyptians
were most vulnerable:

> I say there was negligence which goes up to other levels. Some
> unforgivable   mistakes were committed by the military....The first
> error was that, after the 1956 battle, we insisted that there should
> be concrete hangars at the airports to protect the air force. This
> was done in Israel. It is not new military theory or genius. We saw
> hangars every time we photographed Israeli airfields....There were
> no hangars here. Our planes remained in the open....
>
> ... Planes were put in advanced airfields in Sinai only 5 minutes
> flying time from Israel. The planes were put in those airfields in
> rows....All it would have taken was for an Israeli pilot to hit one
> plane and the rest would have been burned....
>
> ... Defense of airports in the past followed a certain tradition. We
> called it the tradition of independent states. It existed both in the
> government and in the armed forces in Egypt. What is the story of
> the independent states? The air force was an independent state and
> the navy was an independent sovereign state....For this reason, there
> were guns positioned around the airports to defend against low flying
> aircraft and missiles against aircraft flying at high altitude. Fine.
> As we know, the missiles belong to the artillery. The guns around
> the airports, which are to intercept low flying aircraft when they
> descend to strike at the runways, with so called runway bombs, to
> destroy these runways and thus prevent planes from taking off - as
> we know every minute counts - actually these guns existed. But why
> did they not fire?... In the independent states that existed in the
> armed forces at the time, the air force said that the guns should
> have been under the army general command. The artillery said that
> they should have been under the artillery command. They did not
> reach a solution. No orders were issued. The Israelis struck and
> destroyed the runways with runway bombs. They then destroyed the
> planes out in the open.... (105)
>
> ... What was more bitter was that even though we were sure at the
> beginning of June that war was certain and that it might erupt at
> any minute, we continued in our training by the schedules and
> methods followed in peace time. The pilots would take off at
> specific times and end at 0830, after which, they would be in the
> canteen having their breakfast. These methods and schedules were
> not changed, although battles, and preparations for it were to take
> place. Naturally, the Jews monitored all our movements. This, as I
> have said often before, was easy for them, and for us. We can
> monitor what takes place in Israel and Israel can monitor what takes
> place in our country. Thus the Jews noticed that at 0830 our planes
> would be on the ground and the pilots at breakfast. They also

noticed that Egyptian planes had no secure areas. So they set the time to strike at 0830.... (106)

Lower levels of command were equally subject to attack. Among the charges were the following: UAR officers were often promoted for nonprofessional reasons; they did not have the competence required for their positions. Many commanders had been in the same post for up to 15 years; a situation which led to bureaucratic inflexibility. Some otherwise highly qualified officers were taken out of the military, and used in administrative posts, as mayors of small towns and the like. Other officers cared only for pay and promotions; the relations between these and the troops was one of mutual distrust. (107)

General Riyad summed up the military factors: loss of air superiority; lack of organizational coordination and control; and loss of communications. The lessons that he drew from this assessment were as follows:

(1) Entering a battle with the enemy requires prior preparation and coordination. What happened was that the Unified Arab Command had its hands tied up for a year before the battle started. Therefore, there was no coordination in the accepted sense of the word....The advanced command, which was formed a few days before the battle, could not do more than what it had done. This was a grave mistake of Arab politicians (who) had failed Arab soldiership.

(2) There can be no battle without defense from the air and acceptable air assistance together with the airports and communications facilities. I am confident that if the minimum air cover and assistance were provided to the fighting units, the battle would have taken another turn.

(3) Communications had been frequently severed during the battle which led to loss of control in most times. Loss of control means loss of battle.... (108)

Perhaps the most far reaching, nonmilitary analysis came from the eminent Lebanese scholar Cecil Hourani. Addressing himself to Arab decision makers, Hourani argued that the Arabs had been making a serious strategic mistake in their approach to the problem of Israel. Where they had aimed at a policy of conquest and destruction, they should have concentrated on containment. The Arab failure to do this was the result of a culturally ingrained unwillingness to accept an unwelcome reality:

That we were unable to distinguish clearly between containment and conquest was due primarily to a psychological weakness in us: that which we do not like we pretend does not exist. (109)

The goal of the destruction of Israel was unrealistic for a number of reasons; reasons which the Arabs must now admit to themselves:

(1) The first basic truth we must face is that the Arabs as a whole do not yet have the scientific and technological skills, nor the general level of education among the masses, which make possible the waging of large scale modern warfare....Nor do we have civilian populations sufficiently disciplined and educated to collaborate with the armed forces and the civil authorities to the degree which modern warfare demands....

(2) The second truth is that the rate of technological and scientific advance is so rapid in the modern world that even if, in twenty years, we can catch up with the military standards of today, we shall still be outdistanced by the Israelis....

(3) The third truth is that even if we had been able to defeat Israel militarily, we would have been deprived of the fruit of that victory by some of the Great Powers (sic: the United States), who would have intervened to save Israel's political existence.

(4) The fourth truth is that, in twenty years, or even less, even if we succeeded in bringing our scientific and technological skills to a point where we could wage a modern war, warfare itself will have taken on quite another aspect. The possession of nuclear weapons (by Israel)... will offer a choice either of mutual annihilation or of international control; and in neither case shall we be able to get our own way on our own terms. (110)

Hourani concluded that the proper goals of Arab policy should be twofold: The containment of Israel within whatever boundaries the Arabs could get international pressure to agree on; the gradual transformation of Israel from a European dominated "exclusive" Jewish state, into a predominantly Oriental Arab-Jewish state with which Arab leaders could come to an agreement. (111) The weapons that the Arabs should employ to accomplish this were international diplomacy and oil:

Arab oil, and the very considerable cash holdings which it generates for governments and private individuals, gives us the potential ability not only to solve most of our internal problems of poverty and underdevelopment; it could also play an important role in giving us influence in the economic and political life of Europe, with a consequent political influence. In order to be effective, however, there are two necessary conditions to be fulfilled. We must define our long term and short term aims in terms of the possible; and we must coordinate the policies of the oil producing countries, as well as the relations between them and the non oil producing countries. (112)

In an article written after the October War, 'abd al-Quddus summarized Egyptian (presumably al-Sadat's) conclusions in the form of a contrast between 1967 and 1973. Even taking into account that the article was written after the fact and, thus, represents hindsight, it still gives an indication of Egyptian thinking:

The first thing we learned (sic: from 1967) is that Israel is not a
state, but an international organization with influence in most world
capitols....Consequently any war with Israel cannot be planned as a
war between one state and another, but as a war between a Zionist
organization and an Arab organization....As a result, Arab planning
was prosecuted in silence, in the basis of unity of faith and objective
rather than futile unionist appearances of the past.   The Arab
organization also had to be established on economic strength....If the
Zionist organization imposes its control on international banks and
industrial firms, the Arab organization can also rely on its
production of petroleum and raw materials....

We also learned from the Zionist organization, its independent
personality, specifically not belonging to any single bloc; in not
being Eastern or Western, Socialist styled or Capitalist....The entity
of the Arab organization also had to be based on an independent
personality so that it may be able to deal with the Zionist
organization in its arena....We managed through this to gain on our
side almost all African states, most Asian countries, and the
strongest powers in Europe. This global gain represented, to be sure,
a force of pressure on both the Soviet Union and the United
States....

The second thing we learned from Israel is faith in the principle of
initiative. We reached the conviction that the side who starts the
attack is more capable of carrying out its plans, imposing its will,
and costing its enemy - regardless of the outcome of battles. This
was what Israel did in the past three years....Taking the initiative of
attack requires lengthy preparation for war comprehensive of
military, economic, and political aspects, plus a factual assessment
of the international environment, and restrain against precipitous
actions. This compelled us to tolerate many Israeli acts, ...without
letting ourselves be drawn into a battle on the 'reaction' level.

We also learned that localities and dates of wars are not announced
in advance, meaning that armies should move only if they will
actually fight. In 1967, the Egyptian army moved into the Sinai then
stood awaiting orders.

We also learned that the date of launching operations must always
remain an independent decision, known only to the state going to
war and no other. The start of the October 6 War was a surprise to
the whole world inclusive of the soviet Union, the United States and
Israel. This surprise did not give any country the opportunity of
intervening to cancel the attack, as was the case in 1967 when the
Soviet and American Ambassadors called on President 'abd al-Nasir
in the middle of the night to ask him not to start the fighting - on
the basis of pledges and guarantees for a peaceful settlement. The
morning of the same night, Israel started the attack.

Another lesson was not starting the war unless we are prepared to
continue for as long as it takes. Israel depended in its wars on

blitzkrieg blows of days. It was not capable, because of its structure and the nature of its international status, to tolerate a sustained war. Arab planning is based on the ability to continue with the war, even if fighting stops as a result of international pressure.... (113)

What al-Quddus did not say was that the Egyptians had also come to the conclusion that Egypt, in effect, must go it alone. The Syrian performance, or more correctly, nonperformance after the Egyptians had risked everything for them, had left a lasting impression among Egyptians for distaste for their Arab brethren. The popular feeling within Egypt after 1967 was that of "Egypt for the Egyptians"; "Egypt first." Haykal openly stated this feeling in 1968, arguing that Egypt's history could not be ignored in spite of its current pan-Arab orientations. The identity of the Egyptian people could be described as follows:

Name: The Egyptian people

Family: The Arab nation

Race: Descendant of several civilizations

Address: Crossroads of Asia and Africa....

This Egypt first mood received its symbolic expression when the name of the United Arab Republic was officially changed to that of the EGYPTIAN Arab Republic in September 1971. (114) Translated into policy, this meant that the Egyptians could not expect too much from their Arab colleagues (Haykal in a series of articles repeatedly made this point); that such strategies as were developed, would be aimed at Egyptian interests first and foremost. Part of the secrecy and the deliberate specification of limited military goals can be read, in part, as an attempt to avoid the possibility of the intra-Arab escalatory process of 1967. Al-Sadat stated in a response to Syrian and Libyan urgings to embark on an immediate war:

We shall maintain patience and silence, and we shall not allow ourselves to be driven (sic: by other Arab governments) into a battle for which we are not fully prepared. (115)

STRATEGIC DEBATE: 1967-1971

Although Arab analysts had assessed the mistakes of 1967 and were more or less agreed upon what went wrong, there were still considerable differences over the proper strategy to pursue. Two basic schools of thought eventually crystallized: Those strategists who favored unconventional warfare, a war of national liberation in some form, most prominently Palestinians, Syrians, Algerians, and later, the Libyans; and those who favored a conventional struggle, basically the Egyptians. The issue around which these opposing strategies contended was that of how to utilize the Arab numerical advantage to offset Israeli superiority in technology and training. The unconventional warfare school argued that it could best be done through an unending series of fida'iyin raids. Their conventional counterparts claimed that only by inflicting large scale casualties by a war of attrition could anything be achieved.

The several Palestinian organizations were the most vigorous promoters of an insurgent style of operation. These groups, despite differences in interpretation, all drew upon Mao's dictum that:

> The revolutionary war is a war of the masses; it can be waged only by mobilizing the masses and relying on them. (116)

Fatah, in particular, espoused a doctrine of protracted warfare; a long series of small engagements which would wear down the Israelis and in which their technological advantages would be neutralized: (117)

> The current guerrilla war has not reached the stage where it could deal a crucial blow to the army of the enemy because it is still in the infant stage. It would be a mistake to deploy, now, all these growing forces for the achievement of the ultimate objective. The basic objective now is to achieve superiority over the enemy but not to destroy him. The achievement of superiority requires that losing battles with the enemy should be avoided. (118)

George Habash of the PFLP adopted a more classically Leninist interpretation of armed struggle:

> The main point is to select targets where success is 100% assured. To harass, to upset, to work on the nerves through unexpected small changes. Brute force is out: this is a thinking man's game....It would be silly for us even to think of waging a regular war; imperialism is too powerful and Israel is too strong. The only way to destroy them is to give a little blow here, a little blow there; to advance step by step inch by inch, for years, for decades....And we will continue our present strategy. It's a smart one, you see; would you really want to fly El Al? I wouldn't. (119)

Insofar as other Arab governments were concerned, the doctrine of a popular liberation war presented a considerable military and political threat. In military terms, it engendered the spector of a return to the Israeli massive retaliations of pre-1967. If there was any doubt as to Palestinian intentions concerning the role of Arab "confrontation" states, these were made clear in the May 6, 1970 Unity Formula:

> The Palestinian revolution considers Arab land surrounding Israel as legitimate ground for Palestinian struggle and any attempt to close down any Arab country to the Palestinian resistance would be tantamount to treason to the objectives of the people of Palestine and the Arab nation in liberating Palestine. (120)

The security of Jordan and Lebanon was most immediately affected. The issue for Jordan rapidly became that of survival. It was caught between the ability of the fida'iyin to generate chaos and the power of the Israelis to carry out punitive expeditions. From either side, Jordan was threatened. The fida'iyin began to set up a state within a state, subverting the loyalty (if there ever was any) of Jordan's largely Palestinian population. The Israeli attacks destroyed the East Ghor canal irrigation system, bringing further economic disaster. And Israeli raids hit Jordanians more often than fida'iyin, making the population more militant, anti-Hashemite, and anti-American.

King Husayn's Bedouin troops managed to defeat the Palestinians in September 1970, and to destroy most of their military potential in Jordan during the Spring of 1971. But the cost of this operation was the destruction of much of urban Jordan, and the alienation of most of the settled population. Husayn, himself, was henceforth styled "the Butcher of Amman" by his countrymen, or, more colorfully, by al-Qadhafi as the "Dwarf King" of the "Nero of Amman." (121) The Jordanian government became the pariah of the Arab world, diplomatically isolated, and supported only by the Saudis.

Prospects were not much brighter for Lebanon. After their expulsion from Jordan, the Palestinians concentrated on building up a base in the al-'Arqub region in South Lebanon. (122) Beirut became the organizational and propaganda headquarters of the movement. The Lebanese government was faced with two unenviable alternatives:

(a) To attempt to control the fida'iyin and risk the possibility of civil war: Muslims supporting the predominantly Muslim Palestinians and Christians defending the government, with the added risk of a Syrian intervention on the side of the fida'iyin (as happened in 1976).

(b) To do nothing, absorb Israeli search and destroy missions which alienated South Lebanese Shi'a populations, and risk a possible Israeli occupation of part or all of the south (as took place in 1978).

In political terms, the popular war doctrine reproduced a situation akin to that facing 'abd al-Nasir in the middle '60s; the embarrassment of regular governments whose inaction vis a vis Israel would be unfavorably contrasted with the "heroic" exploits of the fida'iyin. 'Abd al-Nasir and the Ba'th, both found themselves confronted by a new claimant to leadership of the Arab world. The Palestinians increasingly disputed the claims to Arab leadership of this older generation:

As for President 'abd al-Nasir, who uses the Palestinian cause to suit his own policies in a bid to lead the Arab world but who was never really interested in Palestine or its people, he is, in our candid opinion, of no account. We have not trusted him for the past two years and we have not taken seriously his promises to free Palestine. After all, he proved himself incapable of freeing the Sinai desert; how on earth, then, can he claim to the liberator of Palestine? (123)

   The Egyptians were among the most vigorous opponents of irregular operations. 'Abd al-Nasir had already cogently argued that such pin prick tactics served no useful purpose except to needlessly trigger Israeli responses. And other Egyptian sources pointed out that fida'iyin activities alone were not enough to compel an Israeli withdrawal; that the Sinai lacked sufficient cover for fida'iyin operations. Moreover, since the UAR had invested large sums in an economic infrastructure, any risk to these installations that might result from an escalation of fighting must be a matter of Egyptian calculation. (124)

   However, in view of the increasing popularity and political clout of the Palestinians, something more than verbal argumentation was needed. The initial Egyptian response, therefore, was to begin a "war of attrition," basically sustained artillery bombardment of Israeli forward positions along the canal. The 1968-1970 policy goals here were two-fold:

(a) To raise local Egyptian military and home front morale by giving the appearance of some aggressive action against Israeli forces.

(b) To counter the intra-Arab political thrust of the armed struggle/popular liberation war camp.

In addition, the Egyptians hedged their bets by sponsoring the Arab Sinai Organization, manned by Sinai Peninsula recruits with Egyptian officers, and publicizing the exploits of regular Egyptian Commando Units. (125)

   The strategy of the "war of attrition," September 1968-August 1970, rested on the belief that Israeli sensitivity to high casualty rates could be utilized to force territorial concessions. This Israeli emphasis on taking as few human losses as possible had been dramatized by a number of articles and books on the 1967 War. These, the Egyptians had apparently read with interest. 'Abd al-Nasir, himself, is said to have pored over Western accounts of 1967, and to have taken up reading the Old Testament to find further clues as to Israeli weak points.

   The war of attrition had many points to recommend it as a "mini/max" option, given the assumption that Egyptian troops could not be expected to mount any sort of offensive action against the Israelis on the Canal's east banks:

   a) The canal formed a barrier between the two armies, thus providing a de facto static situation, a situation in which Egyptian troops could operate in a set piece environment, and not be exposed to Israeli tactics of mobility and surprise. And given the numerical Egyptian superiority in artillery, these troops could be reasonably expected to hold their own.

   b) Any sort of action along the canal could, in turn, be interpreted by Egyptian media as a resumption of the 1967 War, thus proving that Egypt had not really been defeated in both the civilian population and the rank and file military; and solving two morale problems - civilian and military - at the same time.

c) A resumption of active fighting along the canal could disarm the proponents of irregular warfare by preempting headlines on a day to day basis. In theory at least, massive artillery engagements along the canal should overshadow pin prick Palestinian raids. Moreover, any arguments as to the effectiveness of hit and run tactics could be drowned in the thunder of the guns. Egypt could claim preeminence among the Arabs by virtue of being the most militarily active opponent of the Israelis.

d) The apparent escalation of tensions in the area, as a consequence of cross canal fire, could be utilized as part of a diplomatic effort to get Western, especially United States, intervention on the side of the Arabs.

e) By continual bombardment, it might be possible to destroy part of the Bar-Lev fortifications, thus making a future canal crossing operation easier: (126)

> We are watching the battles in the war of attrition against the enemy from a new position that had been prompted by the attitudes of Arab masses in Libya and the Sudan. This helps us continue this phase of the war of attrition while we are confident in the increase of our capabilities and our ability to develop and escalate the situation in future phases.... We find the enemy confronting this war of attrition from static positions where he is unable to develop but, instead, resorts to acrobatic adventures such as stealing the five French-made gunboats. (127)

The consequences, however, were not quite what was expected. The Israelis countered the artillery fire with air strikes, up to 150 a day by Egyptian calculations, which caused heavy Egyptian casualties along the canal. In addition, they broadened the scope of the air war to include targets in metropolitan Egypt, itself. (128) Further, they carried out a series of cross canal search and destroy operations. (129) All of this presented 'abd al-Nasir with an unenviable prospect.

The relative incapability of Egyptian air defenses to stop Israeli air strikes led to a further Egyptian reliance on the Soviets. The Asian Research Centre noted:

> As the war of nerves and attrition along the Suez Canal steadily escalated, Russians became gradually involved in Egypt's defence in a combat capacity: By the Spring of 1970 Russian pilots as well as gun crews had become operational along the western bank of the Canal itself. It is estimated that as many as 20,000 Russians were engaged in combat operations of one type or another in Egypt.... (130)

This further influx of Soviet personnel produced, in turn, more complications between Egyptian and Soviets. On one hand, Egyptian officials increased their demands for offensive weapons, basically tactical bombers with which to strike back at the Israelis. On the other hand, the increasing contact between Soviet personnel and Egyptians generated interpersonal friction on a large scale.

The inability of Egyptian units to actively attack the Israelis, combined with the heavy losses, reduced morale instead of raising it (and raised the possibility of more military-civilian friction). Moreover, the Israeli military successes simply continued to demonstrate Egyptian military incompetence, both in air defense, and in their ability to respond to daring Israeli commando raids. Instead of increasing Egyptian stature in the Arab world, the War of Attrition made them a laughingstock.

However, the war of attrition did produce a political success of sorts in terms of an American proposal. This called for a three month cease fire along the canal, and the beginning of negotiations along the lines indicated by UN resolution 242 under the auspices of Gunnar Jarring. Therefore, at least one conclusion could be drawn by the Egyptians: that a significant escalation of fighting would produce some diplomatic results.

In a July 23 anniversary speech to the ASU congress, 'abd al-Nasir announced his acceptance of the Rogers' initiative and in so doing spelled out the Egyptian assessment of the United States' role:

We say: we do not make war for the sake of war but we want to attain our objectives, the liberation of all the occupied territories and the restoration of the Palestinian people's right. Israel seeks expansion. So that our stand will be clear to all the world, the U.S. President, and the U.S. people, we say: we have accepted the U.S. proposals submitted to us by U.S. Secretary of State Rogers because we believe these proposals include nothing new and we have accepted them before. But Israel rejected all these proposals which were included in the Security Council resolution....We must look toward the future to determine the U.S. stand. We say that if the United States continues its policy after this - that is, its policy of supplying Israel with large quantities of arms - then the situation will be grave. It will show that the United States did not want peace but wanted the Arab nation to fall under Israeli occuption and helped Israel occupy the Arab nation's territories. (131)

The lessons of the war of attrition were quite simple: The Egyptian army could never again be exposed to Israeli air power without sufficient air defense. The Egyptian air force was not going to be ready to provide this air defense in the near future. (132) Any sort of local military action - if its scope could be controlled - would produce at least some favorable diplomatic results. Some offensive action against Israeli forces was thus imperative, if for no other reason than domestic stability. (133)

Almost immediately after the cease fire was effected, Arab sources began to analyze the implications of such a move. In an article in an Arab League publication, The Arab World, the authors questioned the wisdom of Arab acceptance of a cease fire. In their reasoning, the nature of the cease fire agreement was intrinsically pro-Israel since it called for an Egyptian freeze in the military status along the canal, meaning no more missile sites, while the Israelis were free to augment their air force without restriction. (134)

But they also argued that Israeli policy was based on the belief that only Arab realization of the military hopelessness of the situation prevented Arab attacks:

> ... It is a policy predicated on the belief that the all consuming passion of one's enemy is to destroy it; only his realization of Israel's invincibility and of his own vulnerability prevents him from doing so. Hence the overriding concern of his policy is to determine the costs required to maintain military superiority and to preserve a correct estimate of the enemy's awareness of and response to it. (135)

Their conclusion was that continuance of a cease fire would only be to the benefit of this policy, since it would allow Israel to maintain the status quo indefinitely.

Even before the cease fire, Haykal had analyzed the situation as follows: What was necessary in the present situation was that the Arabs (meaning Egypt) needed to score a victory against Israel. This should be done in terms of a battle considerably larger than the artillery exchanges across the canal, but less so than a total war: A battle in which the Israelis would suffer a clear defeat; where their losses would be from 10,000 to 20,000 men; where they would be compelled to withdraw even a few kilometers from their present positions.

> I am not talking about defeating the enemy in war, but defeating him in a battle, because defeating the enemy in a war still has a long way to go. But defeating the enemy in a battle falls within the ability that is available in advance of a long way to war....I am talking about a limited battle, where an Arab victory is definite and an Israel defeat is beyond doubt. Is this possible? I do not claim to be a military expert. Just the same, I would say that such a battle is possible.... (136)

Such an Arab victory, Haykal reasoned, would lead to the following results:

(a) It would destroy the myth of the invincibility of the Israeli army.

(b) This shaking of the Israeli army would result in a shaking of Israeli society, because the Israeli army is the backbone of the Israeli society.

(c) Shaking the faith of Israeli society in the ability of the Israeli army to protect it.

(d) The Israeli military establishment which now runs Israel will be brought down.

(e) Current Israeli strategy of enforcing peace (on Israeli terms) by military action will tumble.

(f) U.S. policy will be affected, because the U.S. will continue to drag its feet on any Middle East settlement as long as Israel remains in a stronger military position than the Arabs. This U.S. stance would change if the Israeli military position were shaken. (137)

In any event, by late 1971, there were wide spread reports that the Egyptians had arrived at a consensus on a similar strategy. The Christian Science Monitor reported that the Egyptians were thinking of some sort of modified war of attrition across the canal. However, the Monitor noted that, to its knowledge, Egyptian canal crossing capabilities were still dubious. The Egyptian army had not held any exercises above the brigade level. The Egyptians lacked any sort of combat experience in major amphibious operations. Further, the Monitor noted, it would be extremely difficult for the Egyptians to prepare a canal crossing without the Israelis discovering it. Egyptian air capabilities were still extremely poor; the Egyptians still lacked sufficiently trained pilots, and their trainees had an accident rate that was higher than comparable Western rates. (138)

5 Arab Coalition Politics, 1970-1973: Strategy for Conflict

The parameters of Arab strategy were more or less set forth by 1970. Not only had Arab analysts in general thoroughly examined the reasons for the 1967 debacle, but also the Egyptians, in particular, had benefitted by the experience of the war of attrition. But the translation of any sort of strategic plan from idea to practice, its operationalization, required the creation of a coalition of Arab states. The membership of this coalition was, in part, determined by the geography of Arab/Israeli relations, in part by the geopolitics of resource distribution in the Arab world:

a) The political givens were straightforward, if those Arab states which had lost territories to Israel in 1967, were to have any military hope of recovering them, some working alliance that would clearly function as a military unit had to be put together. Alternatively, if these combatants were to have any leverage with those Western states capable of exerting political or other pressure on Israel, some ability to utilize Arab economic, i.e. oil, power, had to be generated. Arabian capabilities had to be worked into any Arab planning.

b) Geographically, the givens were likewise deceptively simple: Palestine/Israel was a natural causeway between the Levant and Egypt. Whoever controlled this could mount military campaigns in either direction; into Egypt to the south, and into Syria to the north. From Biblical times onward, the thrust of strategy, either Egyptian or Mesopotamian was, therefore, to dominate this natural jump off point. Conversely, from the Israeli point of view, Israel historically had been constantly under attack from larger neighbors to the south and north. In the contemporary Middle East, the creation of a modern Israel had placed what Arab analysts considered to be a non-Middle Eastern state athwart this strategy causeway. Therefore, in an ideological sense, the unity of the Arab world was split; in a strategic sense, a power with extra regional connections and ambitions was in a geographically

96

central position. In this respect, the Arab analogy between Israel and the Latin Kingdom of Jerusalem was not, strategically speaking, as far fetched as might appear.

The solution, in a military sense, was also "given," at least insofar as Arab analysts were concerned. In fact, there was an historical model found in the October 1973 strategy; it was provided by Salah al-Din, hero of the anti Crusade. Salah al-Din had been able to link Syrian and Egyptian forces, to create a coalition strong enough to defeat technologically superior Crusader armies. In other words, to force the Latin Kingdom in the 12th century (and Israel in the 20th century) to fight a two front war. The strategic "lessons" of Salah al-Din's campaigns against the Crusaders thus formed the basis of contemporary Syrian and Egyptian political/military planning.

> When the order was given to launch the attack the Egyptian army was not lonely in the fight...its brother the Syrian army participated at the same time....Both the Egyptian and Syrian armies worked hand in hand in a perfect coordination...each on its own front...and they together recorded for history an honorable page...full of heroism... sacrifice, and courage....This was not the first time for these countries to join forces: their ancestors were the first to fight together under the leadership of the hero "EL-NASSER SALAH ELDIN"....The man who unified the Arab armies to fight under one flag....The great man whose deeds are still an inspiration to the writers in their famous poems and writings....He was the hero who liberated the Arab land from those who pretended they were fighting in the name of Jesus...when nothing connected them with Jesus. He cleared up the Arab land of these people and their mischiefs....(1)

But before any military coordination could be set in motion, political rapprochements had to be brokered, and this was no easy task given the mutual imagery; the mutual mistrust of Arab governments for one another, especially so, in the aftermath of the escalation of 1967. The creation of an Arab coalition capable of waging war against Israel, therefore, was the product of a complex series of factors involving the same domestic, intra-Arab and international levels of conflict that escalated into 1967:

a) The immediate dynamics of the coalition building process were supplied by the consequences of the June War: increased domestic unrest in Arab states surrounding Israel, most notably in Egypt and Syria; increased intra-Arab instability as the result of the seemingly uncontrolled activities of the Palestinians and Libyans (who had begun to combine their forces by 1970).

b) Added to these Arab world dynamics was the increasing belief, on the part of relevant Arab leadership, that neither the United States nor Russia had any interest in a "just settlement" of the Arab/Israeli problem. Rather that the superpowers were more interested in preserving the status quo; in preserving their own spheres of influences in the Middle East.

These factors, in turn, coalesced to both create a range of shared interests, and provide the impetus to act on these interests. But while these interests may have been the necessary background elements, the key to post-1967 Arab coalition building, lay in the political styles of the newly installed Egyptian and Syrian elites. Throughout the whole labyrinthian process of putting together a politically and militarily viable coalition, one finds a concerted effort on both Egyptian and Syrian parts to conduct their diplomacy on the basis of rational calculations of interests to avoid, wherever possible, the uncontrolled emotionalism that led to 1967. This effort carries through into the entire planning and conduct of the October War. Indeed, it often appears that Egyptian and Syrian decision makers were as worried about their Arab colleagues as they were about the Israelis.

Both al-Sadat and al-Asad, came to be known for their pragmatism, as contrasted with the ideological orientations of their predecessors. Both opted for legitimizing strategies oriented toward creating coalitions based on shared economic or political interests, rather than continuing their respective predecessors' emphasis on the politics of emotion.

Both, to a certain extent, reversed the policies of their predecessors in a number of ways: Away from the ideological rigidities of Arab nationalism (al-Qawmiya al-'arabiya), toward a more flexible local nationalism (wataniya); away from a thorough going secularism, toward a more Islamic orientation; away from stress on domestic socialism, toward a more liberalized economy; and away from police state controls, toward a more open politics. In terms of their Arab neighbors this meant that the old Nasirist and Ba'th techniques of exporting domestic discontent were (at least temporarily) curtailed: That the destabilizing inputs from Egypt and Syria which moved across borders and impacted on the other Arab domestic tensions were reduced. This, in turn, created the possibility of a rapprochement between these radicals and the conservative governments of Jordan, Saudi Arabia and the rest of the oil states.

This possibility had been foreshadowed by the willingness of the oil producers to bankroll the Egyptians and Syrians after 1967. As al-Sadat pointed out, the only countries that came to 'abd al-Nasir's aid were the Saudis, the Kuwaytis, and the Libyans:

It is true that Gamal 'abd al-Nasir was defeated on June 5, but the Khartoum conference was another moral defeat. All the labels, accusations, and false images that the Egyptian information media had attributed to all those Arab brothers fell before him in a single moment...

He was, in fact, taught a lesson in 1967, when he realized that the only Arab countries that helped him after the defeat, belonged to his arbitrary reactionary category - Saudi Arabia, Kuwait, and King al-Sinusi of Libya. He received no financial aid from anybody else.... (2)

In addition, al-Sadat was a long time personal friend with King Faysal, 'Amir al-Sabah of Kuwayt, and Hasan II of Morocco. These personal linkages considerably eased what might have been much more difficult problems of creating the trust necessary for sustained political cooperation.

EGYPT: THE CREDIBILITY GAP REVISITED

Anwar al-Sadat was selected as 'abd al-Nasir's successor for much the same reasons Golda Meir, another compromise candidate, was chosen Prime Minister. Nobody thought either would be a powerful opponent once in power. The condition of al-Sadat's elevation to the presidency was his agreement to operate as a "primus inter pares" in a collegial decision making situation. As such, he was beholden to the army, in particular, for support against the more powerful right of Zakaria Muhyi al-Din, and Haykal, and the left of 'Ali Sabri. (3)

Al-Sadat had a reputation for unswerving loyalty to 'abd al-Nasir, and being a relatively pliable personality. Summarizing his qualifications, the staff of al-Nahar noted:

Anwar Sadat has always been Nasser's man. His loyalty has never been doubted. Even when rebuked or dismissed by Nasser, he always went peaceably home without uttering a word of protest. He thus always came back to power....However, Sadat does not fulfill the requirements (sic: of the Presidency). The workers and peasants do not support him. They regard him as a man who prefers to make concessions rather than fight. Nasser, they feel, would always have fought for their interests, but Sadat would probably give ground at their expense. The army neither likes nor fears Sadat and he has little contact with the police and intelligence network. It is also said that he lacks the courage to make immediate decisions.... (4)

Given the machismo orientation of Arab/Egyptian political culture, the stress on the appearance of power as a requisite for leadership, this image of weakness boded ill for al-Sadat. An Egyptian joke summed up the popular reaction to this image:

We're suffering from two plagues at one time. First Nasser dies. Then we get Sadat. (5)

However, Arab sources also noted another side to his character. Unlike his predecessor, al-Sadat was much more concerned to place Egyptian - as distinct from pan-Arab - interests at the center of policy. Moreover, al-Sadat was an advocate of Muslim and Arab tradition:

The problem was to get Egypt out of the Middle Ages, to turn it from a semi feudal country into a modern, ordered, viable state, while at the same time respecting the customs of the people. (6)

He served as the RCC's contact with the Muslim Brethren, and by his own account was impressed with its Supreme Guide, Hasan al-Banna:

> Hassan El Banna deplored the decline of religion and morals in Egypt, and the common disregard of the precepts of Islam. He said that the revival of Egypt must be based upon faith, and that the dogmas of Islam must be inculcated in all branches of the army....He had a surprising, intuitive grasp of the problems facing Egypt.... (7)

Al-Sadat did not specify whether he was actually a member of the Brethren, but his later policies show at least some evidence of Brethren influence. Because of his special leaning toward Islamic affairs, he was made Secretary General of the Islamic Congress, and was 'abd al-Nasir's envoy to Saudi Arabia on occasion. (8)

In terms of his political philosophy, al-Sadat described himself as a pragmatist:

> I have always mistrusted theories and purely rational systems. I believe in the power of concrete facts and the realities of history and experience. My political ideas grew out of my personal experience of oppression, not out of abstract theoretical notions. I am a soldier, not a theoretician, and it was by an empirical process that I came to realize my country needed a political system which responded to its essential needs and reflected its true spirit.... (9)

And he expressed a preference for cautious, diplomatic, problem solving oriented approaches to national or international issues:

> ... Revolutionary tactics demand patience and lucid thought. We proceeded cautiously. It was useless and dangerous to make ambitious claims if we had not the means to translate them into reality.... (10)

> The glorification of violence is fatal to the hotblooded people of the East, because it unleashed their most animal instincts: the result is a series of hideous crimes committed in the name of an ideal.... (11)

His policy goals as he enunciated them in a series of addresses were:

> 1. The regaining of lost Egyptian territories in terms of the formula that not one inch of Arab territory will be lost, and there will be no bargaining over the rights of the Palestinian people. (12)

> 2. Egyptian economic policies will be based on pragmatic - or as he styles it, realistic - considerations, not on either the ideology of Communism or Capitalism. (13)

> 3. The Egyptian role in the Arab world will be based on a recognition that there are some differences between Egyptian national interests and those of other Arab states, and that these differences exist within a general consensus.

The Arab nationalism, in which we believe, neither stands for narrow
racialism, nor for regional expansion which aims to acquire more
land. It is the movement of a people who lived the same history, and
spoke the same language and consequently took on a unity of
consciousness and thinking. (14)

4. The maintenance of Egyptian independence from both superpowers within the framework of nonalignment:

... nonalignment does not mean a negative policy. On the contrary,
it is a positive policy. In our view it means that we are for peace
and against war, and for freedom and against domination, for
progress and against backwardness....When our sons are exposed to
shelling seventeen hours a day, and find that we can bring missiles
from any place in the world to help them, then we cannot stand idly
by. Under such circumstances, superficial allegations about
nonalignment will not worry us.... (15)

His strategic preferences, in line with his generally cautious outlook,
were for political rather than military solutions:

This is what we want and insist on because we believe the battle is
going to be imposed on us, and that the decisive word will be spoken
on the battlefield. We tried, and are still trying politically. We
shall not close the door or miss a chance. Even if there is a one per
cent chance for a peaceful solution, we shall work for it. But in the
end we shall fight to liberate our land, for this is a duty and a
legitimate thing to do.... (16)

Al-Sadat's initial policy options were constrained by a number of
political considerations: The fact of his succession as a compromise
candidate; the legacy of the Nasir legend; the inheritance of an
expanded intra-Arab policy orientation; the utilization of psychic
mobilization as a technique of control.

In addition to these, the inertial quality of the Egyptian organizational structure effectively prevented any radical new departures
from past policy. Nasirist problem solving techniques had always been
in the direction of bureaucratization and routine, rather than initiative
and flexibility. This "organizational vision," as one writer styled it,
dominated Egyptian decision making. (17) In the aftermath of 1967,
'abd al-Nasir had intensified the trend toward centralization and
hierarchy by reorganizing the Egyptian bureaucracy. His goal had been
to consolidate power in his own hands, but the result was the
creation of an Egyptian technocracy, a government of "yes-men." ('abd
al-Nasir's nickname for al-Sadat was Bikbashi Sah, "Colonel Yes-
Yes.") (18)

To some extent, al-Sadat, himself, reflected this technocratic
outlook. He was concerned to avoid the ad hoc nature of his
predecessor's policies, and especially, to avoid the lack of a clear
definition of goals and military/political coordination that produced the
debacle of 1967. No longer would Egyptian policy be placed at the

mercy of intra-Arab outbidding; instead empirical determination of Egyptian interests would define policy:

> ... no ruler is supposed to be a professor of law or technology, or be an atomic scientist, but he should have around him people who can give him the best solutions so that he can make his decisions not in a vacuum but on scientific bases; on firm bases of science based on the opinions of specialists.... (19)

Al-Sadat moved to consolidate his regime by a strategy designed to buy time while he removed his opponents. Officially the government adopted a policy of economic and political liberalization. This was designed to contrast with the police state methods of the previous regime. By a series of maneuvers, al-Sadat managed to pick off his opponents piecemeal - just like 'abd al-Nasir had managed to consolidate his earlier regime. In a "white coup" of May 1971, al-Sadat ousted his foremost left wing opposition, 'Ali Sabri, and internal security head, Sha'rawi Jum'a. (20) This was followed by a series of measures designed to restructure the elite; the declared aim of these moves was to "eliminate the centers of power." (21)   A new constitution was promulgated which stressed that:

> Islam is the State's religion, Arabic is its official language, and the principles of Moslem Sharia (law), the basic source of jurisdiction. (22)

> Society shall uphold morality, preserve it and boost genuine Egyptian traditions. Society shall also keep a high level of religious education, ethical and national values, the cultural heritage of the people, scientific facts, socialist and public behavior within the dictates of the law. (23)

The ASU was reorganized; its Executive Committee abolished; its Central Committee almost doubled; the office of ASU Secretary General eliminated. In addition, the leaders of all paragovernmental organizations, the Socialist Youth Organization, the Egyptian Press Association, etc., were ousted and new persons elected. A new parliament, now known as the People's Assembly, was elected. (24) These moves were accomplished by the appointment of pro-Sadat figures to editorships, cabinet posts, and military commands. (25)

The outcome was to concentrate power in both al-Sadat's hands and those of a group of conservative, "traditionalist" and rural oriented bourgeoisie. Both sociologically and politically this new elite represented a considerable movement away from Arab socialism and pan-Arabism. (26)

However, al-Sadat's tactic of threatening immediate war to buy time, combined with a lack of military activity, eroded his authority among wide segments of the Egyptian establishment and public. (27) The credibility of the regime had already been strained by inflated reports of military success in 1967 and during the war of attrition, and al-

Sadat's verbal behavior intensified popular disbelief:

> If, as the government claims, it has taken the Egyptian army nine months to destroy 60 per cent of the Israeli positions on the far side of the canal, how long will it take the army to destroy the other hundred per cent?

> The only way to get the Syrian army to advance into Palestine is to ship all their soldiers to Egypt first, and then tell them to advance. When they're ordered to advance, they take the shortest route back to Damascus. (28)

This inaction combined with the political and economic problems of the June defeat permitted domestic strains to build up unchecked. Considerable labor unrest broke out, particularly at the Halwan iron and steel complex. University students faced with diminishing prospects of employment and promotion became progressively more alienated. Junior officers, either left wing radicals or fundamentalist Muslim Brothers, were increasingly dissatisfied. Old line nationalists, hostile to Nasir's Arab Socialism, resurfaced. The Muslim Brethren, hostile to the regime's secularism, began to reorganize. The old pro-Soviet left, which had never forgiven al-Sadat for purging 'Ali Sabri and his supporters, began to openly attack the regime. Also an Egyptian "new left" emerged and began to organize anti regime demonstrations. All of these diverse groups focused their resentments around the "no war, no peace" situation.

The outpouring of discontent was the unforeseen consequence of two decisions taken immediately after the 1967 war: First to triple or even quadruple the size of Egyptian standing forces, and second to recruit as many college graduates as possible into the armed forces. The goals were to create a large military establishment, capable of overwhelming the Israelis by sheer numbers, and to upgrade the combat efficiency of the military by raising its educational level. The former decision resulted in a tremendous strain on the Egyptian economy; already scarce resources were further depleted. This, in turn, intensified working class unrest. The latter decision introduced a leaven of student militancy into officer and NCO ranks. Student impatience with al-Sadat's regime thus was transmitted to its military.

Al-Sadat, therefore, found himself under increasing pressure from a number of quarters:

a) Students: Student strikes and demonstrations against the regime continued throughout 1972 and on into 1973; student outbursts occurred at the Universities of Cairo, Heliopolis, al-Azhar, Alexandria, Asyut, and 'Ayn Shams, as well as at lesser colleges, secondary schools, and even military academies. The catalyst of these demonstrations appeared to be 16,000 Palestinian students. (29) In January 1973, the government cracked down and began large scale arrests. Student activism focused on disenchantment with the "no war/no peace" situation, and rejection of official controls on political activity. Most of the student militancy was organized by the Supreme National Committee of Cairo University Students. (30) This organization declared that:

> The spontaneous action of our university students is not a sudden movement following Sadat's recent declaration (of January 13, in which he claimed that outside agitators were behind the riots). It is an expression of mass uprising against the liquidation of political life in Egypt which has continued for many years and deprived the people of the means for political action.... (31)

b) Intellectuals: al-Sadat came under extremely heavy criticism, particularly from Haykal in al-Ahram, but also from a number of other intellectuals for his movement away from Nasirist tenets. Some elements of this intelligentsia began to develop contacts with al-Qadhafi, on the grounds that he, at least, was sincere in his principles. (32) In March 1973, al-Sadat removed a number of journalists and writers from their positions in the media.

c) Working class: Workers at the Halwan industrial complex were particularly restive, a series of demonstrations broke out at Halwan, Alexandria, and working class suburb of Shubra al-Khayma. Leaflets attacking the regime were regularly circulated among workers, and the regime was seriously concerned over the possibility of a combined student/working class uprising. (33)

d) Religious: On November 5, 1972 a group of Muslims set fire to a Coptic church at Khanikah, north of Cairo. Damage was also done to Coptic shops and houses in the Cairo area; similar incidents were reported in Alexandria. A commission of inquiry was convened, and al-Sadat met with Coptic Patriarch, Shanuda III, and the Shaykh of al-Azharin an attempt to prevent further confessional strife. But religious tensions remained high throughout the year. (34)

e) Military: The near mutinous attitude of the Egyptian military presented one of the gravest threats to al-Sadat's regime. Reports of mutinies and uprisings by individual units circulated throughout 1972. In June, two Egyptian pilots reportedly disobeyed orders and engaged Israeli air patrols; (35) in September, an army battalion stationed on the Canal had to be disarmed by loyal units; (36) in November, a number of air force officers at the Beni Suif Air Base were arrested. (37) The most bizarre incident, however, occurred on October 12, when an officer made a speech to the assembled faithful at Cairo's al-Husayni Mosque in which he urged the belivers to start at jihad. (38)

Al-Sadat's difficulties in controlling his military were compounded by the intermingling of military and civilian politics. The critical factor in this linkage was the 70,000 university graduates that had been incorporated into the military since 1967. These were not only a younger generation of officers, but also opinion leaders within the military. This group had been in a state of maximum mobilization since their induction. Their personal career expectations had been in limbo, and they were becoming increasingly dissatisfied with the situation. Many of them were reported to have argued that either orders be issued for an attack, or that the alert be cancelled. (39)

Matters came to a head between al-Sadat and his younger officers with the dismissal of the Commander-in-Chief and War Minister, General Muhammad Sadiq. Sadiq was enormously popular with both the younger officers and with civilian students. During his tenure in office, he had also succeeded in building up a power base among senior officers by raising their salaries between 50 and 100 Egyptian pounds per month. (40) At the same time, he was the darling of the right wing represented in the ASU. (41) Politically, therefore, he represented a considerable threat to al-Sadat; organizationally, his position as head of the Egyptian military gave him the capability to play the same game of bureaucratic politics that the late 'abd al-Hakim 'Amir had played.

The issues which sparked the dismissal were multiple. Sadiq had been the driving force behind the decision to eject Soviet advisors in July 1972, and his outspoken anti-Soviet sentiments threatened to jeopardize the continued supply of Soviet arms. (42) In addition, he clearly sympathized with dissident elements in the army; he vigorously objected to the execution of the officer who spoke in the mosque. Finally, Sadiq refused to mount any kind of operation against the Israelis (see chapter 6), arguing, among other things, that Egypt should not embark on a war without acquiring sophisticated weapons first. (43)

Al-Sadat, however, was later to state that he dismissed Sadiq because of Sadiq's incompetence and cowardice. According to al-Sadat's version, he was planning some sort of cross canal operation scheduled for November 15, 1972; an operation basically designed to forestall (or at least take the steam out of) expected anti-Sadat student demonstrations in the wake of the Soviet ouster:

> ...I was surprised when I convened the Supreme Council of the Armed Forces. As I told you, I instructed the war minister (sic: Sadiq) in August, to go to the Supreme Council of the Armed Forces to inform it of the decisions and to make the forces ready by November. Two days later the war minister returned and told me I (sic: Sadiq) have convened the council and everything has been prepared. We are ready for November 1, I told him no, our date is November 15....Therefore, at the end of October when I convened the Supreme Council, I assumed it was ready for the first of November. It became apparent that the war minister had not informed the Supreme Council of the decisions....At this moment (sic: after an exchange of questions) the war minister leaned toward me and said: I did not pass the information on because I wanted to maintain secrecy. Do you withhold secrets from the Supreme Council of the Armed Forces? It is the Supreme Council that draws up the plans....
>
> The ministers' decisions were haphazard...I even found out something worse than that (sic: Sadiq's deliberately misleading state-

ments)...The defensive plan collapsed because the Jews increased the height of the sand barrier on the canal to 17 meters while our forces (sic: meaning Sadiq) did not make any effort. The result was that our boys were sitting behind two meters as opposed to 17.... (44)

On October 26, Sadiq was replaced by Ahmad Isma'il 'Ali. The commander of the Navy and more than 100 other senior officers were also either arrested or pensioned off. Sadiq's dismissal brought down a storm of protest by students and others. Pressure for action from within the military was intensified, now led by Chief of Staff, Lt. General Sa'ad al-Din Shadhili. (45)

f) Economy: At the beginning of 1972, a series of austerity measures were inaugurated to prepare the Egyptian economy for the coming war: bans on the purchase of new automobiles, on foreign travel, on the import of luxury goods, and the governmental takeover of wholesale food trade. (46) In addition, a new ten year development plan was launched in early 1973. Its goals were to double national income, to create 3 million new jobs, to increase consumption by 5%, and to improve social conditions in general. (47) Nevertheless, the double pressures of rapid population increase, and the cost of maintaining the large military establishment produced an acute foreign exchange problem. Egyptian ability to purchase needed wheat was jeopardized.

At a crisis meeting of the Committee for National Security held on September 30, 1973, al-Sadat summed up the economic situation:

The situation in which we find ourselves means that two months from this date we will not be able to pay one mil of the payments that will fall due at the beginning of the year. I will not be able to buy a single grain of wheat in 1974. In other words, the people will not have a loaf of bread, the minimum substance. (48)

By his reasoning, it would have been cheaper to lose the entire army in the Sinai than pay for continued mobilization:

I do not withhold the fact from you, my sons, that we reached a difficult economic situation before the decision to enter into battle....My calculation was simple. The army cost us 100 million pounds a month, and if the enemy destroyed our installations and houses worth 200 million pounds, these ultimately were two months' expenses. We could do nothing but enter the battle, and that is what happened. Economically, we had entered the stage of certain danger. Had 1974 come with the situation still unchanged, it would probably have been difficult for use to produce a loaf of bread.... (49)

g) Discontent: The approximately one and a half million persons who were displaced from Isma'iliya and the Canal Zone, became an increasing strain on the Egyptian morale. Many moved in with relatives, but a huge number of homeless remained. Symptomatic of the breakdown of social solidarity, of the increasingly widespread discontent and frustration, were the phenomena of a series of random arsons, one destroying the Cairo Opera House, and mini riots at bus stops, and soccer matches. (50) Insofar as the regime was concerned, it was only a matter of time before one of these incidents sparked an upheaval along the lines of "Black Saturday" of January 1952, when a shooting in the Canal Zone started a chain of events that culminated in mob violence which destroyed much of Cairo.

As 1973 progressed, al-Sadat found himself in a situation that increasingly paralleled that of the late King Faruq. He was dependent on a steadily decreasing power base, as the Guardian's David Hirst reported early in the year:

> Stage by stage, Sadat has been narrowing his inherited power base. First he disposed of Ali Sabri, Sharawi Gomaa and Nasser's apparatchicks. Then he came to rely heavily on the army, but antagonized a substantial portion of that with the dismissal of General Sadek. He has thrown out the Russians without winning over the Americans.... (51)

The remaining conservative and technocratic coalition had become progressively isolated from any source of popular support. The credibility gap was increasing, rather than narrowing. The gulf between the image this new elite was projecting, and its actual appearance to the bulk of the population, were poles apart. (52) In addition, the elite was beginning to split up. Technocrats, as represented by Sa'id Mara'i, were starting to dissociate themselves from the ultras of the right. (53) The military was split among itself. An-Nahar Report, in the first week of October, carried a story to the effect that Ahmad Isma'il had tendered his resignation in protest over pressure within the officers' corps for an immediate attack. (54)

Widespread popular alienation faced this uneasy elite. The possibility of a coup by a coalition of students, workers, intellectuals, and military was extremely likely. The students and workers could control the streets; the military could provide the organized force. All that was needed to reproduce the situation of 1952, was the existence of a Free Officer's Movement, and there was sufficient potential leadership to create that.

SYRIA: THE CULT OF PERSONALITY AND
THE POLITICS OF ISOLATION

The editors of an Arab World Weekly analysis of the Syrian regime characterized the post-June Ba'th as a party of "isolation and secrecy": Isolation because the party had shown over and over again that it was both unable, and unwilling, to share government with any other group; secrecy because the Ba'th kept its organization under a cloak of secrecy and rarely divulged the names of its leaders. In addition, the editors pointed out that the Ba'thists always projected a feeling of arrogance in both their tactics of monopolizing power and their statements of party ideology:

> Every citizen has seeds of the Ba'th in him, but these seeds have not bloomed inside every citizen. Therefore, the role of the vanguard is to contribute to the bloom of these seeds and to transform sectors of the people into organized masses aware of their historical role.... (55)

After the war the Jadid faction, seemingly oblivious to domestic opposition, ruthlessly intensified the drive for a secular, proletarian society. Al-Ba'th described the post war policy line under the headline:

> The Revolutionary Strategy: An Outcome of Education, Experience, Sacrifice, and Legitimate Aspirations. (56)

After admitting that June 5th was a "step backward and even more than that," the paper went on to describe what was needed:

> Liberation from all forms of imperialism as well as from all its political, economic, military, and social centers. (57)

To accomplish this, two conditions were necessary:

> A clear revolutionary strategy, and the will to accept steadfastness and comprehensive confrontation, or the popular armed struggle in all its forms, and the determination to escalate it to the level of an overall liberation war.... (58)

In line with this doctrine, the regime pressed on with its unpopular programs of socialism and secularization domestically, and with its policy of fida'iyin style border confrontation with Israel. These policies rapidly became a source of increasing conflict between the Jadid and al-Asad factions within the party. The issue between them was that of how best to liberate the occupied territories. Jadid's wing took the position that ideological confrontation was the key. Only by operationalizing Ba'th ideology domestically and abroad could any progress be made toward liberating the territories. Therefore economic development at home and the maintenance of ideological purity in terms of intra-Arab contacts was necessary. (59)

In contrast, al-Asad's group stressed the need for immediate military action. All economic projects should be suspended, especially those that depended on Soviet aid, because the Soviets were "pressuring Syria to accept the political and peaceful solution" to the Middle East crisis. Therefore the price of Soviet aid was the acceptance of a political solution. Moreover, the Syrian Ba'th should cooperate with both the old Pan-Arab Command and the Iraqi Ba'th party, even though these were ideologically hostile, for the sake of added military strength. (60)

Ultimately this conflict escalated into the events of September 1970 and led to al-Asad's takeover in November. (61) An Arab assessment of al-Asad pointed out his poor, 'Alawi origins, his long time connection with both the Ba'th and the Syrian Air Force, and his relatively mild and soft-spoken nature. At the same time this source noted his hard line attitude on the Arab-Israeli issue, and his tendency to judge allies, including the Soviets, in terms of their willingness to confront the Israelis:

> What is publicly known about General Assad are two things: he is an "Alawite," a Moslem Shia, and his name means "The Lion." He is known to be married and have children, but his family rarely appears in public, maintaining the strict Moslem tradition....He goes out only to army functions. He smokes locally made cigarettes, but refrains from drinking alcoholic beverages....In the inner circles of the party, he has a reputation for being a firm believer in army and party discipline. (62)

> Assad is as much an advocate of war of liberation against Israel as the rest of Syrian leaders, and was believed to have been among the first Arab officials to see the potential of the Palestinian commando movement (sic: al-Asad and Lt. Col. 'abd al-Karim al-Jundi were apparently the driving force behind Syrian support to Fatah from 1965 onward). He once said in a speech to Syrian troops: "There can be no peace as long as Zionists continue to exist on Arab soil."... (63)

> Reports spread about him in the foreign press that he was anti-Soviet were grossly exaggerated. He is known to have criticised the Soviets, whom he likes to describe as "our friends and allies," on two things: their reluctance so far to give Syria what Assad considers as more effective weapons, and their pressure on the Syrian regime to make it agree to a political settlement to the Middle East crisis. (64)

Al-Asad's own statements bear out this image of undeviating hatred for the Israelis. The Israelis are pictured as the archenemy, bent on a never ending policy of expansion:

> This Zionist danger, the long term aims of which have never been in doubt, has become clearly evident, its ambitions crystallized and its means and methods clearly defined since the 1967 aggression. Our enemy is treacherous and vicious. He now publicly speaks about his ambitions after previously concealing them. He has no scruples in adopting any criminal method in order to implement his plan....What happened in Beirut recently (sic: the Israeli raid on April 10, 1973) indicates how far the enemy can go in his crimes. It also proves that the enemy does not differentiate between one Arab country and another, except insofar as this serves his unchanging strategy, which is aimed eventually at building a greater Israel and at the political and economic domination of the Arab homeland in the interests of Zionism and imperialism.... (65)

Given this perception of Israeli annexationism, the only solution was force, political efforts such as al-Sadat's diplomacy were useless:

> The result of the political struggle waged by some Arab and friendly states has been more Israeli arrogance and impudence. There is no doubt that this struggle has greatly shown to the world what Israel's intentions are, but it has not proceeded one step toward Israel's withdrawal from the territory it occupied in 1967. Because expansion is in the nature of the Zionist entity, we ultimately have to wage an armed battle to defend our rights and liberate our usurped territory.... (66)

Moreover, this military action against Israel must take place as soon as possible. Delay worked only to the advantage of the Israelis:

> The Arab masses, which are angered and pained, wonder how long our Arab forces will remain idle and only the weaknesses of our nation projected. These masses have a right to ask, because every delay in utilizing Arab resources and capabilities means increasing the pains of the Arab masses. It also means the expansion and spread of the Zionest danger to include more Arab countries.... (67)

Directly after taking power in a bloodless (or "White") coup on November 13, 1970, al-Asad and his supporters moved to change both the image and the policies of the regime. Symptomatic of this change was the background music chosen for the regime's first communique, issued on November 16. In contrast to the heretofore standard Syrian practice of broadcasting martial music prior to the announcement of a new government, Damascus radio and TV played classical music. (68)
      Al-Asad was extremely conscious of the hostility with which he and the 'Alawi Ba'thists were regarded by the Sunni community, and attempted to play down the elite's 'Alawi identity:

> We believe that, to a great extent, our party in the past was alienated from the masses on the home front. This is what we sometimes call internal isolation....We believe that mutual confidence between ourselves and the people is the best we can hope for.... (69)

He relied on a number of Sunnis, among them Defense Minister Mustafa Talas and sometime Prime Minister 'abd al-Rahman Khulay-fawi, to serve as links between the regime and the Sunni community. But even here, the tenuousness of 'Alawi/Sunni relations is apparent. In a stratagem not unlike 'abd al-Nasir's earlier technique of creating opposing factions within the governing elite, al-Asad carefully inter-posed a Christian, Major General Yusuf Shakkur, as Chief of Staff, between Talas and the Muslims in the military. The theory behind this move was apparently that Muslim soldiers would not rally around a Christian as opposed to an 'Alawi, since both were equally anathema in the sense that they were not Sunnis.

Bureaucratic (or rather primordial) politics aside, al-Asad went out of his way to inaugurate a number of policies designed to demonstrate the government's piety, and to mollify groups, religious and otherwise, that had been alienated by his predecessors. He, and other officials, began the practice of praying publicly on Friday. Special attention was paid to relations between the government, and the 'ulama,' and with the various Christian churches. <u>Radio Damascus</u> took to broadcasting Sunday services from Christian churches as a gesture of good will toward Syrian Christians. (70) Upon his election to the Presidency (the first time a non-Sunni had become President), al-Assad took the traditional Islamic oath of office, the bay'a .(71)

The overtly police state character of the government was toned down. Restrictions on travel to other Arab countries were eased; extensive and obvious public surveillance was curtailed; some political prisoners were released. Consumers goods were made more plentiful. (72)

More importantly, the Ba'thist hard line emphasis on socialism and revolution as a basis for political community and governmental legitimacy was replaced by a cult of personality. This cult, apparently orchestrated by al-Asad's brother, Colonel Rif'at al-Asad, who was also commander of the elite 70th Brigade, was designed to project a Nasir like image on the theory that the political isolation of the regime could be overcome by al-Asad's personal charisma. As one Arab source noted:

> Why is the glorification of Assad? There appears to be a great deal of psychology involved. Experience has shown that the Arab character rallies around a man as a leader rather than around an institution, like a collective leadership inside of the Ba'th Party leadership. Nasser's popularity - despite the not so strong political machinery expressed in the UAR's Arab Socialist Union - was a good example....After Nasser's death, the Arab masses yearned for a new leader, the Syrians appeared to have centered their attention, at least for the time being, on Assad. In fact, Assad's popularity in Syria started when he decided to follow in Nasser's step.... (75)

Al-Asad replaced his uniform with civilian clothes (like 'abd al-Nasir) and worked at projecting the image of himself as a father figure. Photographs of himself and his family were widely distributed, an unusual procedure for Syrian leaders, along with stories about him spending all his free time with them. Syrian official publicity called him "The Hero Leader." Mass demonstrations and rallies were organized in support of al-Asad and the government; during one of these, Minister of Culture and Guidance Fawzi al-Kayyali was so moved as to introduce al-Asad as "the miracle maker." Placards describing al-Asad as "the hero leader," "the great leader," and "father of the people" were common, as were slogans such as: We are ready to sacrifice our blood for you, Oh Hafiz! (74)

The nickname of "abu Sulayman" after his oldest son, Sulayman ('abd al-Nasir was referred to as abu Khalid for the same reason) was popularized , and crowds took up the chant, "Hafiz, Hafiz," in imitation of the Egyptian chant, "Nasir, Nasir." (75)

The regime's isolation in the Arab world was also of concern to al-Assad, the more so since lack of Arab political, and military coordination served to benefit the Israelis:

> We must realize in this regard that Israel had benefited from the Arab nation's mistakes more than it (sic: the Arab nation) has benefited from its own strength. Israel has never really confronted a united Arab force. It has only confronted divided and dispersed forces. This is our fatal weakness.... (76)

Therefore, al-Asad began to reorient Syrian foreign policy away from its narrow ideological basis. In a statement which echoed the views of his Egyptian counterpart, al-Asad declared:

> On the Arab level we have decided to make reunions with the progressive countries in earnest and to develop these reunions into unionist steps....We have also decided to normalize relations between ourselves and the other Arab countries and not to create tension in these relations unless the liberation cause justifies it.... (77)

The chief progressive country with which al-Asad wished to restore relations was Egypt, and secondarily with Iraq. In order to do this, however, he had to build a base of support within Syria. The technique utilized was that of a "national front," a coalition of chosen parties allowed to operate under the aegis of the Ba'th: The Arab Socialist Union of Syria, a group of breakaway Ba'thists and Nasirists who wanted closer ties between Syria and Egypt; two factions of the Socialist Unionists, who were more or less in favor of some form of unity between Syria, Egypt, and Iraq; the Arab Socialist Party, another fallen away Ba'th faction; and the Syrian Communist Party. (78) With the exception of the Syrian Communist Party, all of these parties had been committed at one time or another to unity schemes involving the Egyptians and/or Iraqis.

These efforts, however, foundered on the rock of Sunni hatred of the regime; a regime which the Sunnis held responsible for the loss of Syrian lands. Al-Asad's attempts to find a solution to this dilemma produced other unexpected contingencies and conflicts. Attempts at rapprochement with Sunni governments, on the off chance that outside Sunni acceptance might mitigate domestic Sunni alienation, created frictions within the Ba'thist elite.   The strategy of overcoming religious differences by the force of personal charisma generated intense personal jealousies within the military. Escalating border tension with Israel in an effort to create in-group solidarity in the face of an external threat, produced unacceptably high casualties.

Al-Asad found himself, like his Egyptian counterpart, under increasing threat from a variety of sources:

a) Sunni Hostility: Sunni sentiments were inflamed by the promulgation in al-Ba'th on February 1, 1973 of a new Syrian Constitution which omitted the phrase, "Islam is the religion of the state." The omission was most probably a gesture in the direction of hard line Ba'th secularists. After two weeks or so of uneasy calm (punctuated by local religious clashes between Sunnis and 'Alawis), full scale rioting broke out on the 23rd. (79) Hama was the scene of the worst violence, but outbreaks occurred in Homs, Latakia, Aleppo and Damascus. According to the Arab World, the demonstrations were organized by the Muslim Brethren. (80) The rioters chanted or carried placards with anti-'Alawi slogans; (81) other antigovernment groups joined in. (82)

The regime hastily added a phrase to the effect that the religion of the head of the state must be Islam, and rushed army units to Hama (under the command of Rif'at al-Asad). Rioting and antigovernment demonstrations continued into March. The regime replied with daily radio broadcasts alternatively pointing out the merits of the new constitution and threatening to deal with insurgents with "an iron hand." Ultimately the new constitution was approved with a 97.6 per cent vote in its favor, but Sunni/'Alawi hostility persisted, and relations remained extremely tense. Rioting broke out again on April 15, the Prophet's birthday. (83)

b) Splits within the Military: These involved a complex set of issues; 'Alawi officers were still split into Asad and Jadid factions. Jadid himself was imprisoned, but his followers were still strong among junior officers; (84) some of these planned an operation to release him in August 1973. This was prevented by security forces; however, the loyalty of many of the younger officers remained a source of concern. (85)

Differences between Sunni and 'Alawi officers over alleged 'Alawi domination of the military were exacerbated by Rif'at al-Asad's meteoric rise to power. In order to hold the loyalty of the 'Alawi community, al-Asad had resorted to a strategy of cooptation: in this case he appointed 'Alawi officers to command positions (including a large number of al-Asad's relatives and personal friends). The result was a bifurcation of the Syrian military, with 'Alawi officers commanding Sunni troops; and a consequent morale problem since these troops were (not unexpectedly) unwilling to fight for the 'Alawis. (86) Rif'at al-Asad, therefore, symbolized, in his person, the preferential career treatment given 'Alawis. These tensions came to a head when War Minister Major General Salih 'Umrani was assassinated in March 1972. Air Force Commander Major General Naji Jamil (a Sunni), and his followers, insisted on a full scale investigation of the assassination on the theory that the perpetrators were adherents of Rif'at. These differences were also crystallized in another direction. Generals Talas and Jamil objected to al-Asad's attempts at rapprochement with Iraq, an objection which engendered considerable ill feeling. (87)

As a consequence of these, and other differences within the military, al-Asad was unsure of his officers. This uncertainty was confirmed by a reported assassination attempt on, or about, July 10, 1973. At that time, al-Asad entered a military hospital in Damascus for

five days. Syrian media gave out the story that he had done so for a
minor operation on varicose veins in his left leg.   Beirut papers,
L'Orient Le Jour and Le Soir, however, carried reports that he had been
shot in the leg during the course of an uprising by rebel army units; that
some   300   officers   and   non-commissioned   officers   had   been
arrested. (88)

c) Intra-Ba'th opposition: Ideologues within the Party vehemently
objected to the regime's modifications of Ba'th tenets. This opposition
increased to the point in late 1973 where the government felt it
necessary to inaugurate daily lectures explaining domestic and foreign
policies to senior Party officials. (89)

By late September, then, the regime faced a situation comparable to
that of pre-June 1967: Sunni antagonism coupled with serious splits
with the elite. The government was very apprehensive that religious
rioting would break out again (possibly during, or after, Ramadan); that
left wing elements in the Party and military would form an opposition
movement; and that a student movement similar to that in Egypt would
emerge. (90)

ARAB STRATEGY FOR WAR

In 1964, 'abd al-Nasir had outlined the strategic preconditions that
must be met before any sort of successful military confrontation with
Israel was possible: The concentration of superior military force, the
isolation of Israel, and Arab unity. That they were not fulfilled in June
1967 was a consequence of factors outside the Egyptian leader's control,
and did not negate them in Egyptian eyes. In developing a strategy to
reverse the events of June 1967, al-Sadat relied heavily on his
predecessor's strategic thinking, but he added to it the conclusions
drawn as a result of the June War.

Strategically, the problem that presented itself to the Egyptians was
threefold. First, in a strictly military sense, a coalition of Syria, Egypt,
and Jordan had to be built. The pattern of 1967, whereby the Israelis
were able to defeat first Egypt, then Jordan, and then Syria could not
be repeated. If the Egyptians were to get across the canal, Syrian
forces had to occupy the Israelis long enough for the Egyptians to
consolidate themselves. Syrian attacks, therefore, had to be vigorous
enough to get the Israelis to move most of their forces to the north.

As it turned out, the Syrians were successful in so doing. A Dayan
press conference on October 9, 1973, later reproduced in the Arab
media, included these comments:

I want to begin at the beginning. I say that now we are facing two
fronts. Egypt and Syria. We want very much to paralyze one of
them - the Syrian front. It has absolute priority because, above all,
it exists inside our country....Had this (sic: Syrian) column stayed in
the Golan Heights, it would have gained control of it and spilled over

in the Houleh valley. This is inside our country, while our problems
with Egypt... are not paramount problems, in the short range at
least, for the State of Israel.... (92)

Jordan was the strategic link between the northern and southern
fronts. As Syrian military analyst Lt. Col. Haytham al-Ayyubi was later
to argue, Jordan was of critical strategic importance in any confrontation with Israel. In terms of its military resources, Jordan possessed the
fourth largest Arab army, some 73,000 men plus 42,000 more in reserves
and paramilitary formations. While the numerical strength was small,
the high quality of Jordanian training more than made up for this.
Moreover, Jordan had the fifth largest air force which could, under
certain circumstances, interdict Israeli aircraft flying strikes into
Syria. (93)

Strategically, the addition of Jordan to an Arab front resulted in
four advantages:

1. Jordan's long borders, between 290 and 295 kilometers -
   excluding the Dead Sea - presented the Israelis with a defensive
   problems. Therefore, Jordanian troops stationed along these
   frontiers could tie down large numbers of Israelis, even if the
   Jordanians took no overt action.

2. Jordanian forces stationed at Aqaba could blockade the Israeli
   port of Eilat.

3. In the event of hostilities, Jordanian territory could be used as a
   route for both Iraqi and Saudi Arabian forces attacking Israel,
   thus avoiding the necessity for these forces operating along a
   relatively narrow Syrian front.

4. Jordanian ground forces could protect the Syrian's southern flank
   in the Dar'a region; its air force could bolster Syrian air
   defenses. (94)

A coalition of oil producing states had to be created in order to
bring to bear Arab oil pressure on Western nations, and through them on
Israel. Assuming that Arab forces, by themselves, could do no more
than dislodge the Israelis from a few kilometers of Arab land, this
diplomatic/economic weapon would be the key factor in a political
victory. If an oil embargo was to be employed, there had to be a unity
of oil producing nations behind it. The piecemeal cut offs of earlier
wars would lack the requisite political threat.

Israel had to be diplomatically and propagandistically isolated from
other sources of international support. A repetition of the 1967
experience, wherein the Arabs found themselves on the wrong side of
world opinion, had to be avoided, especially so, since the Arabs were
planning to attack first, and if any sort of United Nations support was
to be counted on.

As a corollary to these efforts, however, Palestinian opposition to
anything short of all out war against Israel had to be neutralized.

Otherwise, al-Sadat and his colleagues would find themselves attacked for selling out the "rights of the Palestinian People."

Egypt and Syria: Sinai and Golan

Syrian-Egyptian contacts began almost immediately after al-Asad's take over; al-Asad traveled to Cairo in December 1970. From the beginning, negotiations between the two were hampered by radically different outlooks. Although both sides recognized the need for a two front war against Israel, there was no agreement on the timing and nature of this war. Most of these differences stemmed from the status of the occupied territories of the two countries. Israeli statements had made it clear that most, if not all, of the Sinai was negotiable; the Golan Heights, on the other hand, was not. (95)

In turn, this Israeli position led to different Egyptian/Syrian policy conclusions. For the Egyptians, negotiations were at least a possibility; for the Syrians, negotiations appeared unlikely (and ideologically unthinkable, in any event). Israeli lines in the Sinai were on the other side of a heavily defended water barrier, and were some distance from Cairo. Israeli positions in the Golan overlooked the Damascus plain, and were a short distance from Damascus itself. The immediacy of this strategic threat translated into a sense of urgency on the part of the Syrians; its converse enabled the Egyptians to proceed with caution, to avoid the haste which led to 1967:

> Haykal, in an article on the psychology of impatience, had argued that the Israelis were counting on the Arabs to begin another battle with Israel prematurely. He cited an Israeli psychological study which reportedly concluded that Israelis could depend on Egyptian impatience to work in its favor. The Egyptians would opt for one of two courses. Either they would attack without adequate preparation, or they would seek a settlement - any kind of settlement - to the crisis. (96)

There was also a legacy of considerable mistrust to be overcome. The Syrians felt that Egyptian acceptance of United Nations Resolution 242, and other compromise formulae, was an indication that they were prepared to make compromises at Syrian expense. They were, and are, acutely sensitive to the possibilities of an Egyptian "sell out." The Egyptians, for their part, remembered the events of 1967, when the Syrians had dragged them into a war and then refused to fight it. The Egyptians, therefore, were, and are, particularly anxious not to be propelled into some rash policy by Syrian extremism.

Insofar as al-Asad was concerned, continued Israeli occupation of the Golan meant a constant threat to Syria's security. As a consequence, he was an early advocate of establishing a joint Syrian, Iraqi, Jordanian front. The original idea, proposed in 1968, was to headquarter a joint command in Damascus under an Iraqi commander (the Jordanians were unwilling to accept a Syrian commander.) This scheme collapsed when a rival Ba'th faction took power in Iraq. (97)

Syrian goals in a series of talks with the Egyptians can be estimated as follows:

a. To get immediate Egyptian military assistance vis a vis the Israelis.

b. To secure a firm Egyptian commitment to the principle of complete Israeli withdrawal from the Golan.

c. To enlist Egyptian support in Syria's relations with Palestinian organizations.

d. To acquire, via Egyptian mediation, economic and diplomatic aid from Saudi Arabia, including a withdrawal of Saudi Arabian support for Muslim Brethren activities in Syria. (98)

The first two were the most critical in Syrian eyes, and all during the discussions, the Syrians utilized a local "war of attrition" along the Golan to pressure the Egyptians. According to Arab sources, by December 1972:

... The Syrians feel that renewed fighting in Golan will place the Egyptian leadership in an extremely awkward situation and that, given the internal difficulties facing Sadat, Egyptian army officers are liable to press for action along the Suez front. (99)

In response, the Egyptians chose to temporize by dealing with Syrian demands in terms of large intra-Arab frameworks: the Arab League; the Tripartite Federation of Egypt, Libya, and Syria; and the Joint Arab Defense Council. They were apparently counting on intra-Arab divisions to both prevent any sort of concerted action, and to diffuse any Egyptian unilateral responsibility for defending Syria (much as 'abd al-Nasir had done years before). In any event, they did not start serious negotiations until early January; the Egyptian/Syrian Supreme Council, headed by Ahmad Isma'il, was not set up until January 31, 1973.

This Egyptian inaction, and consequent Syrian frustration, produced a crisis of sorts during these initial talks. Israeli air attacks on Syrian positions in the Golan and near Dar'a on January 8 caused heavy casualties. (100) These attacks were coupled by Israeli warnings to the effect that, if Syria persisted in supporting guerrilla activity, Israel would not limit its retaliation:

The dilemma before the Syrians is a serious one because, contrary to their current plans, Israel's reaction does not necessarily bear any proportional relationship to the acts perpetrated by them against Israel.... (101

The Syrians accused the Egyptians of failing to provide military aid as required by the terms of the Tripartite Federation Agreement, and threatened to withdraw from it. Foreign Minister 'abd al-Halim

Khaddam, in reply to a question concerning Arab military preparations, remarked acidly:

> There is no plan, not even a conception of a plan. Even if one existed, it would not be brought before the (sic: Joint Defense) Council, but would be studied only by those concerned. Although we have no confidence in the effectiveness of repeated meetings, we attend them to see what happens. (102)

Immediately prior to the Israeli raids, Minister of War Ahmad Isma'il, al-Sadat's personal envoy, and Hasan Sabri al-Khuli held talks with Syrian leaders. Presumably during the course of these talks, the Egyptians stressed the argument that only a two front war combined with use of the oil weapon had any chance of succeeding. Therefore, the Syrians were most likely asked to, in turn:

a. Accept the principle of a conventional war aimed at securing a negotiated settlement.

b. Allow the Egyptians to set the timing of the war.

c. Moderate their hostility to Jordan.

A combination of two factors both impelled and permitted the Egyptians to start serious discussions concerning a coordinated attack: The crescendoing of student unrest around the turn of the year, and the appointment of Ahmad Isma'il as War Minister and Commander in Chief. The student riots impressed upon the regime the tenuousness of its domestic position, while Ahmad Isma'il's appointment removed that last major military opposition to an immediate attack. Al-Sadat was later to claim that this appointment was the first of a series of decisions that led to war:

> The first actual decision on the October 6 War was taken when I removed former War Minister Sadiq and appointed Marshal Ahmad Isma'il in his place. This marked the fact that the matter had now entered a serious stage.... Within three months - from late 1972 to early 1973 - after the appointment of Marshal Isma'il, 20 million pounds were spent on equipment.... (103)

Contacts intensified over the next three months, with Marshal Ahmad Isma'il travelling regularly to Damascus. Preliminary planning for the Syrian Front was apparently worked out by February; according to Talas, the Syrians started preparations for the attack in that month. (104) Ahmad Isma'il was also in Damascus twice in March; on the 2nd, after his trip to Moscow, and on the 30th for a four day visit. (105) Two days later, on April 4, Saudi Arabia announced that it had given Syria a ten million pound grant to strengthen its army. (106)

Overall coordination was begun during the course of a secret meeting of the Supreme Council of the Egyptian and Syrian Forces in Alexandria in late April (probably either prior to, or during, the time that the Arab Defense Council was in session in Cairo, using this as a cover in the presumption that foreign intelligence services would be focused on events in Cairo). At this time, al-Jamasy presented a report which specified the potential dates for an attack: May, August-September, and October. At, or about the same time, al-Sadat and al-Asad met in Burj al-'Arab (outside of Alexandria) and made the decision for war:

> I said: Hafiz, I am going to war this year. What do you think? He said: I am with you. (107)

On August 22, the ranking members of the Joint Supreme Council (eight Egyptian and six Syrian officers, disguised as civilians) met at Egyptian naval headquarters at Ras al-Tin to complete the plan. Mustafa Talas then flew to Damascus with the plan for the two presidents' consideration. (108)   According to al-Sadat, the final decision as to the month of the attack was made in the course of his stopover in Damascus, August 25-27, on the third leg of his trip to Saudi Arabia and Kuwayt. (109) At this Damascus meeting, he no doubt also informed al-Asad of the commitments made by the Saudis and Kuwaytis to finance Arab military operations (see below).

Jordan and the Dilemma of the Fida'iyin

After September 1970, the critical issue for Jordan was its relationship to the fida'iyin. In order to preserve its national existence, Jordan had fought and defeated Palestinian insurgents; in order to preserve itself in an increasingly hostile Arab environment, Jordan had to make some concessions to these self-same insurgents. Moreover, if these concessions did not meet with conservative Arab approval, Jordan faced the complete loss of any Arab subsidy. If the concessions were considered too pro-Palestinian by the United States, Jordan's chief Western supporter, no United States military aid or, hopefully, pressure on Israel to withdraw from the West Bank would be forthcoming. Either way, it looked like a losing proposition.

Jordan's relations with its immediate Arab neighbors had been nearly nonexistent since the September civil war. The Syrians had invaded it, and then closed off Syria/Jordanian borders to both land, and air traffic; Libya and Kuwayt had withdrawn the budgetary subsidy promised at Khartoum in 1967. Egypt, which had tacitly supported Jordanian resistance to the Palestinians in the 1970 crisis, had broken relations in April 1972 in response to Husayn's United Arab Kingdom Plan. (110)

The Jordanians themselves were split concerning possible options to alleviate the situation. One faction, led by Crown Prince Hasan, the Queen Mother, Sharif Nasir Bin Jamal, and followers of the late Wasfi al-Tal, felt that isolation had not harmed Jordan. This group argued that Jordan had already proved that it could withstand the hostility of its Arab neighbors, and demanded a return to the concept of a "Jordanian Entity" and the designation of Palestinians living in Jordan as residents, rather than citizens. This faction saw no hope of any return of the West Bank, or any use in military collaboration with other Arab states. (111)

A more moderate coalition headed by Husayn's political advisor,

Zayd Rifa'i, supported by Zayd bin Shakir, Adnan abu 'Awda, and Ahmad Tuqan, felt that Jordan's isolation must be tempered in the interests of the regime. But even they believed that Jordan had been victimized by fellow Arabs, that these Arabs were making political gains at Jordan's expense, and that the initiative for rapprochement should come from outside Jordan. (112)

The King, himself, was described as being divided between these opposing views: his heart was with the moderates, but his head was with the extremists. In any event, he could not afford to alienate those (the extremists) who had been his chief supporters in crises. Nevertheless he began to move for better Arab relations, arguing that an Arab detente would have considerable economic benefits. Given Jordan's current budget deficit of some $100 million, any move that would lead to restoration of cut off Arab subsidies was welcome. (113)

Initial contacts began during a conference of Arab Foreign and Defense Ministers in Kuwayt in November 1972, under Kuwayti mediation. These broke down over Jordan's refusal to accept any return of fida'iyin unless under Jordanian supervision. (114) Further discussions were conducted during the January 1973 meeting of the Arab Defense Council. The points of disagreement were several:

1. Egypt and Syria wanted Jordan to reactivate the Eastern Front; the Jordanians refused to consider this until diplomatic relations among the countries were normalized. (115)

2. Egypt and Syria wanted Jordan to permit the return of fida'iyin units; the Jordanians refused. (116)

3. Egypt, in particular, wanted to prevent Jordan from negotiating a separate peace with Israel; the Jordanians demanded Egyptian support for a return of occupied territories to Jordanian, rather than Palestinian, control. (117)

4. The Egyptians also wanted to utilize Husayn's good offices in dealing with the United States. (118)

5. The Saudis wanted to prevent Jordan from developing close contacts with the Iranians. Jordan was actively considering, if not actually implementing, plans for the stationing of Iranian units in Jordan. (119)

Contacts continued throughout the first part of 1973, with 'abd al-Mun'im Rifa'i (Zayd's uncle) being the principal Jordanian emissary. Jordanian reluctance to join forces with Syria and Egypt, however, remained unswayed.   After the April Defense Council meeting, a frustrated Shazili declared:

The position of the Jordanian Command is not satisfactory and we agreed to continue diplomatic efforts to remove the obstacles hindering the revival of the Eastern Front....Facing the Israeli enemy is a national duty. The presence of some financial and military problems are obstructing joint action.... (120)

The Jordanians appear to have known about the decisions taken at Alexandria in April, and were clearly worried. They were not about to repeat the mistakes of 1967. In a secret circular (almost immediately published in the Beirut press) which was distributed to officers, public security officials, and military intelligence, Husayn laid out his reasons for not becoming embroiled in another war. The timing of the circular, dated May 13, coincided with both the Lebanese crisis and with Syrian, Jordanian, and Israeli alerts. As such, it was probably as much a signal to all sides concerning Jordan's intentions not to be involved in the conflict. In the circular, Husayn stated that:

> It is clear that the Arab nation is preparing for a new war....It is painful for me to state that, should this occur, the battle would be premature as regards both the state of preparation of the Arab armies and their capabilities... unless figures and documents showed that there was at least a one in two chance of beating Israel, Jordan will not take part naively and impulsively in a war that we consider the final solution to save our land, our people.... (121)

Other parts of the circular went on to describe Jordan's reasons for not cooperating with the Egyptians and Syrians: Previous Jordanian experience with Egyptian leadership had cost it the West Bank; joint Arab planning was nonexistent; to allow Arab troops (other than Saudi forces) to enter Jordan before Jordanian forces were sufficiently strengthened would mean the "immediate loss of Jordan and its East Bank in spite of everything we have achieved." (122) As for the fida-iyin:

> Regarding the so-called Palestinian resistance, our attitude is clear and so is its attitude toward us. Our wounds are not yet healed and shall not be forgotten. And they were sustained by our nation at the hands of that corrupted resistance.... Israel knows everything about the resistance from within (sic: referring to the April 10 Beirut raid).... Our attitude to this resistance is to wish good luck to those who want it. As far as we are concerned, it has no chance of appearing in our land with its suspect leadership.... (123)

In spite of this, a tradeoff was arranged. Zayd Rifa'i was named Prime Minister on May 26, a move which signified a policy shift in his faction's favor. On May 29, he visited Damascus to begin talks. Impetus for these talks was supplied by Faysal: In response to a plea for help from Husayn, he advised the Jordanian to cooperate with Egypt and Syria. On August 29, Talas informed Husayn of the status of Egyptian/Syrian planning. Though tripartite military coordination might be worked out, the problems of Jordanian/fida'iyin relations remained. If Egypt and Syria were to deal with the fida'iyin, they needed Jordanian concessions on the issue of fida'iyin presence in Jordan.

The Fida'iyin and a Palestine State

Clearly, if the Egyptians were planning a strategy to get some negotiated solution, cooperation of Fatah was imperative. Otherwise the fida'iyin would disrupt any negotiations by attacking Israeli installations and personnel. Given the divisions with the fida'iyin, this would happen in any event, but it could be minimized if Fatah's support could be garnered. Fatah could then be expected to carry other groups along in support of Egyptian strategy.

Moreover, any rapprochement with the Jordanians risked Palestinian hostility. The Palestinians would perceive efforts to bring Jordan into a military alliance as attempts to weaken the resistance. In this event, Egyptian and Syrian internal security might be threatened. The BSO's assassination of Jordanian Prime Minister Wasfi al-Tal in Cairo had demonstrated its ability to strike down unfriendly Arab leaders. This hostility to any efforts to reach a negotiated solution had been underscored by Fatah Central Committee member, Hani al-Hasan, in March 1973:

> This is the resolution of the Palestinian Resistance movement: any Arab leader who signs agreements with Israel at the expense of the Palestinian people will be shot. (124)

However, the resistance was having its own troubles, and these offered the Egyptians opportunity for maneuver.

An Arab assessment of the post-1970 situation of the resistance noted that:

1. The resistance had been militarily neutralized since July 1971. The Jordanians had effectively expelled it; the Syrians had restricted its movement; the Lebanese were pressuring fida'iyin in South Lebanon.

2. Leadership in each of the major organizations, Fatah, the PFLP, and the PDFLP, was being challenged by younger and more radical elements.

3. The movement as a whole was generating more autonomous, terrorist units that were not under the control of established organization. (125)

Fatah, in particular, was affected by these trends. Not only had it lost enormous prestige following the Jordanian defeat, but the relatively conservative "war of liberation" approach promoted by Fatah, was being increasingly upstaged by "spectaculars" carried out by splinter organizations. Moreover, the leadership was badly split between two warring factions:

a. The right, led by Khalid al-Hasan, which wanted a conciliation between Fatah and regular Arab regimes, including Jordan, and West Bank Palestinian leaders. This group also felt that some sort of Palestinian entity under United Nations auspices was a viable solution. (126)

b. The left, headed by Salah Khalaf and Hamdan 'Ashur, which demanded unyielding opposition to any attempts at compromise. As far back as early 1970 this wing had been pressuring for a more aggressive policy:

> Khalaf has charged that 'Arafat has been soft with the Lebanese authorities and also with King Husayn; he has accused Arafat of going too far in his association with the Chinese, and failing to go far enough in his relations with the Soviet Union. At the same time Khalaf has urged the Fatah executive to extend the war against Israel in the same way as the Popular Front (sic: PFLP) has done, attacking Israeli property, aircraft, and interests wherever they may be.... (127)

By 1973, this split had worsened considerably to the point of armed clashes, and had taken the form of a struggle for control of the BSO. The BSO emerged in 1971, following the Jordanian Civil War. (Its name, Black September, symbolizes the dishonor and loss to the Palestinians caused by their defeat in Jordan.) It was composed of a small number (100-300) well trained, younger and better educated (relative to Fatah's membership as a whole) Palestinians. These rejected Fatah's cautious tactics, its emphasis on large scale military confrontations with the Israelis, and its tendency toward bureaucratization. Instead, the BSO's members sought to radicalize the resistance, to create a "revolution in the revolution." Along these lines, therefore, the BSO specialized in small scale operations designed for their propaganda effect, in the same manner that the PFLP operated (the BSO developed an organizational link with the PFLP to carry out these attacks.) BSO operations were, apparently, planned and directed by Fatah intelligence (known as al-Rasd). (128) Its most well known operation was the attack on Israeli athletes at the Munich Olympic Games in September 1972. In terms of Fatah intraelite politics, the left, which dominated al-Rasd, was able to use the BSO for its own ends; Salah Khalaf, himself, is said to have planned the Munich attack. (129)

Although Yasir Arafat originally supported BSO activities, some of these attacks, like that on the Saudi Embassy in Khartoum on March 1, 1973, began to jeopardize Fatah sources of support. Algeria and Libya had already either reduced or withdrawn their budgetary contributions, and Fatah could not afford to lose Saudi and Kuwayti subsidies. The PLO had already been forced to cut salaries in February, a move which led to great bitterness. (130) In addition, these operations further aggravated increasingly strained relations with other Arab countries, notably Egypt and Syria. Moreover, they triggered an aggressive Israeli reaction, both open and clandestine, which cost Fatah several of its leaders. (131)

From an organizational point of view, Fatah was facing an increasingly difficult situation: loss of funds, loss of prestige, loss of control over increasingly autonomous units, and loss of recruits. Therefore, Arafat, and those around him who were concerned for Fatah's organizational survival, moved away from the left, and increasingly attempted to control its activities.

The Egyptians, who had some connections with Khalid al-Hasan, sought to exploit these divisions for their own purposes. Their tactic was twofold. On one hand, they pressed Fatah leadership to accept the idea of government in exile (also vigorously promoted by the Algerians), and on the other, they combined this with efforts to get the Palestinians to cooperate with Syria and Jordan in terms of a unified Eastern Front. The government-in-exile proposal was broached by al-Sadat almost immediately after the Munich attack, and had two immediate goals:

a. To create a less radical alternative to the PLO, in line with Egyptian diplomatic aims;

b. To reassert Egyptian leverage with the fida'iyin in the wake of the Munich attack which the Egyptians perceived as a serious setback for Arab diplomacy. (132)

The idea of a more formalized status for the PLO, which was dominated by Fatah, had some advantages:

a) It would secure PLO/Fatah status as the preeminent Palestinian group, and might even involve international recognition.

b) It would solidify Arab sources of revenue.

c) For Arafat, himself, as head of both Fatah and the PLO, it would mean formal recognition of his leadership of the Palestinians.

There were, however, considerable disadvantages. Such an organization was, as Fatah leaders had argued, more susceptible to outside Arab control. If Fatah acceptance of the idea was not accompanied by some "victory," Arafat and his colleagues risked being branded as traitors to the Palestinian people. Moreover, there was tremendous internal opposition to be met.

As might have been expected, it was instantly rejected by the PDF, the General Command, and the PFLP as an attempt to involve the resistance in capitulative settlements. (133) Fatah leadership, however, considered the proposal (it had already been previously brought up by Khalid al-Hasan) before turning down the idea on the grounds that it would render the resistance more vulnerable to control by host governments. (134) The Egyptians persisted, however, bringing the matter up again in terms of a proposal for the creation of a Palestinian state in the West Bank in June 1973. (135)

These proposals widened the splits in Fatah's leadership. Hamdan 'Ashur accused Arafat of having prior knowledge, and tacit approval, of the plan. (136) By March 1973, Arab sources noted that two opposing views on future strategy had emerged: The al-Hasan argument that the resistance should reevaluate its strategy and tactics, and should cooperate in a Saudi/Egyptian front. In this context, the concept of a Palestinian state could be a stage toward complete liberation; (137) the Khalaf argument that more aggressive operations against all Arab governments should be undertaken, that the resistance intensity operations inside Israel, step up international activity, and launch a propaganda campaign to expose those Arab states that were weak in their determination to fight Israel. (138)   After a bitter debate, the leftists were able to impose their views, but the right, supported by Morocco, Tunisia, Saudi Arabia, Kuwayt, and the Trucials, continued its opposition.

The Syrian sponsored Eastern Front scheme was primarily designed to secure control over fida'iyin operations to prevent the possibility of these activities triggering an Israeli reprisal before Arab forces were coordinated.   Talas, in particular, was concerned over bringing fida'iyin in Syria under control, arguing that they were a danger to Syrian security. (139)   In addition, the espousal of a plan to control the fida'iyin might be expected to lessen Jordanian opposition to allowing resistance units to operate from its territory.   This, in turn, could ease Palestinian opposition to an Egyptian/Syrian rapprochement with Jordan.

The initial Palestinian response was a refusal, but the Egyptians pressed on during the summer.   'Arafat was informed of plans for an impending attack, and repeatedly asked to coordinate Palestinian activities with those of regular Arab forces.

The breakthrough was apparently made in late August.   Al-Khuli spent four days talking to Husayn and 'abd al-Mun'im Rifa'i early in the month.   Following his return, Akhbar al-Yawm carried a story (later denied by Rifa'i) that Jordan had agreed to three Egyptian conditions as prerequisites to resumption of relations: Jordan would permit the reactivation of the Eastern Front under an Egyptian commander.   A Palestinian force would be allowed to operate from Jordan.   Husayn would shelve his United Kingdom plan until all territories were liberated. (140)

This gave the Egyptians and Syrians something to bargain with, and talks between them and Palestinian leaders intensified toward the end of the month.   On August 23, al-Sadat and Ahmad Isma'il met with Fatah, PLO and al-Sa'iqa leaders; on August 30, Shadhili, al-Khuli and Vice President Mahmud Fawsi met with Arafat to discuss reviving the Eastern Front. (141)

The Palestinians remained deeply suspicious of Husayn's motives, however, and considerable behind the scenes pressure was apparently brought to bear, much of it by Syria through the twin media of al-Sa'iqa and the PLA.   Both organizations vigorously promoted the Syrian line that the fida'iyin should acquiesce in any Egyptian/Syrian moves toward Jordan since they were the necessary prelude to any action against Israel.

Behind this seemingly logical argument, however, was a considerable veiled threat: al-Sa'iqa and the PLA, it was said, formed an alternative leadership for the fida'iyin should Fatah lose control.   Al-Sa'iqa's Zuhayr Muhsin was said to be ready to replace Arafat himself.   These rumors were backed up by Syrian restrictions on Fatah operations from Syria; arms destined for Fatah were confiscated in July 1973.

The possibility that Syria might continue these moves, and restrict all fida'iyin activities, presented Fatah with the possibility both of a major split in the movement, and the loss of a major sanctuary and staging center.   If Syrian disfavor were echoed by Egypt and Saudi Arabia, the fida'iyin would be without any allies among the states bordering Israel.   Its only alternative sources of support would be Iraq, which was removed from the area, and Libya, which was an unpredictable ally at best. (142)

The United Nations and the Third World

By al-Sadat's account, the international arena was critical, and he personally exerted diplomatic efforts to line up Third World support:

> Naturally it was not possible to begin the battle from a vacuum and without a prelude. You might recall that in May of that year (sic: 1973) I personally attended the African (sic: OAU) conference in Addis Ababa. I exerted special efforts at that conference to put the Africans into the picture and explain the position to them without saying anything about the battle that had already been decided upon. I told them about our circumstances and that we had no choice but to take some action.... (143)

The final communique of this conference pledged its support for the "legitimate struggle to recover all occupied Arab land, and to safeguard the rights of the Palestinian people," and condemned the Israelis for obstructing all efforts toward peace. (144) In addition, the communique warned that:

> Israel's attitude might prompt member states to take political and economic measures, collectively or individually, in accordance with the charters of the Organization of African Unity and the United Nations.... (145)

This was followed by an Egyptian diplomatic move at the United Nations in July to introduce a full scale debate on the Middle East as a follow up to an earlier Lebanese complaint about the Israeli raid on Beirut of April 10, 1973:

> Actually, there was another aim behind lodging the complaint with the Security Council. I sent al-Zayyat to the United Nations and asked him to include the Middle East problem in Lebanon's request to the Security Council to discuss the Israeli attack....Some people did not understand our move....They said: What is the use of obtaining another resolution that will have no effect whatsoever?....But we had another aim. We could not start drastic action such as the battle in the international arena from a vacuum or embark upon a major action behind the world's back.... (146)

The culmination of these, and other Arab efforts vis a vis the Third World was two-fold: An increasing number of African nations breaking relations with Israel, and the passage of a series of favorable resolutions by the Third Non-Aligned Conference at Algiers.

African disaffection with the Israelis had been steadily growing in direct proportion to an increasing sense of African/Arab identity. A combination of factors operated to foster this feeling. First, continued Israeli occupation of Arab lands grated on African sensibilities concerning the sanctity of their own borders. Second, in 1972, Faysal visited five African countries (Uganda, Chad, Senegal, Mauritania, and Niger) which had large Muslim populations. His goal was to strengthen international Muslim solidarity, (147) and he succeeded to the extent that four countries broke with Israel within two months of the trip. Third, Libya and Saudi Arabia were able to offer the prospect of almost unlimited economic aid, adding economic self interest to territorial principle and religious sentiment. By April 1972, the OAU had begun to pass outspokenly anti-Israeli resolutions. By May 1973, six African states, (Uganda, Chad, Congo-Brazzaville, Mali, Niger, and Burundi) had already broken relations with Israel, two more followed prior to the attack. Summarizing this prewar movement away from Israel, one publication noted:

> It is now clear that the honeymoon is over in relation to Israel's attempt to play the Little David role and keep Middle East questions out of its African relationships.... (148)

The Fourth Non-Aligned Conference which met in Algiers September 5-9, 1973 ended with a series of resolutions which marked a hardening of Third World political and economic opposition to the West. One such document violently attacked Israel, condemned the US for its Third World policies, and declared that the basic division of the world was between the rich countries and the poor countries. (149) A parallel economic statement strongly defended the rights of countries to nationalize their raw materials, attacked the activities of multinational corporations, and noted that imperialism was still the major obstacle confronted by developing countries struggling to reach higher standards of living. (150)

The resolution on the Middle East stated, among other things, that the Conference:

> Demands that the Israeli forces leave at once and unconditionally all the Arab territories occupied since June 1967....

> Reaffirms its full support to Egypt, Syria and Jordan in their struggle by all means to recover their occupied territories....

> Calls on the nonaligned countries to engage in support to the Arab people of Palestine in its struggle against colonialism and Zionist racism, for bringing about its national rights in their entirety. The Conference underlines that the realization of these rights constitutes the basic condition of a just and lasting peace and declares that the Organization for the Liberation of Palestine (PLO) is the legitimate representative of the Palestinian people and its just struggle.... (151)

In addition, Egyptian diplomacy was able to secure the support of Iran and Turkey, two Muslim countries which had relations with Israel. In September, the Foreign Ministers of both Iran and Turkey visited Cairo, and affirmed their countries' support for the Arab position. (152) Neither previously had been particularly sympathetic on the official level to the Arab cause, but elements of their populations were pro-Palestinian.

The Shah, in particular, was acutely sensitive of the problems posed by Iranian ties with Israel. In a postwar interview with al-Hawadith, he stressed Iranian backing for the Arab's war effort. Iran, he said, had put an unspecified number of aircraft at the disposal of Saudi Arabia. It had replied positively to an Iraqi request for friendship in the war, thus allowing the Iraqis to withdraw three battalions from their frontiers and transfer them to the front. (153) He went on, however, to defend an evenhanded stance: Iran's economic relations with Israel were based on the fact that Israel existed. But Iran had not established formal diplomatic relations with Israel because of its ties with the Muslim world:

> I see no benefit for either us or you (sic: Arabs) in closing Israel's economic offices in Tehran. Let us be frank. Deception is useless, and the world is not governed by emotions. (154)

Moreover, Iran had from the beginning backed Arab aims:

> It is not possible that the Muslim holy places be placed in the hands of non-Muslims.... If the rights of the Palestinian nation are not fulfilled, there will be no peace in the area. The Palestinians, more than any others, have a right to decide their own destiny.... (155)

More importantly, neither, heretofore, had friendly relations with Egypt. The Iranians mistrusted the Egyptians because of their sponsorship of radical Arab nationalism in the Gulf; the Turks had not forgiven them for supporting the Greek side in the Cyprus conflict. Both, however, had compelling reasons of their own for a rapprochement with the Egyptians. The Iranians presumably hoped to garner Arab moderate support to offset Iraqi activities in the Gulf; the Turks to bring the Arabs over to their side on the Cyprus question. Both Iran and Turkey, moreover, faced a threat of sorts from the Palestinians. The Turkish People's Liberation Army was supplied and trained, in part, by Fatah; (156) Palestinian elements had figured in disturbances in Iran. (157) From the Iranian and Turkish point of view, therefore, the Egyptians with their preeminent political position in the Arab world, and their contacts with the Palestinians were a useful ally.

From the Egyptian/Arab perspective, the neutrality of Iran and Turkey during another Arab/Israeli war would be a very large strategic gain. Iranian support, even passively, of an oil embargo would enormously increase its effectiveness. Turkish denial of NATO bases to United States efforts to support the Israelis would also prove invaluable. As events later proved, the Egyptians were successful in their attempt.

From all of this, al-Sadat concluded that he could count on extensive Third World support, both within and without the United Nations, and might even get some Western backing therein also:

> As you can see, the atmosphere in Africa was being prepared. Internationally the atmosphere was also suitable after we resurrected the (sic: Arab-Israeli) issue and obtained the world's moral

support through the Security Council's majority vote in our
favor....Before that, the international atmosphere was poisoned with
propaganda against us because of the ferocious psychological
warfare that began in early 1972 when (sic: Secretary of State)
Rogers stood up and said: "We have given Israel and we will give it
more so it will continue to be superior to the Arabs." This meant
there was nothing but despair facing the Arabs.... (158) Thus, the
Security Council resolution was in our favor despite the U.S. veto
because the resolution resurrected the question anew and clearly
presented it before the world. (159)

The Oil Weapon and Its Politics

Arab consideration of the ways and means of using oil to pry
Western countries, especially the United States, away from support of
Israel, had been going on for some time. Directly after the 1967 War, a
conference of Arab Economy, Finance, and Oil Ministers considered an
Iraqi plan to impose a three month total embargo. This was to be
accompanied by a phased nationalization of foreign oil concessions. The
goal of this plan was to force Western European nations to support Arab
diplomatic efforts to force an Israeli withdrawal. After three months,
those countries that had gone over to the Arab point of view would be
rewarded by a resumption of the oil flow. (160) A series of conferences
and seminars had considered alternative ways to use oil since then.

The context of this ongoing Arab hostility toward oil concessions,
and the subsequent Arab oil strategy, is made up of a number of factors:
A widely held image of oil concessions as products of imperialist
machinations; rivalries between producers and nonproducers; Arab
overbidding behavior on the issue of Arab-Israeli relations.

This image of oil concessions as another form of imperialism finds
its expression in terms of a generalized theory that all oil concessions
have been thrust upon the Arabs as a consequence of: The collusion of
conservative regimes with their Western "feudalist" counterparts; an
era in which the Arab World was under colonial domination and did not
have the resources to defend itself; the unsophisticated nature of Arab
negotiators who were easy prey for slick Western diplomats. The
conclusion that was drawn from all this was that concession agreements
must be revised to eliminate these injustices to the Arabs.

Moreover, this generally negative view of oil concession was
intensified by a second set of perceptions concerning the relations
between Western oil companies and their respective governments.
These relations were seen as one of three possible combinations:

a) Imperialist governments controlling the oil companies.

b) Oil companies controlling the Western governments.

c) Both operating as separate entities, but acting in concert.

As a consequence, those Arab governments with oil companies operating in their territories found themselves in an extremely awkward, even dangerous, position. Their policy toward oil companies became a touchstone, a criterion of their fitness to rule. If they appeared to be too subservient to the oil companies, they risked the accusation of being "stooges of the imperialists" and risked the possibility of a coup. If they made life too difficult for the oil companies, or nationalized them, they risked the loss of Western economic benefits.

The solution that most of the governments concerned opted for was to project the appearance of an unfavorable attitude toward the oil companies, and to combine this with the argument that the foreign exchange, thus acquired, would benefit the Arab cause. Thus the principal contributors to the economies of Egypt and Jordan after 1967 were Kuwayt and Saudi Arabia; the same combination plus donations from the Trucial Shaykhdoms financed Fatah. In the case of the Saudis, their initial backing of Fatah stemmed from two considerations. First, the majority of Fatah leaders were opposed to Nasirism. Second, many of these same leaders were members of the Muslim Brethren. During the later '60's when the Saudis were at sword points with the radical camp, support for the Palestinians provided a convenient way to demonstrate Saudi support for the Arab cause. It was more serious for the Kuwaytis. Given the existence of a large Palestinian community, and the relative weakness of Kuwayti defense forces, both internal security and external neutrality could be critically affected by a breakdown of relations with the Palestinians and their radical supporters. Here again, Fatah was the principal beneficiary of Kuwayti aid; some Fatah leaders, Khalid al-Hasan for example, drew salaries from the Kuwayti government. (161)

Saudi Arabia, especially, was faced with a difficult dilemma. On one hand Faysal would have preferred some Western/United States presence to counter growing Iranian and Iraqi strength in the Gulf. On the other hand the possibility of any movement toward the West/United States was limited by:

a) Domestic Saudi nationalism of a decidedly anti-Western variety. The abortive coup of July 1968 was attempted by younger air force officers, and raised the spector of a Libyan style takeover.

b) Extreme anti-Western sentiment among oil field workers. A series of arsons at ARAMCO installations on August 5 and 16, 1973 presented the Saudis with the unenviable prospect of having to use Arab troops to guard United States installations. (162)

c) The necessity to adopt an attitude of separation versus the West in order to maintain credibility within the Arab world. (163)

Given political opposition to any sort of "soft" policy vis a vis the United States concerning its pro-Israeli policies, Faysal's ability to resist Arab pressure to use the oil weapon was limited at best. (164) Because of its position as the foremost oil producer, Saudi Arabia was the chief target of radical pressure to use oil politically. This pressure mounted as Arab leaders perceived increasing Western concern for securing access to Middle East oil. In April 1973, Egyptian media carried the remarks of OEP assistant director, Elmer B. Bennett to the effect that the United States might soon be confronted by the choice of either conserving energy or invading the Middle East. (165) Stories in the United States press describing Marine desert training exercises drew considerable Arab attention in August. (166)   President Nixon's statement to a September 5 press conference to the effect that United States policy toward Israel would not be affected by Arab oil threats, was similarly reported. (167) The conclusions that were drawn were two fold:

1. The Arabs, however, are not convinced by these public (sic: United States) signs of imperturbability, and they point to the apprehensions of Senator Fulbright and the implications of Marine desert exercises. They are certain that the oil weapon could be used with formidable effect, presenting Washington with two choices. Firstly, it could attempt to secure its oil supplies by forcible intervention on a major or minor scale. Alternatively, it could seek reconciliation.... (168)

2. Arab financial reserves have virtually doubled during the 1970-72 peroid and promise to attain uniquely high totals within the decade. These and the rising premium attached to oil have put a big stick in the Arab's hand.... (169)

Like al-Sadat and al-Asad, Faysal came under increasing threat. This sense of shared threat, combined with a perceived need for each other's aid, brought Faysal and al-Sadat together. In July 1971, the Arab World analyzed the elements at the root of the Egyptian-Saudi understanding: An implicit recognition that interest, rather than ideology was the key to inter-Arab relations; and a sense that the Arab world faced dangerous destabilization through the activities of Arab radicals, and the continuance of the Israeli occupation. (170)

For his part, Faysal wanted to stem the trend toward radicalism, communism, and Zionist expansionism in the Arab world. His concrete policy goals in the negotiations were:

a) To prevent al-Qadhafi from taking over Arab/Muslim leadership.

b) To restore Jerusalem to Arab hands.

c) To stabilize his own domestic position.

d) To reduce Iranian influence in the Gulf.

e) To restore, or at least maintain, the radical/conservative balance of power in the Arab World - which meant, among other things, bringing Jordan out of its intra-Arab isolation, and moderating both Egyptian and Syrian policy.

f) In line with the above, isolating Iraq from radical support and thus relieving Iraqi pressure on Kuwayt.

g) Restoring some leverage with the US.

Al-Sadat, on the other hand, was acutely conscious of the need for Saudi oil and revenues:

> We are all waging the battle of the same destiny. The circumstances of this battle have imposed, and destiny has decreed, that Egypt be the basic military base and that Saudi Arabia be the owner of 60 per cent of the Arab oil reserves. Therefore, when Egypt's military power and Saudi Arabia's oil influence have joined forces, each one of them has become more effective.... (171)

His goals in the negotiations were to:

a) Get Saudi financial support for the Egyptian economy.

b) Convince the Saudis to utilize the oil weapon in the form of a boycott, if necessary.

c) Obtain Saudi diplomatic help in dealing with Syria and Jordan.

The catalyst that finally brought these longtime antagonists together was the activity of al-Qadhafi. From Faysal's perspective the Libyan presented a multiple challenge:

1. Al-Qadhafi's insistence that he was the leader of a future Islamic revival both personally affronted Faysal's position as protector of the Holy Places, and politically challenged his claims to Muslim leadership. Al-Qadhafi's spectacular attacks on Western interests had to be matched by comparable deeds. (172)

2. The Libyans were one of the most aggressive proponents of politicizing Arab oil, in contrast to the Saudis' cautious approach. If Faysal were to retain control over the oil weapon, such radical pressure had to be resisted at any cost. (173)

3. Libyan attempts to unify with Egypt raised the possibility of a powerful radical force unbalancing intra-Arab power relations. (174)

From the Egyptian point of view, al-Qadhafi represented a mixed blessing. On one hand, a union with Libya as demanded by al-Qadhafi could both solve Egypt's economic problems and provide additional strategic and military resources for a war against Israel. On the other hand, such a union carried distinct disadvantages:

1. Al-Qadhafi wanted an immediate battle with Israel. The Egyptians felt this would be premature militarily and, if carried on, economically would jeopardize any chance of attracting Western capital.

2. Such a union would most probably lead to a complete rupture with the Russians.

3. Al-Qadhafi had contacts with a number of anti-Sadat groups whose influence might be expected to grow in any unified regime.

4. The importation of al-Qadhafi's cultural revolution would disrupt Egyptian society, since it would intensify already existing Muslim-Christian conflict. (175)

5. Saudi Arabia, Morocco, Sudan, Syria, and Iraq would be alienated by a union. (176)

In the protracted bargaining which took place from roughly mid-1971 to August/September 1973, Faysal asked a number of things from the Egyptians:

a) That Egypt abandon its reliance on Soviet aid which Faysal argued was one of the major factors contributing to the American support for Israel. In this connection, Faysal encouraged al-Sadat in his decision to eject Russian advisors in July 1972 by again arguing that such a move would lead to a change in US policy. When no such thing happened, Faysal was personally embarrassed and felt honor bound to offer to pay for half the costs of rearming the Egyptian forces. (177)

b) That the Egyptians suggest to al-Asad that Syrian dependence on Russia be reduced also. (178)

c) That some of the socialist measures enacted under 'abd al-Nasir be abolished and guaranties protecting foreign investments be made. (179)

d) The Egyptians support the Saudi position in the Gulf; that the conflict with Iran should be settled by diplomatic rather than military means; that radical movements in Oman be controlled in the interests of Arab solidarity against Israel. (180)

In return, Faysal promised extensive economic aid to the Egyptians, aid sufficient to replace anything the Soviets had offered, and to remove any possibility of Egyptian dependence on the Libyans. The high point of Saudi economic offers took place during al-Sadat's secret visit to Saudi Arabia, Qatar, and Syria from August 23 to 27. At that time, Faysal is reported to have promised al-Sadat all the money he needed to confront Israel. Al-Hawadith later in the month reported that some Ł 500 million was promised by a combine of Saudi Arabia, Kuwayt, Abu Dhabi, and Qatar. (181) Thereafter, the proposed but much delayed Egyptian-Libyan union was finally torpedoed by the Egyptians.

Al-Sadat, in return, demanded a more aggressive Saudi stance vis a vis the United States. The Saudis were unwilling to go along, considering such a policy dangerous to their own economic interests. Deputy Prime Minister Sa'ud al-Faysal (Faysal's son) explained this position in an al-Hawadith interview on August 30, 1973:

... Oil is an economic weapon and like all economic weapons it needs study and time to produce results. Every economic weapon has an effect and a counter effect, and it is essential to study the best means of employing such a weapon if one is to ensure that the enemy's loss is going to be greater than the sacrifices you make. The employment of such a weapon must therefore be linked to a specific aim which ought to convey to your enemy precisely what you are after, and what he ought to do if he wishes to spare himself the harm of an economic boycott. Against whom do we want to employ the oil weapon? Our talk of an oil boycott implies that we are threatening the whole world whereas it is known that our object is to apply pressure on the U.S. The truth, which we should bear in mind, is that if we were to implement a decision for an oil embargo today, the U.S. will be the last country to be hurt, because the U.S. will not become dependent on Arab oil before the late seventies.... (182)

The Saudis preferred a gradual approach, freezing production levels, and limiting rate of growth. In addition, they would have liked to avoid punishing Europe and Japan. Finally, by not making either abrupt demands, or any special promises to other Arabs about their actions, they wanted to leave the United States room for maneuvering. Their strategy was to utilize oil monies to obtain arms, not to withhold oil. (183)

In August, however, Faysal began to shift his position in response to Arab pressure and a United States failure to respond to Saudi warnings. (184) In the aftermath of a series of such warnings in both US and Arab media, he announced that Saudi Arabia could no longer be expected to continue increasing its production levels to meet US demand. In order for the Saudis to undertake such expansion in the future, two conditions must be satisfied:

a) The US and the West must assist the kingdom in industrializing itself in order to create an alternative source of income to depleting oil reserves.

b) A suitable atmosphere, hitherto disturbed by Zionist expansionist ambitions, must be present.

The second demand was the critical one for the US:

... Adopting biased attitudes and from giving unlimited aid to Israel, which has increased Israel's arrogance and led it to reject peace and to insist on a retention of its war gains. America is, to a large extent, responsible for rectifying this situation....We are deeply concerned that if the United States does not change its policy and continues to side with Zionism... such a course of action will affect our relations with our American friends because it will place us in an untenable position in the Arab world and vis a vis the countries which Zionism seeks to destroy.... (185)

The Tripartite Summit

The final coordination of the military, diplomatic, and oil strategies was achieved during the mini-Summit of Egypt, Syria, and Jordan (represented by their respective heads of state) and Saudi Arabia (represented apparently by Kamal Adham, Faysal's National Security Advisor, who appeared in Cairo on the 9th), in Cairo, September 10-12, 1973. In the course of the talks a number of agreements were reached:

1. The wartime role of Jordan was clarified; and Jordanian views concerning their long borders with Israel, their limited armed forces and air power were respected. (After all, the Egyptians had General Riyad's report on the Jordanian situation.) Jordan's role was to be defensive. It was to draw Israeli forces away from the other two fronts, and to prevent Israeli attempts to outflank Syrian units from the South. King Husayn, himself, is said to have taken part in planning the Jordanian deployment. (186)

2. The relationship of military action to an oil embargo was clarified, i.e., that a war must be long enough to allow oil producers time to act.

3. Jordan agreed not to seek a separate peace, and Saudi Arabia promised to treat the question of Israeli withdrawal as a whole, i.e., without making any concessions over the Golan Heights as distinct from a Sinai settlement.

4. Additionally Saudi Arabia promised more economic aid to the Syrians on the same terms as they had to the Egyptians, i.e., the relaxation of socialist measures in favor of capitalism.

5. Egypt and Syria agreed to establish diplomatic relations with Jordan, thus ending its isolation in the Arab world.

6. Syria agreed to restrict anti-Jordanian, fida'iyin propaganda.

7. For its part, Jordan agreed to allow the stationing of additional PLA forces on its territory and to release 754 Palestinians taken prisoner over the course of the last several years. (187)

These agreements cleared the way for a three front military action, and they were hailed in the Arabic press as a significant step toward Arab unity. Following immediately after the Algiers Conference whose resolutions indicated a widespread sympathy for the Arab position, the mini-Summit seemed to assure Arab leaders that their strategy had a chance of succeeding. In this, it was one of the critical factors affecting the decision to attack. (188)

Immediately following the summit, Husayn carried out his part of the bargain. A general amnesty was declared, and the Palestinians - including BSO leader Muhammad Da'ud 'Awda - were released. This, in turn, permitted Egypt and Syria to increase their pressure on fida'iyin leaders, arguing that only they could influence the Jordanian government to make concessions. (Parenthetically, the prisoner release strengthened al-Sadat's position at home among both students and army officers who were very pro-Palestinian. Egyptian students, in particular, had been vociferously agitating for the release of these prisoners for some time. The Egyptian media was careful to play up al-Sadat's personal role in securing their release.)

The PLO's executive council met following the mini-Summit, and agreed to the establishment of an eastern front. Significantly, it was al-Sa'iqa leadership that played the crucial role in convincing wavering members to accept a compromise arrangement with Jordan. Al-Sa'iqa's argument was that it would be foolish to attempt to move against the combined weight of Egypt, Syria, and Jordan; that fida'iyin leaders should be guided by political realities and not by emotions:

> Husayn of 1973 is that of 1970, but Jordan of 1973 is not necessarily that of 1970.... We are not calling on the people to forget the September (1970) tragedy. When presidents al-Asad and al-Sadat met Husayn, I do not believe they did so. Rulers are not guided by their personal feelings but by their political responsibilities. Al-Asad and al-Sadat met Husayn or others because they are in need of Jordanian territory and Jordan's support.... (189)

Even as the council was meeting, PLA units began moving back into Jordan. The PLA was considerably more acceptable to Jordan than fida'iyin irregulars. It had been created in 1964 as a conventional military arm of the PLO, during the same set of Arab summits which established the latter. However, it had split off from that organization following Fatah's takeover in 1968, and from that time maintained its own command structure. But PLA commanders took their orders from host countries, Syria and Egypt; in effect, putting the PLA under the complete control of these countries.

Under the arrangements agreed upon during the mini-Summit, two units of PLA forces were to be stationed in Jordan: Syrian backed PLA troops in the north, Egyptian sponsored PLA units in the south. The number of PLA troops was estimated as 5000 men; both contingents were subject to direct Jordanian military supervision. (190)

6 Operation BADR: Calculus of Controlled Escalation

The combined Egyptian-Syrian battle plan, code-named Operation Badr, was the military component of the larger Arab strategy aimed at altering the status quo:

> I have told you what the basis of my strategy was. I told it also to 'abd al-Nasir. I told him: Jamal, if we win 10 centimeters of the east bank of the canal and hold them, we will change the entire situation... (1)

From this simple thesis grew the idea of a controlled conflict: conflict, rather than war, because its elements involved a series of other relations, outside the direct Arab/Israeli military relations. What is notable about the conception of limited conflict as it emerged is the stress on rationality in its genesis and the syncretistic use of Western technology and Arab cultural themes in its operationalization:

> We base our military planning on our estimate of the situation. What does an evaluation of the situation involve? The estimate of the situation should cover the enemy's equipment, preparations, and fortifications. It should also cover our equipment, our forces, air force, and tanks. The first part of our estimation should begin with the enemy and then us. The next part of the estimation is called "the influencing factors", namely, the factors which would affect the enemy and the factors which would affect us. In the end, the plan is drawn up on the basis of the estimation.

> ....it was possible for the Arab nation to restore its position and regain confidence in itself. Arab militarianism, Egyptian militarism in particular, was able to regain confidence in itself. The world is now listening to us because we are speaking the language of the age and because we have absorbed the technology of the age. All our analyses and actions are based on the technology of the age. All soldiers who participated in the military battle, as I have already

said, absorbed this technology. What I have to say about military science could fill volumes. This is the highest military technology and one of the most complicated sciences in the world. I say that we absorbed all this. After all this, I do not say no, no, no as we had been doing for the past 25 years.

....I would say that if we are not serious enough to assume responsibility and make war, manhood will disappear from Egypt and the Arab nation for many generations to come. People were aware of this before 'abd al-Nasir died. Minister Muhammad Fawzi knew it. I told him: Fawzi I am the one who will attack al-Qantara and al-Sharqiya. Make the preparations for the day of attack...My opinion is that manhood and our existence as human beings will become extinct if we do not carry out our battle, even if we lose it... (2)

In a commentary on the Bar-Lev line, al-Sadat at one point argued that this static defense indepth arrangement had been forced on the Israelis by other than military considerations: That the main Israeli concern had been to reduce the number of men required to man it (and thus reduce the total mobilized military manpower) and to reduce the possibility of Israeli losses if war did break out. Hence, they moved away from their traditional military doctrine of mobile warfare, and toward a style of defense that played into Egyptian hands. Here, al-Sadat makes repeated comparisons with the Bar-Lev line and the Atlantic wall (indeed in post-October commentaries, Egyptian spokesmen make increasing reference to the major battles of World War II):

....I looked at the Bar-Lev line and compared it to what Hitler called the Atlantic wall. When he occupied Europe, Hitler took up positions in anticipation of the Allied invasion of Europe and built up what was called the Atlantic wall.

It was all clear there. I told him (sic: al-Jamasy): The Bar-Lev line is all here-but on a smaller scale. All the tactics that Germany used in resisting the Allied invasion of Normandy is here in this book and they will use them against you. You will find that the Atlantic wall had three defensive zones right on the edge of the Atlantic. The Bar-Lev line is a concrete wall right along the canal. The positions are built of more than just concrete. The chambers have double roofs, one of which is built of railroad ties taken from the Egyptian railways in the Sinai. A second concrete roof is built above these ties.

This meant that neither the artillery nor the air force or anything else would be able to penetrate it. The first line in the Atlantic wall erected by Hitler to deter the Allies, namely the reinforced concrete, coincided with the points directly on the canal, right on the canal. The Atlantic wall had a second line including reserves and alternate positions. The same thing applied to the Bar-Lev line. The third line included most of the reserves which, if approached from the front positions or the second line, would move, spread out and encircle and exterminate the enemy. Such was the German military doctrine.

There was one thing: The Jews could not tolerate a loss of men on the Bar-Lev line. That was why they had built it in three lines so that its positions would be strong and save them from using a large number of men. When a position is strong, fewer men and weapons have to be deployed. The impregnability of the position would make it possible to deploy fewer men. That was one Jewish mistake which they copied from Germany. The second mistake was that the Jews were overconfident. They had believed that we could not storm the Bar-Lev line and that if we had wanted to storm it we would have had to storm it from the rear. (3)

The operational plan utilized by Egyptian-Syrian forces in October was apparently the outgrowth of a series of less ambitious plans. Arab sources report that as early as December 1971, Shadhili had been ordered to prepare a report on the feasibility of a limited war. At that time he proposed a surprise attack across the canal, coupled with air strikes in the Sinai. The objective was not so much to produce an outright victory or even military gains, as such, but to end the state of "no war, no peace" and to compel United Nations intervention.
This plan, or one like it, was also presented to the Arab Defense Council (a different body from the later Egyptian/Syrian Supreme Council): It was rejected as being too ambitious. However, both plans mark the crystallization of Egyptian thinking concerning military action along the lines originally set forth by Haykal. Al-Sadat later phrased it thusly:

> Let me tell you today: In the calculations which we made for the battle, the important criterion was not how many square kilometers would be liberated but the shattering of the theory of Israel's security; to destroy the theory was more important than the destruction of the Bar-Lev line; to restore the world's confidence in us, in our words and our ability to act, was more important than the crossing of the canal. To prove that the "invincible Israel" was a mere illusion was more important than winning an additional square kilometer.... (4)

However, there was considerable opposition from senior Egyptian officers, especially General Sadiq. His replacement by Ahmad Isma'il 'Ali opened the way for a more aggressive preparation for war. Al-Sayyad compared the differences in outlooks between Sadiq and Isma'il 'Ali as follows:

> General Sadek used to say: Give me advanced weapons and I shall fight. I will not allow my army to enter a battle the outcome of which is not guaranteed. Therefore, I will not fight before offensive weapons have been ensured, including MIG-23s and long range missiles.

Lt. General Ismail, on the other hand, says fight with what you have
got, and ask for more. Developments of the battle would force your
friend (meaning the Soviet Union) to give you what you want. You
are not strong or able to impose your conditions unless you are
fighting. But as long as the guns are silent, no one would respond to
your demands.... (5)

Immediately upon his appointment, Isma'il seems to have made the
decision to attack without waiting for any sort of advanced weaponry,
and began to plan his operation around in hand equipment.   This
decision, however, rested on two critical assumptions: That tactics
could be devised to enable Egyptian-Syrian numerical advantages to be
successfully utilized; that Russia could be forced to resupply Egyptian
forces if a war developed; that the logic of previous Russian
commitments in terms of weaponry and prestige to the Arab side would
compel it to prevent an Arab defeat.   In this reasoning, Isma'il
apparently drew upon the example of 'abd al-Nasir's success in getting
Russian air defense units during the War of Attrition: when it appeared
that Israeli air attacks might jeopardize 'abd al-Nasir's regime, Russia
stepped in.

Isma'il's views on the political/military situation facing the
Egyptians were spelled out in the course of a speech delivered to army
officers:

Our task as officers is to be ordered to fight.   As military
professionals, we fight when we are ordered to fight, we fight and
die. My mission as an officer is to die for the sake of my country....

American Position.   America is supporting Israel which is our
principal enemy.   There is nothing to be hoped from America, no
matter what we do and try. She will not prefer us to Israel, although
it has many and large interests in our region. It considers Israel as
its aircraft carrier in the area, and uses the Arabs' disunity.
America, as the leader of imperialism, wants to keep us away from
the Soviet Union, and wants to keep the Soviet Union away from this
region, because of the oil. But all this should not prevent us from
talking to America and other countries, because we follow an open
door policy....

Soviet Position.   The Soviet Union helped us, and we do not deny
this. It helped us in 1967, gave us weapons and established an air
bridge, helped us to build the High Dam and to build up our economy.
All this because we have joint interests; both of us are opposed to
imperialism and colonialism; the Soviet Union also considers Israel
as its enemy. We have our socialism, which stems from our land,
and the Soviet Union has its communism....It helps us because we are
the largest state in the region, and because we are friends, but
friendship has its limits. The Soviet Union, as one of the superpowers, has its commitments.

Armament.   I cannot go into the details of the subject of armament. You have to believe that your leadership will not push you into an uneven battle. The leadership is intent on assigning to us the tasks that we can implement.   As we follow our open door policy, we welcome weapons from any state, whether in the east or west. We pay for what we get. The occupied land is our land, and it is we who will have to liberate it. We shall train, we shall fight, we shall expel the enemy from Sinai and liberate the land.

Regarding the future, there is no doubt that you share my feeling that every year that passes embitters the soul, but the state is making a great deal of effort to ensure for us the victory that we wish.   Israel is not a legend, and is not an invincible enemy. We should give the enemy his due, without either exaggerating or underestimating (his strength).   Cunning, deceit and training are necessary. We have the men, the armed forces are full of men and heroes, and we have the weapons.   And as long as we have the elements of war - men, weapons and morale - then we should fight until victory. It only remains to coordinate these elements in order to reach a coordinated plan that will lead us to victory. So let us begin with preparing ourselves.... (6)

Ahmad Isma'il, himself, was accounted one of Egypt's most brilliant military strategists.   He was an outstanding student at the Military Academy in the '30s, graduated from the Staff College with distinction in 1950, studied tactical warfare in England, and was one of the first high ranking Egyptian officers to receive Russian military training. His specialty was intelligence, serving in that capacity in World War II, and 1948. He later fought in the 1956 and 1967 wars. After 1967, he was one of those who designed and constructed Egypt's defense line West of the Canal. He was appointed operations chief in 1968, became Chief of Staff when General Riyad was killed in 1969, was pensioned off by 'abd al-Nasir in the same year following an unopposed Israeli landing on Egypt's Red Sea coast, and was brought back by al-Sadat as intelligence chief in May 1971 following 'Ali Sabri's abortive coup. (7)

During his 17 months as intelligence chief, he introduced the use of electronic equipment, and reorganized the Egyptian intelligence apparatus to make it into a surprisingly effective operation. In addition, he was a strong supporter of Sadat, a technocrat, and an advocate of cautious, calculated, mini/max style of procedure in the Soviet mold. (8) This professional caution was reinforced by his experience as Chief of Staff of the Sinai front in 1967: An experience which clearly appears to have left him with the conviction that Egyptian forces could never be allowed to meet Israeli armored units in any kind of wide open desert fighting.

In a post war interview with Haykal, Ahmad Isma'il described the considerations which shaped his choice of strategy and tactics. The first concern was dictated by the Israeli doctrine of "massive retaliation," as it had been applied along the canal:

The choices open to me....were the following: Should we revert to the "war of attrition"? Or should we make an effort greater than the "war of attrition"?

My view was that the War of Attrition had achieved its aims....and also that Israel would not acquiesce in its resumption, so that any attempt on our part to revert to it would meet a stronger reaction from Israel. This meant that I was faced with the possibility of engaging in small operations in which I should encounter a big reaction from the enemy - much bigger than was justified by their political and military value. So I ruled out a war of attrition.

I therefore had to think of a greater effort, a more extensive and comprehensive action, at least equivalent to the massive reaction we were going to receive from the enemy....That is to say, our blow to the enemy should be a large one, and we should be prepared for a major blow from the enemy in return.... (9)

After his appointment as Commander in Chief of the Tripartite Federation Forces, Ahmad Isma'il added a second dimension to his calculations:

This new situation added a second factor to my thinking. The first had been that the blow we struck must be a powerful one. The second was that the blow we struck must be a joint one on two fronts.... (10)

In the context of this expanded operation, Ahmad Isma'il analyzed Israeli capabilities as follows. The Israelis possessed four basic advantages: Air superiority. Technological ability. Rigorous training. US resupply. However, the Israelis also had a number of weaknesses: Extended lines of communication which were difficult to defend. Limited manpower, incapable of sustaining heavy losses. A weak economic base, unable to sustain a long war. Overweening arrogance concerning Israeli superiority versus Arab forces. (11) The strategy developed to exploit these disadvantages was to:

a) Attack along a broad front; in the Egyptian case, along the whole length of the canal.

b) Attack North and South simultaneously, to prevent the Israelis from concentrating on either front.

c) Retain, again on the Egyptian front, as much armor and aircraft in reserve as possible, for the expected heavy Israeli counter-attack, (12) and for the possibility of a prolonged war of attrition.

As Ahmad Isma'il explained the strategy:

....an attack along the whole line of confrontation would impose on him (sic: Israel) the following:

1. He would be obliged to disperse his air counter strikes against our forces.

2. As a result of this, counterattacks would have to be made everywhere because the line of confrontation was very extended.

3. Because of this extension the enemy would not be able, at an early stage, to discover where the main effort of our attacking forces was being directed, and would not be able to concentrate on it....

4. Again because of this extension the enemy's reaction in the form of counterattacks would be delayed, because he would be waiting to see where our principal effort was being directed before he moved.... (13)

These considerations were, in turn, worked into al-Sadat's general strategy for producing movement on the Arab/Israel issue. Hence, al-Sadat's symbolic use of the term, "operation spark," to refer to the combined political/military action; a catalyst designed to unleash forces which would alter the Middle East stalemate. The goals of operation spark as set forth in a post war interview were:

1. Forcing Israel to fight on two fronts.

2. Inflicting losses on Israel the likes of which it has never suffered before.

3. Forcing Israel to stay under military mobilization as long as possible.

4. Awakening Arab solidarity so that for the first time Arabs would use all their weapons (sic: the oil embargo) in the battle. (14)

BAR LEV AND ALLON LINES

Much Arab planning effort went into solving the problem posed by Israeli defensive fortifications. According to a later Arab interpreta-tion, the basic Israeli war plan for both fronts was to rely on these fortifications to delay any attacking force long enough for Israeli reserves to be mobilized:

1. Frontal lines would stop advancing forces with the support of the air force.

2. If these failed, standing army units would contain the enemy, again with air force support.

3. Once mobilization was complete, invading forces would be destroyed.

4. Invading forces would then be pursued into Arab territory and be totally destroyed. (15)

Accordingly, the Bar-Lev line was a system of 30 strong points, arranged in three defensive lines some two miles deep, behind a sand barrier on the canal bank; each position manned by a battalion of infantry, each surrounded by mine fields to a depth of 200 yards. The whole complex was linked by a system of communications trenches, and the individual garrisons were self sufficient in ammunition, food and water for one month. (16)   The function of these positions was to constrain any Egyptian attack and channel the attacking forces into areas where they could be destroyed by artillery and armor. The main Israeli defense reserves station in the Bir Jifjafa area would then either finish the job or stop the attackers long enough for mobilization to be completed. (17)

The Allon line was a much thinner line consisting of 12 bunkers, anchored by a large underground position at Tal abu al-Nidal. These were strategically positioned on all the avenues of approach into the Golan Heights, and were supported by a tank ditch and mine fields. Like the Bar-Lev line, the purpose of these fortifications was to slow down an enemy advance and channel it into "killing areas" where Israeli armor and artillery could destroy attacking forces. To this end, the Israelis had also built an extensive road network behind the Allon line to facilitate the rapid deployment of defending Israeli forces. (18)

The Egyptians, in particular, spent considerable energy in developing a detailed plan for the crossing, partially because of the complexities presented by Israeli defenses, partially because of the symbolic value of a successful crossing.   Western military analysts had lavished much praise on Israeli prowess, and the Bar-Lev line had come in for its share of admiration:

> The Israelis have previously demonstrated their ability to adapt the principles of offense to their specific situation. Their defense of the Suez Canal and the thwarting of the Egyptian War of Attrition demonstrate an equal capability for imaginative adaptation of the principles of defense. (19)

Chief architect of the crossing operation was Chief of Staff Shadhili, specialist in both guerrilla, and airborne warfare, and a charismatic figure in the Patton tradition. In many ways, Shadhili was the ideal man for the job: Educated at the Egyptian military academy and trained in Russia, he commanded a platoon in 1948, a paratroop company in 1956, held a senior position during the Yemeni civil war, and commanded a special mobile force in 1967. (20)   Like Isma'il, he believed that Egypt should fight with the weapons it already had, relying on Arab support alone.   To this end, he was an aggressive proponent of the Eastern Front concept and a fervid exponent of the idea that Arab forces could defeat the Israelis. (21)

In addition, he was the Commander of the Egyptian Shock Forces (also known as al-Sa'iqa - the Thunderbolt) after 1967 until his appointment of Chief of Staff in 1971. These forces had been created in 1955 and were then active in the Sinai.   They played a role in the defense of Port Said in 1956 and penetrated into enemy territory in

1967. During the War of Attrition along the canal, al-Sa'iqa units made frequent crossings with successively larger units. (22) The missions of these units were described as:

a) Making on the spot studies of Israeli fortifications.

b) Assessing how much damage Egyptian bombardment had done. (23)

These missions increased in importance as Egyptian tacticians began to reason that the Israeli static defense system might be more vulnerable to attack from the rear than were previous, more mobile positions. (24)

As Shadhili analyzed the situation, six problems were involved:

1. The first problem we had to overcome was how to cope with the inflammable material that would be blazing on the surface of the Canal when we started to cross....

2. The second problem was how to remove the earth wall erected by the enemy on the east bank, so that we could install ferries and bridges over the Canal....

3. The third problem was how the engineers were to carry out these vast engineering operations while they were under fire from the enemy who controlled the east bank....

4. The fourth problem was how the infantry was to cross the Canal and secure the bridgeheads until the tanks, artillery, and heavy armament poured across the bridges and ferries installed by the engineers, and how the infantry was to hold out against enemy counterattacks with tanks for from twelve to twenty-four hours, until the crossing of the tanks and heavy armament was completed....

5. The fifth problem was how the infantry was to cross this water obstacle successfully if we did not destroy and silence the automatic weapons and artillery which commanded the terrain from the firing slits of the Bar-Lev line and covered the whole length of the Canal....

6. The sixth problem was how to reorganize our forces on the east bank and how the tanks, guns and ammunition were to reach the infantry units which had crossed before them - and how all this was to be done at night and under enemy pressure, and how the tanks were to find their way and discover their units.... (25)

Most of the detailed planning and coordination was put together by Major General Muhammad 'abd al-Ghani al-Jamasy, Director of Operations. Al-Jamasy was the most intellectual of the three (al-Sadat apparently used to discuss books with him). Like Isma'il and Shadhili, he was a graduate of the Military Academy, and had, in addition, studied in both the United States and Russia. His specialties were training and operations planning: In 1961 he was commander of the Armored School; in 1966 Director of Land Forces Operations; in 1968 Deputy Director of Intelligence; in 1970 Director of Operations and Director of Training. In particular, al-Jamasy had served with Montgomery in the Western Desert during World War II, and both Badr and its covering deception plan are, to some extent, modelled after Montgomery's tactics at al-Alamayn. (26)

Syrian operations were directed by Mustafa Talas. Although trained in conventional warfare, Talas had written extensively about the theory and practice of guerrilla warfare. An Arab review of his writings noted that Talas combined an admiration for Mao, Giap, and Che with an intensive study of classical Islamic tacticians, for whom he had an almost mystical admiration. His theories concerning armed struggle were a blend of Maoism and intense concern for regaining Arab honor. His second book on guerrilla warfare, <u>Armed Struggle in Facing the Israeli Challenge</u>, was dedicated to the "soul of the late martyr, Brigadier General 'abd al-Mun'im Riyad...swearing liberation...pledging revenge, and promising victory...no matter how high the price and great the sacrifices...." In it, he set forth his argument for uncompromising armed struggle with Israel:

> The Israeli enemy defeated, militarily, the Arab armies in 1967. If the enemy withdrew without a fight, this constitutes, in my opinion, the greatest insult to Arab militarism, because the enemy who stripped us of our land by force, insulted our pride, slaughtered our children and aged, and raped our women, and desecrated our shrines, should not, under any condition, get out without punishment....

> This is why the armed struggle is the correct answer to the arrogance and insolence of the Zionist enemy. What is taken by the sword, should be redeemed by the sword if we are to preserve our military honor.... (27)

Talas was apparently unique among Arab senior officers in that he believed in the use of irregular forces in conjunction with regular units (which was done during the war):

> The partisans' war centered on the rear front of the enemy, and which aims at weakening him, occupying his forces, and jamming his communication lines, and which lends its moral support to the regular forces and the people throughout the whole country, etc....is on the whole, coordinated strategically with regular warfare.

> In addition, the partisans' war plays an outstanding role in the coordination of operations during military expeditions. In order to accomplish the various jobs of coordination during military campaigns, the leaders of the partisans' bases located in the rear front, plus the leaders of the partisans' armies that are temporarily sent out of their bases, should distribute their forces in a rational manner. They should - while taking into account the place and time factors and by the use of various methods - launch a strong attack

on the vital and most accessible enemy points, and by so doing, weaken the enemy, hold his forces and hinder his communication lines, thereby helping our forces on the front line. (28)

Arab planning was meticulous in the extreme, especially on the part of the Egyptians (no doubt as a result of the analysis of 1967). Soviet tactics were utilized, but the Egyptians point out that (with variations) these were considerably modified by Arab planners to suit local conditions:

> We come to the subject of Soviet military experience. War is usually the test for any Western or Soviet tactics and the war has confirmed several new theories which we benefited from. Our fighting experience is presently our principal reference in the use of sound Arab-Egyptian tactics.... (29)

In spite of this syncretistic approach, Egyptian and Syrian tactics were constrained by the type of armament received from Russia and the ability of Arab forces to utilize such arms as were supplied effectively. In particular, there were several constraints on Arab planners:

a) The lack of air forces (or more specifically pilots) capable of engaging Israeli air forces;

b) The lack of any real capability for long-range, strategic bombardment of targets within Israel proper;

c) The lack of sufficient number of aircraft able to provide tactical air support with any degree of efficiency;

d) The lack of self propelled artillery. (30)

According to Ahmad Isma'il, the first step in planning was the construction of an extensive series of defensive fortifications on the west bank of the Canal:

> We had to build positions capable of controlling both the west and the east banks of the canal. The Bar-Lev line overlooked our positions; so we proceeded to build up positions overlooking the east bank in order to be able to control it. This was a difficult and expensive job, but it was essential if I was to be able to assist my forces as they crossed over from west to east, and also if I was to protect my forces for the mobilization and conceal them until the time came for the surprise of the crossing....This meant that we had firm positions, and it gave us the advantage inasmuch as if the enemy realized our intentions and tried to strike a blow to frustrate our attack or make it miscarry, we should be able to resist and destroy him.... (31)

Behind this defense line, the Egyptians also constructed an enormous logistics infrastructure: Extensive communications networks were

built, roads, railroads, docks; on these both military and civilian
vehicles, railroads, and water transport were used to move supplies and
equipment to the front.   A series of fuel depots especially secured
against air attack were constructed, most of them underground. Water
tanks were set up from Port Said north, in all sectors of the front, and
an extensive system of pipes was laid to provide water to all
sectors. (32) Clearly, no matter what the outcome of the crossing
operation, the Egyptians did not intend to be caught without adequate
supplies of fuel and water in particular.

Much of this materiel was moved to the front prior to October 6;
special care was exercised to transport it gradually to avoid alerting the
Israelis:

> I also delayed sending the equipment for the crossing as long as
> possible, for it was certain that the withdrawal of this equipment
> from stores would alert the enemy to our intentions. For some of it
> we made special cases so that no one should realize that the huge
> lorries belonged to the engineers. We also dug holes in the ground by
> the canal into which the equipment was put as soon as it arrived at
> night. (33)

Such materiel as could not otherwise be concealed was camouflaged
(see below).

Similar fortifications were constructed on the Syrian front. In this
case, a triple line of fortifications was constructed: The first, a few
miles back from the ceasefire line, was designed to provide protection
for forward air defense and mechanized divisions. The second, the
Sa'asa Line, was some 10 to 12 miles behind the first, and was fortified
with heavy artillery revetments. The third was 8 to 10 miles from
Damascus itself, and likewise heavily fortified. (34)

Like the Egyptian fortifications, these lines were to function as
defense lines in case attacking Arab forces were pushed back across the
original ceasefire lines, and if the Israelis attempted to move on either
Cairo or Damascus. This, in theory at least, prevented a repetition of
the 1967 situation in which both capitals were militarily vulnerable to
Israeli ground forces. (At one point in 1967, 'abd al-Nasir is said to have
told al-Sadat that no organized Egyptian forces stood between the
Israelis and Cairo; al-Sadat later vowed that this state of vulnerability
would never occur again.)

The combined Egyptian/Syrian operation as it developed was given
the code name "Operation Badr." Ahmad Isma'il claimed that this
name was chosen for "good luck", (35) but it had a more symbolic
meaning. The term badr, itself, means "full moon," and could also be
used to refer to the Egyptian requirement for a moonlit night (see
below). (36) This was due to the fact that the date of the attack was
scheduled to be sometime in October. October was also the Islamic
month of Ramadan, the month of fasting, and a time of great religious
and historical significance.

Ramadan was chosen as the month for fasting because the Qur'an
was first revealed during it. (37) October 6th, which corresponded to

the 10th of Ramadan, was even more symbolic because it was the day
when the prophet began his preparations for the battle of Badr in
January 624 AD. During this engagement, a small force of Muslims led
by the Prophet defeated a much larger contingent of Meccans. Badr is
thus considered the first victory of Islam and is interpreted in the
Qur'an as a divine sanction of the new faith. (38)

The battle of Badr is also known as the furqan (testing, proof) in
Islamic dogma because it is conceived theologically as the first trial of
strength between the powers of good and evil: Evil was defeated by the
strength of faith and discipline of the Muslims, and those who had real
faith were weeded out from those with insufficient faith to follow
Islam:

The battle of Badr brought to an issue
The fight between Truth and Unbelief.
It was the Day of Differentiation.
Not for spoils was it won, nor by numbers;
But by courage and planning, union of wills,
And pooling of strength and resources,
And above all by the help of God,
Whose help is ever all sufficient. (39)

The choice of the term "Badr," therefore, concisely expressed the
emotional and religious significance of the impending attack: Not only
was it to be the "test" of Arab manhood, but also a reaffirmation of the
strength of Islam, a reversal of the sense of Muslim impotence that had
spread throughout the area in the wake of the 1967 War. (40)

The orders of battle with which Egyptian and Syrian planners had to
work were outlined in an article in al-Usbu' al-'Arabi published during
the first week of the war. Although somewhat sketchy in details, it
represents an Arab assessment of Egyptian/Syrian forces which varies
to some extent from Western accounts. Notable is the comparison
between Egyptian and Syrian ground forces as a consequence of their
differing operational environments: the Egyptian army being trained
and equipped primarily for water crossing and desert operations, and the
Syrians being organized to engage in tactics designed to break through,
and encircle, enemy forces in mountainous terrain.

EGYPT:

a) Ground forces: Regardless of the time it has taken, the
rebuilding of the Egyptian armed forces after the June 1967 debacle
will go down in history as the most costly project the government has
ever carried out. Egypt's land forces are divided into three armored
divisions totalling around 300,000 men. The army also has 4 mechanized
infantry divisions, 5 infantry divisions, 2 parachute brigades, 16
artillery brigades and 20 commando battalions....Like the Soviet
weapons which are predominant in the Egyptian armed forces, training
is also predominantly Soviet oriented....When fully mobilized, the
Egyptian army grows to the size of around 850,000 men....

It is estimated that the armored corps have around 1,950 tanks, of which 1,550 can do frontline jobs and 400 can perform well on the second line of defense. They are all suitable for combat action day and night. The huge T-54 and T-55 tanks are equipped with radar to facilitate combat action at night....In addition to these tanks, there are 50 heavy duty tanks usually kept as part of the strategic reserve. The Egyptians use their tanks as part of armored units which include artillery and mechanized infantry, engineering corps and signal corps...

The most significant development in the Egyptian armed forces since the 1967 War has been the introduction for the first time, and on a large scale, of Soviet made amphibious tanks. It is estimated that there are around 100 of these BT-76 amphibious tanks...

The Egyptian army is characterized by the huge size of its field artillery (there are around 1,500 cannons and guns of various calibers). These are distributed among the infantry units. The size of the field artillery reflects the Soviet tactical action in warfare which relies on heavy and concentrated artillery fire for offensive and defensive purposes....

b) Air Forces: The Egyptians are said to have around 586 combat aircraft which include a wide variety of the MIGS (17 and 21 and various versions of the two), the SU-7, TU-16 fighter bombers, Il-28 light bombers, and a variety of the Mi-helicopters....The SU-7 and MIG17 are used as ground attack fighters capable of flying at low altitudes to provide support to the ground forces...While the SU-7 can go into action immediately after the battle starts, the MIG-17 can operate better in areas where the enemy does not have air superiority or if there is a protective air umbrella to provide the SU-7 with cover....The MIG-21s include the multipurpose planes, interceptors, and fighter bombers. They are equipped with air to air missiles and are essentially used to engage enemy aircraft.

c) Air Defense Forces: Following Israeli deep penetration raids during the War of Attrition, the Egyptians had to build a strong air defense system that would curb these raids and deter Israel from undertaking them. Now Egypt's frontline, principal installations, and densely populated areas are protected by one of the most sophisticated air defense systems in the world....Although defensive in character, this system could quickly be transformed into one for offensive purposes. Among the first (sic: missiles) to be installed in Egypt were the SAM-2s and SAM-3 missiles. Only during the current fighting did it become known that the Egyptians have also been supplied with the mobile....SAM-6 missiles, which have been most effective in Syria....The SAM-2 missiles are set up on fixed launchers, whereas the SAM-3 and SAM-6 missiles can be moved around on tanks or even trucks....

d) Naval Forces: The Egyptian navy is perhaps the strongest in the East Mediterranean. It is believed to have around 12 submarines, 5 destroyers, 2 corvettes, 10 submarine chasers, 4 fleet mine sweepers, and 12 Osa-class, and 8 Komar class patrol boats with Styz SSM. The

Egyptian navy also has around 30 motor torpedo boats and 20 landing craft....The navy is capable of undertaking offensive action as well as defensive action in the sense of providing adequate protection to Egyptian shores, both on the Mediterranean and the Red Sea....

SYRIA:

a) Ground Forces: The total strength of the Syrian armed forces is estimated at 120,000 men divided between land, naval and air forces. Divisions, brigades, and detachments are the basic units of the armed forces....The larger part of the hardware is Soviet made, and almost all military tactics are Soviet oriented. In a state of full mobilization, Syria can raise an army of 320,000 men.

The armor corps of the Syrian army, like its Egyptian counterpart, is characterized by the large size of its medium tanks (totalling around 1,140) of which around 900 are suitable for operations on the first line of defense, and 240 are suitable for operations on the second line of defense....The Syrians have paid considerable attention to the strengthening of their armor corps on the grounds that this would be the main strike force which would have the task of making a breakthrough into enemy defenses on a very rigorous terrain. Until 1972, the Syrian army had 1 armored division, 2 mechanized divisions, 2 infantry divisions, 1 parachute battalion, 5 commando battalions, and 7 artillery regiments. The army has about 30 JS-3 heavy tanks, 600 T-54/55 medium tanks, 150 T-34 and PT-76 light tanks....

These army units have been trained for breakthroughs, pursuit of the enemy, and encirclement tasks. They have also been trained as part of the operational and strategic reserves with the main tasks of launching counterattacks. The T-34 tanks are supplied to the infantry for support purposes....The T-54/55 tanks are equipped with 100mm guns which have reduced the army's reliance on separate SU-100 SP guns which had been used to support the T-34 tanks....Another important force in the Syrian army is the antiaircraft and artillery guns which are used in large quantitites.

Since the 1967 War, Syrian ground forces have been supplied with a variety of surface to air missiles including SAM-2s and SAM-3s. The latest addition were the SAM-6 missiles which have done remarkably well during the current fighting....Syria has also got several batteries of the "Frog" type ground to ground missiles and the wire guided missiles which are mainly antitank missiles known as "Sagger."

b) Air Forces: The Syrian air force consists of around 10,000 men and 310 combat aircraft. Of these, there are 200 MIG-21 and 30 SU-7 fighter bombers. The rest include MIG-17s, transport planes, and helicopters. The Israelis have spread rumors that the Syrians are also using the sophisticated....SU-11 which flies at 2.5 mach and can put up with the Phantoms and Skyhawks....

c) Naval Forces: Syria has a small naval force which consists mainly of 2 mine sweepers, 2 coastal patrol vessesl, 6 Komar class patrol boats equipped with Styx SSM, and 12 motor torpedo boats (less than 100 tons).... (41)

Many of these arms, particularly aircraft and missiles, reached Syria and Egypt in the later stages of 1972 and throughout 1973. Because of the friction between Russia and Egypt, there was apparently considerable unwillingness on the part of the Soviets to provide extensive arms to the Egyptians. As early as 1971, al-Sadat had been faced with this reluctance, a reluctance which seemed to stem from two Soviet considerations:

a) A suspicion of al-Sadat, himself, especially after the 'Ali Sabri ouster:

When I declared last summer that 1971 would be decisive, there was a misunderstanding with the Soviet Union as a result of the events in the Sudan and the boys who had the centers of power here (a reference to 'Ali Sabri and his colleagues), for these boys had told the Soviets that I sold the country to the Americans.

When I visited the Soviet Union along with Lt. Gen. Mohammed Ahmed Sadek, we spoke with the Russians frankly. I asked why should this happen between us, since we are friends. I am not obliged to the Americans in any way. But I am obliged to my friends (the Soviets) who are helping me militarily and industrially and have built the High Dam for me. So we talked on October 11th and 12th, and I asked them why the misunderstanding. Was it because the boys of May (Sabri and colleagues were ousted in May, 1971) had told you that I sold the country to the Americans?

It is clear I never sold the country to anyone. I am also not selling it to the Americans or even to you. (42)

b) Refusal to provide any sort of weaponry that might enable the Egyptians to reopen large scale hostilities. Presumably one of the "lessons" of 1967, insofar as the Soviets were concerned, was that Arab forces could not handle such equipment as they had already received, and therefore should not be given the opportunity to start another disastrous war. Friction on this account steadily developed over the course of time, culminating in the Egyptian expulsion of Russian advisors. The Egyptians reportedly even went so far as to ask the Syrians to remove their Soviet advisors also:

In October 1971....We dissipated the clouds in relations between us and the Soviet Union and agreed on specific (arms) shipments to reach us before the end of 1971....It was supposed that when these weapons begin arriving, I will be able to take our decision on the battle (sic: "the Year of Decision"). But October, November, and December went by, and no weapons arrived....

In the middle of December (1971) I sent them a message saying that the weapons had not arrived, and that the time of their arrival was not clear, and asking to visit them to discuss the situation....By delaying the visit, they wanted to cool me down, because they had not agreed about 1971 being the year of decision, and were, in fact, opposed to any move, but political and diplomatic moves.

I visited them in February and again in April, at their request, because Nixon was scheduled to visit Moscow for his first summit (with Brezhnev) in May 1972....The center of discussion between us....I always argued that the problem will not be solved without military action. And the view of the Soviet Union was always opposed to military action. The discussions always ended in that....so that we may be able to talk to Israel from a position of strength (we should get more weapons) and they usually promised to send us weapons.

....We agreed that following Nixon's summit with Brezhnev, Egypt's capability should be speedily strengthened. For our assessment was that nothing new will happen in the American position, since 1972 is a year of election.

Fourteen days after the summit, I received a message from the Soviets and their analysis was identical to the one I had forecast, which is that there is nothing new in the American position....I sent them a reply saying that since our assessments of the situation were identical, then I am expecting the weapons we had agreed on to begin arriving, so that we may be on firm ground following the American presidential election....But one month went by, before I received any reply, and the reply did not contain anything about the battle, except in its last three lines....

Before that, the communique on the summit had been issued, and it talked of military relaxation in the Middle East....If this relaxation took place while Israel is in a superior position, it will mean that the problem will not be solved, and it will mean that the strong will impose their conditions....When I received their reply, I took my decision on (sic: expelling) the Soviet experts in the summer of that year.... (43)

Alarmed, the Syrians set about mediating Egyptian/Soviet relations, beginning in August/September 1972. These efforts, culminated by the personal intercession of al-Asad, apparently succeeded according to al-Sadat:

Relations throughout the summer (of 1972) remained frozen until our brother President Hafez Assad visited Moscow in October....As a result, there was an activation of relations, but this was only on the surface....In early 1973 Marshall Ismail visited the Soviet Union and Hafez Ismail also visited the Soviet Union. The Soviets concluded a deal with Marshall Ismail, and it seemed that relations began to take their normal course again as of February 1973. Some parts of this deal actually began arriving after the return of Marshal Ismail from the Soviet Union. The decision of the battle was taken in April

1973, and some parts of the deal began arriving, and we hoped that relations would return to normal. But the Soviet Union continued to insist that a military battle should not be considered, and that we should await a peaceful solution. (44)

The Syrians, however, continued their activities: On May 2, al-Asad visited Moscow in an effort to get more aid for Syria and Egypt, especially in the area of air defense. Arab sources claimed that, at that time, both Syria and Egypt had been receiving large quantities of weapons and spare parts, including MIG-21s, SAM-7s and 8s, radar and electronic equipment. (45) According to these sources, Russia had done this because it was convinced that the Egyptians were about to resort to war. In such an event, Russia would be blamed for an Egyptian defeat if they withheld arms (Ahmad Isma'il's reasoning). The arrival of this equipment was a major factor in significantly changed Egyptian estimates of their military capabilities. By May, Egyptian leaders were said to be convinced that their armament was sufficient to enable them to begin hostilities. (46)

But, the Egyptians (or Syrians either) were not satisfied that the Soviets had delivered either in quality or quantity the necessary gear. Al-Sadat commented on Soviet arms deliveries thus:

Yes, our armament was not up to standard. I will tell you a secret which no one has learned until now. When we entered the battle, half of our helicopters were out of order because of the shortage of spare parts... (47)

These complaints were extended to include Soviet resupply efforts during the fighting:

From the second day of the battle, I asked for tanks from the Soviet Union. For history, on that day, and before we hit 400 Israeli tanks in 4 days, I predicted, and told the Soviet ambassador that the battle would be a battle of tanks. Send me armor quickly, because the one who has more tanks will be the one who will stay in the battle longest. However, the required armor only reached me from the Soviet Union a week after the cease fire! The tanks that reached me were from Algeria and Yugoslavia as well as 100 tanks from Libya. (48)

Additionally, Egyptian/Syrian planners could expect at least some aid from Iraq and Jordan. These had remained in position until late 1970, when they were pulled out after 'abd al-Nasir's acceptance of the United States sponsored ceasefire proposal which ended the War of Attrition. The Iraqi army had considerable experience in combat over rough terrain because of its more or less continuous engagement with Kurdish insurgents in Northern Iraq. In the Arab view, therefore, the addition of Iraqi units could be a major factor if fighting in the Golan continued for any length of time. The Arab World staff assessed the capability of Iraqi forces as follows:

a) <u>Ground Forces</u>:   Since the 1967 War....the total number of Iraqi ground forces has risen to around 100,000 men divided into 2 armored and 5 infantry divisions....The Iraqi army is predominantly equipped with Soviet made hardware, just like the Syrian and Egyptian armies....The Iraqi army's armored strength is estimated at about 450 T-54/55 and 140 T-34 Soviet tanks, 55 British Centurion mark 13 medium tanks, 40 M-24 Chaffe light tanks, 55 AML-60 armored cars, 20 Ferret scout cars, and a number of BTR-152 armored personnel carriers. The artillery includes Soviet 120mm and 130mm guns.

b) <u>Air Force</u>:   The Iraqi air force is believed to have around 7,500 officers and men, and about 229 combat aircraft, which include 8 TU-16 medium bombers, 10 Il-28 bombers, 50 SU-7 all weather fighter bombers, 36 Hunter mark 9 ground attack aircraft, 20 T-52 jet Provost light strike aircraft, 60 MIG-21 interceptors, and 45 MIG-17 and MIG-19 fighters....The air force also flies 4 MI-1, 20 MI-4, and 11 Wessex helicopters, some SAM-2 guided surface to air missiles, and about 45 transport airplanes.

c) <u>Naval Forces</u>:   The small Iraqi Navy has about 2,000 officers and men, three submarine chasers, 12 motor torpedo boats, and 10 patrol boats, both less than 100 tons. The Iraqi paramilitary forces include a national guard of around 10,000 men, plus one mechanized brigade of security troops of some 30,000 men. (49)

Jordan's military establishment was summed up by quoting a Jordanian saying, "King Hussein is the army and the army is King Hussein": (50)

> For the army is his right hand arm for consolidating his regime. It is overwhelmingly loyal to the King and the monarch is himself extremely devoted to his army. Continued loyalty to the crown is basically due to the fact that the bedouins form the core of the Jordanian officer corps and enlisted men, both in quantity and quality. These tribesmen have little or no awareness of political issues, and look down upon the life style of the townspeople. Their powerful loyalty to the tribe has been transformed into blind allegiance to the King, army and commanding officer. All this is reinforced by their religious tie to the King as a descendent of the Prophet....

> Ever since the 1967 War, King Hussein has taken personal responsibility for the army. He immediately began to expand it and to strengthen it by acquiring mainly U.S. made weapons and aircraft. Hussein is thoroughly knowledgeable about military affairs, and the small and big things in his army. Almost nothing could be decided as far as the army is concerned without the King's knowledge and, perhaps, approval.... (51)

a) <u>Ground Forces</u>:   British trained, well disciplined and consisting of capable fighters, the Jordanian army is equipped with exclusively western made weapons....The Jordanian Armed Forces comprise some 73,000 men. Reservists number some 20,000, and some 22,000 men are in the paramilitary forces. By way of weapons, the Jordanian Armed Forces have about 400-500 medium size tanks (M-47, M-48, M-60, and Centurions), 270-300 armored cars ("Salahiddins" and "Ferrets"), 400 troop carriers (M-113 and "Saracens"), around 200 guns of various types, M-42 antiaircraft guns, and ground-to-air "Tiger Cat" rockets. Two armored divisions, a mechanized division, an infantry division, and a number of brigades, regiments, and companies handled this equipment.... (52)

b) Air Force: Jordan now owns....52 fighter planes. Of these, there are 20 F-104 planes, and 32 Hawker Hunters. It has a limited number of carrier helicopters. (53)

The Egyptian plan, as finally worked out, called for a canal crossing operation, seizure of a defensible position on the east bank, a strip some 10 to 26 miles deep, and either the defense of this area, or a further advance into the Sinai - depending on conditions. (54) The operations order which al-Sadat issued to Ahmad Isma'il immediately prior to the attack specified these objectives:

> The strategic aim for which I shoulder political responsibility in entrusting it to the Egyptian armed forces - on the basis of all I have heard and know about the state of preparedness - is summed up as follows: Defying the Israeli theory of security by means of a military action based on the capabilities of the armed forces whose aim would be to inflict the heaviest losses on the enemy to convince him that his continued occupation of our territory imposes on him a price which he cannot pay, and consequently, defying the Israeli theory of security based on psychological, political, and military armament, showing that this is not a steel shield that can protect him now or in the future. If we succeed in defying Israel's security theory, this will lead to certain results in the short, and in the long run.... (55)

The Egyptian main force was to be kept under the protection of its air defense system; the Egyptian air force was to be utilized primarily in a ground support role, engaging Israeli aircraft only where surface batteries were unavailable.

Such was the Egyptian understanding of the overall plan for conducting the war. But it was clearly not what the Syrains understood to be the case. Indeed, the later Syrian-Egyptian break in the final stages of the war appears to have been the product of a misunderstanding at the planning stage. In a postwar interview (and the fact that it is a postwar statement has to be taken into account), Mustafa Talas outlined the Syrian strategy:

1) To achieve the element of surprise...

2) To begin the offensive simultaneously on the Syrian and the Egyptian fronts to curb the enemy's air and land effort and disperse his forces...

3) To penetrate deep into enemy defenses in Sinai and the Golan...and to maintain a high frequency of advance on <u>both</u> fronts to force the enemy to split his forces throughout the battle and to prevent him from dealing separately with each of the two fronts... (56)

At this point, it is clear that the Egyptian and Syrian strategies are already divergent. But Talas goes on: While it was clear that Syrian forces would force the Israelis to confront them at the outset, to give the Egyptians time to break through the more formidable Bar-Lev line, it was expected that the Egyptian army would break out and move to the Sinai passes. This would give the Syrians breathing space to consolidate their foothold. But the Egyptians instead unaccountably delayed their breakout:

> What happened on the Egyptian front was that, when the fraternal Egyptian army crossed the canal and stormed the Bar-Lev line, it spent many days repelling the tactical counterattacks...which enabled the Israeli command to expose the intentions of the Egyptian command (sic: not to break out) and transfer its reserves to the northern front. The Egyptian command continued in this manner for a whole week...without considering marshalling its other forces and following up the attack, despite our continued insistance that the plan should be followed...

> The way the plan was implemented on the Egyptian front proved that the Egyptian political command contrived a different plan than what we agreed on... (57)

Other than this, Syrian forces were to occupy as many Israeli positions as possible, to continue fighting until a ceasefire, and to withdraw to previously prepared defensive positions to engage in a "war of attrition" if the Israelis mounted a successful counteroffensive. Syrian air war strategy was essentially the same as that of the Egyptians.

TIMING: ESCALATION AND THE FORECLOSURE OF OPTIONS

As noted above, Egyptian and Syrian planners were considering three sets of dates, "windows" during which an attack could be launched under optimum conditions. According to Egyptian versions, these windows were arrived at by a careful study of the physical conditions necessary for successful military operations: among other things, currents in the Canal and atmospheric conditions. Within these technical parameters, however, there was considerable latitude as to when to actually attack. As the joint Egyptian/Syrian decision making progressed, all of the dates before October were considered and then rejected. What appears to have happened is a complex process where, on the one hand, all options except the military option came to be perceived as unworkable, while the military option - because of the increasingly concrete planning - came to be seen as the most promising. On the other hand, the time frame for action appeared to be steadily narrowing: not only did the military requirements place their own limits on time, but background pressures for action continued to steadily build up:

a) The earlier military dates were progressively forecluded: in May the planning was not sufficiently complete, moreover, the Israelis were informed of a possible attack and mobilized to forestall it. In August, the plan had been completed, but not yet fully operationalized; moreover the Israelis again mobilized (see note 99 for details). By October, however, all the military elements had been put together.

b) Paralleling this increased military possibility was a concurrent decrease in the perceived likelihood of a political solution: a number of al-Sadat's diplomatic initiatives had failed, and the Israelis were giving every sign of settling into the occupied territories. In addition, Arab perceptions of Kissinger were such that they believed that he operated entirely in terms of a calculus of power, and would respond only after Arab military power was demonstrated.

c) Tension in both Egypt and Syria were clearly on the increase, and these were reinforced by a deteriorating Arab situation in which the Palestinians were steadily expanding the Arab/Israeli conflict into Europe and elsewhere via international terrorism. Indeed, the possibility of an Israeli retaliation for one of these attacks appears to be a major factor in the final Arab decision to attack. The attack was to start in the last hours of daylight, and then continue to move equipment across the Canal during the night, thus giving themselves several hours of darkness before the Israelis could counterattack. The Syrians wanted a morning operation, to attack from out of the sun, a Muslim cavalry tactic utilized by Salah al-Din at the battle of Hittin in July 1187 to defeat Crusader forces: (58)

> As for the fixing of H-hour, the timing was discussed between us and our Syrian brothers until a few days before the fighting started. For various reasons, including the fact that the sun would be behind them and in the enemy's eyes, the Syrians wanted the operation to start at first light....We, on the other hand, for various reasons, including, in addition to the direction of the sun, the requirements of the crossing, erecting bridges, and opening the way for the passage of heavy equipment such as tanks, preferred to take action at last light, in the evening.... (59)

The Egyptians, however, had other problems to contend with, such as the speed of currents in the Canal, and the necessity of an Israeli stand down. They needed, therefore:

1. A moonlit night, with the moon rising as we needed it, in the decisive hours.

2. A night in which the speed of the current in the Canal would be favorable to the crossing.

3. A night when action by us would be the last thing the enemy expected.

4. A night when the enemy himself would not be prepared for action. (60)

The dates when these prerequisites were met were clustered in four months:

Afterwards (sic: after the April meeting between al-Sadat and al-Asad) we were in constant contact in order to fix the most suitable date. This is because, during the meeting in question, we had a study before us by the operations branch on the conditions of every day of the year and which of them were more suitable from a military viewpoint....It is now possible to make precise calculations about natural phenomena and weather conditions from the beginning of the year right up until the end of the year....Thus, during my meeting with President al-Asad, and with these scientific studies on hand, we chose three groups of dates that were suitable for the attack. The first group was in May, the second in August and September and the third in October.... (61)

If the attack was not carried out by the last of these dates, i.e., October 1973, it would have to either be postponed until the following year, or put into operation under less than optimum circumstances. (62) The former, prolonging the increasingly unacceptable status quo and raising the possibility that the laboriously forged Arab coalition might, in time, split apart from its own inner tensions; the latter increasing the risk of an already chancey operation.

These considerations came to have increasing weight as options other than that of war became progressively eliminated. According to William Polk, al-Sadat and al-Asad had at least three other possible courses of action:

1. To accept the military defeat of 1967 and negotiate with the Israelis.

2. To maintain the military/political status quo and hope for the best.

3. To mount a diplomatic "forward policy" aimed at bringing both international and superpower pressure to bear on Israel. (63)

For obvious reasons, alternative number one was out of the question: The weakness of both the Egyptian/Syrian leadership ruled out any display of conciliation. (64) Moreover, an admission of defeat was as psychologically impossible in 1973 as it was in 1967. In addition, as al-Sadat argued, negotiations with the Israelis while they were still in possession of Arab lands was tantamount to a surrender of these lands:

....Assuming there was any idea that we would sit down (sic: and negotiate with Israel), how can we while Israel is occupying our land? If we sat down with Israel while it is occupying our land, it would ask for so much land. I would say no. Israel would say: Then I will retain the land in my possession. What would I do in the game of tricks? (65)

The second alternative was also increasingly unsatisfactory. Time was clearly not on the Arabs' side; the domestic situation in both Egypt and Syria was becoming rapidly more tense, and the Israelis were giving every indication of preparing to colonize Arab lands. Settlements were being built in the Golan Heights and along a strip leading to the Sharm al-Shaykh. The demography of the Old City of Jerusalem was being changed by the extensive construction of apartment houses, and the relocation of Jewish families in them.

This "creeping annexation" had been watched by Arab governments with great concern for some time. In April 1973, King Husayn voiced these fears with an appeal to Arab governments to foil the "terrible Israeli plan to wrest the ownership of occupied Arab territories." (66) This was followed by a joint Jordanian, Syrian, Egyptian petition to United States Secretary General Kurt Waldheim concerning:

....the persistence of the Israeli occupation authorities in changing the physical, geographic, and demographic structure of the occupied Arab territories....the Israeli cabinet is now considering a proposal for the authorization of Israeli individuals to purchase land and property in the occupied territories....Such a decision would obviously be carried out in the context of Israel's policy of pressuring the Arab inhabitants of the occupied territories to acquiesce in Israel's continuous steps of settlement and absorption of the occupied territories.... (67)

Arab feelings of frustration were heightened by pronouncements by General Dayan which were duly carried in the Arab press. In late June 1973, Dayan proclaimed that the Palestinians:

....had buried the idea of a Palestinian state ....That the refugees will have to find some places in the Arab states. Sooner or later the Arab countries will have to absorb them....Israel will not accept them willingly and not by force....There was a Palestine, but there is none any more. Part of it became Israel and part of it became Jordan .... (68)

In response, Jordanian Prime Minister Rafa'i, joined now by Iranian Prime Minister Amir Abbas Hoveda, issued a communique:

> Expressing intense concern about the gravity of the situation in the Middle East, the two premiers stated that the occupation of territories belonging to a number of Arab states through the use of force constitutes a serious violation of international laws and threatens the security of the region and the peace of the world.... (69)

This was followed in September by Dayan's announcement of the proposed establishment of new settlements in the Sinai, for security reasons. (71)

Moreover, it appeared that both the United States and Russia were tacitly underwriting this Israeli expansionism. The United States had vetoed a Security Souncil resolution which "strongly deplored" the Israeli policy of consolidating its position in the occupied territories. (72) The Soviets had begun to allow Jews to emigrate to Israel; an estimated 70,000 had left between 1971 and 1973. In 1973 alone, the rate had increased to about 30,000. (73) Thus, not only did the Israelis seem to have Great Power diplomatic support, but also to have an unlimited source of immigrants with which to colonize Arab lands (a set of facts which appeared to confirm decades of Arab propaganda about unlimited Israeli territorial ambitions, from "the Nile to the Euphrates.")

The issue of Jewish emigration came in for vehement attack by Arab leaders, especially Faysal and al-Qadhafi. According to Faysal, the Soviet emigrants to Israel were worse than the weapons being supplied by the United States. Al-Qadhafi had a more explicit theory: The United States and Russia were in collusion. While the United States supplied the arms, the Soviets provided the military manpower. (74)

But it was the Syrians for whom Jewish immigration was particularly threatening, since the most aggressive Israeli plans for settlements were in the Golan. Al-Asad, himself, raised the question during his May 2 visit to Moscow. According to Arab sources, al-Asad expressed the fear that as many as 10,000 Russian Jews might be settled in the Golan, raising the number of Israelis in the region to some 50,000 within two years. Accordingly, he urged the Soviets to give strong military support to efforts aimed at recovering occupied Syrian land. (75)

The Syrians then moved to stop Jewish emigration more directly. On September 28, two fida'iyin styling themselves the "Eagles of the Palestine Revolution" hijacked a train carrying Jews from Russia to transit facilities at Schoenau, Austria. Al-Sa'iqa officials later admitted that the "Eagles" were actually an al-Sa'iqa unit. (76) The fida'iyin took three emigres and an Austrian customs official hostage, releasing them only after Austrian Chancellor Bruno Kreisky promised to:

a) Discontinue transit facilities for Soviet Jews, and

b) Close the Schoenau camp itself. (77)

In addition, the "Eagles" released a statement (printed only in al-Nahar) warning Russia:

A warning to the Soviet Union: we, the Eagles of the Palestine
Revolution, issue this first and last warning to the Soviet Union, our
friend, that its embassies and interests in the Middle East will be
targets for strikes by our revolutionaries unless it stops the
emigration operation to Israel.... (78)

(The Eagles' raid is a considerably more complex phenomenon than
merely a direct Syrian response to Jewish immigration: Its timing
suggests that it may have been part of the Syrian deception strategy,
but even this interpretation has problems. In any event, see the
discussion below.)

The third option likewise appeared increasingly unlikely. The
superpowers were clearly more interested in detente than in doing
something about the Arab situation:

In June 1973, the second summit was held in Washington between
Nixon and Brezhnev....The communique issued afterwards made it
clear that the two superpowers had taken a big step forward, and
agreed that nothing (to disturb the peace) should take place in any
part of the world....There was nothing left in the world but the
Middle East, because an agreement on Viet Nam had been reached
already....The communique meant that our cause was being put on
ice, and that we should wait for a peaceful solution....We all know
about the American stand, that Egypt and the Arabs were a dead
body that could not move and that had no value. Hence, the
importance of our decision to fight. It was a 100 percent Egyptian
decision, because the two superpowers were opposed to any move,
and had declared it twice to the world in their communiques issued
in Moscow and Washington in 1972 and 1973. (79)

The United States seemed more and more committed to backing
Israeli occupation:

I have just completed contacts with all of the Big Five, with China,
with the West and East Europeans and the non-aligned countries.
There is only one conclusion - if we don't take our case into our own
hands, there will be no movement, especially given Washington's
ridiculous ideas evidenced by Hafiz Isma'il's trip....All the West
Europeans are telling us the same thing. And what's more they are
right. Everyone has fallen asleep over the Middle East crisis. But
they will soon wake up to the fact that the Americans have left us
no other way out.... (80)

The basic policy of America and Israel is to maintain the ceasefire.
The ceasefire suits Israel because it wants to change the character
of Arab lands and impose the status quo. America and Israel, in the
meantime, launch a psychological campaign aimed at convincing us
that we are no match for Israel, which is backed by America
politically, economically, and militarily. What they want is to kill
our cause.... (81)

Moreover Russia was not far behind the United States. But where the United States at least backed its client, Russia did not: instead it had attempted to restrain the Egyptians. (82)

As a consequence Russian/Egyptian relations became progressively more strained. The Egyptians undertook a series of harassing tactics aimed at Soviet personnel in Egypt. The plan for the evacuation of Soviet personnel, put into effect in October, was said to have been drawn up by the Soviet ambassador in response to Egyptian provocations. (83)

As a backdrop to these disillusionments with the United States and Russia, rumors about their hostile intentions began sweeping the area. The Soviets were about to restore diplomatic relations with Israel, an intention buttressed by intelligence and diplomatic reports. (84) The United States was planning some kind of military action against Arab governments, either to seize oil installations or to force an acceptance of Israeli occupation:

The question which is raised today is this: Is it true that the United States will occupy the sources of Arab oil to insure a supply of Arab oil? Before we answer this question we must talk about the sources of Arab oil. These sources are the Arab Gulf area, the Kingdom of Saudi Arabia and some other Arab states....What then does the United States lack that it has to occupy the sources of Arab oil, especially when these sources are already occupied by the United States in actual fact? What then is the reason for the call for the United States to occupy the sources of Arab oil? Is it really the fear of the Arab states using oil as a weapon to pressure the United States to change its policy toward the Zionist enemy? But there is a wider angle than this. It is U.S. policy in the Arab area. The U.S. threat to occupy the sources of Arab oil is part of U.S.-Zionist strategy which seeks to place the entire Arab area under U.S.-Zionist influence. The threat to occupy the sources of Arab oil is the final chapter in this strategy. Thus area states will remain within the framework of the U.S.-Zionist policy. That is, the Arab states will remain neutral toward the issue of Zionist occupation of Palestinian and neighboring territories, whereas those Arab states whose territory is occupied, if they lose all hope of using oil as a weapon, will be inclined to agree with U.S.-Zionist liquidationist solutions. (85)

Kissinger was said to be planning to "unleash the Israelis":

Kissinger is convinced that a political solution can be achieved only when a crisis becomes acute. In Viet Nam he was able to reach a practical solution only after the escalation of air raids on North Viet Nam and stepped up fighting. In regards to the Middle East, Kissinger aims at getting a solution by a resumption of fighting. But since he cannot push the Arabs into fighting, he must therefore utilize Israel.... (86)

We must get ready for a confrontation with Henry Kissinger, because this confrontation, one way or another, is forthcoming, and it would be dangerous for us if we were not prepared... (87)

The publication of a purported United States plan for settling the territorial issues served to confirm these fears; clearly the United States and Israel were about to act. Al-Jumhurriya tied together Dayan's remarks concerning Israeli plans for Jerusalem with the United States plan. According to it, the Israeli moves and the plan's publication revealed collusion:

(Dayan's) statements uncover not only Israeli expansionist ambitions, but also a new strategy to impose the status quo....(Dayan's) statements come at the same time as doubtful plans proposed by the United States....(These) require an awareness on the part of Arabs of collusion.... (88)

In short, by the fall the psychology of paranoia which gripped the Arab world in early 1967 was repeated. The United States and Israel were planning something; the 1967 coup in Greece was replaced by the 1973 coup in Chile (89) as evidence of these ominous intentions. Al-Sadat articulated Arab forebodings in terms akin to those used earlier by 'abd al-Nasir:

....What we are facing today....is a ferocious imperialist invasion. There have been two similar invasions in our history. The Tatars invaded us once and the Crusaders the next time. The third invasion, the Zionist invasion, is the worst, because the United States, which used the veto....(sic: on a UN resolution condemning Israeli occupation of Arab territories), stands behind the ferocious Zionist invasion. The aim of this ferocious Zionist invasion is to control our area politically and, actually, as the dean of the Alexandria University said, to control the civilization of our area as well.... (90)

The precipitant of the decision to attack, however, was the aforementioned Israeli/Syrian air battle: In Arab eyes, the Israeli attack was a deliberate attempt to destroy the newfound unity of the Summit, (91) a prelude to larger operations. In his book on the 1956 War, Dayan laid out three conditions which would necessitate an Israeli preemptive attack:

1. Interference with Israeli shipping in the Gulf of Aqaba.

2. Increased fida'iyin terrorism.

3. Creation of a joint Egypt/Syria/Jordan military command. (92)

After the minisummit, the last two of these conditions were present: widespread fida'iyin activity and an Arab military coordination. (93) The

Israeli/Syrian air battle, therefore, took on added significance; the Syrian reposte at Schoenau almost assured another Israeli reprisal; both were accompanied by a barrage of Israeli warnings concerning increased fida'iyin attacks. These were promptly played up in the Arab press. Al-Thawra (Damascus) noted: "That a comparison between current Israeli statements and those made prior to June 1967 shows, unequivocally and clearly, the similarity in tactics and aims that Israel is now trying to play the previous game preliminary to commiting an aggression." (94)

This combination of military action and verbal warning triggered a complex of Arab responses which stemmed from years of experience with Israeli "massive retaliations":

a) A feeling that Israel would respond with overwhelming force; force out of proportion to original Arab incursion, a retaliation "much bigger than was justified." (95)

b) A belief that any Arab government was a potential target, irrespective of whether it was actually the instigator; "to the Israelis we were all alike." (96)

c) A willingness to take Israeli threats at their face value: even though Arab commentators were aware that these threats occurred in the context of an Israeli election campaign, and could plausibly be interpreted as attempts to generate support among an increasingly Hawkish Israeli electorate. (97)

Reports of Israeli troop manuevers in both the Golan and Sinai added weight and urgency to Israeli utterances:

News agencies confirm that Israel concentrations along the cease-fire line with Syria have noticeably increased. Quoting enemy sources, the news agencies report that a state of emergency has been proclaimed in Israeli settlements near the occupied Syrian Heights. Political observers pointed out that the Israeli officials' statements on the so called Syrian concentrations and their claim that the Syrians would carry so-called Syrian concentrations and their claim that the Syrians would carry out certain military operations actually aim at covering a premeditated agression planned by the Zionist circles against the Arab countries and Syria in particular. Political observers point out that the enemy used a similar propaganda method before the 1967 June aggression and that the enemy's information campaign and his talk about peace was to pave the way for a new aggression against the Arab countries. Press reports from Beirut said that Zionist enemy planes were carrying out an air survey of the southern areas and that enemy armored reinforcements were seen taking up positions in the Golan Heights. Meanwhile MENA reports that the Zionist enemy has also concentrated his forces along the Suez Canal. The agency adds that Egypt has declared a state of alert in the northern and central sectors of the Canal due to the Israeli concentrations. (98)

Obviously, these Israeli troop redeployments were in response to large scale Arab exercises carried out at about the same time: Dayan in responding to intelligence analysis of these exercises had decided to augment Israeli defenses.

Whatever doubts the Egyptians may have had concerning the necessity of a first strike were swept away. (99) The Syrian/Israeli air battle occurred on September 13; by the 16th, Egyptian naval units were on station; ground units were deployed by the 26th; Syrian units moved up also. On the 28th the Eagles' raid took place: Clearly the events of 1967 were being repeated; the stage was set for another Israeli attack on Damascus. Events moved swiftly: On the 30th the Committee of National Security met to consider the situation: Al-Sadat delivered his pessimistic assessment of the "no war, no peace" status quo, and its effects on the Egyptian economy. The same day, Ahmad Isma'il notified the Syrians to be prepared for momentary action (see below).

On October 1, the Egyptian Supreme Council of the Armed Forces met; its members reviewed their respective roles in the forthcoming attack.   During the course of this meeting, al-Sadat told his commanders:

> I thank God that we have reached this moment to put the final touches to work, to tell the world that we are alive, and so that our people will regain their confidence in themselves and in you. I am fully confident that every member of the armed forces will fully discharge his duty out of his sense of responsibility for his homeland. I assume with you the full responsibility - historically, materially and morally. At the same time, I am totally confident in you and that you will act with all confidence, reassurance and freedom... (100)

Following the meeting, al-Sadat signed the strategic order for to set the date for the attack. Field Marshal Isma'il flew to Damascus the next day to coordinate the final date and time of the attack with the Syrians.

On October 3, al-Sadat signed the order to attack. The date set was October 6, chosen for the following reasons: (101)

1. Astronomical calculations showed that there would be a moon rising at the beginning of the night and setting at the end of it.

2. Egyptian scientists had studied reports of the Suez Canal Authority and discovered that the current in the canal was most favorable for crossing on October 6.

3. The Israelis would not be expecting the Arabs to attack during the Islamic holy month of Ramadan.

4. The Israelis were preoccupied also with their own upcoming general elections. (102)

SECRECY AND DECEPTION: ARAB IMAGE PROJECTION

The ultimate success of Arab planning hinged on the ability of their forces to score quick victories in both the Sinai and the Golan, and to entrench themselves prior to the expected Israeli counterattack. To do this, considerable attention was devoted to securing projected operations from Western and Israeli intelligence. This problem was indeed formidable, as the Israeli assassination of Fatah leaders in Beirut on April 10, 1973 had demonstrated. Not only were the Israelis able to target selected Fatah leaders, but they were also able to execute the attack without meeting significant opposition. (103) After this raid, the Arab media devoted considerable attention to the purported activities of Israeli and, more particularly, United States intelligence in the area. (104)

The general lack of secrecy concerning Egyptian/Syrian intentions to attempt an attack in May added further impetus to the drive for secrecy. Not only did the Israelis, the United States and Russia know about the attack, but the Jordanian and Iraqi governments were also informed. A report to the Iraqi Ba'th Party Congress released in January 1974 stated:

> For a relatively long time the command (sic: of the Ba'th party) had expected the possibility that the Egyptian and Syrian, under the direction of some foreign as well as Arab circles would take some form of military action against Israel with the aim of activating the situation in the area and facilitating the implementation of a peaceful solution which the two regimes....were seeking. Preliminary estimates indicated that military action would take place in May or June 1973. (105)

(Al-Sadat was later to argue that this May crisis was part of his deception plan. See below.)

This insistence on secrecy, however, derived as much from inter-Arab political considerations, as from the need to preempt the Israelis. If any of the lessons of 1967 were valid, surely that of the necessity of preventing other Arab governments from escalating the situation out of control was preeminently so. (106) Altogether, then, secrecy was imperative on a number of counts:

1. Prevent the Israelis from mobilizing their reserves and thus negate any surprise factor Arab forces might achieve.

2. Prevent superpower interference, and a repetition of the events of June 4/5, 1967. (107)

3. Prevent a repetition of Arab outbidding, in terms of escalating the goals of the war. (108)

4. Prevent Israel from creating an unfavorable international climate.

The problem,   as conceived by the Egyptians especially, was not only to conceal both intentions and operational preparations - the total volume of men and material moving to the front - but also to produce alternative explanations for such activities.   Thereby hopefully confusing Western and Israeli analysts as to their true nature for as long as possible. Al-Sadat later summarized the matter:

> Studies show that after the world and its great powers became confident of what science has achieved in terms of obtaining information and studying the movements of armed forces by means of artificial satellites, reconnaissance planes, and others, October proved that knowing about movements is one thing and knowing about the intentions of these movements is another, and that strategic diversion and the element of surprise are still possible if they are well prepared despite all listening and photographic devices....This is proven by the fact that the United States was watching our movements but did not understand them.... (109)

In so doing, they seem to have relied heavily on Western negative images of Arab behavior, engaging in a sophisticated piece of imagery whereby these images were utilized against their originators. (110) In particular, Arab planners appear to have counted on three factors:

a) Western tendency to discount much of what Arab leaders said concerning their intentions to start another war:

> ....Perhaps you can recall that on this very day last year....I was talking to you and to the nation. I told you at the end of my address that I would not talk about the battle anymore....Perhaps no one understood this reference to the battle: Our enemy, in particular, did not.   For the enemy had based his calculations....on the assumption that we had lost our fighting spirit and the will to resist. It occurred to nobody that when I was talking to you here, making no more than a brief reference to the battle, zero hour had been set; battle orders down to the minutest detail had been issued. Our men, our brothers, and sons in their hundreds and thousands were already taking up their combat position....I was talking to you while hundreds of thousands moved in silence.... (111)

b) Western beliefs that Arabs could not keep anything secret:

> In turn, the Egyptians are capable of having a preemptive strike of their own.   The question is, however: could the Arabs keep something like this quiet? I think it would be very difficult for them to do that....The Israelis have one of the finest intelligence groups in the world.   In order to make such a preemptive strike fully effective, several governments would have to be brought in on this. For example, whether they would bring in Jordan, I don't know. Anyway, several governments would be involved. When you get

more than one government involved, automatically the chances of
having the news out are escalated.... (112)

c) Western feeling that periodic Arab crises and troop concentrations were fairly standard phenomena; that full-scale response to each
and every crisis was not feasible. In a postwar address, al-Sadat
produced this interpretation of previous crises:

> We had to have a coverup for the three groups of dates we thought
> suitable for battle. For each group of days we used to make
> preparations for a complete battle....As Dayan said after the war,
> the other side took these preparations seriously at first. It spent
> funds on preparing its forces vis-a-vis our deceptive operations. As
> you know, spending funds is very painful for the Israelis....After
> going through this twice, Dayan and his friends gave up, considering
> our preparations as nothing more than agitation and solely intended
> for local consumption. (113)

Secrecy was maintained by rigidly controlling the number of people
with knowledge of the attack. According to Arab sources, less than
eight heads of state apart from al-Sadat and al-Asad were utlimately
informed. Initially, only the two Presidents, Field Marshal Isma'il and
General al-Jamasy knew of the decision. (114)   Later, the Egyp-
tian/Syrian Joint Military Command Council was brought in along with
both respective planning staffs.   However, aside from personnel
immediately engaged in the planning, only the following were informed,
and not all equally so: Hourari Boumedienne, Faysal, Husayn, 'Arafat,
Hasan II, the Iranians, and to some extent, al Qadhafi. (115)
Boumedienne and Faysal were kept continuously informed; King
Hasan was brought in sometime before July 1973, at which time
Moroccan troops were dispatched to Syria. Faysal and Husayn were told
of the general play to attack, but not of the actual date. In a later
interview, Husayn remarked with some annoyance:

> We were surprised by the resumption of military preparations at a
> time we considered ourselves in the heart of the case which is the
> case of our people. (116)

'Arafat was informed some three days in advance, at which time he
installed himself in Fatah Headquarters in Damascus. (117) However,
the Palestinians were aware of the impending attack for some time
prior to 'Arafat's move (see below):

> It is no secret that we of the resistance were aware of Egypt's and
> Syria's intention to fight a few months before October 1974. The
> military coordination in this area was wide open to the extent that
> we placed all our fighting abilities under the Egyptian chief
> commander. We were informed of the starting date of the war a
> few days beforehand.... (118)

Iranian Foreign Minister Abbas 'Ali Khalatbari was told of Egyptian plans during his visit to Cairo in September. (119)   Al-Qadhafi, apparently, was originally scheduled to play a major role in the war. Al-Sadat sent him a letter early in the year requesting the Libyans to:

1. Prepare Tobruk port to be an alternative to Alexandria and an auxiliary to it.

2. Contract for spare parts and the ground equipment needed for the Mirage squadron, because without this equipment, the Mirages would be of no use in the fighting.

3. Pledge to supply us (sic: the Egyptians) with four million tons of oil over a period of one year from the beginning of the fighting, because at the start of the battle we would close all the oil wells we have, and because these quantities could not be stored before the battle.... (120)

Al-Qadhafi's response to these requests was not wholly satisfactory, particularly concerning payment for spare parts for the Mirages:

As for the equipment of the Mirage squadron, there was a delay in the payment until June 1973. We used to hear in whispers that the excuse was our lack of seriousness of purpose.... (121)

Nevertheless, al-Qadhafi was aware of Egyptian/Syrian planning and openly disapproved of it, leading to the possibility of a major security leak. Al-Sadat described the situation, beginning with a paraphrase of his earlier letter:

....However, all this and many other things (sic: Libyan knowledge of Egyptian efforts to secure arms for the projected attack) could not change your doubting tone. Indeed, this doubting - and I can almost say sabotage - reached a strange stage when the colonel (al-Qadhafi), who had information the secrecy of which he should have at least respected, delivered a public speech weeks before the battle, in which he declared his disavowal of the battle plans which Syria and Egypt were preparing and predicted a calamity. I need not explain the effect of such a public speech by an Arab head, whose close relationship with us is known by all, on the morale of the soldiers and officers who were preparing to fight.... (122)

As a consequence, al-Sadat was forced to ask Faysal to make up the Libyan's financial aid, and al-Qadhafi was excluded from further participation:

When the hour came, we had to enlist the help of the Kingdom of Saudi Arabia to expedite the purchase of this equipment. The Kingdom of Saudi Arabia actually paid - thanks to it - the price of this equipment, which (ironically) Libya has obtained part of.... (123)

Later, after a particularly acrid outburst by al-Qadhafi in which he attacked Egyptian/Syrian conduct of the war, (124) al-Sadat dismissed the Libyan's role with this comment:

There was no need to notify Colonel Mu'ammar al-Qadhafi. Since he declared before the start of battle, and after it started, on the radio station on October 8, and in the Lebanese press, that he was innocent of all this and did not approve of the plan.... (125)

However, up to the final moment, only al-Sadat, al-Asad and Ahmad Isma'il knew of the target date. And even here, al-Asad was only to be informed of the hour of the attack upon receipt of the code word, "Badr," which Ahmad Isma'il conveyed to him:

But now I want to tell you that we maintained secrecy to the extent that D-day, when it was decided upon, was, in principle, known to two men - only myself and the President. And even when we began the countdown from D-day, a month before the start of operations - D minus 30, D minus 29, D minus 28 and so on - the secret was still restricted....As Commander in Chief of both fronts, on September 30 I sent the Syrians a signal warning them that the operation might start at any time, on receipt of the signal "badr"....I myself went to Syria on October 2 and we discussed the timing of the operation, and, after detailed study endorsed by President Hafiz al-Asad, H-hour was fixed for 1400 hours.... (126)

Senior Egyptian officers were briefed on the attack at a Supreme Council meeting on October 1; some naval commanders were issued sealed orders earlier in September; some local army and air force commanders were informed about 48 hours in advance; the troops themselves were told 10 to 15 minutes in advance; some air force units were given their orders just before takeoff:

A few days before D-day, these details were passed on to the Army Commands, then to the divisional commanders, the brigade commanders and the battalion commanders...Some of the soldiers who were in the vanguard of the attack knew about it 48 hours before; others were told on the morning of D-day.... (127)

The basic deception plan was to take advantage of the cover provided by annual late fall and early summer manuevers along the Canal and in the Golan. Actual troop movements (which could not be concealed) were coupled with a barrage of fake orders, news stories and rumors designed to mislead Israeli intelligence:

We prepared a watertight plan for camouflage that was put into effect with great precision...The last three days were especially difficult...but we did not expect the enemy to be taken in the way he was... (128)

Among these deceptions were:

a) Attempts to conceal the extent of troops and material moving to the front:

When we began mobilization, as I knew the enemy was carrying out reconnaissance every day, I would dispose a brigade in the field, for example, and then at night withdraw a battalion, so that the enemy would think that the forces deployed had been engaged in a training operation which they had completed, and then returned.... (129)

b) Stories put out to the effect that Arab forces could not man sophisticated Soviet weaponry:

Another part of the strategy of deception was the report that was leaked out after the departure of the Soviet experts from Egypt. The report was purposely leaked out to the West and Israel...The report said that the missiles and complicated technological weapons in the Egyptian army had become useless with the departure of the Soviet experts...It was so "well served" that the West and Israel believed it. They slept peacefully, believing that we were finished technologically.... (130)

c) The use of news stories concerning a possible Israeli attack as a cover for Egyptian/Syrian troop movements and alerts: The stories, themselves, focused on Israeli redeployments in the Sinai and Golan; deployments which could have been in response to Arab movements (although the London Times claimed the Israelis were actually contemplating an attack).   Syrian forces in the Golan were initially deployed in a "defensive" configuration; armor being dug in to static positions, much like the 1967 deployment of Arab forces. The Egyptians added an elaborate wrinkle to this configuration. An al-Akhbar reporter described it:

We had to exert superhuman efforts, and our plan included 61 camouflage items, the funniest of which was perhaps the "lazy squads" - soldiers who sucked sugar cane, ate oranges and bathed in the canal waters just before the crossing started... (131)

d) Other news stories were spread concerning activities that would draw attention away from the troop buildup. The Egyptians published information that reservists called up for the fall maneuvers would be allowed time off to return home in order to perform the "Little Pilgrimage." Israeli intelligence was also allowed to acquire a bogus secret order for the discharge of reservists recently called to active duty. Still other stories were floated describing the forthcoming visit of the Rumanian Minister of Defense. Finally, in the week immediately preceding the attack, the Egyptians mounted an operation in Europe designed to create the impression that al-Sadat was going to be out of the country from October 6 onward:

In the first week of October, under a tight veil of contrived secrecy, a group of Egyptian intelligence officers flew to Paris under the pretext of seeking a quiet resort near Orly Airport. It was specified that this resort should be fitting to house a high level Egyptian personality during a recuperation period that was intended to be top secret - even from the ears of the Egyptian people. Our officers floated whispers that they deliberately wanted to reach Israeli intelligence's ears that Egypt did not want the visit to be official or even semiofficial. Of course Israeli ears monitored this and also learned that this leading Egyptian personality was scheduled to arrive on October 6th.... (132)

In addition to this operation, stories were circulated to the effect that al-Sadat was going to visit the United Nations in October. This story was given added plausibility by presenting al-Sadat's moves as a logical extension of the mini-Summit diplomacy: the trip to New York was said to be in coordination with King Faysal; and there was a suggestion that King Husayn might accompany al-Sadat. (133)

e) The Eagles attack in Austria may have been designed to draw Israeli attention away from the Middle East. Indeed, one of the reasons put forward for the so-called Israeli "intelligence failure" is that Israeli intelligence manpower was heavily committed in Europe and elsewhere in dealing with Palestinian international terrorists. The timing of the raid, however, raises some problems. Since it was launched some two weeks after the Syrian/Israeli air battle, it could logically be construed (at least insofar as the Israelis were concerned) as a Syrian response to the defeat. Therefore, it was more than likely that the Israelis would respond by some military action against Syria. And since the Syrians were planning a surprise of their own, it does not seem to make sense that they would want to trigger an Israeli preemption - and there is evidence that Arab leaders were very concerned about the possibility of just such a preemption. (134)

However, there are some alternative theories, so far without any hard evidence to make them more than that. First, the raid was designed to do just what it did and raise the possibility of an Israeli attack. In turn, this possibility would either serve as a cover for Arab military movements already in progress, but which now could be pictured as a response to this threat. Or, it might genuinely have been a Syrian attempt to create a crisis of sufficient magnitude to force the Egyptians to set the date for the attack. Up to this point a number of dates had been discussed and rejected. It is just possible that the Syrian leadership had come to the conclusion that the Egyptians would not act, and needed to be prodded into action. Second, the raid might have been an independent phenomenon: There is some evidence that the Eagles' plan of attack was worked out between al-Sa'iqa and other terrorist groups, notably the BSO and PFLP. (135)

Arab commentators were, naturally, delighted by the success of these measures. In one of a series of postwar articles, Haykal analyzed the surprise that the Arab forces were able to achieve. The Israelis, he argued, were possessed of the belief that the Egyptians would never dare to begin a new war, that the Bar-Lev line was capable of stopping the indifferent troops that Arab armies would field, that the IDF was capable of crushing any Arab force that did get across, and that Arab governments were unable to coordinate their military activities. Further, they were bitterly divided among themselves over the forthcoming elections. Thus, they were both supremely confident about their military situation, and totally absorbed in domestic politics.

Even so, the Arab surprise was not complete: Strategically, the Israelis were surprises; Israel failed to obtain information beforehand concerning the Arabs' intention to attack, the scope of the attack, and its objectives. Tactically, however, the Israelis saw indications that fighting might break out along the Egyptian and Syrian fronts, and made an estimation of the possibility of Arab military operations set to begin on the evening of October 4. This estimate was the subject of controversy.

Senior Israeli officers held that the forces massed along the Syrian front were due to the general tension which followed the Syrian-Israeli air battle of September 13, that the massing of Egyptian forces was either a show of solidarity with the Syrians (sic: like 1967) or the result of annual fall exercises. A group of younger officers opposed this view, arguing that the size of the forces were larger than before, and that it was not possible to determine whether they were deployed offensively or defensively. Senior opinion held sway until October 4, when the Israelis received word that the possibility of an Egyptian/Syrian attack was immediate. This information accurately fixed the attack for sunset, October 6 (i.e., the original zero hour). Electronic and air reconnaissance data received on October 4/5, confirmed this information.

The matter was referred to higher levels: Meir, Dayan, Elazar, and others debated the issue. The military evidence was clear, but they found it difficult to believe. They decided to contact the United States, both for confirmation and to get a Russian warning to Egypt/Syria. A preeemptive air strike was considered, but not ordered. As for the United States, the CIA could not give Kissinger definite confirmation of Israeli conclusions. Nevertheless, Kissinger informed President Nixon, and contacted the Soviets. The Soviet Ambassador to Egypt attempted to contact al-Sadat, but he was already in the operations room.

The morning of the 6th, the Israelis again discussed an air strike. They decided that it was too late to order such an attack. The Egyptians had built up formidable air defenses; there was no surprise element; Israeli aircraft would be exposed to heavy losses. Even at this late date, the Israelis remained convinced that the Egyptians would change their minds, or bungle the attack, or be easily thrown back. They intensified contacts with the United States, ordered up reserves, and issued alert instructions. The Israeli command post at Umm Khasib in the Sinai was sending out warning signals when it was hit by missiles. The time was 1400 and the surprise had been accomplished. (136)

According to Ahmad Isma'il, this surprise on the Egyptian front was virtually complete: (137) Israeli communications from frontline units indicated complete surprise and confusion. Israeli return fire was initially aimless (firing either on their own units or on empty desert); the first Israeli counterattacks were disorganized. (138) On the Syrian front, however, the Israelis were alerted: Al-Asad later indicated that captured Israelis were unanimous in declaring that their command knew of the impending attack, and made preparations to confront it. (139)

Air War: The Missile Defense

The primary concern of both Egyptian and Syrian strategists was to avoid a repetition of the 1967 destruction of their air forces, and consequent Israeli control of the air space over the battlefield. This problem of having to defend against Israeli air bombardment had been a constant worry:

> When I asked Ali Boghdadi, the Commander of the Air Force, what does it mean to supply Israel with 40 Phantoms and 80 Skyhawks, he told me it means Israel would be able to make between 1000 and 1200 sorties per day. We are military men and cannot calculate haphazardly, I must prepare my people for 1000 and 1200 sorties. (140)

It was also equally clear that Arab air forces were no match for the Israelis. This lesson had been driven home again in September according to al-Nahar's thinking:

> The air battle earlier this month showed Syria to be suffering from the same problem - namely the lack of electronic and radar equipment for the early detection of Israeli aircraft. Assessment ot the battle has shown that the Syrian planes were drawn into an Israeli trap. The Israeli planes that the Syrians thought they were attacking were a few, but numerous enemy jets which the Syrians were not able to detect were apparently flying at a very high altitude. When the dog fight developed, these Israeli jets descended on the Syrian aircraft and shot them down. (141)

(The Syrians had a different version of this air battle. See below).

The solution chosen by the Egyptians and Syrains was threefold: a) To protect their aircraft by constructing concrete hangars; b) to deploy an extensive air defense system composed of SAM-2, 3, 6, and 7s and ZU 23-4 guns to protect ground forces; c) to utilize available air forces in ground support roles, engaging Israeli aircraft only as a last resort.

Much of this system had been installed in Egypt during the "War of Attrition." (142) Syrian installations were considerably newer, being constructed mostly in June 1973. The SAM6s around Damascus were reported emplaced in June. (143) The Guardian estimated that the Egyptians had 130 fixed SAM sites to the Syrian's 12, a comparison which gave an idea of the relative density of the two systems. (144) Efforts were made by both Egyptians and Syrians to conceal the true extent and location of these defenses. The Egyptians utilized dummy sites; the Syrians favored mobility, moving SAMs around to confuse Israeli targeting. (145)

The Syrians, in fact, claimed that much of their initial success in destroying large numbers of Israeli aircraft was due to a clever ruse which involved repositioning their missiles. L'Orient Le Jour carried a story to the effect that the major reason for the heavy Syrian air losses on September 13 was a Syrian decision not to expose the positions of these missiles by firing them at the Israeli jets. Instead MIG-21s were assigned to engage the Israelis, regardless of losses. The idea was to give the impression that the missiles were in fixed emplacements. They were then repositioned; when the Israelis attacked what they thought were missile sites, they were caught unaware and shot down. (146) According to Talas, Syrian air defense techniques were unexpectedly successful:

> We had hoped that we could shoot down one Israeli plane for every Syrian plane or even two planes shot down. But the result was astounding. We shot down three Israeli planes for every two Syrian planes shot down. We shot down 91 Israeli planes (sic: a substantial revision of the initial Syrian claim of 157 Israeli planes downed in the first 5 days) for 64 Syrian planes shot down. (147)

Eyewitness accounts from the Golan tended to bear out Talas that the missile defense was successful in forcing Israeli aircraft to fly too high for accurate bombing:

> We had no trouble at all from the Israeli air force this time. They flew too high and were unable to harm us. (148)

> The crucial difference between then and now was the Israeli air supremacy in the last war. We never had an opportunity to fight then, but now there was no Israeli air domination and we were able to put up a great fight. (149)

> SAM, nothing but SAM. Believe all that is said about SAM. (150)

On the Sinai front, the Egyptians reported similar success in defending against Israeli air strikes. When asked why the Israelis failed to destroy Egyptian bridges, Shadhili replied:

> First, I would like to say that the crossing operation would not have succeeded without the air defense and missile network covering the area. The air defense umbrella provided protection for the efforts exerted by infantry and engineers. The enemy's air attacks were severe and successive....they did hit some points, but military bridges are constructed from linked parts which can be replaced. Repairing a birdge usually required between half an hour and a full hour. We moved bridges from one location to another to confuse enemy pilots who had specific reconnaissance information. Heavy smoke screens were created to make aim even more difficult, while

dense anti aircraft fire contributed further to this. The enemy was using extremely low flying attack tactics in attacking bridges, and the SAM-7 rockets proved a magnificent success in downing numerous raiders. (151)

Nevertheless, Israeli air strikes caused considerable damage on both Egyptian and Syrian fronts. Although forced by Jordanian and Lebanese fire to attack Syrian air defenses directly, rather than laterally, Israeli aircraft were able to suppress the Syrian missile system: especially after the destruction of the Baruk radar site in Lebanon which provided the Syrians with critical early warning. Syrian spokesman later admitted that Israeli bombing of strategic targets within Syria had been effective. Syrian economic losses were estimated at $650 million; oil installations at Banias and Tartus were bombed, as were power stations at Homs and Hama, airports, and communications facilities. (152)

The Syrians discounted their own inability to hit Israeli heartland installations by arguing that a counterforce strategy better suited their military objectives:

...Any of our pilots could have dropped his bombs on any town in the occupied lands, to destroy its houses. But our feeling of our ability, our self confidence and awareness that our principal objective is to liberate the occupied lands made us concentrate our attacks against the enemy's war machine.... (153)

The Egyptians, likewise, admitted to considerable losses in and around the Canal Zone, but turned this into a propaganda advantage of sorts by paralleling Syrian accusations that these were strictly civilian targets. If the Egyptians had wished to hit similar targets in Israel, according to al-Sadat, they could have done so by using their missiles (in this case, the Zafir "Triumphant," which the Egyptians claimed was operational). (154)

Egyptian and Syrian Air Forces did, however, play a significant role during the initial attack: 222 Egyptian and 100 Syrian aircraft hit Israeli targets. (Syrian Air Force units had been practicing in preparation, just prior to the Syrian/Israeli air battle of September. (155) Egyptian aircraft attacked in two waves, preceding the opening artillery barrage: the first wave hit Israeli communications centers; the second bombed Israeli ground forces. (156) According to the Egyptians, these attacks were low level and extremely accurate:

I stood there dazzled and forgot myself, because I was watching the pilots swooping down on the tanks, one after another and with complete ease, taking accurate turns, striking and then going up, followed by another and so on. Every attack was followed by a column of smoke. (157)

Throughout the rest of the war, Arab air forces played a minor role, although Syrian (and Iraqi) aircraft continued to engage Israeli air and ground forces, suffering heavy losses as a consequence. Egyptian aircraft remained largely inactive until forced to come out in force to help defend against Israeli advances after October 15. Egyptian jets then engaged the Israelis in extensive air battles, at which time they, like the Syrians, suffered heavy casualties. During these battles, the Egyptians claimed their pilots fought with great courage and achieved at least 7 sorties per aircraft per day. (158)

Ground War: The Hedgehog Tactic

Syrian forces stationed along the Syrian/Jordanian border were moved to the Golan on/before September 28. Jordanian troops then moved over to cover the Syrian left flank, taking up positions in the Umm Kamal area. Moroccan units were deployed on the Syrian right in the Golan. On October 2, the Syrian army went on extreme alert, followed by the Egyptians and Jordanians; the Syrians also began calling up reserves. (159) On the night of October 5, Egyptian patrols made their final reconnaissance of the Bar-Lev line. Egyptian frogmen cemented shut pipes designed to spray napalm on the canal surface, a tactic which, according to Shazili, was arrived at only after considerable experimentation:

> At first we thought that it would have to be extinguished, and we conducted experiments, with this end in view, in places similar to the Canal. But it became clear to me that immense efforts would be required....We then started thinking along the lines of making it impossible to use this material before the crossing....reconnaissance of all the enemy's preparations showed that he kept this material in large tanks buried underground so that it would be difficult to destroy them by artillery fire. These tanks were connected to underwater pipes so that the inflamable material could be forced to the surface of the water. Thus it was clear that if it was possible by any means to close these pipes...there would be no fire. (160)

Preceded by the air strikes, the ground assault began at 1400/1405: Syrian and Egyptian artillery opened fire; Special Forces and other airborne troops were dropped behind Israeli lines to disrupt communications. The Egyptian bombardment was especially intense; some 2000 artillery pieces fired successive salvos designed to pin down the Israeli defenders:

> ....After the aircraft passed over the canal, our artillery began bombarding all the enemy positions in the Bar-Lev as well as his tactical and mechanized forces in the rear for 53 minutes. The bombardment then stopped until the enemy forces came out of their shelters. They surprised once more with artillery shelling. This operation was repeated several (sic: 4 salvos in all, according to Ahmad Isma'il) times so that when our forces crossed the canal the enemy forces did not come out...The enemy believed that the periodic suspension of shelling was an effort to "hunt" him with artillery, but he was surprised by the waves of the first forces which crossed the canal... (161)

In the Golan, three infantry divisions supported by two armored divisions stormed forward in three echelons. The leading echelon consisted of mixed infantry and armor, along with bulldozers and bridge crossing equipment. The weight of the Syrian attack was in the southern sector of the Golan, to both avoid Israeli strongpoints there and to take advantage of the easier terrain to the south (Moroccan troops were assigned to the north). The tactical disposition of Syrian forces followed more or less standard Soviet procedure: armor to the front, infantry to the rear, the whole advance moving behind an enormous artillery barrage. (162) Arab sources estimated that the Syrians committed forces sufficient to give them an 8-to-1 initial advantage; Western sources gave figures of 900 to 1200 tanks, 45,000 men. (163)

Syrian tactics called for bypassing Israeli positions, driving as far into the occupied Golan Heights as possible, and later eliminating bypassed Israeli positions. The Israeli outpost on Mt. Hermon was taken by airborne Syrian units; Syrian ground forces split, bypassing al-Qunaytira, turning north and south to execute a pincer movement around this town. By October 7, Syrian forces had pushed to the pre-1967 lines, in the Lake Tiberia area somewhat beyond them, in heavy fighting:

> On the first day, we destroyed the enemy's fortifications in Sinai and the Golan and, afterwards, fighting fiercely, aiming primarily at destroying the enemy's forces on the land and in the skies...our forces managed to liberate Jabal al-Shaykh, al-Qunaytira, Jabin, Jukhdar, Rafid, Tal al-Faras, and other villages in the Golan.... (164)

By the 8th, however, Israeli forces had regrouped and begun to counterattack; the Syrians were halted. Israeli units then managed to break through the Syrians in the north (where the Syrians never had much success, in any event). According to the Iraqis, the reason for the Israeli breakthrough was because Syrian strategists had never understood the problems of movement and logistics in the Golan:

> ...The battle plans drawn up by the Egyptian and Syrian regimes...would have led to a definite military disaster on the northern front after five or six days of fighting....After the Syrian forces had stormed areas in the Golan Heights during the first and second days of the war, they found themselves...surrounded by an enemy defensive antiarmor missile network as well as by armor...The enemy launched a counteroffensive bringing it to the outskirts of Damascus....(165)

Syrian forces began an orderly retreat, reinforced by Iraqi troops on the 10th (the Iraqis later claiming that their intervention had saved the Syrians from defeat), and Jordanian troops on the 13th. Syrian, Iraqi, and Jordanian units managed to stabilize the front at the Sa'asa line, and were able to fight a static "war of attrition". However, in the post-mortem after the war, al-Asad was at great pains to explain the reasons for the Israeli breakthrough, and at the same time to scotch rumors that the breakthrough was the result of Druze treachery. The story had

spread, aided by Israeli radio broadcasts, that a Druze Colonel in charge
of the northern sector had refused to advance when ordered. The
political implications of such a story in terms of anti-Druze hostility;
Druze-'Alawi conflict; anti-Shi'a/anti-regime Sunni hostility were
enormous and ominous:

> But when the fighting developed, and the enemy threw in the
> fighting, his huge reserves of equipment, and the continuous supplies
> from the United States, Israeli superiority reached a percentage of
> seven to one and sometimes ten or fifteen to one. In view of this
> superiority...the breakthrough on the Damascus axis was realized. I
> was in the operations room when the commander of the post
> telephoned to say that the enemy had broken through his position,
> and that he would continue to fight until the end...I hailed his
> courage, asked him to remain steadfast and promised speedy
> reinforcement.   And this is what actually happened.   The brave
> leader was martyred - the brave leader about whom the enemy
> spread lies, and said he was court martialed and executed... (166)

In the Sinai, Egyptian troops executed a textbook operation: under
cover of the artillery barrage, al-Sa'iqa units blew holes in the
embankments on both sides of the Canal; before the smoke from these
charges cleared, 100 men in rubber boats swarmed across the Canal:

> If only you had seen how impetuous they were. If only you had seen
> them as, with flags in their hands, they crossed the bridges under
> heavy fire. If only you had seen them storming the fortified
> positions with their own bodies before they used their arms - if you
> had seen all this you would have been amazed....

> (They) shot off like arrows as soon as they heard the order to cross,
> paying no attention whatsoever to what was coming from the other
> bank. Rubber boats in which we crossed were moving with the speed
> of a motor boat because of the frantic rowing of our men....

> I never thought the battle field would be easier than the training
> field, but this is the way it was. Do you know that we crossed the
> canal while we were still fasting - vowing to take our iftar (first
> meal after sunset on Ramadan) meal on the eastern bank. (167)

Egyptian engineers using high pressure water hoses made 60 gaps in
the embankments; they installed ten bridges and fifty ferries in six to
nine hours. Infantry carrying lightweight packs and utilizing hand carts
to move heavier equipment, crossed the canal and set up a defensive
line on the east bank: the first Israeli fortification was taken in 12
minutes. (168)   Egyptian losses, which were expected to be in the
neighborhood of 10 to 15,000 for the crossing operation, were less than
200. (169)   Armor and other vehicles followed the infantry; the first
vehicles moved across the Canal in a little over two hours after the
start; 2nd army units moved across as planned, but 3rd army units were
delayed by a combination of difficulties in breaking through and traffic
jams caused by armor getting stuck in the sand.   Nevertheless, the
Egyptians moved large forces across in 24 hours:

On October 6 and 7, we moved five divisions to the eastern bank of the Canal, including three from the 2nd army and two divisions to the south from the 3rd army, and an armored brigade with each division and another armored brigade toward Port Said opposite al-Qantara al-Sharqiya. (170)

These units were reinforced at night, and dug in to engage in what an al-Nahar reporter described as the "hedgehog" tactic:

The Egyptian forces play the role of the "hedgehog" who concentrates strongly on fortifying himself. He advances slowly while, in certain instances, he allows the Israeli "snake" to advance so that he can effectively attack it... (171)

In practice, this tactic meant that Egyptian infantry took up positions in front of the Egyptian armor, dug in, and waited for Israeli armored counterattacks. In the first few days of the war these tactics were extremely successful - until the Israelis changed their own tactics and began to send in infantry along with armor to neutralize Egyptian defenders. Except for a large scale attack on the 14th, designed to take Israeli pressure off the Syrians, the Egyptians adhered to this defensive tactic. Israeli forces broke through Egyptian lines on the 15th, the breakthrough giving rise to unofficial stories of Coptic treachery, stories which contained a long term political threat, apart from the military aspect.

The official version of the Deversoir breakthrough was expounded by Haykal: The infiltration began at exactly 1305 local Egyptian time on October 13, when two SR-71A reconnaissance aircraft from Turkey or Greece (the Egyptians later asked the Turkish government for clarification of the reasons why Turkish bases were being used to accommodate spy planes overflying Egyptian territory) (172) broke into Egyptian airspace at an altitude of 25 kilometers and flying at three times the speed of sound. (173) The aircraft flew over Port Said, over the entire Egyptian front, the Red Sea coast, veered over Nag Hamadi, flew over Cairo, recrossed the Egyptian front laterally, and returned to base after overflying the Syrian front. During this flight, they photographed the "seam" between the 2nd and 3rd armies. This information was communicated to the Israelis. (174)

It came at a time when the Israelis were debating their response to the Egyptian canal crossing. Two alternatives were being considered:

a) To continue to fight it out along the entire front to prevent the Egyptians from enlarging their beachhead. But this carried the disadvantages that Israeli forces would be subject to both Egyptian artillery and anti aircraft missiles, and that the area was too constricted to utilize tactics of mobility and encirclement.

b) To avoid the unfavorable situation in which the Egyptian deployment had placed them, and apply the tactic of penetration and encirclement which was more suited to Israeli capabilities. (175)

If the latter alternative were chosen, the best point for such a thrust would be the area where enemy units joined each other:

For, at that point where two armies meet, measures for safe-
guarding this joint must be drawn up in accordance with a document
bearing the signatures of four staff officers from each of the two
armies....It follows that one of the most important and closely
guarded secrets in military operations is that joint where armies link
together for that point, is where the responsibility of one army runs
out and that of another begins, and it is the weakest point in the
front....The enemy was bound to locate that joint eventually by
means of reconnaissance and battle engagements, but the important
factor was when the enemy would be able to do so. It had to be
found at the right moment and not later as that would render the
discovery of no value....Needless to say Israeli forces chose the
latter alternative, and the American SR-71A aircraft were not
promenading over the Egyptian front. (176)

The Israeli crossover began after dark on October 15. The first units
across the Bitter Lakes were Egyptian vehicles captured in 1967 which
Egyptian soldiers mistook as their own units. The Israelis wore Egyptian
uniforms and spoke Arabic. (177)   Even so the surprise was not
complete: PLA units ('Ayn Jalut Brigade) stationed in the area had
reported to their Egyptian counterparts that the Israelis were preparing
a crossing operation. This information was disregarded by Egyptian
officers who reportedly remarked "you must be dreaming"; some of
these officers were later shot. (178) Egyptian military communiques
initially described the breakthrough force as consisting of seven tanks
which were immediately engaged and either destroyed or scattered. (179) Subsequent communiques (180) announced the encirclement
of this force and called upon it to surrender. (181) Nevertheless, there
was a hiatus of over a day before the seriousness of the Israeli crossing
was assessed by the Egyptians. Apparently no one informed either the
2nd or 3rd army commanders or Ahmad Isma'il until sometime on the
16th. (182)
Ahmad Isma'il later gave this account of the breakdown of
command:

....I admit the picture before us was somewhat shaky for several
reasons....The initial reports about the (sic: Israeli) operation were
before me as soon as I returned to my headquarters from the
People's Assembly meeting on October 16. The reports indicated
that a small batch of amphibious tanks had infiltrated....and it was
the conviction of the local command that they could be wiped out
quickly....in fact, the commander did give orders to a sa'iqa
battalion to confront them....A second reason was the reshuffle of
responsibilities which was made among some of the commanders for
emergency factors. This led to an interrupted flow of information....A third reason was that the enemy managed to hide his
tanks....in a fruit growing grove, thus getting through a critical
stage in the operation....I had evidence that assured me that the
enemy had failed in his first attempt to open the loophole and was
about to drop it. This was when we broadcast that we had destroyed
the enemy's infiltrating forces....All the same, the (sic: Egyptian)
forces were alerted; we succeeded in encircling the loophole area
and tried to put pressure on it by all available means.... (183)

Israeli goals were military, psychological, and political. The military objective was to destroy as many of the Egyptian missile sites as possible, to harass the rear of the 2nd and 3rd armies. Psychologically, the aim was to put pressure on Cairo's nerves, to create a situation of panic akin to that of 1967. To this end, Israeli communiques reported Israeli forces as being at so many kilometers distance from Cairo. There was no military value in these communiques, but they weighed heavily on the nerves. (184)

Politically, the crossing was designed to:

1) Coincide with Meir speech to Knesset so she could announce that Israeli forces were operating on western side of canal.

2) Raise morale after shock of Egyptian crossing.

3) Give a false impression of Israeli strength to assert its political power. (185)

Israeli tactics on the west bank consisted of rapid sorties by small groups of tanks which were sent in every direction:

It was a guerrilla war with tanks operating in groups of tens, fives, and even three in many cases, which made their sudden appearance on roads and in front of positions....Another point to be taken into consideration was that Israel was expecting a ceasefire resolution and, therefore, sought to spread out as far as possible, however thinly that might have been, in order that her presence might be felt over the widest possible area. (186)

The Egyptian High Command was apparently thrown into a panic resembling that of 1967, and was split between two alternatives: To either withdraw from the Sinai or to meet the Israeli thrust with available forces on the west bank. Al-Sadat later described the situation in the operations room:

On Friday, October 19, the Deversoir bulge was three days old....On this particular day, at exactly 0010, Marshal Ahmad Isma'il asked me to go to the general command. I went there. It was obvious that there were certain viewpoints regarding the Deversoir bulge. Marshal Ahmad Isma'il, Lt. General al-Jamasi and corps commanders were on one side, and Major General al-Shadhili was alone on the other side. It was the opinion of the Marshal and the rest of the commanders that the Deversoir operation was only a political television theatrical to save Israel's reputation and to affect us psychologically. (187) Al-Shadhili had returned from the front on a mission I had assigned to him concerning the bulge. He returned to say that it was inevitable that we would have to withdraw all (the forces in) the east to preserve the west....Faced with this, and he the Chief of Staff, I must admit that a convulsion shook my command. (138)

Unlike 1967, however, al-Sadat chose to stand fast and avoid what probably would have become a disastrous retreat:

> It ended only when I personally went to the operations room and made the decision that the armies would stay exactly where they were with the understanding that our reserves would deal with the bulge in the west.... (189)

Most Western accounts view the Deversoir operation as the decisive move in the war, the beginning of the collapse and destruction of Egyptian forces. (190) However, Arab commentators have argued that the situation facing the Egyptians was not as desperate as Western sources indicate: That only two divisions of the 3rd army were actually surrounded; that these units were not as hopelessly cut off as described; that most of the 1st army was uncommited and available for an attack on the bulge. (191) The Egyptians, themselves, insist that this was a minor incursion; that it was a "television operation" designed for propaganda purposes; that it was surrounded and would have been quickly destroyed had the Egyptians so desired:

> The view of the Marshal (Ahmad Isma'il) and the other commanders was that the Deversoir operation was nothing but a political television operation to save Israel's reputation, and was doomed to failure. (192)

> Regardless of the size of the force that wanted to cross to the west, that force had only fifteen kilometers wide and was surrounded, with all its arms and equipment, by two complete armies in the east. The operation was totally doomed because the 400 tanks they had in the west were surrounded by 800 tanks, in addition to the forces of the two armies deployed in the east. Their withdrawal after the ceasefire emphasizes this fact. Had their presence been of any value, they would not have withdrawn it at all.... (193)

Naval War: The Bab al-Mandab

Although overshadowed by the land fighting, nevertheless significant naval engagements took place in both the Mediterranean and Red Seas. At the outset of fighting both Egypt and Syria declared areas of both seas to be war zones and asked commercial ships to stay out of them:

> The Mediterranean Sea area north of latitude 33°, 6' and east of longitude 34 is considered a prohibited area. All ships are banned from entering the area and run the risk of being fired upon... (194)

> ...the Arab Republic of Egypt announces that it considers the regional waters of Egypt and Israel and the high seas adjacent to them to be an area of naval operations, defined as follows:

1. The Mediterranean: area up to latitude 33° north and east of longitude 29° 5' east.

2. The Red Sea: area up to latitude 23° north. (195)

In these areas, a series of naval battles took place between Israeli and Arab patrol boats. Israeli Reshef and Saar class boats using Gabriel missiles were extremely successful against Osa and Komar class boats using Styx missiles, the relative losses being 13 to 3 in favor of the Israeli units. (196)

In this respect, Syrian naval forces - which were made up of various types of patrol boats - were confined, either by design or tactical necessity, to defensive roles: protecting coastal installations, especially port facilities at Latakia and Tartus, and countering Israeli efforts to cut maritime supply lines between Syria and Russia. (197)

The Egyptian navy, considerably larger, and equipped with destroyers and submarines in addition to patrol boats, played a substantially greater part in the fighting. Its missions were given as:

1. Coastal defense.

2. Support of ground forces; bombardment of strategic targets.

3. Interception and destruction of enemy naval units.

4. Strategic blockage. (198)

As with Egyptian ground forces, naval forces underwent detailed and prolonged training. Planning for naval operations was coordinated with air and ground plans; coordination was also established with Syrian naval forces:

In the light of the operations plan, a plan was drawn up for training under conditions identical to those of actual battle. There was continuous training. We made a point of training under various sea conditions to increase the efficiency of the units. (199)

Like the ground units, also, Egyptian naval units moved into position under the guise of training exercises. (200) Of these, the units blockading the Bab al-Mandab were strategically the most important.

The Israeli declaration that it intended to keep Sharm al-Shaykh, was of great concern to both the Egyptians and the Saudis. Israeli access to the Red Sea threatened both the Sinai and the Eastern Egyptian coast, and Israeli claim to Sharm al-Shaykh implied continued Israeli occupation of the Abu Rudays oil fields. It also threatened the Western coast of Saudi Arabia, and, in the Saudis' minds, their oil resources. This mutual sensitivity to the possibility of Israeli expansion into the Red Sea was one of the factors leading to the Faysal/al-Sadat understanding in 1971.

This concern was intensified by the PFLP's attack on an Israeli chartered tanker, the Coral Sea. The Saudis were especially worried about the implications of this attack for two reasons:

a) The threat by Israel following the attack to resort to security measures to protect its shipping in the Red Sea.

b) The declaration by the PFLP that the attack was also aimed at Saudi Arabia, which the PFLP accused of providing oil for the Israeli pipeline from Elath to Ashelon.

In the Saudi view, any expansion of Israeli activity in the Red Sea would add to the military/naval burden on Saudi Arabia. It would also lead to the possibility of a direct Saudi/Israeli confrontation. As a response, the Saudis began planning an increase in their own naval forces, and pushed for a working arrangement with Egypt concerning the Red Sea. (201)

The Israeli lease of two islands off the coast of Ethiopia (given in Arab sources as Dahlak and Halib) intensified these fears. According to an article published in Ruz al-Yusuf in September 1973(202), Israel and the United States were developing a cooperative maritime strategy to dominate the Red Sea. The United States was said to be vitally interested in controlling the Arabian Peninsula oil fields; hence it was moving to oppose Egyptian/South Yemen efforts to control the Red Sea. In fact, the United States interests were so important that it was considering the overthrow of the South Yemen government, in order to prevent hostile influences from utilizing South Yemen as a jumpoff point for taking over the oil fields. Israel, on the other hand, was concerned to extend its military influence into the area to protect the security of its shipping. Ruz al-Yusuf quoted Dayan on this point:

> The building up of the Israeli navy is part of a plan aimed at building up an Israeli strategic force that can impose Israeli influence and protect it at areas which are far from the region of the principal conflict on the current ceasefire lines.... (203)

The moves in this strategy were listed by Ruz al-Yusuf as:

1. The movement of a United States naval base at Serte to Mussawa in Eritrea, and the installation of a radar network for tracking naval movements in the region.

2. The aforementioned Israeli lease of Ethiopian islands.

3. Purported Israeli plans to settle these islands with Ethiopian News, members of the Falasha tribe.

Ruz al-Yusuf concluded that these twin pressures from the United States and Israel "constitute an immense force of pressure on the Aden government. This is why the near future will always be full of surprises on the lands of South Yemen...." (204)

The blockage was imposed from October 6 to December 2/3. (205) Unlike their dramatic announcement of the closure of the Straits of Tiran, the Egyptians this time did not formally announce the existence of a blockage (although they did claim the right to blockage under international law. See below). Egyptian media, however, played up the fact of the blockade. South Yemen later officially proclaimed a blockade, and in this connection there is some discrepancy as to the South Yemeni role. One story states that the Egyptians contacted the Aden government the day of the attack, and requested it to close the Straits. The South Yemenis are said to have agreed, but to have asked the Egyptians to do the actual blockading, since Yemeni naval forces were insufficient. (206)

Egyptian units, given variously as a destroyer and frigate, two destroyers and two submarines, or a combination of destroyers, submarines, missile and torpedo launches, then enforced the blockade. These were supplemented by North and South Yemeni gunboats and shore batteries. In addition, mines were laid along the coasts; according to Egyptian sources, a small Israeli tanker (2,000 tons) and three troop carriers were sunk by mines off the Sinai coast. (207)

The mission of Egyptian forces was to patrol the area and prevent vessels carrying war or strategic materiels from sailing through the Straits to Eilat. Additionally, these units were to disrupt Israeli Red Sea communications, and stop the Israelis from utilizing oil from the erstwhile Egyptian oil fields in the Sinai:

> Under international law, Egyptian warships in the straits area had a right to intercept any merchant ship...to ask its identity and destination...to board it, search it, and verify its papers and cargo...In case the cargo of the ship consisted of strategic material that would benefit the enemy's war effort, both the cargo and the ship became liable to confiscation....

> Throughout the days of the war, some 200 ships carrying strategic materials, petroleum, and arms shipments from South Africa to Israel complied with such orders....As for ships sailing under the Israeli flag, they avoided the test of passing through the straits from the beginning and were ordered by their headquarters to go around the Cape of Good Hope so as to discharge their cargo in Israeli Mediterranean ports. Naturally, these ships arrived at their destination after the ceasefire... (208)

According to the al-Nahar staff, Egyptian commanders were under orders not to fire on, or at least avoid sinking, any vessels for fear of adverse international reaction. However, al-Ahram later reported that, in fact, Egyptian submarines had sunk two ships, an Israeli 20,000 ton refrigerator ship (early in the war), and a 45,000 ton tanker (whose sinking was not immediately announced). On October 24, a warship (presumably a destroyer - but this is not clear from available accounts) fired a warning shot(s) across the bow of the La Salle, and prevented it from entering the Red Sea. (209)

Arab sources also reported the Egyptian airborne and naval troops took up positions on a number of islands in the Bab al-Mandab, itself. The islands in question were said to be ceded to Egypt by South Yemen for a period of 99 years; Saudi Arabia and Abu Dhabi were to pay the rent.   The Egyptians were apparently considering developing these islands into a permanent naval facility capable of blocking access to the Red Sea for some time into the future.   Thus, reinforcing Egyptian claims to strategic control of the Red Sea, and negating the value of the Israeli held islands. (210)

The second version of Egyptian-Yemeni cooperation concerning the blockade held that Aden was not informed until after the fact, and that, as a consequence, the South Yemenis were seriously worried by the blockade.   This was because the government of Aden found itself in an extremely uncomfortable position.   On one hand, it could not express public indignation at the Egyptian move while every other Arab nation was demonstrating solidarity with the Egytians and Syrians.   On the other hand, there was no benefit to be gained from the blockade, and possibly some long term disadvantages:

a) The blockade could create a major international issue over control of the Bab al-Mandab, leading possibly to some form of internationalization.

b) The blockade raised the possibility of an Israeli strike against Aden itself, a strike the South Yemeni defense forces could not deal with, and one which might severely damage an already shaky economy.

c) The blockade could trigger an increased American presence off the South Yemeni coast. (211)   (South Yemen did, in fact, protest the presence of 7th fleet units off the Bab al-Mandab.) (212)

The blockade was successful in shutting off the port of Eilat: Only one ship entered Eilat - a vessel already in the Red Sea when the blockade was begun. (213)   Ships destined for non-Israeli ports were not stopped . (214) Egyptian spokesmen later quoted an Israeli claim that 13 freighters had been bottled up by the blockade. (215) In analyzing the strategic effect of the blockade, an Egyptian commentator claimed that Eilat handled up to 30 percent of Israeli oil imports, and the bulk of its trade with Africa and Asia, some 20 percent of its entire foreign trade. The blockade therefore had isolated Israel from some of its major markets and sources of fuel: "For Israel Bab al-Mandab is a vital necessity of its economic life...." (216)   Its continuation after the ceasefire provided the Egyptians with additional bargaining lever-age. (217)

Fida'iyin Operations

Palestinian units, both fida'iyin and PLA forces, supplemented regular Arab armies. In most cases, they functioned as an extension of Arab Special Forces, hitting targets behind Israeli lines in both the Golan and the Sinai, providing additional manpower in the Golan. In so doing, they added another dimension to Israeli military problems.

'Arafat, himself, left for South Lebanon a week before the attack, and camps in Lebanon, Syria, and Iraq were alerted for possible action. (218) In this, 'Arafat had agreed to participate in a "modest role" alongside regular Arab armies. (219)   A Fatah force arrived at the Egyptian front on October 3, and fida'iyin forces went on full alert on October 5. (220)   According to Palestinian spokesmen, some 26,000 fida'iyin were mobilized under a unified command to fight on all three fronts.   At least 500 fida'iyin were said to be operating within Israel. (221)

Fida'iyin target selection was the product of a combination of Fatah doctrine, and the requirements of regular Arab tacticians. In the Fatah doctrine Israeli military forces are divided into two categories: the "shield" consisting of paramilitary border settlements, and the "spear," the regular armed forces. The function of the shield is to lighten the defense burdens of the spear, while that of the spear is to strike at regular Arab forces which threatened Israeli security. In line with this analysis, Fatah tactics call for hit and run attacks on settlements; ambushes of patrols; raids on outlying installations. The objective of these tactics is to tie the Israelis down to defensive positions, reduce their mobility, and force the diversion of regular units to protect settlements and the like. In addition, the occupation and holding of defensive positions in Israeli territory is called for, if conditions permit. Here the objective is to nullify the effectiveness of the shield completely and thus compel the spear to move over to a defensive role. (222)

Most of the fida'iyin operations were carried out along the Lebanese/Syrian border. Operations from Jordan were hampered by the Jordanians; 14 operations were carried out, including an attack on a military convoy on the Jerusalem-Latrun road and the destruction of a radar site at Kafr Malik. (223)

Altogether, fida'iyin sources claimed a total of some 200 operation, including attacks on 42 settlements, on convoys, on air fields, on fuel depots, on troop staging points, and on one radar site. (224) In the Golan, three battalions of PLA (Hittin) forces fought alongside Syrian regulars. These were transported by helicopters for action ahead of Syrian forces along with Syrian Special Forces. PLA units operating with the Egyptian army were stationed along the Southern sector of the canal. Their mission was to function as a tripwire should the Israelis attempt to cross the canal (see above). (225) Fida'iyin units struck at the rear of Israeli forces in the Golan. Settlements in the Kiryat Shmoneh area were attacked. (226)   In the Sinai, fida'iyin units operating out of Gaza attempted to cut Israeli supply lines in an area between Khan Yunis and Beersheba. Fida'iyin units crossed over from Jordan to attack targets in the Jerusalem area. Units operating from South Lebanon managed to occupy the heights of abu Ru'us, south of Mt. Hermon. These heights dominated a series of Israeli settlements in northern Galilee. (227) During the battle for Mt. Hermon, fida'iyin joined with Syrian forces in attempting to defend it. (228)

Media War: The Lessons of 1967 Applied

In marked contrast to the verbal exaggerations, threats, and general bombast that preceded the 1967 War, Arab media treatment of the events of October (although not of those of September) was restrained, and for the early stages of the war, at least, relatively accurate and uncensored. This was partly due to Arab analyses of the failings of 1967, partly due also to the necessity of stressing the fact that the Ramadan war was a limited operation: an operation designed only to recover the occupied territories and not to destroy the state of Israel. This was a critical consideration, since the problem was to dislodge an enemy whose own propaganda machinery had successfully promoted the notion in non-Arab minds, at least, that it was only defending itself. And it had garnered the backing of the foremost power in the world, the United States, for its conception of a peaceful solution. The goals of this strategy would logically seem to be the following:

a) To prevent, or at least reduce, the possibility the Israelis would resort to air strikes against Egyptian industrial and civilian targets. (In this connection, al-Sadat's warning to Israel that Egypt had missiles and would use them if the Israelis struck in metropolitan Egypt was a similar attempt.) (229) Although this was the hope of the Egyptian strategists, they were not particularly optimistic that it would succeed. Al-Sadat later remarked, with some exaggeration, that he expected the home-front losses to be in the neighborhood of one million casualties. (230)

b) To forestall, as long as possible, United States intervention on Israelis behalf.

c) To preserve the international support for regaining the lost territories that had been built up by diplomatic means.

d) To prevent a repetition of Arab outbidding on the goals of the war that occurred in 1967, and also to prevent Arab accusations of a "sell out", if and when a ceasefire was arranged, and Arab forces had not moved into Israel. This charge that the Egyptians had accepted a ceasefire too soon was, in fact, made by Libya and Iraq.

e) To restore Arab credibility, both domestically and in the international arena.

From the Egyptian point of view, the guidelines for this strategy were laid down in the April 21, 1973 policy program of the Egyptian Cabinet:

Information media have had great and delicate responsibilities before, during, and after the battle; in view of these responsibilities, the government has paid special attention to these media. The government is intent that these media reflect our clear battle strategy, and confront the methods of psychological warfare launched by the enemy's media....The government will also extend every available assistance to the press to facilitate its effective role in this phase of confrontation.... (231)

Immediately after the announcement of the Egyptian/Syrian attack (which echoed the 1967 Israeli claim that the other side had moved first), (232) a communique was sent to all Arab League offices which set forth the official rationale action:

In a final analysis, Arab action is justifiable, moral and valid under articla 51 of the Charter of the United Nations. There is no aggression, no attempt to acquire new territories. But to restore and liberate all the occupied territories is a duty for all free, self-respecting, peoples. (233)

This theme of commitment to a limited war designed solely to recover Arab territories only was repeated by al-Sadat in the course of an October 16, 1973 speech:

Firstly, we made war for the sake of peace. We have made war for the only peace that is entitled to be described as peace - a peace based on justice.

Secondly, we did not make war for the sake of aggression against the territory of others. We made war, we are making war for two objects: to recover our territories which were occupied in 1967, to find a way to recover the rights of the people of Palestine and to ensure that they are respected. It was with these goals in view that we accepted the risks of fighting. We accepted them in reply to intolerable provocations. It was not we who started it; we were defending ourselves, our territory, our right to freedom, and life. Our war is not for the sake of aggression, but against aggression.

We are ready to accept a ceasefire on the basis of an immediate withdrawal of Israeli forces from all occupied territories, under international supervision, to the pre-June 1967 lines.

We are ready, as soon as the withdrawal from all these territories has taken place, to attend an international peace conference at the United Nations.... (234)

Al-Asad echoed this theme in the course of an address carried by Syrian radio and TV on the evening of the 6th:

Brother citizens, our brave men, nco's, and officers, sons of our brave people: While greeting every one of you, I address your noble Arab spirit today - the spirit of courage, heroism and sacrifice - I address the love of the homeland with which you were brought up, and your faith in the cause that you are determined to defend....For a week or so the enemy has been concentrating and preparing, believing that he could deal us a treacherous blow. We were alert and vigilant, watching the enemy's movements and activities. We were getting ready to repel his latest aggression....We are not fond of killing and destruction. We are defending ourselves against death and destruction. We are not aggressors and have never been so. But we have been, and still are, defending ourselves against aggression. We do not desire anyone's death, but are defending our people against death....Today we are defending ourselves so that our people will enjoy their freedom....Today we are defending ourselves in order to live in peace.... (235)

Arab media presentation of events was remarkably restrained, with the exception of some battlefield claims (especially by the Syrians). (236) Western newsmen were allowed access to the battlefronts, in a self conscious effort to offset Israeli reportage - in line with the conclusions reached concerning media failings in 1967. Efforts were made to produce actual evidence of claims: photographs, prisoners, and wreckage. Egyptian information policy was governed by two principles laid down by Ahmad Isma'il:

a) That all information possible should be communicated without disclosing anything injurious to national security.

b) That whatever was disclosed "must be true or - let me be frank with you - it must be near the truth." (237)

The reasoning behind this was:

I knew from the start that a great part of success in the war depended on people having confidence in what we said we were doing, and I therefore demanded strict adherence to this principle in the framing of communiques.... (238)

In this connection, there was considerable Arab sensitivity to Western accounts of the fighting. Early in the war, the Arab World noted, with some relish, that Western news sources had begun to doubt the credibility of Israeli statements, while at the same time being impressed with Arab handling of press relations. (239) Later, when Western sources began to carry news of Israeli successes, the Arab League Office in London submitted a note to the BBC protesting its pro-Israeli slant. (240)

Morale and Discipline:
Modern Weapons and Traditional Values

By all accounts, both Arab and Western, the morale and discipline of Arab troops was extremely impressive and remained largely intact throughout the war. Arab renditions of the bravery of their soldiers were, naturally enough, exaggerated. However, Western observers bear out accounts of Arab willingness to fight. (241) Egyptian infantry units readily engaged Israeli armor, accepting heavy casualties in order to get close enough to utilize their relatively short range Sagger and RPG-7s. Even the surrounded 3rd Army units showed little inclination to either desert or surrender (although part of this is due to the fact that their officers had orders to shoot deserters). As one Israeli soldier lamented concerning the attitude of these troops:

> We've drawn them pictures in the sand here when they come over to pick up supplies and we try to show them how they're encircled. But they think they're encircling us.... (242)

Syrian forces fought with an exceptional ferocity. Syrian tank crews refused to abandon disabled equipment, turning their tanks into static firing positions, until ultimately destroyed. Syrian helicopters made suicidal attacks on Israeli armor. In a passage reminiscent of Shakespeare's Henry V, al-Asad described Syrian feats of arms:

> Imagine a mountainous front, 70 kilometers wide, but smaller in depth, in which some 2500 tanks, thousands of artillery pieces, and tens of thousands of soldiers equipped with the latest weapons, are massed....Imagine fierce fighting continuing day and night for days on this narrow front, where men, armor, and planes were engaged in pitched fighting, where no inch of land was devoid of fire, wreckage or victims....That was the Golan battle fought by the Syrian army, which made legendary feats, the greatest in the history of modern and ancient wars. To give you one example, Syrian helicopters, while the fighting went on fiercely, used to land, with their cargo of bombs and soldiers on enemy tanks to destroy them and be destroyed in the process. Our troops used to collide their armored vehicles with the enemy to paralyze their movement, then leap out and engage enemy soldiers in face to face fighting, which sometimes took the form of fist fighting and strangulation. The examples of the courage and sacrifices of our troops are countless... (243)

Even allowing for considerable exaggeration, the reversal of form from 1967 was completely unexpected. Dayan, himself, later admitted that, while he had advance knowledge of the quantity and quality of arms at the Arabs' disposal, his assessments of the effectiveness and fighting ability of Arab forces were mistaken. (244) The question then arises as to why or how this reversal occurred, and to this, a number of tentative answers can be given:

a) Western-Israeli underestimation of Arab military capability, based on the 1967 War: changed Arab military behavior in 1973 appeared the more dramatic because of its contrast with the generally poor conduct of Arab armies in 1967. After that debacle, any improvement would appear all the more impressive because it was unexpected on the basis of past Arab performance. But, it should be noted that Arab forces in 1967 fought under the twin handicaps of being the victims of surprise - hence disorganization - and lack of air cover. Presumably any army, Western or non-Western, would look bad under these conditions. In 1973, Arab forces had the advantage of surprise, and it was the Israelis who were initially disorganized. (245) Nevertheless, some Arab units did fight bravely, but this fact was generally overlooked because of the generalized picture of Arab incompetence. (246)

In addition, Western assessments of 1967 Arab performance were not themselves free from their own historical/cultural context. Western armies had been defeating non-Western troops for over two centuries (Japan is an exception); the legacy of this continued success was (and is) an image of Western superiority. (247) The swift Israeli victory in 1967 merely confirmed the validity of this image. Moreover, this victory was over Arab/Muslim forces that already had an especially negative stereotype in Western eyes, the consequence of centuries of hostile interaction with Christendom. (248) Hence, an unfortunate acceptance of analyses of Arab behavior which made inferential leaps from the fact of military defeat, to the fiction of national cowardice. (249)

b) Clearly defined Arab objectives: Unlike 1967, where both the issues and objectives were clouded, Arab troops fought for clearly defined national, strategic, and tactical objectives. Egyptian and Syrian soldiers knew precisely what was expected of them. Ahmad Isma'il described the essentials of Egyptian indoctrination:

1. The forces should be convinced that fighting was inevitable and that there was no alternative solution without it.

2. The men should have confidence in their arms.

3. There must be intensive training.

4. The forces should be allowed to see with their own eyes what they were going to be up against, so that they would not be afraid of it. (250)

c) The emotional advantage of attack: Arab forces had the initial advantage of being the attackers, for the first time in any campaign; prior to this:

The problem for our forces was that circumstances had obliged us to be on the defensive for six or seven years - most of the time an immobile defensive - and forces in such a situation... are liable to suffer from what is known in military parlance as "trench sickness." We had to rid ourselves of the effects and complexes of trench sickness.... (251)

d) More effective Arab leadership: The widespread incompetence in senior officer echelons, the tendency of higher commands to panic in difficult situations was remedied, to some extent, by the dismissal of large numbers of higher range officers and their replacement by men of demonstrated ability. The gap between officers and men that existed in 1967 was also partially closed, and a reasonably consistent chain of command had been established. In the interwar period, Egyptian military schools in particular had graduated a cadre of young, professional officers, officers who apparently responded to Shadhili's charismatic leadership and sense of mission. But there was clearly more to Egyptian morale building than the creation of cadres of young and dedicated officers: the honor of the officer class was deliberately tied to the success of the Canal crossing by a number of techniques. At the outset of the planning process, al-Sadat took those officers who would be involved to the Egyptian ramparts on the west bank, and made each examine the Israeli fortifications to be attacked. Thus, he associated them with his own policies. During the period of intensive reorganization and training, the theme that Egyptian honor was at stake was a standard feature of Egyptian indoctrination techniques. But, in respect to the officer corps, it was focused on their role as Guardians of Egypt. (252) Later, a more practical device was used: All senior officers were required to cross the Canal within 15 minutes of the start of the fighting, automatically placing them at the head of their men.

e) Arab familiarization with weapons systems and, therefore, confidence in their ability to utilize them: In 1967, Arab forces were only marginally trained in the use of Soviet supplied weapons, especially in terms of aircraft. In addition, Arab logistics capabilities in the sense of being able to keep aircraft and vehicles operational (let alone repair damaged items) was minimal. Moreover, Arab personnel were not familiar with some Soviet equipment that arrived during the crisis. As a result, large numbers of vehicles were abandoned when in need of only minor repair.

Part of the problem was a simple lack of training, but part of it also was the difficulty of combining non-Western troops with culturally alien Western equipment. From the outset, Egyptian planners recognized that overall military strategy and tactics would have to be tailored to the character of the manpower available, i.e., small cadres of highly trained individuals (senior officers with extensive backgrounds, academy graduates, and some pilots), but also large numbers of Egyptian peasants: Peasants who were still very traditional in their outlook and behavior. (253) Ahmad Isma'il described the basic planning mix used:

We come to the subject of Soviet military experience. War is usually the test for any Western or Soviet tactics, and the 1967 War has confirmed several new theories which we benefitted from. Our fighting experience is presently our principal reference in the use of sound Arab-Egyptian tactics... (254)

Unlike Israeli strategists who had for years been able to benefit from ongoing social institutions designed to change traditional behavior, Egyptian planners had neither time nor facilities to engage in large scale modernization programs. (255) Fortunately for the Egyptians, the Soviet equipment utilized by the army had already been adapted to the needs of a peasant based ground combat force. The problem became, therefore, to integrate simple to operate Soviet equipment, e.g., the AKM Assault Rifle, with the existing values and attitudes of the Egyptian peasant, in a manner that would produce an acceptable battlefield performance.

The first area to be remedied was the overall inability of Egyptian troops to handle Russian (or any Western) arms. In 1967 Egyptian forces were only marginally trained in the use of their weapons, and this lack of familiarity contributed greatly to the breakdown in morale. The key here was intensified training at all levels:

> ....I wanted to change the old concept that arms make the man; whereas in fact it is the man who makes the arms. If he has no confidence in himself no arms will protect him, but if he is confident, all the arms he bears will protect him... (256)

The technique chosen was to simplify the skills required of the average Egyptian soldier insofar as equipment operational requirements would permit. Egyptian troops were drilled meticulously on each skill. The attention to detail was impressive, ranging from a calculation of the effects of the weight of equipment each soldier would carry, to the building of full size models of sections of the Bar-Lev defenses for troop exercises. The technique of realistic training was basically Western, basically an extension of Russian training methods. But the learning emphasis was pure Egyptian, a stress on rote memorization which characterizes the entire Egyptian educational curriculum. (257)

Egyptian troops repeated drills until they were memorized. Nothing was left to either imagination or personal initiative; the stress was on mechanical repetition of acquired skills. Drills ranged in scope and complexity from the daily practice of sagger firing to some 1200 full scale water crossing exercises. This rigid and authoritarian approach had both positive and negative consequences: On the one hand, the vast resources of Egyptian manpower were put to military use, but on the other hand, this use had to be tightly structured to fit existing preplanned contingencies. As long as Egyptian troops could operate in a structured and memorized operational environment, they were effective. When they were forced out of it by Israeli tactics, they became increasingly disorganized.

f) Motivation to fight: In 1967, Arab troops lacked any sort of motivation to defend either territory or regime. Sunni Syrian troops could not have been expected to fight well for either the secularist Ba'th regime, or its predominantly Shi'a officer corps. Egyptian soldiers had only the nebulous slogans of Nasirism, an unfocused ideological appeal, to motivate them. Neither secularism nor pan-Arab nationalism had sufficient behavioral linkages with Arab/Islamic culture to provide the emotional impetus to fight.

In an effort to rectify the motivational vacuum, the Egyptians replaced Nasirist appeals with slogans designed to be meaningful in terms of the psychological makeup of the Egyptian peasant soldier. In 1967, Egyptian troops were both confused and unmotivated: Confused because there was no clear definition of what Egyptian national interests were being defended. Unmotivated because the slogans of the Nasirist regime, "Unity, Discipline, Work," required an ideological sophistication and commitment which was irrelevant to the values of the average Egyptian soldier. Not only were these slogans outside of this soldier's immediate personal convictions and concerns, but they were also cast in a Western, rather than Islamic mode. As a consequence, Egyptian troops simply were not motivated in any organized fashion.

In 1973, the motivational appeals were then very much in the Egyptian/Islamic tradition: defense of the land, defense of honor, and defense of Islam. All of these were keyed to existing peasant values. Defense of the land tied in with peasant attitudes toward land holding, but stressed that the land in question this time was part of mother Egypt. Photographs showing the first Egyptian troops across the canal kissing the earth testify to the operative success of this motivational theme. Defense of honor presented yet another aspect of traditional Egyptian values. Further, this definition of honor is very much rooted in an aggressive, varrior tradition. Egyptian military communications stressed the theme that Egyptians must regain their lost honor. Two examples will suffice, one from Shadhili, the other from Isma'il:

So let us, together, regain the glory of Arabism and prove to the whole world that we are men of war, who either live proudly or die honorably... (258)

You should know that we are facing an enemy that is beginning to set little store by us, thinking we are not capable of fighting, which makes him rampage in the region without fear of being repelled or punished... (259)

The Islamic theme was also heavily emphasized. From the choice of the name Badr onward, the forthcoming battle was conceived and depicted as a "jihad," a traditional term which connotes a collective defense of the faith. Not only was Badr to be a test of Egyptian/Arab manhood, but it was also to be a reaffirmation of Islam. Indeed, al-Sadat personally replaced Nasirist slogans with that of "Allahu Akbar" (God is Greater), the traditional Muslim battle cry:

There is no foresaking freedom, socialism, and unity. This (slogan) existed before 1967 and will continue to exist after it. This matter is connected with our basic principles. But "God is Greater" was the battle cry, while laying emphasis on the fact that there is a great change in the military moral guidance.... (260)

The Egyptians then tied these traditional appeals together in a sophisticated piece of battlefield psychology. Egyptian assault units that first crossed the canal carried Egyptian flags (in many cases emblazoned with the phrase "Allahu Akhbar"). When these units reached their assigned crossover positions, they planted these flags in locations visible to troops on the Egyptian side. The effect on troops waiting to cross the canal produced by the spectacle of a sea of Egyptian flags suddenly arising on the far bank can easily be imagined. One Egyptian officer commented afterwards:

> As the banners began to rise, it seemed as if a powerful electric current ran through the troops... (261)

Other units shouted this "Allahu Akbar" as they crossed the canal, apparently adding to the existing emotion. Later Shadhili was to comment:

> Did Dayan take into account the moral effect of thousands of men crossing the Canal and shouting in unison "Allahu Akbar"? I do not think he did. (262)

Communications

Although Arab sources naturally do not go into detail concerning communications tactics, it is clear that communications were of great concern. Arab planners attempted to rectify the failings of 1967. Arab forces apparently made extensive use of land lines to prevent Israeli electronic interference. In addition, Egyptian units were directed into position by a system of road markers of different colors, units being instructed to follow a particular color to reach their assigned positions, lessening the necessity for extensive communications traffic before, and during, the attack. (263)

The Egyptians and Syrians appear to have been able to monitor Israeli communications: Ahmad Isma'il indicated an awareness of the content of Israeli messages, (264) and Haykal was informed that Israeli communications centers in the Sinai were broadcasting when the Egyptian attack began. (265) Al-Asad claimed that the Syrians had been able to break Israeli codes during the war. (266)

The Oil Embargo, Incremental Escalation

In al-Sadat's strategic analysis, the oil weapon was the critical factor; the military operation was secondary, designed to create a political situation in which Arab oil producers would have to act. Initial Arab military successes do not seem to have been anticipated, despite the postwar rhetoric; they came as an unexpected bonus. (266) The problem in this connection was two fold: to compel Arab oil states to adopt a unified oil policy vis-à-vis the West, and the United States, in particular; to arrive at an oil strategy which would do the least harm to Arab oil interests, especially Saudi Arabia's.

In terms of inter-Arab politics the form that any oil embargo might take was frought with implications. The Saudis did not want any action

which might disrupt relations with the United States; Kuwayt and the
Trucials were concerned with protecting their United States/European
markets. Iraq and Libya saw the possibility that a blow might be dealt
both against the West and also conservative Arab regimes. (268) At the
same time, all sides were concerned with avoiding the possibility of a
Western military takeover of the oil fields.

The risks and benefits of various oil strategies had already been
analyzed, at some length, in a paper delivered to the Conference of
Arab Economy Ministers in December 1972. According to its author,
Dr. Yusuf Sayigh, the ultimate goal of Arab oil policy was to exert
pressure on countries that have been, or are still, supporting Israel:
specifically, the United States and Britain. Two basic options were
available: total or partial nationalization, or total or partial embargo.
In terms of the second option, embargo, the halting of Arab oil flow
could take either of two forms:

a. It could be withheld from all western companies, and consequently, from their mother countries. This would paralyze the
economies of all western states, including Japan, within a few months.
It would also expose the weakness of the United States, its inability to
provide alternatives to Arab oil. But such a policy would be utterly
unwise and shortsighted. It would risk the high probability of western
military reaction: not necessarily a military blow aimed at all Arab oil
producers, merely an attack on one. Moreover, Russia could not be
expected to intervene to prevent western states from carrying out their
military action: This would create the conditions for a United
States/Russian confrontation, which the Soviets did not seem prepared
to face.

b. It could be withheld from the United States and Britain only, or
even expanded to include West Germany and Holland, all countries
which support Israel more than other European states. With a complete
halt to America's friends in Europe, pressure would then be generated
by these states on the United States: The United States would be "put
in a corner" by its European friends who would be clamoring for oil to
keep their own economies going. Moreover, this was a relatively low
risk policy; withholding oil would simply mean that Arab countries
would refuse to sell their oil to those countries which were hostile to
them. (269)

In order for any one of these strategies to be inaugurated, however,
the necessary political conditions had either to occur, or be created.
This would require:

1. evidence that the United States was directly helping Israel in an
open conflict.

2. a willingness on the part of oil states to risk jeopardizing
relations with the United States. (270)

Both of these conditions were met when the United States began
arms shipping to Israel. Arab media played up news concerning these

deliveries, creating both enormous popular resentment, and steadily intensifying pressure on oil states to act against United States interests. Even so, these states delayed action while their leaders, including Faysal, warned the United States to desist. (271)   Israeli successes in the Sinai (widely interpreted as a direct consequence of United States aid) (272) coupled with the United States declaration that even more equipment would be forthcoming, triggered the Arab response.

On October 17, Arab oil ministers meeting in Kuwayt rejected Libyan and Iraqi demands for the nationalization of United States oil holdings and inaugurated a series of incremental cuts in oil production, opting for a low risk strategy. (273)   The reduction was to be in the form of 5 percent increments, starting at once, and continuing each successive month until

> ...such time as the total evacuation of Israeli forces from all Arab territory occupied during the June 1967 War is completed, and the legitimate rights of the Palestinian people are restored, or until the production of every individual country reaches the point where its economy does not permit of any further reduction without detriment to its national or Arab obligations... (274)

Although an embargo on the United States was discussed, it was made optional (only Libya and the UAE/Abu Dhabi enacting it) - principally at the insistence of the Saudis, who wished to give the United States time to consider its "hostile" attitude toward the Arabs. (275)   On October 20, however, when the United States was clearly not going to alter its policy, the Saudis banned all oil exports to the United States and led the move for a series of embargos. Even here, the approach was extremely cautious: Countries were classified into three categories: (276)

1. hostile, which were subject to embargo.

2. friendly, which conferred exempt or most favored status.

3. neutral, which conferred nonexempt, but nonembargoed status. (277)

In order to get on the "friendly" list, a country had to: (a) break relations with Israel; or (b) apply some economic sanctions against Israel; or (c) afford some military assistance to the Arabs. (278) This combination of embargo and reduction in output was continued until December 1974, when it was ended, except for the United States and the Netherlands. All restrictions were ultimately lifted following the Syrian/Israeli disengagement agreement of May 29, 1974 (the first Egyptian/Israeli disengagement was effected on January 18, 1974): Arab oil ministers meeting in Cairo formally lifted the embargo on July 11, 1974. (279)

Algeria	October 20	10 percent cut United States ban
Behrayn	October 20 October 21 October 30	5 percent ban United States ban Netherlands ban
Kuwayt	October 21 October 21 October 23	10 percent cut United States ban Netherlands ban
Libya	October 19 October 19 October 30	5 percent ban United States ban Netherlands ban
Oman	October 25 October 25	United States ban Netherlands ban
Qatar	October 19 October 21 October 24	10 percent cut United States ban Netherlands ban
Saudi Arabia	October 18 October 20	10 percent cut United States ban
UAE/Abu Dhabi	October 18 October 12	United States ban Netherlands ban
Dubay	October 21	United States ban

Iraq publically disassociated itself from the decisions taken at the October 17 and November 4/5 meetings of Arab oil ministers, and criticized the oil strategy as being both counterproductive and a victory for Saudi Arabia which then directed events "in accordance with United States and reactionary plots." Acting independently, Iraq nationalized the United States (Exxon and Mobil) share of the Basra Petroleum Corporation on October 7, and the Dutch (Royal Dutch Petroleum) share on October 21. It also imposed a destination embargo on the United States and the Netherlands.

Fig. 6.1. Arab oil measures (October 1973).

Sources: Arab World Weekly, October 13, 20, 27, 1973; Arab Report & Record, October 16-31, 1973; Strategic Survey 1973, pp. 30 ff.

CEASEFIRE AND AFTERMATH

In spite of official Egyptian optimism concerning the course of the war, the deteriorating situation was far too uncertain to be tolerated. Even if further fighting went in favor of the Egyptians, there was no reason to jeopardize an already successful operation.

If Egyptian public statements concerning the objectives of the war are accurate indicators, these objectives had been achieved early in the fighting. The Egyptians had managed to cross the canal, the Syrians were holding on at the Sa'asa line, the oil embargo had been instituted. In short, there was nothing further to be gained, either militarily or politically.

Therefore the problem facing al-Sadat and his staff was one of halting the conflict at the most opportune time. In this, there were a number of considerations due to the several factors involved:

1. The Egyptian military which was eager to continue fighting, and opposed to a ceasefire. (280)

2. Egyptian allies, the Syrians and Saudis, who were opposed to an indecisive end to hostilities.

3. Some Arab governments, notably Libya and Iraq, which would use an Egyptian acceptance of a ceasefire to their own political advance vis a vis al-Sadat.

4. Russia, which was pressing for an immediate ceasefire: Kosygin was said to have shown al-Sadat reconnaissance photographs of the front in an effort to convince him of the gravity of the military situation. (281)

5. Still other Arab governments, Jordan and Lebanon, which also wanted a ceasefire, and - in the case of Jordan - whose postwar cooperation would be needed. (282)

Timing, therefore, rather than the acceptance itself, became the critical factor. If al-Sadat stopped the fighting while Arab forces were obviously in the ascendency, he risked being charged with a "sell-out," in much the same manner that 'abd al-Nasir was accused of quitting too soon in 1967. If, on the other hand, al-Sadat delayed too long and the military situation turned too clearly to the advantage of the Israelis, then most of the political benefits of the war would be lost. He might even risk the possibility of another disaster along the lines of 1967.

Therefore, some compelling and face saving reason must be found to justify accepting a ceasefire: United States aid to Israel provided the excuse. The official Egyptian explanation as offered by al-Sadat harked back to 'abd al-Nasir's resignation speech:

Brother Hafiz al-Asad. We have fought Israel for 15 days now. In the first four days, Israel was alone, and we exposed it on the Egyptian and Syrian fronts and they (sic: the Israelis) lost, with their own admission, 800 tanks on the two fronts and more than 200 planes. As for the last ten days, I have been fighting America and its latest weapons on the Egyptian front....To put it simply, I cannot fight America or shoulder the responsibility of having our armed forces destroyed again. (283)

However, if this logic seemed to be true from the Egyptian viewpoint, it most emphatically was not so from that of the Syrians. Where the Egyptians could afford the political risks attendant on protracted diplomatic maneuvering, the Syrians could not. Therefore, the two allies parted company; the differences in their political prospects and strategic positions resurfaced (see above). In a later comment on the Egyptian action, al-Asad minced few words:

In the meantime, we were preparing for a counteroffensive all along the front, after it had become clear to us that the enemy had been weakened to the point of collapse. We were confident that our offensive would yield important and positive results, and we were surprised by the ceasefire. God be my witness that I am not saying this to censure, or ignore the circumstances that necessitated this resolution...But this should not prevent us from admitting the fact that the ceasefire has made the Arabs, and particularly the Syrian army, lose a golden opportunity... (284)

In effect, by laying the full responsibility for events at the door of his major ally, al-Asad was protecting himself. As the ead of the Shi'a dominated government, he could not risk Sunni accusations that the Shi'as had lost yet another war. As leader of a moderate faction within the Syrian Ba'th, he had to justify his actions in response to radical Ba'th criticism. As an officer dependent on the support of his military, he had to preserve his credibility or risk a possible coup.

In spite of these differences, the Egyptians accepted a United Nations sponsored ceasefire which was set for October 22. According to Arab sources, the Egyptians did so only after receiving Russian assurances that it would produce an Israeli withdrawal under the terms of United Nations resolution 242. The original ceasefire resolution did, in fact, call for a return to the framework of 242. In 338, the UN:

1. Calls upon all parties to the present fighting, to cease all firing and terminate all military activity immediately, not later than 12 hours after the moment of this decision, in the positions they now occupy.

2. Calls upon the parties concerned, to start immediately after the ceasefire, the implementation of Security Council Resolution 242 (1967) in all its parts.... (285)

Jordan immediately followed the Egyptian lead in accepting the ceasefire; Kuwayt, the PLO, Libya, and Iraq rejected it out of hand. Syria delayed its acceptance until the 24th, and according to one source, stopped shooting only after Russia threatened to halt all arms shipments. (286)

The first ceasefire broke down almost at once, and the Egyptians charged the Israelis with cynically exploiting the ceasefires:

> The enemy has taken advantage of the ceasefire resolution. He sent a number of his tanks last night into the Deversoir area, trying to gain some new positions in which he had no presence before the ceasefire resolution... (287)

Israeli forces rapidly expanded their bridgehead, moved to the outskirts of Suez city, cut the Cairo-Suez road, and completed the encirclement of the 3rd army. The Security Council, meeting at Egyptian request, passed Resolution 339 (jointly introduced by the United States and Russia) which called for a return to the positions of October 22. When this failed to have any effect, al-Sadat called on both the United States and Russia to intervene. In the hiatus that followed, Russia (which had been pressing for a ceasefire with great urgency since the 19/20th) moved unilaterally. Seven airborne divisions, already on alert, appeared about to be moving into Egypt; indeed, there were reports that advance parties of Soviet troops had already arrived. (288) In addition, Brezhnev sent a note to Nixon which left no doubt about Soviet intentions:

> I will say it straight, that if you find it impossible to act with us in this matter, we should be faced with the necessity urgently to consider the question of taking appropriate steps unilaterally. (289)

To underscore the gravity of this already serious threat, there were reports that the Soviets were also sending nuclear warheads to be used in connection with Scud missiles in position in Egypt. (290) A calculation of United States ability to oppose Soviet forces by conventional means disclosed an extremely unfavorable military situation in the Mediterranean. The option chosen was to order a worldwide alert of United States forces to signal United States intentions not to permit massive Soviet intervention. (291) Not surprisingly, the ensuing United States/Russian confrontation was widely interpreted by Arab editorial writers as yet one more instance of United States support for Israel.

In spite of the official explanation, al-Sadat still found himself the target of considerable attack for ending the fighting. Arab popular opinion had been mobilized by the war, by the spectacle of Arab troops holding their own against the Israelis, and was not appeased by its sudden ending. Both domestic and foreign opponents, sensing this public disaffection, took the opportunity to outbid al-Sadat in their protestations of desire to continue fighting.

As an attempt to offset this behavior and build support for postwar Egyptian negotiating strategy, al-Sadat dispatched emissaries to Arab capitols to explain his position. But within six weeks of the ceasefire, he found himself opposed from within the Egyptian elite. He removed both Shadhili (al-Sadat later explained that he had secretly done this at the height of the debate over the appropriate response to the Israeli Canal crossing) and the Commanders of the 2nd and 3rd armies. All of these were violently opposed to his acceptance of a ceasefire. Although the MENA explanation for these dismissals was the argument that they were necessary to rejuvenate the higher officer corps, and to utilize combat experience gained in the war, (292) the real reasons were more complex. On the one hand, al-Sadat clearly wished to avoid a postwar coup attempt such as occurred after 1967, when the military similarly felt that the political leadership had made the wrong decisions (a theme since stressed by Shadhili). Moreover, Shadhili himself had acquired enormous popularity as the "hero of the crossing"; his pictures had begun to appear throughout the Arab world. Therefore, Shadhili represented a very real (and continuing) threat to al-Sadat: like 'Amir before and Sadiq later, Shadhili could have used his position in the Military to overthrow al-Sadat. Moreover, there was clear evidence of disaffection within at least the 3rd army which marched on Cairo in December (Egyptian sources claimed it was instigated to do so by al-Qadhafi) to protest al-Sadat's acceptance of the ceasefire. (293)

But there was also another, and potentially more important, reason. A rumor had sprung up which asserted that the reason the Israelis were able to cross successfully was because Coptic officers had betrayed the Egyptian army. As with the rumor concerning Druze treachery in Syria, this story carried the spector of sectarian conflict, especially as Coptic/Muslim tensions had already been running high before the war. Al-Sadat's response here was the same as al-Asad's: to stress the loyalty of the Coptic community, and to document this by appointing a Copt as Commander of the 2nd army.

7 Conclusion: History, Politics, and Conflict

The War of 1973 is an extremely complex phenomenon on a number of different levels of analysis. Historically it is both the outcome and the forerunner of a series of changes in relationships between: (a) the Arabs and the West, especially the Arabs and the United States; (b) various combinations of Arab states themselves; (c) Israel and the Arabs. Politically, it is the culmination of the strains and tensions existing since 1948, and intensified by the events of 1967. In this sense, it is the logical political and military extension of an ongoing and selfreinforcing Arab/Israeli conflict system. In addition, it is an acculturation phenomenon: an example of Arab learning in terms of the ability to use Western techniques, both political in the sense of propaganda strategy and military in the sense of operating Western weapons. Psychologically, the War resulted primarily in an abrupt change in the Arabs' image of themselves, and secondarily in Western image of the Arabs.

In a strategic sense, the War represents a problem for Western analysts because it presents new and difficult problems for the prediction of future Arab behavior. The Arab environment has been changed in the sense that, as Kissinger once put it, there are new "objective realities" in the Arab world which must now be taken account of, meaning that Arab decision makers are able to project their power in ways that can directly affect selected Western interests (especially those of the United States). The relationship between Arab politics, or the Arab world as a system, and the larger international system has been altered by the impact of the energy crises.

In a technical sense, the analysis and projection of Arab political behavior has become more complicated by the new found Arab ability to alter existing patterns, and to do so on the basis of an analysis of Western preconceptions about Arab behavior. For the Western analyst, some of the problems raised by this Arab ability to break with their own past are Arab propaganda: how does one analyze it, when can one believe it? Arab intentions: is an assessment possible, given Arab disinformation abilities? When is a situation in the Middle East not normal: when is a fact pattern sufficiently different enough to say that things have changed? (1)

PSYCHE AND HISTORY: ARAB IMAGES OF THE WORLD

One of the themes that has run through the material presented has been that of the preeminence of perceptions, attitudes, and emotions in Arab decision making. This is not to say that Western decision makers do not have similar perceptual, attitudinal, or emotional approaches to decision making, but that these are emphasized in the Arab world. In each case, the projection of emotions and images has provided the dynamic for the ensuing crisis - not just personality, but the projection of an image system, a conflict model of human interactions.

Arab decision makers operate in terms of a complex system of threat perceptions, of images of the environment as being over-whelmingly hostile. These images are tied together by a nexus of cultural values which stress the preservation of individual or group honor at the expense of any other consideration. When this honor is endangered, it must be restored by violence – either verbal or physical. (2) If action is not taken immediately, honor is lost. As a consequence, Arab decision makers are prone to perceive all acts or utterances as actual or potential threats. They are prone to interpret the motives of others as being suspect, prone, in a general sense, to a paranoid outlook. As a consequence, Arab assessments of themselves, and their actions tend to overcompensate for this sense of threat, of vulnerability. These assessments tend, therefore, to be highly colored by this concern for honor; they tend to glorify the decision maker in question at the expense of others in his environment.

For a variety of historical reasons, mostly the outcome of Western domination of the area, the West became the most salient threat, both politically and culturally. The Arab cognitions were dominated by an overwhelming perception of Western threat and a sense of profound in-ability to do anything about it. The creation of the state of Israel introduced still further anomalies into this imagery. Arab forces lost a series of wars, each slightly larger than the last. In the interims between these wars, Israelis replied to Arab irregular attacks by well publicized, efficiently executed "massive retaliations" (3) These were intended to deter further Arab action, but they served only to intensify Arab perceptions of threat.

Early on, therefore, a pattern of stimulus and response developed. Arab leaders would engage in all kinds of threats against Israel, and they would follow these up with cross border attacks. The Israelis would then reply with a punitive expedition, and thus demonstrate Arab military weakness. The 1967 escalation was an extension of this process. In its aftermath, Arab self pride was completely destroyed. Arab postwar reaction was that of utter despair. The already well developed sense of threat was magnified: Fear of Israeli annexationism; fear of an Israeli invasion of Syria in the wake of the Eagles' raid; fear of a Western expedition against Arab oil producers; fear of a Kissinger sponsored Israeli preemptive war against Egypt, Syria or both at once.

OCTOBER 1973 AND THE ARAB SELF-IMAGE

The October War, as accurately predicted by Haykal, was an event of significant magnitude in its impact on this heretofore negative (or if not entirely negative, then at least frought with considerable self doubt and possible self hatred) image. Arab spokesmen themselves have articulately expressed the psychological impact of the war. October is usually depicted as a great military victory, a feat of arms which vindicates Arab honor. The Egyptians have, understandably enough, gone furthest in this respect, but the image of the victory of Arab arms is widely shared in the Arab world, and indeed outside it. For example, the Pakistani paper Dawn ran this headline on October 23, 1973: ARABS REGAIN HONOR. (4)

Al-Sadat put forward what appears to have become the official Egyptian view in an address to the People's Assembly:

In the name of God, brothers and sisters....I do not think that you expect me to stand before you to boast together and to show pride over what we have realized in eleven days....during the most glorious days of our history. Yes, the day will come when we will sit down to tell about what each of us did at his post, how every one of us played his role, and how heroes came out of this people and this nation at a time when the light of torches illuminated the path so that the nation was able to cross the bridge between despair and hope....

I pledged to God and to you that we should prove to the world that the 1967 setback was an exception in our history and not the rule....I pledged before God and before you that our generation would not hand over flags at half mast or humiliated flags to the coming generation.

I never doubted that these armed forces were among the victims of the 1967 setback, and that they were never one of the reasons for the setback....In 1967, these forces were able to fight with the same courage and solidarity with which they are fighting today, had their military commanders maintained their nerves against the air strike....had their commanders not issued a decision for withdrawal....These forces were not given the opportunity to fight for the nation, for the honor of the nation and for its soil....

According to any military standard, the Egyptian forces realized a miracle (sic: of rebuilding). It is no exaggeration if I say that military history will for a long time come to scrutinize and study the operation of October 6, 1973....The risk was great and the sacrifice was great, too. But the achievements of our six hour battle were great. The arrogant enemy has to this moment lost control; our wounded nation has restored its honor; the political map of the Middle East has changed.... (5)

Field Marshal Ahmad Isma'il echoed it:

We have changed the image the whole world had of us. It used to think of us as a lifeless corpse, but now it has seen that we are capable of movement, capable of fighting, capable of victory. And it is not only the image of Egypt that has changed, but the image of the whole Arab nation. (6)

King Faysal phrased it in Islamic terms:

O Brothers, we have returned to our God. He supported us, fulfilled his promise, and has given us victory. Almighty God has said: "It is our right to support the believers." Thus, all of us should adhere to God fearing to consolidate our victories and to continue the steps for the liberation of the land sacred places.... (7)

In line with these comments, the fighting qualities of Arab troops are extolled. According to Ahmad Isma'il:

It has been proved before my eyes that the Egyptian soldier is one of the toughest soldiers in the world; he is extremely patient and daring....There were days when we had soldiers living on half the ration, but their combat readiness was unimpaired.... (8)

Similar accounts were given of the bravery and morale of Syrian forces:

Our soldiers were ready to fight and die to recover our occupied territories and morale was very high. (9)

As for relations with Israel, the heretofore predominance of Israeli power has ended. The Israeli security theory (that expanded frontiers are necessary) has been disproven and the myth of Israeli invincibility has been destroyed. Al-Sadat put this notion in the form of a parable:

We proved to the world the incorrectness of Israel's security theory....When we were small children in the village we used to imagine that the king wore golden slippers. Before October, Israel's security theory was such a false golden slipper. Now the world knows, and the owners of the slippers also know, that those are wooden slippers and that their destruction is possible.... (10)

Ahmad Isma'il stated it with reference to the canal crossing:

We have proved to Israel that her theory of secure frontiers is worthless. The Suez Canal was not a sufficient impediment to a resolute will, nor was the Bar-Lev line a sufficient obstacle to preparedness for sacrifice.... (11)

In addition, there is a tendency, especially on the part of the Syrians, to resurrect some of the pre-1967 Arab imagery of Israel as a small state whose existence is due to United States power. Syrian Minister of Information, George Saddiqni, argued that post October politics in Israel were symptomatic of a crisis of confidence, that Israel would fold up, if it were not for United States aid, and that the Israelis no longer have the will to fight. (12)

Although not as extreme as the Syrians, the Egyptians also have suggested that, were it not for United States invervention, things might have gone quite differently later in the war. As al-Sadat declared:

I admit that the Israelis are militarily efficient, whether from the aspect of planning or the aspect of implementation, but from the days of October 15 and 16, i⁺ had become totally clear to me that this thing we were observing was not Israeli planning. In the first four days, we struck at Israel's main force and hit more than 400 tanks on our front by Israel's own admission. Then how was it possible later that I should suddenly find before me, armored battalions "coming down like rain"? The strength of Israel's tanks became clear in the first four days, and as regards their air force, Israel recently announced that it had ordered its pilots not to approach the canal area at that time. The operation had been concluded....The situation was completely clear. Well then, what had happened after October 11, 12, 13, 14 and 15? What happened was new planning - a new blood force. The United States had officially announced the air "bridge". In fact, it was not an air bridge, but was actually United States intervention to the extent that some modern United States tanks had not traveled more than 104 kilometers, that is, only the distance between al-'Arish and the Deversoir. (13)

The war demonstrated the Arab Nation's power vis-à-vis the West; the Arabs had become a new and powerful actor on the international scene. Al-Sadat continually stresses this view:

We have fought for generations to achieve the kind of Arab solidarity which resulted from the October War. The future outlook is that the Arab nation will rise even higher. It has weapons which it has used. It has the ability to absorb modern technology. This is what the armed forces did in the Golan and on the canal....We have the energy weapon and the funds weapon. What is left is to coordinate work to build a new future. (14)

At the economic, political and military levels taken collectively, the Arab world emerged as a third power on this earth. This Arab world has always had all the elements of power....: a decisive strategic position between three continents....and the vital arteries and passes from the beginning to the end of the Mediterranean, the Suez Canal, the Red Sea, and Bab al-Mandab, and Arabian Gulf up to the approaches of the Indian Ocean. The Arab world also has natural resources which modern civilization feeds on - oil....But all this lacked one basic thing - it lacked the driving force....October came to turn on this driving force. The world suddenly became aware that the Arab potential has become a reality and that it is inevitable when dealing with Arab countries....to adopt another method. Europe and the United States have repeatedly been compelled to accept increases in oil prices and a reduction in oil production.... (15)

In particular, the United States must now come to the realization that its policies toward Israel are inseparably linked with the preservation of its oil interests. For the United States, the war has presented two new realities:

The first is that there are American interests in the area that cannot be protected without Arab good will, and second, that the image which world Zionism has tried to portray to the world of Israel being capable, with its striking force, of dictating its will in the area is a distortion.... (16)

The Military "Lessons" of October

In addition to the new found self image, a number of more concrete military lessons were drawn from the war. Here, some care must be used in accepting Arab commentary at its face value: There appears to be a good deal of historiographical rewriting of some aspects of the war to suit Arab strategic (and deceptive) purposes. For example, the editors of Aviation Week were treated to some elaborate discussions as to the limited value of ECM (electronic counter-measures) in future wars. Yet at the same time, it is clear that the Egyptians are going out of their way to develop as sophisticated an ECM capability as possible. (17) However, some general conclusions appear to have been reached. There is a widespread feeling that Arab strategy and tactics, which focused on quantity and the use of prepared positions which would force the Israelis into the role of the attacker, are basically correct.

Obviously, although the technological inferiority of the Arabs can be remedied, the numerical inferiority of the Israelis is irremediable. One is reminded of the famous 'mot' to the effect that one Finnish soldier is worth eight Russians, but what happens if the ninth turns up? Space and numbers are the weapons that Israel will increasingly have to reckon with.... (18)

Insofar as the Egyptians seem to be concerned, this strategy of numbers should be carried out in terms of the minute planning and training used in 1973:

Any action which has been well and scientifically planned, and for which there has been good practical training, is capable of achieving 100 percent success. (19)

However, a Palestinian expert on military matters took issue with Egyptian/Syrian commitment to routinized operations which cost them the initiative:

The main lesson to be learned from the Arab strategy resulted from the adoption of (sic: Soviet) "steam rolling" tactics as against Israeli general practice of mobile warfare and penetration in depth....

Such a strategy of penetration would have better suited the Syrians and might have enabled them to reach the western ridge of the Golan, under air cover provided by the mobile SAM-6 and the Syrian air force....Israeli supply lines in the Hula Valley would then have been endangered....The Syrians fought according to the book, and the military consequences were not as favorable as had been expected....

The Egyptian strategy was extremely successful in the first phase of the war, but later there were fatal mistakes. The Egyptians ought to have attempted to take the Sinai passes before the arrival of Israeli reserves, thus securing an advanced geographic defense line....As a price for not following this course, the Egyptians, like the Syrians, failed to exploit the full advantages of their initial success, and lost the initiative to the Israelis. (20)

In addition, the Egyptians appear to have concluded that the use of missile equipped infantry can neutralize both armor and aircraft:

After all, the armies established their theories and training on the basis that planes and the tank are the decisive weapons, it appeared that rockets and infantry can still turn this concept upside down if they are given the use of weapons, if there is brilliant planning and dependence on the courage of fighters like our sons from the universities, farms and factories. Our fighters used to wait courageously for the tank with its thick armor, heavy fire, and frightening rumble, and then blow it up when it got a few yards away from them. (21)

This is supported by other sources:

The other surprise of the war was the deadly effectiveness of guided anti-tank missiles at various distances. These missiles allowed infantry to face tanks on equal and even superior terms. A new era in military history has opened when a couple of soldiers armed with missiles that cost only a few thousand dollars can destroy several tanks which cost a few hundred thousand dollars each.... (22)

Two interpretations of the value of air superiority have emerged:
The above Egyptian argument that missile defenses have substantially
reduced the role of air forces, and an opposing view put forth by
Palestinian analysts:

> As for the air, contrary to what many analysts have concluded, the
> October War proved once again that the major key to military
> victory is the mastery of the air - in particular possessing air
> superiority over the battlefield - at any price in terms of aircraft
> and pilots lost. For, in spite of the formidable Arab air defense
> systems, the Israelis were able to destroy many tanks and vehicles
> from the air, and this advantage became overwhelming once SAM
> missile systems on the West Bank were destroyed. It may be
> observed that if the Arabs had an air force comparable to the
> Israelis, and Israel were compelled instead to rely on the combined
> air defense systems of Syria and Egypt, the Israelis would have been
> outclassed.... (23)

Egyptian comment on naval operations took the form of an analysis
of the strategic effects of the Bab al-Mandab blockade:

> The war has decisively proved that Sharm al-Shaykh is not as
> important as Israel thought when she built her ambitions in Sinai
> upon it. Sharm al-Shaykh is no longer the key to Eilat; the key
> moved to to the far South, when we discovered an Arab strategy for
> the Red Sea in accordance with which we have decided to close the
> Bab al-Mandab.... (24)

To the extent that these views are representative of Arab thinking,
and not entirely designed for local consumption, Arab leaders have
probably reached the following conclusions:

1. That a successful military confrontation is possible. Therefore
   war can be resorted to in the last resort.

2. That Western Europe and the United States are dependent on
   Arab oil. Therefore, another embargo would have telling effect.

3. That, as a consequence of the foregoing, Arabs need not make
   concessions on what they consider vital issues: Israeli withdrawal, the rights of the Palestinians, and a return of Jerusalem
   to Arab/Muslim hands.

What the foregoing Arab commentaries (whether expressing a
regained sense of self worth or celebrating a successful strategic/mili-
tary policy mix) have as an underlying theme is the sense that October
was a victory in an ongoing clash of civilizations. One of the major
perceptual elements in the Arab imagery of the environment is the
belief that the Arab world is in a state of confrontation with the West
(which, of course, includes Israel). This feeling runs like a thread
through all the planning and preparation for war: from the general idea

of a two pronged attack based on Salah al-Din's exploits, to the symbolic title Badr for the operation itself.   Equally, it percolates through Arab training and indoctrination procedures.   Emphatically, however, this observation is not meant to conjure up counter images of wild eyed Arabs charging out of the desert screaming "jihad, jihad." What it does mean is that the Arabs have a profound sense of their own history, and the dominant image in that history has been that of endless conflict with the West.   The October War has become part of that image.

THE ARABS AND THE WEST I: THE DECISION TO ATTACK

The Arab decision to attack was made in the face of a series of military defeats, each successively larger than the preceding.   As such, it was the product of a very pessimistic projection of the future, e.g., the vision of permanent Israeli occupation of Arab territories,   plus an overwhelming set of circumstances which impelled a decision to launch a preemptive war. (25)   The key perceptual factor in the situation as Arab (but especially Egyptian) decision makers saw it was the link between the United States and Israel: Israeli military power could be offset by United States diplomatic leverage. In this case (and clearly taking their text from the 1956 War wherein Eisenhower had been able to force the Israelis to withdraw) the real problem was to move an actor external to the Middle East.   And here, postwar statements (and contemporary Arab diplomatic and propaganda policy) indicate that the war was aimed at changing United States policy by demonstrating that: (a) United States interests could be adversely affected, and (b) Israeli theories of the need for expanded territorial holdings as an indepth defense were incorrect. Additionally, the Arabs acted out of a perception that their erstwhile ally, Russia, was not going to do much to alter United States policy.
Even within the general context of Arab mistrust of both super powers, there was a pronounced Arab concern that the positions of Russia and the United States were asymmetrical vis-à-vis their respective clients. In a prewar interview, al-Sadat explained:

A comparison of the attitudes of both powers in regard to the Middle East alone shows that the United States provides Israel with the most modern weapons and with economic aid without which Israel would not be able to pursue its aggressive policy. The United States used the veto in favor of Israel, and had previously used it twice. The funny thing is that in the last instance, the United States resorted to the veto just because the other 14 United Nations Security Council member countries stood against Israel.   On the other hand, Russia supports a peaceful solution and does not want war.   The proof of this is that it does not supply us with the most advanced modern weapons.   The United States uses Israel as a bridgehead to defend and preserve its interest.   We are not a bridgehead for Russia and it has never asked us to be.... (26)

Therefore, United States policies geared to the maintenance of the status quo were the primary Arab target. The Arab decision to act in this regard stems from two conclusions: (a) That the United States had accepted the argument that a strong Israel could protect United States interests in the area. (b) That only the United States had the power to alter what was becoming an increasingly unacceptable situation in the area. Early in the war, the Monitor summarized Arab understanding of US/Israeli assumptions which underlie this policy, and the reasons why Arab diplomats believed these had been made obsolete by the attack:

1. There was no real chance of a settlement while the Russians remained in the Middle East. The Egyptians ejected them last year.

2. The Arabs were unwilling to fight, and if they did, would be incapable of inflicting serious damage. Israelis have not only encountered tougher resistance this time, but also Prime Minister Golda Meir has personally expressed distress over the extent of Israeli casualties.

3. No political unity existed among the Arabs. President Sadat lined up overwhelming political support for military action even from the outset of battle.

4. Israeli claims that secure borders are geographic and not political, and that the Suez Canal, in particular, is a secure border, have been challenged by massive Egyptian military crossing. (27)

The attack was timed to take advantage of several trends which the Arabs saw as favoring action:

a) A shift in international opinion to their side, principally as the result of Israeli intransigence.

b) The creation of an Eastern Front following the September mini summit.

c) Increasing Western concern over the energy crisis, making the threat of oil sanctions that more effective.

d) A dramatic shift of African sentiment away from the Israelis as measured by the number of African nations breaking relations with Israel.

e) The existence of a large bloc of pro-Arab nations in the United Nations General Assembly, which was in session.

This was juxtaposed to what appeared to be a deteriorating local situation: Increased Israeli settlement in the occupied territories, something which confirmed the worst Arab fears of Israeli annexationism, increasingly uncontrolled and dangerous Palestinian activity, aided and abetted by the Libyans, an activity which threatened to bring down Israeli reprisals and further aggravate already tense domestic situations in Egypt and Syria; the looming threat of some sort of Western action, either against the oil producers or in the form of a United States sponsored Israeli attack on one or more "confrontation" states.

The attack was the outcome of a complex set of prior factors, each autonomous in its own right, but interacting to foreclose options and impel a certain course of action:

a) The decision made by 'abd al-Nasir to reorganize and expand the Egyptian military had the latent consequence of building up an organizational momentum. By rebuilding Egyptian military capabilities and at the same time recruiting highly politicized students, 'abd al-Nasir set in motion the forces within the military which put enormous pressure on al-Sadat to act.

I would not be exaggerating if I said that the October War was decided upon after the defeat. Since the 1967 defeat, we were working on the basis of regaining our position by means of another battle. (28)

b) The actual planning by Soviets and Egyptians for a canal crossing operation functioned to generate sets of expectations within the military. Al-Sadat's decision to order Shazili to prepare a report on a limited war added to this impetus and increased pressure on al-Sadat to act.

c) Al-Sadat's decision to replace Sadiq with Ahmad Isma'il was critical in the foregoing context. It, in effect, removed the major counterweight to Shazili and the hawks. With Ahmad Isma'il's appointment, the restraint imposed by lack of technologically sophisticated weapons was eliminated as a bar to action.

d) The annual fall Egyptian military exercises, partly designed for domestic political reasons, introduced input of their own. Once men's expectations and careers were locked into training for action, once resources were committed, an irresistable push for action was generated.

e) Soviet decision in February to deliver large quantities of arms in response to Syrian/Egyptian requests. This was probably a Soviet attempt to maintain leverage with restive Arab clients, a move to protect an already large investment in the Arab World: something the Egyptians, apparently, were counting on. But it had the effect of altering both Egyptian and Syrian assessment of their military capabilities vis-à-vis the Israelis in favor of action.

f) The Syrian insistence on the necessity for immediate action, in opposition to Egyptian and Saudi caution, and Jordanian reluctance, slowly gained ground as all sides began to perceive that the time to act was growing short.   This feeling crystallized during the September summit:

> Nevertheless, after 1971 and 1972 it had become clear that there was no hope for diplomatic efforts, intensified or otherwise, and that we had no choice but to prepare for the battle and to continue with such preparations.... (29)

g) Build up of popular expectations concerning an eventual attack: Whether or not al-Sadat's threats were perceived as merely bluffs, the very fact that they were consistently repeated served to create a climate of expectations, both in the Egyptian public, and in relevant segments of the elite and military.   The consequence was a "self-fulfilling prophecy" wherein al-Sadat had ultimately to act to preserve his position.

All these factors began to reinforce each other and "snowballed" in the later stages of 1973.   The outcome was a decision to fight a war that the Egyptians and Syrians thought they might lose.   To use de Rivera's terminology (30) a "forced consensus" was generated by the combination of these factors; a consensus on the proposition that it was necessary to attack both Israel and the West.

THE ARABS AND THE WEST II:
CULTURE, TECHNOLOGY AND WAR

In their resume of the war, Arab analysts have stressed the fact that its conception and conduct were totally an Arab innovation. This is true in the sense that Arab planners took standard Soviet military techniques and hardware and put them together with Arab behavioral traits; the whole then became a strategic gestalt which was different from any of its components. There are really two issues involved in the assessment of this gestalt. The first involves a phenomenon which anthropologists have dealt with for years in terms of the concept of acculturation: The configuration of conditions which will induce, or facilitate, the transmission of cultural elements from one culture to another. Here it should be obvious that a given military technology is an outgrowth of its underlying cultural system. The problem of acculturation occurs when this technology is exported in the form of arms transfers. Second, and closely allied, is another issue: How does a non Western state combat the technological superiority of a Western state? Here the problem is not so much one of using Western technology (although it clearly is involved), but of bringing indigenous resources to bear on the conflict. This problem of translating traditional cultural and social elements into military strategies capable of defeating Western technological sophistication is at the heart of most theories of guerrilla war (which of course grow up in the context of a confrontation between Western imperialism and non-Western nationalism).

In this context, the Arab strategy for war was both an attempt to selectively assimilate Western (in this case Soviet) military technology in certain critical areas, and combine this with a strategy of large numbers. Here, the blend, the syncretism, is important. Arab (and Ottoman) armies had been losing battles to smaller Western forces for decades as a consequence of superior Western military technology, which usually translated itself into superior firepower. As Hurewitz argues, Arab and Turkish military reformers usually failed to match their Western opponents because they were basically engaged in imitating existing technology. The problem was that while the imitation was reasonably good, the technology it copied had changed in the interim. Arab and Turkish reformers, therefore, were always "shooting at a moving target." They were always slightly obsolescent in their new-found military techniques. (31)

From this perspective, the conception and conduct of the October War was a product of intensive Arab analysis of this technological lag, a lag whose dimensions were brought home all too dramatically by 1967. The strategic, organizational, military (with considerable Soviet help), and propagandistic failings were corrected insofar as possible. The consequence was a dramatic reversal of Arab behavior, and Arab political-military fortunes:

> The June 1967 defeat revealed many of the negative aspects in our life which distorted the shining face of our revolutionary experience....The Arab nation has been driven to war with Israel several times during a quarter of a century without any calculations based on facts and realities and without any prior determination of the goal and aim of war and without any consideration of the eventualities that might accompany it. Thus, what has happened, happened again and again and the Arab soldier was consequently deprived of the opportunity to have a real confrontation on the battle field. As we look through the pages of the past quarter century of Arab-Israeli confrontation, we find that the general Arab line of thinking was marked by extreme confusion which manifested itself in numerous ways: Irresponsible disregard for the adversary and the strength of those behind him, extreme overestimation of the adversary's power, and fear of it, and conflicts among various forces, regimes and currents in the Arab World in which confrontation with Israel was used as one of the cards in the conflict and squabble. Instead of being the subject of real study and planning, confrontation with Israel was always the subject of constant altercation....It is our right to say that the method of our action which reached its peak on October 6 proves that we have learned the lesson and that we have been able to calculate, to draw up a plan and take a military initiative for the first time since the inception of Israel... (32)

According to Arab spokesmen, the central element of this plan was the doctrine of limited war:

Liberation was the objective of the battle and reactivation (sic: of active warfare) was one of the means we used to shock the enemy, those behind him, and the entire world, to make them understand our cause and compel the enemy to retreat. We understand and realize the dimensions of the international balance as well as the sensitivity and importance of the Middle East to the West and the East. Thus, the October War was a limited war which was intended to strike the Israeli theory of security at the core. We were aware that this would result in important changes leading to the complete liberation of the land. (33)

Western analysts have pointed out that the Arabs managed to achieve two sorts of surprise in 1973: strategic and tactical. (34) Strategically, they were able to conceal the extent of their coordination and preparation for war until late September. Because of this, they were able to bring to bear their superior numerical resources before the Israelis could mobilize. Tactically, they employed a manpower/weapons mix that enabled them to counter Israeli technological superiority. In so doing, they limited Israeli tactical options and forced the Israelis to fight on Arab terms for the first part of the war.

Arab strategists had debated this problem of bringing Arab man-power and resources to bear in a war against Israel for years. The doctrine of a war of attrition had likewise been openly discussed in the Arab media; the conception of a limited war had been in existence for at least four years prior to 1973.

The conduct of the 1973 War was an extension of the strategy, deployment, and tactics of 1967: a broad Egyptian deployment in the Sinai which was designed to force the Israelis to attack a series of prepared positions, on the theory that the defender in a desert environment has more cover and is less exposed to casualties than the attacker. (35) Other Arab forces were positioned on the Syrian and Jordanian fronts to force the Israelis to split up their forces. A strategic blockade was maintained in the Red Sea to cut Israeli maritime access to war materials.

In 1973 the critical difference was the surprise element on the side of the Arabs. Egyptian and Syrian forces attacked before digging in, the Egyptians East of the Canal and the Syrians falling back to prepared positions in the Damascus plain. In tactical terms, the Arabs applied existing Soviet tactics plus a few innovations to the local desert situation. The general disposition of Arab forces, their organization, disposition, and tactics were the same in both 1967 and 1973. (36) But at least four tactics were introduced:

a) The utilization of a rolling missile umbrella to protect ground forces against Israeli air strikes.

b) The widespread introduction of infantry equipped with handheld missiles to counter superior Israeli armor.

c) The use of light "dune buggy" type vehicles armed with antitank weapons to nullify heavier, slower Israeli armored vehicles. (37)

d) The use of high pressure water hoses to cut through sand banks more swiftly than bulldozers. (38)

The immediate result of these efforts was the surprising performance of Arab troops in the first stages of the war. But the broader implications concern the mixture of Russian technology, Arab culture, and a self-conscious strategy that shaped these efforts. Arab planners were able to construct a battlefield situation in which existing cultural attitudes and values could be brought to bear on the performance of Arab troops. They were able to analyze those elements of Arab behavior that contributed to the disastrous performance of 1967 and reintegrate them into a successful motivational mix in 1973. Specifically, existing Arab/Islamic cultural values were utilized to motivate troops; existing authoritarian social patterns and practices were incorporated into training techniques, and existing elitist attitudes were structured into officer corps performance.

In the anthropological sense, this Arab strategic syncretism, then, is a form of cultural borrowing. A borrowing that occurs under very special conditions, but basically when there is a combination of both a perceived need on the part of the members of the borrowing culture, and some sort of functional "fit" in a cultural sense. In other words the borrowed item - in this case military technology, and its attendant strategic thought - must be at once useful in policy terms, and compatible in cultural terms. The consequence is a complex behavioral process by which the recipient in an arms transfer learns to adapt both the imported technology and his own cultural institutions in order to effectively use the equipment. The outcome of this process is a mixture of technology, culture and strategy which is different from both that of the original source and that of the arms transfer recipient. (39)

In the case of Arab forces engaged in the war, this process of cultural assimilation was uneven: Arab forces performed much better under conditions where the role of Western technology was minimal. Therefore, Arab forces were able to match the Israelis reasonably well on the ground, (40) less well in air defense, hardly at all in air-to-air combat, (41) and not at all in naval warfare. (42)

In a broader historical sense, however, the October War is an extension of non-Western military strategies aimed at the West. As noted, the essence of these strategies is to convert the strengths of traditional social orders into weapons to be used against a superior enemy. (European theories of partisan warfare deal with the same problem, except that they are in all European environment.) Elements emphasized by non-Western strategists vary - mobility, time, and space, kinship linkages, honor - but they all have the same underlying equation: the combination of a minimal technological infrastructure, e.g., some Western arms, with non-Western culture and behavior. (43) In this instance, the Arab version of a limited war was designed to limit impact of Israeli technological superiority. Key to this conception was the employment of missiles: Ground to air missile to blunt Israeli air superiority, ground to ground missiles to blunt Israeli superiority in armored warfare. In each case, the introduction of these missiles allowed Arab strategists to take advantage of both the numbers and the stolid qualities of their troops.

The use of missiles to defend ground operations had advantages and disadvantages. On the plus side, it enabled technologically inferior forces to engage an enemy who could expected to have air superiority; it also permitted a large number of relatively inexpensive ground units to defend against a smaller number of very expensive aircraft. Even if the attrition rates were staggering in favor of the aircraft, the ultimate victory would go to the defenders. On the minus side, the use of a slow moving missile defense system severely limited ground tactics. Speed and maneuverability were sacrificed because of the necessity to move only under the missile umbrella. (44) As Ahmad Isma'il explained it:

> We began our operation under the protection of our famous network of missiles. In order to advance, I had to wait till my armor entered the field, and then I had to give a chance for my mobile anti aircraft missiles to enter, regardless of the chances others might have seen or, indeed, the chances I might have seen....If I had thrown in my forces after that available chance experts are talking about, without adequate defense against the enemy's air superiority, I would have been putting the whole burden on the Air Force which would have exceeded its capacity.... (45)

More fundamentally, the problem of training and maneuvering large numbers of brave, but essentially traditional troops, imposes restrictions on tactical options. Arab educational techniques stress rote learning, the memorization of materials. These presumably are carried over into training practices, and in turn reinforced by Soviet tactical doctrines. Initiative is downgraded; the emphasis is on programming troops to respond to certain scenarios gamed out in advance. Contingencies not thought of in advance are not easily handled. (46)

Egyptian strategy therefore was aimed at the avoidance of any sort of fluid battlefield situation, on protecting the integrity of the Egyptian army at all costs and thus avoiding a repeat of the experience of 1967. Ahmad Isma'il expressed this mind set in a revealing exchange with Haykal:

> Haykal: Why wasn't our total offensive developed as quickly as it should have been?....Why was our planning confined to the great crossing? Did we not see a chance available?....
>
> Ahmad Isma'il: It was not a question of chances. There were calculations. Whatever chances might have seemed available, I could not take the risks....Were we too slow? I don't know. What I know is that I kept to the plan, the original plan which called for a staging pause after the crossing, in order to make the bridgeheads secure, reassess the situation according to the enemy's reaction and prepare for the next move.... (47)

Isma'il's sentiments were later echoed by al-Sadat in answer to a question concerning his acceptance of a ceasefire (for which he had drawn considerable criticism from both his Syrian allies and other Arab states):

I managed to keep my forces sound because I predicted the ceasefire. Had we delayed the ceasefire more, it was very possible that we would have come out battered, yet with the same results.... (48)

Parenthetically, Israeli strategists have been quite sensitive to the Arab equation: numbers versus technology. Their response has been to accelerate the technological gap by acquiring weapons of great sophistication and destructive power. (49)   In addition, Israeli military acquisitions policy has aimed at securing a variety of delivery systems capable of hitting targets behind Arab front line defenses. (50) Moreover, it appears that a nuclear option is being considered;   the strategic value of this is that it would hold hostage the very sources of manpower which Arab strategists propose to utilize. (51)

MIDDLE EAST CONFLICT AND
THE INTERNATIONAL SYSTEM:
STRATEGY, LINKAGE AND SUPERPOWER INTERESTS

It is a truism that Middle Eastern conflicts have tended to ramify outward and involve successively larger segments of the international system. Four Middle Eastern wars have been fought in less than three decades, and each war has brought ever greater involvement by powers external to the region. In 1948, European states supplied small amounts of arms to combatants in Palestine; in 1956, British and French troops were involved on a small scale; in 1967, the United States and Russia actively backed their respective clients; in 1973, the same superpowers undertook massive arms transfers, and nearly came to a nuclear confrontation.

The critical factor in this increasing linkage between Middle Eastern conflict patterns and the outside world has been that of the nexus between several strategies. On the one hand, there are the Arab and Israeli strategies aimed at securing favorable superpower intervention; on the other hand, there are the superpower strategies aimed at securing various interests, however defined.   The reciprocal and complex interaction between these strategies has supplied the dynamic for the escalation of Middle Eastern conflicts outward from their source.   This dynamic has been especially operative since the 1967 war. (52)

One of the consequences of 1967 was an upsurge in anti-Western particularly anti-American feeling. Since Israel was perceived as being part of the West, the West was logically responsible for the "set-back". (53) Most Arab governments broke relations with the United

States, and pressure was put on United States installations and interests throughout the area. United States military bases, especially Wheelus AFB, were progressively closed, and United States Naval access to port facilities became nonexistent, with the tenuous exception of Bahrayn. Pro-Western governments were placed in the extremely awkward position of balancing between the need for United States military hardware and the anti-United States sentiments of their populations. Considerable pressure was put on these governments to replace United States with Soviet arms. (54)

Russia was similarly affected, but managed to recoup its losses by a two fold strategy: First, an extremely vocal championship of Israeli withdrawal; second, a massive and well publicized resupply operation to Syria and Egypt. (55) At the same time, however, Russia privately pressed Arab leaders for moderate and pragmatic approach to the problem of Israeli occupation. This push for moderation translated itself into the issue of what Soviet arms would be supplied and in what quantity. This issue rapidly became the focal point of intense Soviet-Arab friction. (56)

The key to Russian exploitation of the post-1967 situation was two fold: First, the relative military weakness of the "front line" states which effectively prevented any military alteration of the territorial status quo. Second, the inter-Arab division between radical and conservative camps, a division which deprived these same "confrontation" states of support from conservative oil producing states.

As Tuwayni concisely phrased it:

The Arabs make war with Russian armaments and peace through American diplomacy. (57)

To the extent that Syria, Egypt and Jordan could not regain the occupied territories by use of force, they were compelled to attempt diplomatic means. These means had, ultimately, to be directed at the United States, which the Arabs perceived as the Israelis' chief benefactor, and the only nation that could influence an Israeli withdrawal. Without, however, any sort of leverage, these efforts met with little success. Therefore, reliance on Russia was the only alternative option.

US policy at the time seemed to rest on two assumptions:

a) That by keeping Israel sufficiently stronger, direct United States involvement in the complicated Arab-Israeli conflict could be avoided.

b) That at the same time a policy of relative noninvolvement would dissociate United States oil interests from the conflict, and minimize Arab pressure on these interests.

In so doing, it was hoped that the economic interests of oil producing countries would prevail over their political commitment to the "Arab Cause." (58)

2422422444

Western oil interests nevertheless came under considerable pressure from their host countries. A series of disputes arose between oil companies and Arab governments: disagreements over oil pricing arrangements, disputes arising out of conflicts between Western producers and state run Arab oil companies, generalized political tensions between United States companies and Arab governments as an outgrowth of United States support for Israel. All of these conflicts slowly began to crystallize around the issue of United States arms supplies to Israel. From the Arab point of view, United States shipment of F-4s to Israel had become the touchstone of United States Middle East policy.

Supplying Israel with such "offensive" weapons, in Arab eyes at least, meant that the United States was underwriting both continued Israeli occupation of Arab lands and continued Israeli attacks on other Arab populations. United States decisions on whether to ship F-4s or not became a critical event for Arab governments. In particular, the Saudi Arabians and Kuwaytis were extremely anxious about the domestic repercussions of further shipment of F-4s, and repeatedly warned United States officials of the possible draconic consequences of such moves. (59)   (Parenthetically, the same set of perceptions accompanied the announcement that the United States was to give Israel some two billion dollars in arms and other aid--including both F-16s and Pershing missiles (later dropped from the arms package) in connection with an Israeli agreement to Sinai II. (60)

By early 1972, Arab sources estimated that the United States strategic position in the Middle East had been reduced to an all time low:

The main United States interests in the Arab world remain the petroleum interests - and even these are in a precarious position....the Western oil interests are under heavy pressure in the Middle East. Governments of the producers are presently demanding a 20 percent share in the existing concessions of Western oil companies. Libya is demanding 51 percent. What's more, the right wing governments, led by Saudi Arabia, are leading this campaign.... (61)

Veteran Middle East observer Tom Little summarized Arab feeling behind this pressure:

The Arabs hold the Western powers to blame for the situation, and have done so ever since the Balfour Declaration of 1917 right through to the United States supply of long range Phantom bombers to Israel. They argue that Western interests in the Middle East - oil and the resistance to Russian penetration - lie essentially with the Arabs; they have never understood why what they see as the usual policy of self interest has not applied to them; and because they do not understand, they concluded that Israel must be a special instrument of Western policy. (62)

The October War altered the applicability of both Soviet and American policy assumptions. Russia can no longer count on Arab political/military weakness, and the front line states have acquired an economic/diplomatic alternative to Russian arms. The United States cannot count on either Israeli military superiority, or separation between oil politics and a territorial settlement. Territorial questions are now directly tied to the accessibility of oil.

The Soviets are the most affected by the emerging Egyptian/Saudi axis. A prewar RAND study analyzed the Soviet position in terms of the risks and benefits of such a dependence.

On the benefit side were the following:

1) An expanded Soviet presence in the Middle East could enable it to turn NATO's flank.

2) Such a position could also provide a base for future operations in Africa.

3) It would make possible increased maritime communications with India.

4) Access to Middle Eastern oil was also made possible.

5) Western influence in the area could slowly be restricted. (63)

On the risk side of the ledger were the following:

1) Such a forward policy, coupled with the volatility of the area, raised the possibility of a United States/Soviet confrontation.

2) Due to endemic governmental instability, there was always the possibility of the overthrow of a client state.

3) In certain circumstances an Arab client might "betray" its Soviet patron.

4) Any settlement of the Arab-Israeli conflict would reduce Arab need for Soviet support. (64)

It is in the area of the last two categories that the consequences of the war have impinged on the Soviets. As the RAND staff noted, there were three ways in which risks 3 and 4 could come about: First, as a consequence of the reorientation of radical Arab states away from Russia, either because of frustration at Soviet inability to deliver, or because of a successful Western/United States attempt to woo them away from the Soviets. (65) Second, as the outgrowth of a deescalation of the Arab-Israeli conflict via some sort of solution to the refugee question, thereby causing the conflict to lose its saliency for the Arabs. (66) Third, by the Arabs coming to the conclusion that they could regain the lost territories without direct Soviet intervention. (67)

The October War has raised the possibility that all of these factors might occur. In a psychological sense, the Arab "victory" has increased their ability to make overtures to the United States. The Arabs' ability to negotiate with the West-United States is inversely proportional to

their Arab Islamic self-esteem.   In the post-1967 atmosphere, any
leader that counseled moderation did so at his peril (a situation that
seems to be recurring in 1978-79):

> The return to the 1967 territories has already been rejected by the
> Palestinian resistance movement.   President Nasser and King
> Hussein, among others, believe that such a settlement could be made
> acceptable to the majority of Palestinians and that, without a broad
> base of popular support, the resistance movement would not have
> the continuing strength to resist....That the moderates in the
> resistance, as much as governments and Kings, are silenced by the
> current impasses is one more sign of the power the situation gives to
> the extremists.... (68)

Arab conduct since the war has been unexpectedly rational and pro-
Western. Arab governments which had broken relations with the United
States have now moved to restore these relationships. Arab govern-
ments that heretofore discouraged Western economic investment have
now moved to encourage such investment.
    The titular leader in these moves has been al-Sadat, and the
Egyptian movement toward the West has seriously jeopardized the
Soviet position. Not only was Egypt the capstone of that position in the
Mediterranean, but future Russian utilization of the canal is threatened.
Moreover, Egypt and to a lesser extent, Syria and Iraq, provided
springboards for Russian penetration of contiguous areas in the Middle
East/North and sub-Saharan Africa.
    Egyptian betrayal was all the more dangerous because it was linked
with the openly anti-Communist policies of Saudi Arabia. Combined
Egyptian/Saudi pressure might also dislodge Syria and Iraq from the
Soviet orbit, an intensified form of the pressure that occurred after
Egyptian expulsion of Soviet personnel in July 1972, and appeared to be
surfacing again in the fall of 1973. (69)
    Russia has moved to reduce the impact of this new Saudi/Egyptian
alliance in a number of ways:

a) Increased Russian presence in both Syria and Iraq, especially in
terms of military assistance: This gives Russia direct land and air
access to oil producing areas, strengthens Russian position in the
Eastern Mediterranean, isolates Turkey on both sides and Iran from the
West. In effect, this cuts across any conservative Arab/Iranian axis,
and amounts to an extension of the Eastern bloc buffer into the Middle
East.

b) This is supplemented by the encouragement of radical Arab
nationalism, under the formal aegis of Iraq. In an Arab view, the use of
Iraq as a "front" center (replacing Egypt) fits in with Russian plans for
developing Iraq as an Arab World power, making it a more dependable
ally, and consolidating Soviet influence in the area. (70) By encouraging
radicalism in the Gulf, Russia intensifies domestic pressures on oil
producers not to make concessions to the West on oil related issues. (71)

c) Undermining United States efforts at arriving at a negotiated settlement encouraging hard line Arab factions: As noted above, one of the conditions of Russian resupply efforts in Syria was that the Syrians harden their negotiating position. In addition, Russia has attempted to bolster Palestinian opposition to a peace settlement on two counts: By indirectly encouraging the "rejection front" via Iraq which is its major supporter (and to some extent via Libya also), and by assuring the PLO of complete Soviet backing and of Soviet rejection of any settlement which does not take into account the "legitimate rights of the Palestinian people." (72) Thus, in effect, exploiting differences between the PLO, Jordan, and Egypt. In August 1974, 'Arafat went to Moscow and received unexpected Russian support: Russia officially recognized the PLO and allowed the PLO to open an office in Moscow, declared its backing for an independent PLO delegation at Geneva, and promised to provide the PLO with sophisticated weaponry (which apparently includes some SAMs). (73)

d) In addition, it has resurrected a 1972 notion of an "anti imperialist front," this time to include Algeria, Libya, Somalia, and South Yemen (the PDRY) and the Palestinians, as well as Syria and Iraq. The two objectives of this "front" are to fill the void left by the defection of Egypt, and to provide the nucleus for a grouping of all elements in the Middle East hostile to increasing United States, and conservative Arab influence in the region. This front, now called the "Steadfastness Front," forms the chief organized inter-Arab opposition to both al-Sadat's peace initiative, and the Camp David Accords (for details on its evolution, see below).

The Soviets have also moved to exploit Egyptian/Libyan hostilities: in this case by shipping large amounts of arms to Libya--shipments whose size and sophistication have alarmed the Egyptians. (74) In this connection, it is clear that Libyan personnel do not have the capability of using these arms: the Egyptian/Libyan war demonstrated that. Therefore, it is conceivable that the Soviets could be using Libya as an arms cache: A stockpile of weapons in the Middle East which could be moved around to support pro-Soviet actors in the area. In this sense, the arms influx into Libya would strategically and functionally parallel arms transfers to Syria, and more especially, to Iraq. (75)

e) Moves in the Horn of Africa. Soviet policy immediately after the October War appeared to be aimed at solidifying the Soviet presence in Somalia and South Yemen (the PDRY). (76) President Podgorny visited Somalia in July 1974 and received PDRY National Liberation Front Secretary General 'abd al-Fattah Isma'il in Moscow the same month. 'Abd al-Fattah's visit resulted in a massive increase in already extensive Russian aid to the PDRY. (77) By 1978, there were reports not only of sizeable arms transfers, including advanced aircraft and armor, but also of an influx of East German and Cuban personnel in addition to Soviet cadres. (78)

The left wing coup of June 1978 has solidified the Soviet position in South Yemen. The coup itself was apparently triggered by PDRY

President Salim Rubayyi 'Ali's acceptance of Saudi financial aid, and movement toward both Saudi Arabia and North Yemen (the YAR). This was clearly unacceptable to the Soviets and their supporters in the PDRY and they apparently struck at conservatives in both countries: YAR President Ahmad Husayn al-Ghashmi was killed by a suitcase bomb said to have been delivered by the PDRY; Rubayyi' 'Ali was overthrown, and executed after a brief but bloody civil war (where Soviet aircraft and naval units were reported to have assisted the victorious insurgents). (79) From this position the Soviets have mounted staging operations East and West: To the West, the Soviets have used South Yemen as a conduit to supply PLOAG (now PFLO) insurgents operating in Oman; to the East, Cuban troops were transited through Aden in their way to Ethiopia (PDRY troops were also said to be in Ethiopia). (80)

Initial Soviet policy toward Somalia paralleled their policy toward the PDRY. Immediately after the October war, Russia began to extend its links with the Somalis: both military and economic aid were increased; and in August 1974 Russia and Somalia signed a treaty of friendship. (81) The rolling coup in Ethiopia that began in 1974, however, opened up the possibility that the Soviets might be able to move into Ethiopia as well, and indeed, this appeared to be the case, as the left-wing military junta asked for and received Soviet aid. However, the July 1977 Somali invasion of eastern Ethiopia, the Ogaden desert region, put the Soviets in much the same position that faced the United States in Cyprus: backing two clients who were at war. The Soviets responded by diplomatic pressures on Somalia to end the invasion, and when these failed, began large scale assistance to the Ethiopians. (82) The net result was a reversal of military fortunes, with the Ethiopians first containing and then driving back Somali troops. As Somali fortunes declined, relations with the Soviets became more strained. Ultimately the Somalis expelled the Soviets in November 1977 (83) and moved into the Egyptian/Saudi camp. (84)

Arab analyses of these moves stress the point that with the clearing and opening of the Canal, the narrow straights at the Bab al-Mandab become more important. By strengthening the Russian position in both Ethiopia and the PDRY, the Soviets will be able to control both sides of the Bab al-Mandab. (85) With naval control of Aden, the Soviets would be in a strong position to dominate the approaches to the Arabian Gulf; the use of Perim and Qamran islands off the Yemeni coast would give them advantages in patrolling the Red Sea; naval and air facilities on Socotra would provide a base for Indian Ocean operations. In addition, the Soviets are apparently interested in developing naval installations in the Mukalla area which would give them even more presence on the South Arabian coast. (86)

f) Tactics aimed at isolating al-Sadat at home, and in the Arab world would either force him to abandon his "west-politik," or create the conditions for his overthrow. By exploiting existing differences between Egypt on the one hand and Syria, Iraq and Libya on the other, the Soviets appear to have geographically isolated Egypt. (87) By creating a radical alliance, the "anti imperialist front," they have, at a minimum, strengthened forces opposing Egyptian policies and potentially set the stage for a radical Arab anti-Egyptian axis. (88) By reducing economic and military assistance, they have compounded al-Sadat's postwar problems. The slowing down of Russian economic aid adversely affects the Egyptian economy, and exacerbates already widespread social unrest. (89)

The stoppage in Russian arms coupled with a dramatic resupply operation in Syria intensifies discontent in the Egyptian military. The Egyptian military is said to be both extremely worried about the state of Egypt's preparedness, and jealous over the sophisticated arms being delivered to Syria. (90) These feelings are intensified each time tension increased along the ceasefire lines. (91)

The net effect of all this is to dramatize al-Sadat's complete reliance on the West. And the Soviets have taken to warning the Egyptians about "the danger of illusory promises from imperialist quarters," (92) to drive home the point to al-Sadat's Arab colleagues. Although these Soviet warnings applied initially to promises of United States economic aid, which appeared for a time to be stalled in Congress, they now apply to the seeming inability or unwillingness of successive United States administrations to extract any meaningful - in Arab eyes - concession from the Israelis.

In addition to stabilizing the prewar Russian position, and thus preserving the strategic benefits noted by the RAND staff, postwar Soviet policy has the potential of adding the following:

1. Sealing off oil producing areas by land and sea.

2. Protecting Russian maritime access and transit through the Indian Ocean.

3. Providing Russian control of choke points in the Red Sea, Gulf, and Indian Ocean.

4. Creating new access points from which to encourage anti-Western nationalisms in the Arabian Peninsula, and sub-Saharan Africa.

5. With the addition of Libya, expanding Russian maritime facilities along the Southern Mediterranean coast.

6. Flanking Iran on three sides: Iraq to the East, Russia to the North, and India to the West, thus containing to some extent growing Iranian power. (93)

However, Russian efforts to extend its influence are hampered by roughly the same factors that impeded it before the war:

1. Arab resentment at Soviet acquiescence in allowing Jewish immigration.

2. Friction over weapons deliveries.

3. Arab suspicions of Russian intentions concerning Arab "rights," the feeling that Russia is using the Middle East crisis for its own ends.

4. Splits and antagonisms among its Arab clients: splits among the Palestinians, Syrian/Iraqi hostility, friction between these and al-Qadhafi.

5. Soviet inability to produce a satisfactory settlement on its clients' terms.

For the United States as well, the post-1973 situation presents both positive and negative features. On the positive side is the fact that the coalition which fought the war is basically conservative in nature, rather than radical. Its goals are parallel to those of the United States in many respects: Stability within the region, exclusion of Communist influence, and maintenance of working economic relations with the West. The critical point of difference, however, lies in differing conceptions of what constitutes a workable peace settlement. And here also is the chief negative feature: The fact that United States/Western European oil interests are now tied directly to the outcome of such peace negotiations.

United States' interests as defined by a House Subcommittee are as follows:

1. To preserve peace in the area.

2. To maintain a balance of power.

3. To restore, retain, or expand United States reservoir of goodwill in the region.

4. To secure United States economic interests, particularly oil interests. (94)

All of these are threatened by a combination of three factors: Arab/Israeli tensions, Arab expectations concerning United States policy, and Soviet efforts to exploit the postwar situation.

Arab/Israeli tensions obviously threaten United States interests because of the inherent potential for war, which in turn leads to both potential superpower confrontation and an Arab oil embargo. From the material reviewed in this study, the obvious background factor in this continued tension is the mutual incompatibility of Arab and Israeli definitions of national interests, definitions which have taken on an almost theological aspect with time. (95)

The precipitant of major conflict, however, has been the Syrian sector. Domestic conflicts within Syria have twice, in 1967 and 1973, been projected outward into Arab/Israeli relations. As long as the Syrian regime continues to be dominated by minorities, and thus reamins unstable, this situation can be expected to continue. This basic instability interacts with institutionalized Ba'th radicalism, the geographical sensitivity of the Golan to both sides, and the extremely hostile perceptions of the enemy.

In this connection, border warfare itself does not seem to be a precedent. In the Lebanese and Jordanian sectors, it serves to raise the level of background tension. Only where it becomes linked to Syrian politics, however, does it become critical. (96) In each case, the Egyptians have become involved. However, in both cases, basic differences in outlook have led to short lived coalitions (in the Lebanese fighting of 1976/77, Egyptian sponsored PLA units actually opposed the Syrians and Christians). On the face of the matter, points of friction between Egyptians and Syrians should outweigh points of accommodation. The respective leaderships come from different branches of Islam; their ideological outlooks are different; they are politically separated by the legacy of Egyptian activities in Syria during the short lived Union of 1958/1961. (97) Nevertheless, Egyptian decision makers have consistently been willing to interpret threats to Syria as being threats to Egyptian national interest. (98)

If the changed psychological situation following the October War presents the United States with an unexpected chance of recouping its lost position in that area, it also presents extreme risks. These have to do with one aspect of Arab imagery concerning the West: the legend of the "Great Betrayal."

In the back of Arab decision makers' minds is the memory of British promises to Sharif Husayn of Mecca during the course of diplomatic exchanges between 1915-1916. In return for the promise of British sponsorship of a greater Arab state, Husayn engineered the Arab revolt against the Ottomans. These exchanges, however, took place in the context of a series of negotiations between Britain and other Western powers.

One of these exchanges concerned a British-French plan for dividing up certain areas of the Levant and Mesopotamia between them, to assure a certain amount of political stability. Another concerned British efforts to get Zionist aid, in return for promises of British sponsorship of Jewish immigration into Palestine. Husayn was to some extent informed of the progress of these talks. (99) Nevertheless, when the dust of World War I settled, the Arabs felt that they had been betrayed. (100)

This legend of the great betrayal is indelibly stamped on Arab consciousness, and has been reinforced by subsequent events. For example, United States and Soviet efforts to prevent an Egyptian preemptive attack in June 1967 are still bitterly remembered. To requote from al-Quddus:

This surprise (sic: of October 6) did not give any country the opportunity to cancel the attack, as was the case in 1967 when the Soviet and American Ambassadors called on President 'abd al-Nasir in the middle of the night to ask him not to start the fighting - on the basis of pledges and guarantees for a peaceful settlement. The morning of the same night Israel started the attack.... (101)

Soviet attempts to get the Egyptians to go slow in October were likewise perceived as an attempt to cheat them, as al-Sadat declared in an al-Anwar interview:

> I was surprised when he (sic: The Soviet Ambassador in Cairo) told me that Syria was asking for a ceasefire and she requested this from the Soviet Union....I refused to order a ceasefire and I asked the Ambassador to convey this to his government....Then I cabled President Assad. On October 7th, I received a cable from President Assad denying that Syria was asking for a ceasefire....The Soviet Ambassador then asked for another meeting and again told me that Syria was asking for a ceasefire. My reply to him was violent. I simply said to him, 'I am satisfied with President Assad's answer. I take the truth from his message only'.... (102)

Given Arab expectations of a radical shift in United States policy as a consequence of October, United States "promises" take on added symbolism. In spite of the very sophisticated analysis of military and propaganda strategy that the Arabs undertook after 1967, Arab decision makers have apparently little feel for the way United States policy is made. In retrospect this should not be surprising: Arab political processes are basically authoritarian - the head of the government is just that, the ultimate decision maker, the ra'is, the "boss." It is not really comprehensible to Arab officials that a president of the United States may not be able to override all objections to his chosen course of policy. Therefore, some early hesitations about the implementation of President Nixon's promises of aid, or agreements to build nuclear power plants, or wheat shipments, were interpreted as a cynical attempt to buy Arab goodwill without doing anything concrete (a perception that Soviet propaganda has taken advantage of by emphasizing the object lesson that the West is really not to be trusted).

In reality, of course, United States presidents have, indeed, lived up to their commitments: Not only has the United States provided the Egyptians with substantial aid, as promised, but has also gone further and supplied Arab governments with war materiels; the sale of F-15s to Saudi Arabia, F-5Es to Egypt for example. (103) Nevertheless, it is the perception that counts, and the Arab perceptual world is a world dominated by intense suspicion of Western intentions. In this context, any United States "failure" to live up to its promises will inevitably be interpreted as another great betrayal. Hence the argument that the United States should avoid, at all costs, any role in Middle Eastern peace making which gives the appearance of a United States unilateral commitment. (104) So far, one of the key Arab actors insofar as the United States is concerned, al-Sadat, appears to perceive United States policy as being favorably inclined (or at least is willing to wait and see):

> This has a story which I will repeat. The peace process began here in Egypt. I started it with President Nixon and his Secretary of State, Dr. Kissinger, in 1974 with the first disengagement. Then President Ford came, and we concluded the second disengagement.

It was agreed that after the second disengagement the next step in the peace process would be that of going to Geneva and achieving a comprehensive solution. This means that after the second disengagement, there is no room for a third disengagement or anything else but peace.

When President Carter became president, he committed himself to this. Last September he received all of the Arab foreign ministers and the Israeli foreign minister. I then discovered - and I said this to the 2nd Army about two days ago - that, regrettably, as we were preparing to go to Geneva last summer, the disputes among ourselves as Arabs were greater than our disputes as Arabs with Israel because regrettably, some of us, Syria in particular, had a different line. It later transpired that Syria, in agreement with the Soviet Union, had no intention of going to Geneva.

I received a personal handwritten letter from President Carter. I cannot disclose its contents because it was personal. However, President Carter's explanation of the picture made me answer him with my own personal, handwritten letter.... (105)

Carter and I usually review the international situation, and I review my calculations with his international calculations. That man is serious, sincere and wants to help in peace moves. He also wants to succeed. From the very beginning he took up the energy issue, and the Middle East crisis. Israel wanted to play for time. The energy problem will take seven to eight years during which Israel will have established more settlements in the occupied territories and will have turned the old settlements into a fait accompli. Israel will also put pressure on Carter during his next election campaign. (106)

But al-Sadat has also advanced what could be called the forerunner of the contemporary legend of the great betrayal, in this case:

By a simple calculation, strategic and tactical or the maps, and a study of Israel's situation, which had become quite clear, as it was recently explained by the Israeli defense minister, it became evident that America has thrown all its weight in the battle, and sent new weapons which the American Army itself has not used. It became clear that they were seeking to disfigure that victory we and Syria had scored and use it, if possible to serve Israel.... (107)

To paraphrase Haykal, the crash of Arab expectations from the "sky above to the earth below", from exaggerated expectations concerning United States policy to total disenchantment with it, is likely to produce spectacular anti-American outbursts.

The forward movement of Russia into the Red Sea/Indian Ocean areas is also a prime concern. Russian activities in these areas represent a potential threat of United States/Western European access to oil, and a potential Russian chokepoint strategy aimed at Western shipping through the Canal, into and out of the Persian Gulf, and East-West through the Straits of Malacca. Moreover, these Russian naval facilities provide potential access points for shipment of Russian material to Arab and African insurgents.

All of this adds up to a very difficult situation facing United States policy makers, a situation that, because of the escalatory qualities of inter-Arab and Arab/Israeli relations, has built in constraints in terms of the time available to solve the Arab/Israeli problem. As Kissinger is said to have apocryphally remarked, the "history of the Middle East is a history of lost opportunities." It is another truism of Middle Eastern politics that after each war, there is a period of flux in which some solutions can be achieved: After 1948, it may have been possible to resettle the Palestinian refugees; after 1956, another albeit more restricted opportunity presented itself; after 1967, no Arab state was in a position to resist an imposed settlement. But by August of 1967, the Khartum formula of adamant rejection of all peaceful solutions had been agreed upon. In a sense, a comparable time situation exists in the post-October Middle East.

The opening for a negotiated settlement has been provided by the domination of Arab leadership by the moderate leaders in Egypt and Saudi Arabia. In stark contrast to previous Arab leaderships, these have been willing to try for a negotiated solution. The original Egyptian/Israeli meetings at Kilometer 101 may have dealt substantively with the technical concerns of a disengagement of forces, but their symbolic importance was enormous. Here, for the first time in almost three decades, Arab and Israeli negotiators had met face to face (even in the aftermath of 1948, Arabs and Israelis did not deal directly with one another. The armistice agreements were the outcome of the "Rhodes formula" - negotiations in which United Nations personnel shuttled between Arab and Israeli delegations). The willingness of this leadership to directly negotiate led to the Rabat Summit of November 1974 which, in effect, replaced the Khartoum formula with a strategy of negotiation.

Al-Nahar editor Ghassan Tuwayni summed up the effect of this leadership in the form of a comparison between 1967 and 1973. In contrast to the earlier war, the October War was a war of moderation, a war of Arab "doves," a war which was a victory for rationality.

The first paradox lies in the fact that while bellicose Arab radicalism led to total defeat in 1967, Arab moderation won a half victory in 1973.

Nasser, the militant, was defeated in war and could not get peace even when he offered it to the Israelis. Sadat, the moderate, made war and still holds many trumps in the peace game.

The Syria of Hafiz al-Assad, of the moderate wing of the Ba'th, was more effective than the Syria of Salah Jadid, leader of the radical wing that lost the Golan in 1967.

In 1967 it was the axis of the progressive and anti-Saudi regimes that waged the war. In 1973 it was the triple alliance of Egypt, Syria and Saudi Arabia that conducted the operations.

The militant states, like Libya, did not participate in the hostilities, while the moderate states, like Morocco, played at least a token part.

The participants in the last conflict deliberately excluded both the leftist radicals (Iraq), and the rightist radicals (Libya). Radicalism had had its day, and revolutionary war had been found wanting. It was the age of reason that triumphed. (108)

The importance of the Egyptian/Saudi axis in moderating Arab behavior cannot be overstressed. Throughout the labyrinthian negotiations that preceded the attack two factors stand out: The Egyptian commitment to some kind of coherent strategy based on concrete policy goals, and the Saudi insistence on a plan which would not irreconcilably split the Arabs and the West.

Although the Egyptians supplied the conceptual framework, the Saudis provided the wherewithal to operationalize it. Behind the scenes, Saudi efforts are apparent in a number of areas, utilizing a combination of money and Muslim solidarity: Saudi promises of money to the Egyptians strengthened al-Sadat's already conservative orientations. In relation to the Syrians, the Saudis were able to exploit Syrian/Soviet differences by offering funds for alternative sources of arms. Their point of entry was the Sunni faction around Talas (whom the Soviets once described as a "Syrian Sadiq"). (109) Saudi (and Kuwayti) mediation brokered the Jordanian/Syrian/Egyptian agreement. Saudi support of conservatives within Fatah strengthened their bargaining position, especially when the issue of continued supplies of Arab funds became critical. Fatah leadership itself is dominated by Muslim Brethren adherents, a factor that the Saudis probably also used to work out a Jordanian/Fatah understanding.

Both the Egyptians and Saudis have been stressing the need for a pragmatic approach to a settlement: on Arab policies based on concrete interests, on avoiding outbidding, on avoiding emotionalism:

Actually the Arab stand is cohesive and strong, but, regrettably, there are some of us (sic: especially al-Qadhafi) who are suffering from the demise of outbidding each other. We should admit this as long as we are rational. We have had enough of emotionalism and we admit that there are outbidders and sick people.... (110)

As to points of weakness now, regrettably this is an attempt by certain persons to build leaderships through methods repudiated by all men (sic: the rejection front). The building of leaderships by means of extremism, outbidding and emotionalism is obsolete. (111)

The ability of these moderates to get their view accepted by diverse Arab elements depends on their ability to project an appearance of success. As Harkabi pointed out before the war, Arab leaders were severely constrained in their ability to move away from the rigidities of the Khartum formula. They were trapped in an Arab version of the game of "prisoner's dilemma," where conflict is preferable to rational compromise: (112)

> The Arab leadership is not free to do as it wishes without limitations, however. One difficulty lies in the fact that as long as change does not encompass all the Arab states, a retreat by one would be exploited by its rivals to attack it; Arab leaders are vulnerable to each other, for criticism in one Arab country is liable to influence public opinion in another. From the political point of view there is no Arab union but where the inter-Arab (sic: verbal) abuse is concerned, the Arab world is united in what is almost a single system....
>
> For the (sic: Arab) leadership to change its attitude, there is need for adequate motives, or a significant, spectacular event that will make a change necessary (sic: or possible). If not, the momentum of the existing situation - if only for the reason that it exists -is decisive, for a change means creating something new. (113)

In this sense, the impression that there is movement on the question of Israeli withdrawal becomes a critical factor. Egyptian glorification of the victory of 1973 is a holding action. Given the tactical fluidity and perceptual mistrust that characterizes Middle Eastern politics, the image of the "hero of October" is a wasting asset. It has to be continually refurbished by later dramatic actions, and in this sense, al-Sadat's reliance on this imagery has placed him in a position similar to that of 'abd al-Nasir, much earlier. Like 'abd al-Nasir, al-Sadat having worked one miracle, the "miracle of October," now finds that maintenance of this charisma requires new miracles (in another sense there is also a certain irony: al-Sadat, the chief exponent of the value of pragmatism and rationality, was forced to adopt the politics of emotion to legitimate his pragmatic policies, to reintroduce the political style which the October strategy was supposed to end.) Therefore, the dramatic and unexpected act or gesture has become institutionalized to some extent in al-Sadat's political strategy, as it was in 'abd al-Nasir's. In a letter written to President Carter, al-Sadat articulated his theory of the necessity of the dramatic gesture: (114)

> I told him: I believe that what we need now is some daring action. Until that moment I had no idea at all as to what I was going to do but I was convinced that something daring had to be done. (115)

This perception that something dramatic was needed became more intense as 1973 receded. By 1975, the leverage that the Egyptians and Saudis had been able to exert was dissipating. The relative moderation, pragmatism, and unanimity of the Rabat Summit was replaced by escalating inter-Arab conflicts: The phenomenon of "outbidding" which al-Sadat criticized was accompanied by an escalating level of covert and overt inter-Arab attacks on installations and personnel (see below).

In this context, al-Sadat's peace initiative, his dramatic visit to Jerusalem and his equally unexpected agreement to the Camp David formula, and his assent to a separate peace with Israel, is a response to a deteriorating domestic and inter-Arab situation (the immediate context of al-Sadat's decision to act is discussed below):

> It is only natural for the Arabs to present new papers and new discussions, and also new amendments and amendments to amendments. However, it would be better and more important just to go to Geneva with any paper. The important thing is to go and meet and not to continue discussions and dialogues which might last for a quarter century, as is the case with the disarmament conference, which has recently celebrated its silver jubilee. Then, a Ba'th envoy came to me and said that the United States could not (presumably achieve peace) and even if it would, it did not want to. This was to prejudge things or to insure that they did not take place. This was before anybody could move. The Arab region was engaged in linguistic and semantic discussions, and time was slipping away. Years and generations would have passed before such discussions were over. If we remained silent regarding this damage, we would not have been honest. We are responsible for people's destinies. Today I am convinced that Syria does not want peace; I am sure it does not.
>
> I simply cannot admire the skilled empty discussions the Syrian Ba'th Party is specializing in. I cannot. What they say today, they repeat tomorrow, and the day after tomorrow; they begin anew with all vigor and vitality....
>
> The patience we see today is one of repeating empty talk, and the sincerity is for keeping positions of power. The garment they are making is the garment of hatred for Egypt, and of obstruction of peace moves. Now they are indulging in their vanity. Syria thought that since it had invaded Lebanon, shed its blood, and intimidated Jordan it was the great power and able to do anything. In any event, the mistake was ours because we gave Syria more than it deserved and raised it higher than necessary. The age of harmful pleasantries is over; everybody must know his weight and stature and his true nature must be demonstrated to the Arabs and the world. The pretext of peace behind which they are hiding must be made to fall, as must the bragging about glory and dignity. Where is dignity when a state sends its foreign minister to ask his masters in Moscow what to do next against Egypt, against peace and against the Arabs and how to act under the command of al-Qadhafi...
>
> We also want to exploit the time element and not lose it by listening to the speeches, the heroes in Damascus, Baghdad and Algiers. (116)

In one sense, Jerusalem and Camp David were the product of an emerging charismatic element in al-Sadat's political style. Alternatively, however, they were a calculated and logical extension of his underlying foreign policy assumption: that the United States was the only country with sufficient leverage to force Israeli concessions. Not only that, but this strategy of opting for an extremely high risk policy appeared to be based on his assessment of United States support, and more particularly, on his perception of President Carter himself:

> Nixon left office, Ford lost, and the Carter administration came to power. The peace process was supposed to begin in January 1977 by the reconvening of the Geneva conference to include a peace agreement. The new United States administration needed time to familiarize itself with United States domestic and foreign problems. I met Carter in April this year, and he agreed that the next step would be Geneva. Carter could have made any excuse. For example, he could have said that he had not studied the issue sufficiently or let us settle it step by step, but the man is a first class politician, an excellent statesman, and completely honest. I believe what he says. He agreed with me that we should proceed to Geneva for a comprehensive settlement. (117)

However, by unilaterally moving toward the United States, al-Sadat has acted to increase his isolation in the Arab world. After the trip to Jerusalem, he was tried symbolically and condemned by an Arab People's Congress; prior to his trip to Camp David, his remaining Arab allies (in this case, basically the Saudis) mounted an intensive diplomatic campaign to both convince him to moderate his go it alone policy, and return to some unified Arab negotiating framework. Al-Sadat himself is clearly aware of the political and personal risks of his go it alone strategy (a strategy, as noted, based on the lessons of 1967) and appears willing to take the risk involved:

> I arrived in Iran but I did not discuss this matter (i.e., the Jerusalem trip) with the Shah. I discussed with him the affairs of the area and the bilateral relations between the two countries. I then went back to Saudi Arabia, and there I met with King Khalid, but I did not broach the subject with him. (118)

> This decision was purely Egyptian, and I acted in my capacity as President of Egypt - the biggest Arab state. What prompted me to do this was that I did not know the reaction of the Arab brothers. Hafiz al-Asad was shocked. He believed that nobody had ever done this. He also believed that this action was not traditional, and I must not do it. What would I have done if three quarters of the Arab presidents and kings had disagreed with me - although I was sure that they would?

> Saudi Arabia, for example, issued a statement denying its prior knowledge of this decision or even its approval, simply because the press said that Shaykh Kamal Adham met with me prior to my departure. So to avoid any suspicion of prior knowledge or participation, Saudi Arabia issued the statement.

Therefore, how could this decision be a surprise if I informed all the Arabs about it. There was no need to consult anybody, or to obtain his approval of a fateful Egyptian decision. Nobody consults me regarding increasing or decreasing oil prices. Egypt is free, and will continue to be free to choose its course and fate. I told Hafiz al-Asad that I place my history in one scale, and this initiative in the other. If I fail I will say that al-Asad was right, and that I was wrong, and I will submit my resignation to the People's Assembly immediately. (119)

By insofar as the United States is concerned, this strategy (by design) puts even more pressure on the United States policy makers: Hence President Carter's unusual exercise of coercive diplomacy, sequestering Egyptian and Israeli leaders in virtual isolation until they reached an agreement.

By acquiescing to United States views of the situation, at considerable risk to himself (a risk al-Sadat has been careful to point out), al-Sadat in effect puts the onus on the United States to act to protect him: A sophisticated political version of Ahmad Isma'il's military strategy of forcing Russia into a position of having to resupply the Egyptions during the October War.

In addition to the implications of being maneuvered into a de facto alliance with al-Sadat, an alliance whose limits have not been fully articulated, there are two other problems: (a) Egyptian expectations of United States backing will inevitably be heightened; and (b) U.S. Middle Eastern policy will not be tied to what may become charismatic foreign policy strategy on al-Sadat's part. If this proves to be the case, the United States may well find itself in much the same position vis-a-vis al-Sadat as the Soviets found themselves in relation to 'abd al-Nasir. The combination of expectations, plus charismatic politics, plus an emphasis on surprise may present yet another difficulty for United States Middle Eastern policy makers. Note that, according to al-Sadat, President Carter was surprised by the Jerusalem trip: "The initiative was born while I was on my way from Saudi Arabia to Cairo. I did not speak about it with anyone. When President Carter heard of it, he as well as the news agencies said that it was very stunning. They used the English word "stun." President Carter had no inkling whatsoever of this." (120)

THE ARAB WORLD AS A CONFLICT SYSTEM: POLITICS OF INSECURITY

These linkage relationships are, in turn, embedded in and affected by existing patterns of Middle Eastern conflict. To sum up what has gone before, Middle Eastern escalatory dynamics are the product of an interlocking net of conflicts: Conflicts which have their origins on a number of levels. Politically, these conflicts are the products of a lack of territorial and political stability. As Leonard Binder (121) noted, all boundaries are subject to some form of revisionist attack because they are basically demarcations introduced by Western colonial administrators. Therefore, they lack legitimacy. The foci of political loyalty have not been clearly settled; there are a number of referents, political symbols in the area that compete for Arab political loyalties. The result is that the territorial framework for political action is unclear, irredentism is, in effect, institutionalized. Within these boundaries, political elites find themselves faced with the problem of legitimizing their rule. The fact of this lack of legitimacy has led these elites to opt for legitimizing strategies geared either to sublimating conflicts over legitimacy by generating a sense of external threat and then demanding internal loyalty to deal with this threat, or to projecting domestic tensions outward onto inter-Arab targets.

Political and territorial conflicts are reinforced by conflicts originating in Middle Eastern culture and society. Culturally the area is characterized by (a) a common culture whose value system tends to accentuate the pervasiveness of conflict and (b) a common language, Arabic, whose grammatical sophistication allows the expression of nuances of meanings including nuances of conflict. Sociologically, the area is cross cut by ethnic and sectarian divisions, divisions which have become identified as foci of primordial loyalties. The affect of the interplay of culture and society is to create a matrix of conflicts, conflicts which are then worked into the uneasy structure of political relationships.

Linkage politics (122) both objective in terms of the actual interaction of groups and individuals, and subjective in terms of perceived linkages between conflicts is the dominant pattern that has emerged. Take the Syrian attacks on right wing Christian forces begun in the first week of July 1978, and intensified in the aftermath of Camp David. This escalatory cycle involved a progressively wider range of conflicts. At the level of Lebanese domestic politics, the July fighting had its origins in rivalries with the right wing of the Christian community: In this case between Pierre al-Jumayyil's Phalangists, Camille Sham'un's National Liberal Party, and the followers of ex-President Sulayman Franjiya. (123) During the fighting from 1975/76, these groups operated in an uneasy coalition as they opposed a left wing Muslim/Palestinian alliance. (124) These already complex political and familial conflicts were translated into uneasy coalition politics during the fighting of 1975/76 as Christian forces opposed a Muslim/Palestinian alliance. Here, two sets of additional conflicts were involved: Christian/Muslim tensions inherent in the bifurcated makeup of Lebanon, and an extension of Palestinian/Israeli fighting. (125)

With the entrance of the Syrians in June 1976, whose primary goal was to preserve Syrian dominance over Lebanon (an extension of the Eastern front policy) (126), a further escalation took place. On one hand, the Christians had developed working relations with the Syrians on the basis of a shared interest in preventing a Muslim/Palestinian victory. On the other hand, the Christians had also created links with the Israelis, who also wanted to prevent a Muslim/Palestinian victory. The result was an odd de facto coalition of Christians, Syrians, and Israelis. This coalition, however, quickly broke up in the wake of al-

Sadat's visit to Jerusalem which polarized the Arab world (see below), and the Israeli invasion of South Lebanon in March 1978. The Christians found themselves being forced to choose between the Israelis and the Syrians, and their coalition broke up with the Phalange and NLP opting for the Israeli side, the Franjiyyas moving toward the Syrians. Open Christian/Israeli collaboration was anathema to the Syrians, particularly as it appeared to foreshadow the creation of an Israeli backed Christian entity in South Lebanon. On June 13, Phalangists assassinated Tony Franjiya (Sulayman's son), the Franjiyas responded with a retaliatory attack two weeks later, and Syrian forces began systematically bombarding rightist strongholds the following week. (127) The Syrian response itself was the product of equally complicated foreign and domestic considerations: (a) Syrian strategic interests in Lebanon; (b) Syrian relations with the Franjiyas - they are related by marriage to the al-Asads which added a kinship consideration; (c) the growing resentment of Syrian Muslims at the spectacle of Syrian troops fighting other Muslims for the benefit of Christians. The Syrian bombardment, in turn, nearly triggered an Israeli response; and with that, the possibility of another war (in fact Arab sources on the eve of Camp David were predicting just such an escalation; see below). Here the linkages are complex: intracommunity conflicts, religious conflicts, strategic conflicts, but the point is not that any given set of Middle Eastern conflicts has an escalatory potential.

These objective conflict linkages are supplemented by a perceptual system which emphasizes conflict. Middle Eastern cognitions take the form of a conflict model of the environment; and these conflict oriented cognitions are, in turn, worked into both political strategies and political ideologies. These perceptions are in turn mediated through a set of symbols, in this case articulated in Arab media, which add their own psychological impact. Again, the impact of these symbols and the emotive quality of Middle Eastern politics is accentuated by the prevalence of the "politics of personality": A phenomenon generated partially by authoritarian Arab values which promote hierarchical decision making, and partially by the relative lack of bureaucratized decision making structures. (128) The consequence is a systematic interaction in which no decision maker can afford to trust any other decision maker: each perceives himself to be vulnerable to outside threats on a number of levels. And, given the larger patterns of social change and consequent social tension which are superimposed on Middle Eastern political life, the environment does, in fact, contain a high level of threat. The net effect is the institutionalization of elite insecurity, (129) and a concomitant political style based, as Lasswell once put it, on the "expectation of violence":

> The expectation of violence exercised a profound influence upon the distribution of other symbol formations and upon direct adaptations to the environment. The political processes which are favored by the expectation of violent conflict may be stated in these terms (an equilibrium analysis). The participants tend to array themselves in two conflicting camps (except a neutralized few who

are protected by favorable positions with reference to the general balancing process, as is modern Holland). The dominating pivots of the twofold division are the strongest rivals. Putting the whole matter tersely, the process is:

A seeks to associate C against B.

B seeks to associate C against A.

A or B, failing C, seek to associate D or E (and so on among the various participants).

It will be noticed that one consequence of this process is the tendency toward the universalization of the conflict until the position of all parties of similar status is defined... (130)

Although Lasswell was referring to European politics when he argued that there was a tendency toward polarization in an unstable conflict system, his analysis applies equally to the Middle East. In the period of intense uncertainty following the October War, two major coalitions have emerged: the "Arab Entente," a loose coalition dominated by Egypt and Saudi Arabia, (131) and the "Steadfastness Front", a coalition (132) uneasily led by a Syrian, Libyan, Iraqi triumvirate. Analyzed in terms of Lasswell's Freudianesque theory of an international extension of personal needs for security, this polarization is the inter-Arab consequence of culturally induced security oriented behavior. It is the political expression of Kardiner's security systems. Alternatively, viewed from the perspective of conflict theory, this coalition building behavior is an extension of defensive group formation. Historically, the post-October polarization resembles that of the 1960s when the Arab world was divided between the radicals and the Islamic alliance. In the present situation, a major actor, Egypt, has shifted from the radical to the conservative camp. This is a critical factor because the dynamic for both coalition formation processes was supplied by Egyptian alliances with outside powers, alliances which were perceived to threaten inter Arab balances: first with the Soviets in the 1960s and then with the United States in the 1970s.

Note that although the membership in the post-1970 coalitions is different, the impetus to coalesce was supplied by the same actor, and the structure of background tensions remained the same, although the level of tension has steadily increased:

(a) Cultural conflicts: The upsurge of Islamic fundamentalism that had begun following the 1967 War has increased dramatically. A number of factors, all more or less connected with the Arab-Israeli conflict apper to be responsible: (1) the immediate and exacerbated irritant of Israeli occupation of Muslim holy places; (2) the Islamic imagery that surrounds the October War itself - in this case the presentation of the war as a victory against the West, with all the latent emotional implications that presentation entails; (3) a larger reaction against accelerated social change, in this case change which was induced as part of policies of military modernization. (133) In any event, this ground swell of "Muslimness" has become one of the major factors in contemporary Middle Eastern politics and has been exploited for political purposes. In Egypt, Muslim Brethren antiregime activities have increased, abated to some extent by the Libyans. (134) In Syria, Sunni hostility to the government is on the increase, here because of the Lebanese war. In Iraq, Shi'a/government tensions have exploded into rioting (amidst allegations of Syrian manipulation). (135) In Iran, not an Arab country, Shi'a hostilities to the Shah's programs have also led to riotings, here in connection with the activities of a coalition of anti-Shah nationalists. (136)   The upshot of all this is an increase in primordial, specifically Christian/Muslim tensions throughout the area. And here the Lebanese civil war has become both the focal point and the generator of these tensions as Christians and Muslims outside Lebanon lined up on the side of their coreligionists, and Arab governments sent in troops.

(b) Inter-Arab Conflicts: In addition to a generalized upswing in religious tensions, the Arab world was increasingly wrecked by a series of regional conflicts, conflicts which had their antecedents in pre-October tensions.

(1) In the Arab Northeast, a complex and convoluted rivalry between Syria and Iraq spilled over into proxy conflicts involving both Lebanese and Palestinian factions (and to some extent the Jordanians also). The origins of Syrian/Iraqi hostilities stemmed from the fact that each government was dominated by ideologically hostile branches of the Ba'th: the Iraqis were, in the main extensions, of the old line Ba'th cadres overthrown by the neo-Ba'th. Michel Aflaq, himself, for some time operated out of Baghdad. These differences were temporarily papered over during the October war, and Iraqi forces were utilized in the defense of Damascus. However, they were reasserted with a vengeance as the Iraqis took issue with what they felt was an ignominious Syrian acceptance of the ceasefire, and Iraqi forces were promptly withdrawn amid a hail of invective. (137)

The immediate casus belli of Syrian/Iraqi warfare, however, was a Syrian plan to dam the Euphrates; a plan which the Iraqis felt would either reduce the amount of water left over for Iraqi irrigation purposes, or increase its salinity, or both. At one point both countries came close to open war. Syrian and Iraqi forces remained concentrated on their mutual border throughout 1975 (at the highest level of this tension, some five Iraqi divisions were said to be in position opposite two to three Syrian divisions). While conventional forces were thus poised, Syrian and Iraqi "hit teams" planted bombs in each others capitols. Iraqis, in particular, seem to have made use of their links with the Resistance to carry out those attacks. The Popular Front for the Liberation of Palestine units were said to be involved, as well as members of the Arab Communist Organization (ACO), which had some connections with the PFLP. Later, the Iraqis apparently used a Fatah splinter which styled itself "Black June" (after the June 1976 Syrian attacks on Palestinians in Lebanon). Among other attacks, Black June terrorists hit the Semiramis Hotel in Damascus, the Intercontinental Hotel in Amman, and attempted the assassination of Syrian Foreign Minister Khaddam. (138) These hostilities were, of course, translated into the Lebanese arena as Syrian and Iraqi forces, and their Lebanese and Palestinian surrogates fought each other.

(2) To the Arab Northwest, a similarly explosive situation had developed: Egyptian/Libyan hostilities, steadily escalating after October, were intensified by Libyan moves into the Sudan and the Chad. In July 1976, the Libyans sponsored an abortive attempt to invade the Sudan and overthrow its government; at the same time, the Libyans were providing assistance to Frolinat insurgents in the Chad (and also laying claim to a considerable piece of the northern Chad. A claim, it may be added, that had some basis in fact: the region claimed was originally part of Libya, and had been transferred to Chad in the context of a colonial redrawing of boundaries). The consequence here was direct Egyptian intervention in the Sudan, later formalized into a defense treaty; and some military assistance to the Chad. (139) These tensions, along with more direct Libyan/Egyptian cross border forays, escalated into the open conflict of August 1977: A conflict that threatened to become much larger when the Algerians threatened to intervene on behalf of the Libyans (Algeria and Libya signed a defense agreement in 1975). This conflict was, in turn, linked into another in the Western Sahara: A four-sided struggle involving local insurgents, the Polisario Front, Morocco, Mauritania and Algeria. In this case, the Libyans were backing the Algerians.

(3) To the Arab South, the war between Ethiopia and Somalia and its counterpart between North and South Yemen pitted still other constellations of Arabs against each other. At one point in later 1978, North and South Yemenese forces were massed on each other's borders, in addition to Saudi, and even Pakistani troops. (140) Here again, this conflict had had extensions to the east: South Yemen had been backing insurgents in Oman (PFLO), which in turn led to Saudi and Iranian involvement.

All of these conflicts added up to a situation frought with danger insofar as Arab decision makers were concerned. The Egyptians were fearful of a two front war: with the Libyans on one side, the Israelis on the other (one of the major reasons for al-Sadat's peace initiative). The Saudis were extremely worried that yet another escalation of the Arab/Israeli conflict was about to explode out of the fighting in Ethiopia (an extension of pre-1973 fears). The Syrians were fearful of being maneuvered into a one sided war with Israel (a basic Syrian concern since the early 1950s). These conflicts would have added tension within the Arab world, but they were exacerbated by still other tensions:

(c) Domestic and intraelite conflicts: In the wake of October a number of Arab regimes were shaken by domestic disturbances: reports of demonstrations, arrests, and various forms of martial law were commonplace. The sources of these disturbances were two fold: (a) an extension of the ongoing problems of establishing legitimacy in a situation of social change, and (b) bitter divisions within ruling elites over the conduct of post-October policy. Expressed in terms of Huntington's formula: The rates of social and psychological mobilization, with concomitant increased mass economic demands, outran economic growth rates in most Arab countries. The consequent gap between mass aspirations on one hand, and mass perceptions of economic realities on the other, generated intense frustration. This frustration, in turn, was translated into a variety of antiregime activities, ranging from unfocused mob violence to specific coup attempts. This was accompanied by demands for participation in decision making by a variety of groups: old-line factions and individuals which preexisted October, and new groups mobilized into politics by the war. The upshot was that most Arab regimes were caught on the horns of the dilemma posed by Samuel Huntington: If they opted for efficiency and controlled economic and political development, they alienated increasingly wider segments of their populations, reducing their base of political support. If they opted for increased participation, they reduced the possibility of controlled growth. In either case, the tensions thus generated strained already marginally legitimate institutional structures and made resort to conflict politics almost inevitable. (141)

Most Arab countries were affected, but Egypt and Syria were hardest hit by this pattern of domestic discontent (with Iraq a close third). In Egypt, al-Sadat's "corrective movement" which was economically a policy of moving toward a more capitalistic economy (designed to attract Western money) (142) and politically, an attempt to "de-Nasirize" Egyptian politics, generated unforeseen consequences: The loosening up Nasirist economic controls triggered a wave of popular expectations concerning a rising standard of living; when these were not met, a burst of mass violence broke out in the form of bread riots in January 1977. The worst day of rioting was promptly dubbed "Black Wednesday" after the "Black Saturday" that shook King Faruq's regime. (143) The mass arrests that followed (some 2000 immediately after the riots, another 2000 or so within the year) and the subsequent crackdown on actual or potential opponents of the regime, further alienated large segments of the population. (144)

Politically, the de-Nasirization campaign also produced unexpected consequences. On one hand, the temporary relaxation of press controls permitted opponents of al-Sadat to publicly attack his policies (here Haykal was the most vigorous critic). When press controls were reasserted, however, not only the original opponents were outraged, but now also new groups. Further, al-Sadat's criticisms of Nasirist social and political controls emboldened heretofore quiescent opponents of Nasirism: specifically, the Wafd and the Muslim Brethren (who were opposed to each other in addition). The Wafd attempted to take advantage of a brief experiment with a multiparty system to build a power base in the People's Assembly; the Brethren utilized the crackdown on the left which followed the January riots to press for Islamic legislation and a general return to Qur'anic principles (this in in turn triggered a Coptic reaction, and religious tensions, punctuated by Church bombings, soared). The upshot was that al-Sadat found his regime opposed by pre-Nasir nationalists (the Wafd), Nasirists, an emerging radical left (spearheaded by a rejuvenated Egyptian Communist Party), and the Islamic right.

The problem of defending against this formidable array of opponents was made more complex by uncertainties as to the loyalty of colleagues and subordinates. In an elite already semi isolated, the pattern of pre-October bureaucratic politics reasserted itself, as factions maneuvered for control using divisions over policy issues as access points. In al-Sadat's case, the loyalty of the military was critical (just as it had been before October); and the military itself was split over his arms policy and peace initiative. (145) These splits were exacerbated by the activities of ex-Chief of Staff Shadhili (who appears to consider himself a viable alternative to al-Sadat): Shadhili had managed to garner the support of a number of al-Sadat's opponents, both within and without Egypt, and he made the most of this, dramatically touring the Arab world, offering his services to the Palestinian cause, denouncing al-Sadat's policies, and openly calling for a coup. (146) The consequence was return to the early years of al-Sadat's rule, a situation where he had to utilize 'abd al-Nasir's techniques of control: purging opponents, shifting coalitions of supporters, isolating opponents. Here al-Sadat was, of necessity, constantly suspect, reassigning or purging his officers (especially those officers with any previous connection with Shadhili). (147) In the wake of Camp David, for example, al-Sadat reshuffled his high command (in addition to a number of cabinet posts). The official rationale given was that this change would allow new faces access to the top positions; but according to Arab sources, it was to forestall a coup. (148)

In Syria, the situation was not much better. Here, al-Asad's version of the corrective movement had equally released popular expectations. But these, in turn, were worked into the structure of primordial loyalties: discontent in Syria was focused on the 'Alawi community, which was said to be benefiting (by widespread corruption) from the economic changes at the expense of the Sunni majority. (149) These discontents were aggravated by the spector of Syrian troops fighting Muslims in Lebanon, and by a breakdown of public order in the wake of a series of bombings and assassinations (some carried out by Iraqi sponsored agents, others by indigenous opponents), including an attempted uprising in Aleppo, and North Syria in April 1978.

In the Syrian elite this external Shi'a/Sunni tension was reflected in a series of interconnected conflicts ostensibly over policy issues (i.e., how to deal with the emerging Egyptian go it alone policy, how to react to the situation in Lebanon, how to deal with the Iraqis), but actually over the primordial composition of the elite. The focal point of this conflict was al-Asad's brother Rifa'at al-Asad, nominally the Commander of the Syrian Special Forces, but actually one of the major strategists behind al-Asad's regime. Rifa'at's spectacular rise to power set off antagonisms within the Sunni community; Sunni officers felt that Riaf'at and other 'Alawis, mostly relatives of al-Asad, were being promoted at the expense of Sunnis.

This Shi'a/Sunni struggle was particularly intense in the military, where two factions had emerged. A Shi'a faction, headed by Rif'at and composed of relatives and friends of the al-Asads who had been systematically promoted through the years, and a Sunni faction, organized around Defense Minister Talas and his Deputy Jamil (also Commander of the Air Force and Coordinator of Intelligence). In an attempt to retain the loyalty of the Sunnis, al-Asad had promoted these Sunnis, along with Chief of Staff Hikmat Shihabi (ex-intelligence chief, who replaced Shakkur as Chief of Staff in 1974). However, Jamil and Rif'at al-Asad were apparently personal enemies, as well as sectarian and bureaucratic rivals, both maneuvering to become successors to al-Asad. In the infighting that occured after October, Rif'at succeeded in installing a cadre of officers loyal to himself and was able to wield sufficient leverage to have Jamil summarily dismissed in early 1978. (150) Although intra elite disputes were temporarily papered over, the elite remained badly split; and these splits took on added significance in the wake of reports that al-Asad was seriously ill, possibly dying from leukemia, an event which could set off a full scale power struggle between Shi'as and Sunnis. (151)

In addition to the Egyptians and Syrians, other elites found themselves faced with internal challenges. Jordanian units originally sent to Syria in October engaged in a short lived mutiny in 1974, the causes of which were ostensibly discontent over low pay, but appear to have been connected with divisions within the Jordanian elite. (152) The Saudis were shaken by the assassination of Faysal, and given King Khalid's apparent ill health, appeared to have a potential power struggle in the offing between rival factions of the Royal Family. (153) The Palestinians were badly split as pre-October divisions were intensified by a bitter disagreement over whether to accept some negotiated settlement: In this case, a "Palestinian entity" in the West Bank. In the summer of 1974, the moderates in the PLO managed to pass a program calling for such an acceptance. The consequence was an organizational split as first the PFLP, and then other groups, withdrew to form a rival organization, the Rejection Front. (154) In the face of al-Sadat's initiative, this split widened to include splits in the leaderships of various groups. The consequence was an escalation of intra-Palestinian violence as factions (aided by Arab allies) fought pitched gun battles. (155)

(c) Personal Insecurities: In addition to the other, more generalized patterns of threat and conflict there was one last level: That of personal attacks on Arab leaders. Assassinations in the Arab World are by no means new. The term "assassination" itself is of Middle Eastern origin, (156) and a number of Arab leaders had been assassins' targets in the past (in the 20th century, King Husayn probably holds the record for being the most targeted Arab leader). (157) But, in the 1970s, these attacks increased both in frequency and sophistication. Following the BSO murder of Wasfi al-Tal, it was clear that any Arab leader might well be the victim of an assassin. Especially after the October War,

however, as various factions sought to prevent any negotiated settlement, assassination became a major weapon in intra-Arab conflict.

In April 1974, some 27 people were killed in an attempt to seize
weapons from the Military Academy at Heliopolis in a prelude to an
attack on al-Sadat. (158) In March 1975, King Faysal was shot during a
Friday audience by a disaffected member of the Royal Family, Prince
Faysal ibn Musa'id (whose brother was involved in an attempted coup in
1965). (159) Druze leader Kamal al-Junblatt was ambushed in March
1977. (160) The presidents of North and South Yemen were killed
within days of each other in the summer of 1978. And from there, the
roster of assassin's targets grew: Attempts, successful and not, were
made on the lives of various Egyptian, Syrian, Jordanian, Iraqi,
Lebanese, and Palestinian figures. In addition, there were reports of
plots to kill non-Arab personalities: Americans Henry Kissinger and
Cyrus Vance, the Shah's sister, Princess Ashraf. (161)

The terror inspired by news of actual assassinations was augmented
by open calls for the murder of Arab leaders, and stories of far reaching
international plots to kill selected leaders, (162) and even plots to kill
whole delegations of officials (in the wake of stories that a plan was
being hatched to kill the entire Egyptian delegation that accompanied
al-Sadat to Jerusalem, some 4000 new security officers were said to be
detailed to protect Egyptian officials). The not unexpected result was
that Arab leaders very much feared for their personal safety. Security
forces were increased, suspected plotters were purged, and a range of
security measures were taken.

The systemic consequence of these conflicts was that the level of
conflict in the Middle East as a whole increased, and along with this
increase was an increase in the perception of threat and an increase in
the sense of elite and/or personal insecurity throughout Middle Eastern
establishments. To sum up, a number of factors contributed to this
rising level of conflict. Autonomous social changes, some accelerated
by attempts at military modernization and other social engineering,
which generated a complex background of diffuse discontent. The
impact of media technology, a technology which facilitated a "linkage
politics of discontent" in the sense that news of riots and demonstrations provided behavioral models for yet other uprisings. An increase in
ideological politics, with some exceptions, wherein the ideologically
defined strategies of conflict articulated expanded conflict goals, i.e.,
the overthrow of regimes, the destruction of whole elites, and the
assassination of perceived opponents. A concomitant increase in the
technology of conflict, both in the sense of weapons destructiveness,
and in that of organizational capabilities, e.g. the ability to employ
large conventional forces on one hand, or to engage in international
terror on the other. (163)

Insofar as Arab decision makers were concerned, the response was a
chain reaction of coalition building behavior. Each elite sought to
defend against an increasingly hostile environment by securing allies.
This, in turn, was perceived by yet other elites as an escalation of
threatening behavior. These reciprocated in kind, which set off both
the original and additional elites, in a sequence of ever-expanding

defensive coalitions, coalitions whose membership patterns supplied the
linkages between heretofore separate conflicts.

This coalition building process was accompanied by intensified
attacks, both verbal and actual. Arab media attacks increased in
frequency and stridency (see the excerpt in Chapter I); the resemblance
between these attacks and those of the media war of the 1960s was
remarkable. The media war was supplemented by extensive cross
boundary intervention, ranging from regular forces, to commandos, to
groups of assassins, bombers, and hijackers (the Egyptians, for example,
claim that the Libyans sponsored more than 38 raids into Egypt between
1974 and 1977.

The narrowly based coalition that planned and fought the war, as
noted, began to split up during the war itself. Strategic differences
between the Egyptian and Syrian position were translated into
differences over the conduct of the war and the timing of the ceasefire.
Without pressure of local, inter-Arab, and Israeli threats sufficient to
override these differences, the legacy of mistrust and suspicion
reasserted itself with a vengeance. Egyptian and Syrian differences
were almost at once translated into policies designed to safeguard the
immediate security interests of each. The Egyptians began a series of
negotiations with the Israelis over Israeli withdrawal from the Sinai, the
negotiations of Sinai I (January 18, 1974) and II (September 4,
1975). (164)

In response, the Syrians, feeling that the Egyptians were about to
negotiate a separate peace with Israel, began a series of initiatives
designed to secure both the Golan Heights and the approaches to Syria
on both sides, i.e., through Jordan and Lebanon. In August 1975, even
before Sinai II was concluded, the Syrians and Jordanians had initialed
an agreement that ostensibly called for extended economic cooperation.
However, the military implication was obvious: Jordanian ground forces
would block any Israeli move to outflank Syrian defenses in Golan from
the south, Jordanian air defense would attempt to interdict Israeli
aircraft making a "right hook" over Jordan. (165)

The consequence of these moves was to set off a wave of reactions
in the Arab world. The Palestinians perceived these agreements as part
of a plan by Arab leaderships to betray them a second time, the
Egyptians, by concluding a peace with Israel and leaving the Palestinian
issue unsolved, the Syrians, by allying with the Hashemites in Jordan
(who, it may be added, had never relinquished their claim to Palestinian
territories in the West Bank). The Palestinian response was to intensify
their efforts to secure a safe base in Lebanon - efforts which cycled
together with existing tensions in Lebanon to produce the Lebanese civil
war, and to revive terrorist strategies that had been temporarily
suspended in the later part of 1974 when it appeared that the resistance
was going to be granted substantial international recognition.

The Libyans perceived Egyptian acts, in particular, as a "sellout" of
the Arab cause: a sellout that, insofar as the Libyans were concerned,
began with the Egyptian acceptance of the ceasefire. (166) The Libyan
response was threefold. They sought to intensify already existing
efforts to overthrow al-Sadat, to join in Russian efforts to isolate al-
Sadat (see below) to the extent of becoming the recipient of large scale

Russian arms transfers, and to increase its linkages with more radical groups in the resistance and become one of the major resource suppliers for Palestinian international terrorism. (167)

Similarly, the Iraqis, already isolated politically and psychologically in the Arab world, and directly threatened by the Syrians, perceived the new Syrian/Jordanian axis as a major extension of the Syrian threat. The Iraqi response, in addition to attacks on Syrian targets, was to move toward the Libyans and the Palestinians in the rejection front. This emerging nucleus was, in turn, backed by Russia for its own reasons, and later the Algerians were drawn in on the basis of a composite of Soviet and Libyan ties.

The outcome was an emergence of two extensive and opposed coalitions: The Steadfastness Front which evolved out of the older Rejection Front; and the Entente which was an extension of the original Egyptian/Saudi axis. Not only were the members of these alliances opposed on a number of substantive issues, but they were also commited to different strategies of conflict. The Steadfastness Front opted for a strategy of expanding to goals and means of conflict, of dramatically altering the balance of power within the Arab world, and moving it away from the West. Entente strategy aimed at stabilizing the region by disengaging the different subregional conflicts from each other and mediating them. In addition, it opted for retaining Arab linkages with the West. (168) But even with these fundamental differences, the perceived threat from a possible Egyptian-United States, or even Egyptian-Israeli alliance was sufficient to override existing conflicts. In an extraordinary summit, brokered by the Iraqis, leaders of both coalitions met at Baghdad from 1-5 November 1978. During the course of the negotiations two major trends emerged: (a) a movement of Entente states away from their heretofore full support of al-Sadat, and toward the anti-peace treaty stand of the Steadfastness Front; and (b) a rapprochement between Iraq and Syria as a strategy of extending and strengthening the Eastern Front in the event of an Arab-Israeli war fought within the Egyptians.

ARABS AND ISRAELIS: THE ESCALATORY IMPERATIVE

The tensions inherent in this unstable Arab conflict system are transmitted to Arab/Israeli relationships as well. Not only are they transmitted, but they are also amplified by the "lessons" of October. As Pranger and Tahtinen point out, there are two basic lessons: That a preemptive attack is imperative given the type of weaponry now employed in the Middle East. (169) That given the demonstrated ability of each side to conceal its plans for an attack, anticipation, rather than a response based on hard intelligence, becomes the mode by which an attack is launched. (170) In this situation of extreme uncertainty, any event can trigger a preemptive attack. An intensification of Palestinian terrorism like the Fatah Raid into Israel in March 1978 (the raid itself was the outgowth of splits within Fatah leadership over the al-

Sadat peace initiative), a re-escalation of the fighting in Lebanon - as for example the Syrian/Christian fighting of the mid-Summer 1978, the invasion of Lebanon, itself, first by the Syrians in 1976, and then by the Israelis in 1978, could have escalated into a more general conflict. Pranger and Tahtinen have pessimistically described the situation:

> Two preemptive capabilities posed for knock out blows will undermine any concept of a stable deterrence in the Middle East. The 1976 military status in the Arab-Israeli conflict is highly unstable and likely to become more so if current patterns of weapons acquisition continue....The military solution in the Middle East, with deficient or nonexistent deterrence mechanisms, will be accident prone, vulnerable to a wide range of mistaken judgments... (171)

The point is that not only is there an enormously heightened sense of threat by all major parties concerned, but that this pervasive threat perception opens the way for otherwise minor actors to dramatically alter the course of events.   A major peace initiative by Egypt - the Jerusalem trip - was effectively stalled by the actions of an eleven man Fatah raiding party, (172) and in the aftermath of Camp David, Palestinian leaders have vowed to use the same strategy to block a separate Egyptian-Israeli peace. (173)

In this psychological system of interlocking insecurities, tensions, and perceived threats, combined with an uncertain environmental situation between war and peace, the dynamics of inter-Arab, and Arab-Israeli relations led to a steadily increasing sense that war was inevitable. Each side, Arab and Israeli, increasingly perceived the other as preparing for war. Each side saw the other as becoming increasingly intransient on issues concerning a settlement. The result was a wave of statements, warnings, and forecasts of increasing bellicosity: indeed, in a manner startlingly reminiscent of the pre-1967 psychological climate, as all sides seemed to be engaged in generating a series of self-fulfilling prophecies proclaiming the imminence of war.   These were accompanied and reinforced by a series of mobilizations and troop movements, designed to gain local diplomatic advantages. Here pre-October techniques of threat generation were utilized as components of the post-October negotiating process. Each of the major Arab-Israeli agreements so far has been preceded by deliberately escalatory moves by one or more actors. The results, however, were more escalatory than intended, as these moves interacted with existing conflicts, each with its own dynamic, and the consequence was an escalatory cycle considerably more intense than originally calculated. The use of pre-October techniques, already incredibly risky as 1967 proved, were made even more dangerous by the lessons of October, and the calculus of threat and escalation was even more uncertain.

On a number of occasions, events seemed to be escalating out of control. In the late summer of 1974, in the context of uncertainties caused by the Syrian refusal to renew the United Nations Disengagement Observer Force mandate in the Golan (with the concomitant possibility of a renewed Syrian war of attrition along the Golan), the Israelis began a partial mobilization. This was clearly intended as a warning to the Syrians that a renewal of hostilities would lead to unforeseen and dangerous consequences insofar as the Syrians were concerned. However, this "signal" was interpreted by Syrains as signalling an Israeli intention to invade, along the lines of similar Israeli moves as far back as 1967. The consequence was not only a dramatic escalation along the Golan, but also in the Sinai.

The Egyptians, in turn, anxious about the possibility of an Israeli preemptive strike, and operating with a well developed theory of what events would trigger such a strike (see below), were prepared to interpret any Israeli military activity as foreshadowing such an attack. Especially, in this case, when these troop movements were accompanied by veiled warnings, such as a statement by Shim'on Peres to the effect that the Arabs "were not to think that the element of surprise is confined to one side." (174)

In any event, both sides began maneuvering in the Sinai. The Egyptian, in particular, claimed that their buildup was to forestall an Israeli attack. (175) Apparently only some very active United States intervention prevented escalation into a full scale war. Parenthetically, in an interview a little over a year later, Chief of Staff Gur detailed the Israeli perception of just how such a war would start:

> I assume it would be the Arabs who would start the war. There is a possibility of a war of attrition opening on the eastern front. Such a war would be liable to draw reactions from us, and this could turn into a real war. This can be with the Iraqis or without them, and it has, of course, many implications. It is possible that nothing might come of the agreement with Egypt (sic: Sinai II) because of internal developments there, or for pan-Arab reasons, and then a war might develop. Such a war might spread to other fronts as well. If the agreement with Egypt goes into force, an Egyptian offensive is less foreseeable... (176)

During 1975 the drum fire of warnings continued. But now the more strident Arab warnings of an impending blowup were reinforced by an undertone of Western comments along the same lines: Warnings, in this case, that stressed the argument that an Arab/Israeli stalemate would result in a new and potentially more dangerous war. (177) These warnings were counterpointed by a literature which argued that Western powers should forcefully intervene in the Arab world, especially in the oil producing areas, to assure that Western interests would be safeguarded. (178) The upshot here, of course, was that Arab decision makers read these reports and articles and drew their own conclusions: That either the Israelis really were up to something, or that the Western powers, principally the U.S., were really planning some massive exercise of military force in the Middle East. Apropos of the stories about invading and holding Arab oil fields, the Kuwaytis are said to have responded by mining the oil fields. Here again, the latent image of the West as being hostile to the Arabs was translated into Arab interpretations of Western literature.

The tempo of threats increased in 1977, in the wake of tension generated by the Syrian intervention in Lebanon. Arab sources now spoke of an Israeli "blitzkrieg" against selected Arab targets: Targets ranging from Syria and Egypt, to Libya, (179) to the Arabian Peninsula oil fields. (180) In addition to the increasing scope of perceived Israeli threats, now extending outward into North Africa and the Arabian Peninsula, two other elements were added to Arab perceptions of the post-October situation: An increasing belief that the Israelis intended to stay in the occupied territories, a belief of long standing, but now buttressed on one hand by the September 1976 publication of the "Qenig Plan," a document which dealt with the problems of permanently integrating Arab populations in Israel, (181) and on the other, by the election of Menachaim Begin's rightwing coalition in May 1977, a coalition committed to retaining the occupied territories. (182) A concurrent appearance of waffling on Middle Eastern issues by the newly elected Carter administration. The situation in 1977, appeared to be, and was increasingly represented in Arab media, as being an analogy to that immediately preceding the October War. But with the added difference that, unlike October, the Begin government coalition was composed of the same Israeli "hawks" (e.g., Dayan) that made up the coalition that launched the surprise attack of 1967.

In Arab/Israeli relations, it is against this background of increasing tension, tension which was translated into Israeli air strikes on Lebanon, Syrian "tactical exercises", and Egyptian and Israeli mobilizations toward the end of Summer 1977, that the al-Sadat initiative must be viewed:

> We talked about all this, but when you stop to think that, for a period of 10 days, because of a mere miscalculation and the existing psychological barrier, which entailed mistrust and suspicion of each other in any move made, plus the sudden blow dealt by our armed forces - a blow that is extremely respected in Israel, as I said, a blow that gave them a psychological complex - we could very possibly have been led to a battle.... (183)

As noted above, the November 1977 Jerusalem trip was a bold gamble to restore al-Sadat's leadership in the Arab world; it was also a calculated ploy to further U.S./Egyptian rapprochement. However, it was also the product of inter-Arab and Arab/Israeli considerations. Given the increasing level of conflict within the Arab world and the tactical gamesmanship of "outbidding" that accompanied it (i.e., the inter-Arab version of prisoner's dilemma), one strategy, and indeed, the most logical strategy in a situation of mutual Arab mistrust, was the go it alone option. To, in effect, "bail out" of inter-Arab conflicts, providing one could bring one's major source of support, the Saudis, along.

The advantages here were obvious: It would ensure U.S. support, diplomatic and, more importantly, military and economic, which would enable al-Sadat to deal with domestic discontent and have a powerful ally against Russia. And it would cut Egyptian policy loose from the vagaries of the Nasir legacy, or having to act as spokesman for contradictory and shifting Arab interests (another lesson of 1967). By reducing the ever present Israeli threat to the East, Egyptian military and diplomatic energies would be released to deal with pressing problems to the West; Libya, the Chad, and the Sudan, and the Red Sea. (184) Finally, it would end the situation of uncertainty, the "no war, no peace," situation that had driven al-Sadat to attack in October (here al-Sadat was particularly concerned with the desultory nature of the peace negotiations, not only with the U.S. constantly shifting position (presumably because Carter, although honest as al-Sadat notes, was, nevertheless, inexperienced in Middle Eastern complexities, some dramatic action was imperative to move Carter out of his indecision), but because peace negotiations were being tied up at the outset by procedural matters, i.e. who would go to any given Geneva Conference.

But it is important to note that, aside from these more calculated reasons, the driving factors behind al-Sadat's peace initiative were a fear of a preemptive Israeli attack and a belief that if the present situation continued, the psychology of threats would lead inevitably to another war:

> In a session with the Israeli defense minister, 'Ezer Weizman, he asked me: "Why did you want to attack us in the past ten days (sic: immediately prior to the Jerusalem trip)?" I told him: "Never, you started maneuvering in accord with your practice following the October War and with our method - the method of civilized states which are aware of their responsibility - when you started your maneuvers, al-Jamasi also began his maneuvers of equal size. All the intelligence reports are here before me; he showed them to me. The reports say that you were going to deal us a surprise strike...." (185)

> As soon as I became convinced that 75 percent of the problem was the psychological barrier and thought that if we went to Geneva with this psychological barrier we would not achieve or reach any result, I made my decision and made one jump to cross the psychological complexes, the psychological barrier and suspicion - all this so that we would be able to sit down in direct talks and put everything on the table.... (186)

The Jerusalem initiative, however, was short lived: In December 1977, Prime Minister Begin put forth his own understanding of a peace settlement, one which specifically excluded an Israeli withdrawal from the occupied West Bank. (187) In January 1978, the Rejection Front met in Tripoli, Libya, to consider its strategy of opposition to the initiative. In March, Palestinian commandos took matters into their own hands and attacked Israeli civilians, triggering an Israeli attack into Southern Lebanon. All of these moves effectively raised the level of tension to such an extent that discussions of a peace settlement were effectively blocked. Al-Sadat found himself completely isolated within the Arab world (a risk he was willing to run under other circumstances), and in addition, unable to secure any apparent aid from the United States or concessions from the Israelis. Even in the wake of desultory talks in Europe, his request for some face saving gesture, the return of al-'Arish (symbolic key to the Sinai) and St. Catherine's Monastery, were rejected (with Begin's reported comment, "Nobody can get something for nothing.") (188)

The result was an increasing sense among both Egyptians and other Arabs that the Israelis had no intention of withdrawing (a perception reinforced by hawkish comments concerning the West Bank by a variety of leaders, including the newly appointed Chief of Staff, Rafa'el Eytan) (189); and an increase in warning of Israeli intentions to engage in a preemptive strike - especially warnings by no less a figure than King Husayn, otherwise noted for his moderation.

> There will be a couple of more carefully orchestrated interviews by Eytan, perhaps by Arik Sharon...Then, perhaps before October, we are going to see an Israeli strike at Syria and Jordan, aimed at wiping out both armies before they can consolidate the Jordanian forces with the Syrian ones, and above all, before Sadat changes his course 180 degrees and swings around - perhaps after receiving the Nobel Peace Prize - to bid for leadership of the former rejection front....(190)

The Egyptian response was to escalate. The Egyptian political delegation was pulled out of Israel in January, the Israeli military delegation from Egypt in July. This break in communications was accompanied by a renewal of propaganda attacks and threats (191) in general, and increasingly harsh statements by al-Sadat including a May 5, 1978 threat to resume fighting, made in a speech to the 2nd army, and a declaration in August that further talks were useless. These threats, which were accompanied by an escalation in fighting in Lebanon, an escalation in which Israeli and Syrian forces appeared about to become directly engaged, set the background for the United States insistance on face to face talks at Camp David.

The al-Sadat initiative and the Camp David negotiations illustrate the dynamics of this Arab/Israeli conflict system. In both cases they were last ditch responses to what appeared to be a situation of certain war. Parenthetically, even as the Camp David talks were going on, Begin himself threatened military action against the Syrians, (192) and Arab analysts were predicting a blowup. The Arab Press Service produced a war scenario, one which its editors claimed was representative of official intelligence estimates of the situation. Noteworthy is the assumption of Christian-Israeli collusion which underlies this scenarios (an assumption that does not bode well for Christian communities in the Middle East); noteworthy also is the hypothesis that the real flashpoint of war will be an air battle between Israeli and Syrian aircraft (a replay of both 1967 and 1973):

A concentrated artillery attack on the village of Ayshiya...by the Israel backed Christian rightwing militia forces...At about the same time, the Christian militia forces of the "Lebanese Front" will provoke the Syrian troops to bombard their areas in East Beirut. From the northern side of the Front's area...the Syrian troops will be provoked to advance southward on the Christian positions, while other Syrian forces from the northeast will also advance, to complete the encirclement of the rebel Christian enclave. Concentrated Syrian shelling from all sides would then be provoked by Christian militias and snipers....

This should create the "desperate situation" which will prompt the Israelis to intervene "to save the Christian community of annihilation" at the hands of the Syrian army. The Israeli move would be at first limited to Air Force strikes at Syrian military positions around the Christian area....

The Syrian forces are well prepared for such an attack, with their SAM-6 and SAM-7 batteries already established in the Bekaa plateau. At first, the Syrian Air Force would avoid encountering the Israeli planes....But a Syrian Air Force intervention may be unavoidable.... (193)

Arab Press Service editors then go on to describe two possible outcomes: a Christian-Israeli victory, in which case the Christians attempt to set up a Christian state in the central and north of Lebanon, or a Syrian victory in which case the extremists of the Christian right and Muslim left are subdued, and a coalition of moderates under Syrian hegemony assumes control. The escalatory process does not, however, stop there since neither of these solutions would be acceptable to most, or all, of the parties concerned, and the war would expand in scope, now involving Israeli-Soviet collusion:

Israel would attack Syrian military positions in various parts of Lebanon in a two pronged blitzkrieg, starting simultaneously from Lebanon and from across the Jordan River into the east bank of Jordan and then into Southern Syria from both the Jordan valley and from Mount Hermon. At the same time, Israel will strike at Syria's vital economic and military installations along the Mediterranean coast....

Shortly after, or during, the Israeli blitz on the Eastern Front..., Soviet troops would move into South Yemen from the Indian Ocean and will have Perim Island...under their control...Tactical, but well camouflaged Israeli-Soviet collusion in that area will then be "the big surprise" for the Americans... (194)

So far, the tension has been deescalated each time, but the pattern remains: Mobilizations, undertaken for a variety of reasons, an escalation of perceptions of imminent conflict, and then countermobilizations, as all sides operate on the basis of the lessons of

October.

A number of scenarios can be developed based on this systemic interaction pattern. Assuming that the factors which have heretofore structured Arab/Israeli conflicts remain relatively constant, as they have for the last quarter century, the following future states are possible, from the most optimistic to the most pessimistic:

(a) <u>Some movement toward a settlement</u>: A diplomatic solution of Arab/Israeli questions and the creation of a geographical "entity" which would satisfy minimal Palestinian political aspirations. This would no doubt require an extremely skillful (and lucky) diplomatic policy which would have to offer:

1) Guarantees to the Israelis, probably in the form of a defense treaty and the physical commitment of United States troops, which would enable them to satisfy their security requirements, and thus allow territorial concessions.

2) Guarantees to Egypt and Saudi Arabia that their policy goals will be met: i.e., Israeli withdrawal from the Sinai and some form of an internationalized Jerusalem, thus allowing them a "victory" with which to hold off Arab critics.

3) Guarantees to the PLO leadership that they will receive the West Bank, thus giving them something with which to hold off other Palestinian groups.

4) Guarantees to Jordan that the United States would not abandon them to the Palestinians, thus preventing a military move by Jordanian hawks, with or without Husayn's approval.

5) Mediation with the Syrians, using possibly the good offices of the Saudis, to get Syrian acceptance of a partial, rather than total, Israeli withdrawal from the Golan. Here the idea of a Druze buffer zone might be exploited.

For the United States, this would be the optimum strategy. However, it would be, and is being, opposed by:

1) Russia which would perceive it as counterproductive to Soviet interests.

2) Israeli hawks who would suspect a United States "sellout."

3) Extremists among the Palestinians who would object for the same reasons as the Israelis.

4) Elements in Egypt, Syria, and Jordan who do not want a settlement for local political reasons.

5) The Libyans who want all Western influence excluded from the Middle East.

In addition, this strategy would have to overcome both the problem of timing and of psychology. It would have to be worked out swiftly enough to permit Arab moderates to accept it while still basking in the glow of their "victory" of October 1973. Yet it must also be delayed sufficiently to allow Israeli moderates to overcome the shock of the Arab attack, and consequent extreme insecurity.

Although Arab attitudes seem to have become significantly more flexible since the war, the legacy of decades of conflict remains. Malcolm Kerr, who was raised in the Arab world, described this legacy thusly:

> It is fashionable in some circles, after describing the tragedies and complexities of the Arab-Israeli conflict to public audiences, to profess to see light at the end of the tunnel. I see none. What I have tried to suggest is that the hard line political strategies predominantly pursued by both sides over the past two generations have been continuously reinforced by the accretion of psychologically comforting, but politically destructive, self justifications and distorted perceptions of the adversary, culminating in a spirit in each camp of rigid self righteousness. The prospects for settlement would be dim enough were God thought to be a partisan of either protagonist; but alas, He has emerged as the ally of both.... (195)

Here, the Camp David formula which looks first to an Egyptian/Israeli disengagement and peace treaty and later to a negotiated settlement of West Bank issues, runs into this psychological barrier. (196) On the one hand, U.S. pressure can not really be applied to the Israelis on sensitive West Bank issues because such pressure will be instantly perceived as a United States "sellout" to the Arabs. On the other hand, to push for a separate Egyptian/Israeli treaty, without linking it to West Bank issues will be perceived by Arabs as a hostile U.S./Egyptian/Israeli alliance. This perception, or at least interpretation, has not been slow in coming. In a statement almost immediately after the announcement of the Accords, al-Asad charged the Egyptians and Israelis with planning a joint military operation against Syria; a statement that was strongly reminiscent of the conspiracy theory of the 1960s, except that Saudi Arabia has now been replaced by Egypt in a new anti-Arab cabal. (197)

b) Protracted period of indeterminant negotiations: An extension of the preinitiative, pre-Camp David situation in which a number of things can be expected to happen:

1. Arab attitudes toward concessions will continue to harden appreciably. This will be as a consequence of Arab political patterns of "outbidding", where, in a situation of uncertainty, the hardest line is perceived as the safest.

2. Moderate Arab leaders will be under increasing pressure both domestically and externally to produce some kind of breakthrough.

3. Extremists will utilize the opportunity to escalate their attacks on both Arab moderates and the Israelis.

4. Border tensions will rise, partly because of these attacks, partly because of local "jitters" and subsequent military alerts.

United States interests will be placed under increasing Arab pressure, initially in terms of verbal threats, but later followed by restraints on oil production. The problem in this sort of situation is to maintain Arab expectations that something can be achieved by rational bargaining behavior, and to support moderate Arab leaders to the extent possible.

c) 1967-style unplanned escalation: An escalatory variant off of b); a situation in which border tensions increase appreciably as a combination of several factors:

1. Local military alerts called for local purposes: Either to generate threats and thus improve a bargaining position, or to control a deteriorating domestic situation by creating the appearance of an outside threat. The Syrians are particularly prone to utilize this tactic.

2. Possible cross border fire by regular units as a consequence of 1); thus escalating the threat level and generating other alerts in response.

3. Unexpected terrorist actions by elements anxious to prevent any negotiations. Logical candidates for this type of activity are those Palestinians in the "rejectionist front", and the Libyans, either separately or in combination. The Palestinians, particularly the PFLP, are committed to preventing any peace negotiations on the theory that:

    a) No such partial negotiations should be permited, since this would mean a compromise concerning "Palestinian Rights."

    b) A general war, in which moderate Arab leadership suffered a defeat and the Arabs lost more territory, would radicalize the Arab World.

The Libyans would equally like to see a breakdown in negotiations, because:

a) It would probably mean the end of al-Sadat.

b) A war could force the Egyptians into the Libyan orbit, either out of military or economic necessity.

c) If moderate leaders were to be defeated, al-Qadhafi could claim to be the logical leader of the Arabs.

d) Such a defeat in war would prove al-Qadhafi's theory that an Islamic Revival is necessary for the Arabs to regain their strength.

The problem in this scenario is to deter open warfare by any means possible, and to prevent, if possible, extremists from taking advantage of the situation.

d) Arab preemptive war: Most probably started by the Syrians, less so by the Egyptians. This would occur if the Syrian leadership decided that it was useless to try further diplomatic approaches, that the Israelis were not going to withdraw from the Golan. The impulse for this decision would be heightened if the Syrians perceived the possibility of an Israeli move; therefore, the urge to strike first would become insurmountable. In such a situation, the Egyptians would most probably join in. Although they are leery of being pushed into a war by the Syrians (continued Egyptian emphasis on their lack of military prepared- ness indicates this), they have made so many commitments to the Syrians that it is unlikely they can remain aloof. In any event, once large scale fighting started on the Syrian Front, the Egyptians would probably be impelled to attack to forestall Israeli moves in the Sinai. Jordan would try to remain outside the conflict as long as possible, but probably would be forced to enter it in some form.

The factors that would set off this scenario are:

1. Perceived Israeli intransigence.

2. Perceived United States inability/unwillingness to act.

3. Deteriorating domestic situation(s).

4. Perceived changes in the military balance:

   (a) Either by increased Russian aid favoring the Arabs; or
   (b) By increased United States aid favoring the Israelis. In either event, a decision to attack while the balance remains most favorable.

The problem here is to either deter confrontation or minimize its impact on United States interests. Once such a war began, the critical factors affecting the United States' ability to prevent either an oil embargo or destruction of the oil fields themselves are:

1) Military aspects of the war, i.e., if Arab forces appear to be holding their own, the less the chance of an embargo, conversely, if they appear to be losing. (198)

2. The nature and timing of Egyptian involvement. If the fighting is localized to the Syrian front, the oil producers will probably delay action. If the Egyptians become immediately involved, oil action is that much more likely.

3. Nature of United States/Saudi relations, and the willingness of the Saudis to withstand Arab pressure.

e) Israeli preemptive war: Not surprisingly, the Egyptians have produced their own scenario for an Israeli attack. According to

Egyptian reasoning, the Israelis may be expected to launch a preemptive strike of considerable dimension to achieve the following goals:

1) Destroy Arab military capabilities for another six to seven years.
2) Reverse the Arab psychology of victory and the Israeli psychology of defeat.
3) Destroy, if possible, the leadership of the PLO.
4) Prove again that a strong Israel is the key to protecting United States interests in the Middle East.

The factors which would precipitate such an action would be:

1) Western hostility towards the Arabs as a consequence of oil price increases.
2) Greater Israeli military advantages due to increased shipments of United States sophisticated arms, coupled with a cessation of Russian arms supplies to Egypt.
3) Iraqi military involvement in the Kurdish problem, leading to a complete withdrawal of all Iraqi military forces on the Eastern Front.
4) Jordanian withdrawal as a consequence of Egyptian/Syrian support for the Palestinians.
5) An effort to acquire United States/Western aid to offset a local, Israeli economic crisis, along the lines of the one in 1966/67. (199)

In the curious and inverted logic of Middle Eastern politics, every time Israel, the United States ally, wins, the United States loses. Every time Russia allies, the Arabs, "win," Russia loses.

As long as the next war appears to be even, there is little likelihood of Russia/United States confrontation. Each major power will be able to resupply its clients. If, however, Israel begins to threaten the survival of Arab countries either by another canal breakthrough, by air bombardment of large civilian centers, or by a breakthrough of Syrian defenses on the Damascus plain, direct Russian involvement is a very high probability. As a major power, Russia cannot allow its credibility in the Arab World, or the world at large, to be threatened by local powers. The same logic that impelled Russian intervention in 1973 will operate in a later situation, i.e., to protect both its credibility and its investments in the area.

For the United States, any extended war would be disastrous, particularly so if Arab forces begin to lose badly. The postwar consequences of 1967 would be repeated with a vengeance:

a) Pro-United States leaders, al-Sadat and Husayn would most certainly be overthrown; moderate Arab leadership would be forced to eject everything Western merely to preserve their own positions.

b) The "Great Betrayal" syndrome would operate to create a psychological climate which would shift the Arab world completely out of the Western orbit for years to come.

c) Oil resources would be seriously jeopardized, either being completely cut off, or the installations destroyed by militants; pipelines would be destroyed; ships passing through the Straits of Hurmuz or the Bab al-Mandab would be subject to rocket attacks or mines.

Appendix:
Partial List
of Arab Sources

NAME	COMMENTS
Egypt	
al-Ahram	Controlled, Semi-official
al-Akhbar	Controlled
Akhbar al-Yawm	Controlled
Akhir Sa'a	Controlled
Egyptian Gazette	Controlled, in English
Egyptian Mail	Controlled, in English
al-Jumhuriya	Controlled
al-Musawwar	Controlled
Ruz al-Yusuf	Controlled
October	Controlled
MENA (Middle East News Agency)	Controlled
Syria	
al-Ba'th	Ba'th Party
al-Thawra	Ba'th Party
TISHRIN	Ba'th Party

Iraq

al-Jumhuriya	Ba'th Party
al-Thawra	Ba'th Party
INA (Iraqi News Agency)	Ba'th Party

Jordan

al-Difa'a	Pro-Government
al-Dustur	Pro-Government, Semi-official

Kuwayt

al-Ra'y al'Amm	Independent, Conservative
al-Siyasa	Independent

Saudi Arabia

al-Bilad	Pro-Government, Semi-official
al-Madina	Pro-Government, Semi-official
al-Nadwa	Pro-Government, Semi-official
al-Riyadh	Pro-Government, Semi-official
'Ukaz	Pro-Government, Semi-official

Lebanon

al-Anwar	Pro-EAR
Arab Press Service	Independent, in English
Arab World Daily	Independent, in English[1]
Arab World Weekly	Independent, in English[1]
Daily Star	Conservative, in English
al-Hawadith	Pro-EAR
al-Hayat	Conservative
al-Muharrir	Leftwing

Lebanon - continued

al-Nahar	Independent
an-Nahar Arab Report	Independent, in English[1]
al-Nidal	Pro-EAR
al-Rayah	Exiled Syrian Ba'th
al-Safir	Pro-Libya
al-Sayyad	Pro-EAR
al-Usbu' al-'Arabi	Independent
Events	al-Hawadith in English

Palestinian

Action	Published in New York
Ila al-Amam	General Command
Fateh (Fatah)	Fatah, several languages
al-Hadaf	PFLP
al-Hurriya	PDFLP
Journal of Palestine Studies	Published in Kuwayt
al'Tali'a	al-Sa'iqa
Sawt al-Filastin	Palestinian media

Europe

al-'Arab	London
al-Dustur	London
al-Manar	London
al-Watan al-'Arabi	Paris
al-Mustaqbal	Paris
al-Nahar al-'Arabi al-Duwali	Paris

Notes and References

NOTES

Chapter I

(1) The term, War of the Day of Judgment, comes from Israeli Chief of Staff Elazar's reply to a newsman when asked if the new war could be called the "Yom Kippur War." Elazar replied that it would be better called "The War of the Day of Judgment."

(2) Already a considerable body of literature has grown up concerning the October War. For example see John Bullock, The Yom Kippur War (London: Andre Denton, 1975); Moshe Davis, ed., The Yom Kippur War: Israel and the Jewish People (New York: Arno Press, 1974); Galia Golan, The Soviet Union and Egyptian-Syrian Preparations for the Arab Israeli War of 1973 (Palo Alto: Stanford Research Institute, n.d.); Matti Golan, The Secret Conversations of Henry Kissinger (New York: Quadrangle/New York Times Book Company, 1976); Mohamed Heikal, The Road to Ramadan (New York: Ballantine Books, 1975); Chaim Herzog, The War of Atonement, October 1973 (Boston: Little, Brown and Co., 1975); Foy D. Kohler et al., The Soviet Union and the October 1973 Middle East War (Miami: University of Miami Center for Advanced International Studies, 1974); Walter Laqueur, Confrontation: The Middle East and World Politics (New York: Bantam Books, Inc., 1975); London Times Insight Team, The Yom Kippur War (Garden City, NY: Doubleday and Co., 1974); Elizabeth Monroe and A.H. Farrar-Hockley, The Arab-Israeli War, October 1973, Adelphi Papers no. 111 (London: International Institute for Strategic Studies, 1975); William B. Quandt, Soviet Policy in the October 1973 War (Santa Monica: RAND, 1976); Riad N. El-Rayyes and Dunia Nahas, eds., The October War (Beirut: An-Nahar Arab Report Books, n.d.); Zeev Schiff, October Earthquake (Tel Aviv: University Publishing

Projects, 1974); US Congress, Committee on Foreign Affairs, The Impact of the October Middle East War (Washington: Government Printing Office, 1975); Martin Van Creveld, Military Lessons of the Yom Kippur War: Historical Perspectives, The Washington Papers, no. 24 (Beverly Hills: Sage, 1975); Lawrence L. Whetten, The Arab-Israeli Dispute: Great Power Behavior, Adelphi Papers no. 128 (London: International Institute for Strategic Studies, 1977).

(3) Heikal, Ramadan, pp. 263-267. Haykal, whatever his current political fortunes, is one of the foremost Arab strategic thinkers.

(4) See the comments of William A. Rugh, "Arab Media and Politics During the October War," The Middle East Journal 29, no. 3 (Summer 1975): 310-328. Rugh is the Deputy Assistant Director for the Near East and North Africa section of USIS. This newfound media behavior was, of course, the product of a carefully thought out policy. But it should be noted that part of its sophistication, at least where the Egyptians were concerned, was due to President al-Sadat's own experience in journalism, and his consequent sensitivity to the political uses of media, especially where Western public opinion was involved. The publication of his memoirs, In Search of Identity (New York: Harper & Row, 1977), in English and his extensive use of the Western media via interviews are postwar indications of this sensitivity. It was no accident, therefore, that the Deputy Prime Minister of Egypt, Muhammad 'abd al-Kadir Hatim, had written an extensive analysis of the political uses of information. See M. Abdel-Kader Hatem, Information and the Arab Cause (London: Longman Group Ltd., 1974).

(5) Avi Shlaim, "Failures in National Intelligent Estimates: The Case of the Yom Kippur War," World Politics, 28 (April 3, 1976): 18-50.

(6) E. Shouby, "The Influence of the Arabic Language on the Psychology of the Arabs," The Middle East Journal 5, no. 3 (Summer 1951): 284-302; Anwar G. Chenje, "Arabic: Its Significance and Place in Arab-Musim Society," The Middle East Journal 19, no. 4 (Autumn 1965): 447-470.

(7) MENA, August 9, 1976.

(8) Musa Sabri, al-Akhbar, August 2, 1976.

(9) Shlaim, "Failures." Clement Henry Moore, "On Theory and Practice Among Arabs," World Politics 27, no. 1 (October 1971): 106-126.

(10) Geoffrey Godsell, "Will Egyptians Have to Extend 1971?" Christian Science Monitor, October 6, 1971, p. 11. One fairly typical (and reasonable, given the circumstances) Western reaction to this barrage was summed up in an article in The Guardian:

They have done it so many times that the whole elaborate maneuver has become a well practiced routine...After quickly conceding that Israel retains a crushing military superiority in all dimensions of military power, Egyptian spokesmen go on to say that

Arab patience is at an end; they will go to war,   and soon, and in a big way - even though they fully expect defeat...All things considered, Arabs and Jews have done very well in keeping Western interest in the perpetual Middle East crisis---Nevertheless, behind the flow of words there are only more words; there is no significant action in sight...In the absence of a genuine readiness to go to war, the war scares orchestrated from Cairo are a vital ingredient of Egyptian diplomacy..."
Edward Luttwak, "The Diplomacy of Threats," The Manchester Guardian Weekly, January 20, 1973, p. 6.

(11) Arab World Weekly, April 6, 1974.

(12) Foreign Broadcast Information Service, Daily Report: Middle East & Africa, September 6, 1973, hereinafter cited as FBIS.

(13) FBIS, September 21, 1973.

(14) FBIS, October 1, 1973.   Three years after the war, Syrian spokesmen were to claim that these statements made them "live in tension and anxiety for days" because they were contrary to the heretofore agreed deception plan and could warn the Israelis--especially if taken together with evidence of Syrian and Egyptian troop movements.   This in turn heightened the possibility that the Israelis would preempt.   Mustafa Talas in al-Thawra, October 5, 1976.

(15) See Alexander L. George, Propaganda Analysis (Evanston: Row, Peterson and Company, 1959), for the problems associated with the masking of intentions behind an ideological "line".   Arab World sources are acutely sensitive to ideological orientations of the various media.

(16) In June 1978, the Lebanese government decreed a new and tougher press censorship law as part of a policy aimed at reducing inflammatory coverage of an already bloody civil war.   Almost immediately after the law came into effect, the magazine al-Hawadith was suspended for attacking the government's policy.

(17) Arab World Weekly, June 21, 1969, pp. 12-15, and ibid, February 15, 1975, pp. 8-9.

(18) Al-Qadhafi has reportedly gone this tactic one step better and financed his own publishing house in Beirut.

(19) Leonard Binder, "Egypt: The Integrative Revolution," in Lucian Pye and Sidney Verba, eds., Political Culture and Political Development (Princeton: Princeton University Press, 1969), summary of Egyptian communications elites.

(20) Arab World Weekly, February 9, 1975, pp. 5-9; an-Nahar Arab Report, February 11, 1974, pp. 2-3.   Haykal was dismissed after a series of articles which became increasingly hostile to al-Sadat.   However, the two had been at odds since late 1972 when Haykal

attacked al-Sadat for dismissing War Minister Muhammed Sadiq. This hostility increased as Haykal took to criticizing all of al-Sadat's policies, domestic and foreign, and in addition began to promote the cause of al-Qadhafi. In fact, Haykal became so identified with al-Qadhafi that al-Sadat repeatedly declared in his memoirs (in the Arabic version) that Haykal had become al-Qadhafi's chief advisor. October, May 29, 1977, pp. 11ff., contains this accusation. For Haykal's version, see The Sunday Times, February 10, 1974.

The Removal of Haykal was followed by a wholesale replacement of the directors of Egyptian publishing houses and their replacement by men loyal to al-Sadat. At the same time official press censorship was ended. The net effect, however, was to secure a favorable press for al-Sadat. Haykal continued his attacks from other Arab states, writing in either the Lebanese or Kuwayti press. Interestingly, Haykal's book, The Road to Ramadan, was later serialized in al-Ahram as The Ramadan War, beginning in early May 1975.

(21) Arab World Weekly, June 7, 1969, pp. 9-12. In December 1976, the Kuwayt Information Ministry announced that it was forming a press censorship committee. This action apparently was part of a larger governmental response to increasing domestic disorder, disorder in part caused by an exodus of Palestinian Resistance groups from Lebanon to Kuwayt.

(22) Donna Robinson Devine, "Why This War...", International Journal of Middle East Studies no. 7 (October 1976): 523-43.

(23) Graham T. Allison, Essence of Decision (Boston: Little, Brown and Company, 1971).

(24) J. David Singer, "The Level of Analysis Problem in International Relations," in Klaus Knorr and Sidney Verba, eds., The International System: Theoretical Essays (Princeton: Princeton University Press, 1961), pp. 77-92, discusses the problems associated with selection of a level of theoretical abstraction.

(25) For an overview of image analysis as used in international relations theory, see Kenneth E. Boulding, "National Images and International Systems," in James N. Rosenau, ed., International Politics and Foreign Policy, rev. ed. (New York: The Free Press, 1969), pp. 422-431. For two excellent studies applying image analysis to Israeli decision making see Michael Brecher, The Foreign Policy System of Israel (London: Oxford University Press, 1972), especially pp. 23-64, and Abraham R. Wagner, Israeli Perceptions of American Security Policy: Current Trends and Future Alternatives (Beverly Hills: A.R. Wagner & Company, 1976).

(26) Edward Mead Earle, ed., Makers of Modern Strategy (Princeton: Princeton University Press, 1943), p. viii.

(27) See Heikal, Ramadan, pp. 7-8.: "Another unlooked for bonus was that in the Spring of 1973 General Yariv, who was an exceptionally astute officer, had been replaced as Director of Military Intelligence

in Israel by General Ze'ira, who had a rigid conviction that in no
circumstances would Egypt be able to mount an attack. It was
fortunate too that the Israelis drew the wrong conclusions from the
disastrous air battle over Damascus on September 13, 1973 in which
they shot down thirteen Syrian planes." Also, William B. Quandt,
Decade of Decisions: American Policy Toward the Arab-Israeli
Conflict, 1967-1976 (Berkeley: University of California Press,
1977), pp. 166ff. According to Quandt, CIA analysts monitoring the
Syrian press came up with an incorrect interpretation because of
some preconceived notions about Arab behavior.

Chapter II

(1) See Boulding, "National Images." The schema of dividing an actor's
perceptions into cognitive, affective and evaluative categories was
first popularized by Talcott Parsons and Edward Shils in Toward a
General Theory of Action (New York: Harper & Row Publishers,
1951), pp. 53-189, and has since been used in a number of studies. In
the study at hand, this more formal approach has been softened: the
three categories of perceptions have been combined in the thematic
context of Arab imagery.

(2) K.J. Holsti, International Politics: A Framework for Analysis, 2nd
ed. (Englewood Cliffs, N.J.: Prentice-Hall, Inc., 1971), p. 360.

(3) Peter L. Berger and Thomas Luckmann, The Social Construction of
Reality (New York: Doubleday & Company, Inc., 1967).

(4) Robert Jervis, Perception and Misperception in International
Politics (Princeton, New Jersey: Princeton University Press, 1976),
pp. 117ff; see also Milton Rokeach, The Open and Closed Mind
(New York: Basic Books, 1960); Leon Festinger, A Theory of
Cognitive Dissonance (Stanford: Stanford University Press, 1957),
which along with the literature cited in Jervis summarize the field
of research in cognitive psychology. However, in conceptualizing
Arab perceptions as a cognitive model, one must be careful to
distinguish this from conceptions of an "Arab mind." As Michael
Hudson points out, Arabs are far too diverse, and to make such
sweeping generalizings is to engage in stereotyping. See Michael C.
Hudson, Arab Politics: The Search for Legitimacy (New Haven:
Yale University Press, 1977), pp. 392ff.   The image analysis
presented here is far more general and conceptually much less
closed than any notion of an Arab mind.

(5) Charles F. Gallagher, "Language, Culture and Ideology: The Arab
World" in K.A. Silvert, ed., Expectant Policies (New York: Vintage
Books, 1961), pp. 199-231.

(6) The phrase "appear to have" is critical here in the sense that Arab
image formation is different only in degree from that of Western
decision makers.   There is a growing body of literature concerning

Western "crisis" decision making which demonstrates the proposition that Western leaders also operate in terms of well developed image systems; and that in crises situations, these images tend to predominate other, more rational considerations in determining the decisional outcome. See for example: Dean G. Pruitt and Richard C. Snyder, Theory and Research on the Causes of War (Englewood Cliffs, New Jersey: Prentice-Hall, Inc., 1969), for summaries or some of the earlier literature. Also: Charles F. Hermann, ed., International Crises: Insights from Behavioral Research (New York: The Free Press, 1972), and Ole R. Holsti, Crisis Escalation War (Montreal: McGill-Queen's University Press, 1972).

(7) Raphael Patai, The Arab Mind, (New York: Charles Scribner's Sons, 1973), p. 311. See also, John S. Badeau, "The Arabs, 1967," reprinted in Majdia D. Khadduri, ed., The Arab-Israeli Impasse (Washington: Robert B. Luce, Inc., 1968), pp. 97-113, for the same viewpoint from a Western official; in this case, coupled with the argument that one of the contributing factors to the 1967 War was the fact that Israelis responded to Arab verbiage which had no real intent behind it. In 1973, the reverse was true. And the following from Arab historian Edward Atiyah, The Arabs (Harmondsworth: Penguin Books, 1958). "It is a characteristic of the Arab mind to be swayed more by words than by idea, and more by ideas than by facts. Transcendental principles, especially when put into resonant speech, seem to the Arabs to have a power capable of conquering the greatest practical realities..." p. 97.

(8) Hisham Sharabi, Palestine and Israel: The Lethal Dilemma, (New York: Pegasus, 1969), pp. 124-127. Also Patai, The Arab Mind, pp. 60ff; and Morroe Berger, The Arab World Today (Garden City: Doubleday, 1954), pp. 160ff, for similar analyses and literature.

(9) Y. Harkabi, Arab Attitudes to Israel (Jerusalem: Israel University Press, 1972), p. 414.

(10) Ibid.

(11) For example, see John Dollard, et al., Frustration and Aggression, New Haven: (Yale University Press, 1939), contains a Freudian theory of conflict; Robert Ardrey, The Territorial Imperative (New York: Atheneum Publishers, 1966) and Conrad Lorenz, On Aggression, (New York: Bantam Books, 1967), use instinctive theories also based on Freud. See also James E. Dougherty and Robert L. Pfaltzgraff, Jr., Contending Theories of International Relations (New York: J.B. Lippincott Company, 1971), pp. 138-171, 196-278, for the various ways conflict models are used in the analysis of international relations; and also Clinton F. Fink, "Some Conceptual Difficulties in the Theory of Social Conflict," Journal of Conflict Resolution, 12, no. 4 (December 1969): 412-460.

(12) Ralf Dahrendorf, Essays in the Theory of Society (Stanford: Stanford University Press, 1968), pp. 126-128; and "Toward a Theory of Social Conflict," Journal of Conflict Resolution 2, no. 2 (June 1958): 170-183.

(13) Lewis Coser, The Functions of Social Conflict (New York: The Free Press of Glencoe, 1956), p. 8.

(14) See Georg Simmel, Conflict and the Web of Group-Affiliations Trans. by Kurt H. Wolff and Reinhard Bendix (New York: The Free Press of Glencoe, 1955),or Max Gluckman, Custom and Conflict in Africa (Glencoe, Illinois: The Free Press, 1955), for demonstrations of this proposition.

(15) Kenneth E. Boulding, Conflict and Defense: A General Theory (New York: Harper Torchbooks, 1963), pp. 5ff.

(16) Thomas C. Schelling, The Strategy of Conflict (New York: Galaxy Books, 1963), pp. 9ff; Philip Green, Deadly Logic: The Theory of Nuclear Deterrence (New York: Schocken Books, 1968), especially pp. 93ff; Anatel Rapoport, Strategy and Conscience (New York: Schocken Books, 1964), for summaries and critique of game, bargaining and deterrence theories that assume both the ubiquity and rationality of conflict.

(17) Brecher, Foreign Policy System.

(18) Kenneth N. Waltz, Man, the State and War (New York: Columbia University Press, 1959), pp. 12ff.

(19) Ibid.

(20) Robert Jervis, The Logic of Images in International Relations (Princeton: Princeton University Press, 1970), p. 31.

(21) Joseph de Rivera, The Psychological Dimension of Foreign Policy (Columbus, Ohio: Charles E. Merrill Publishing Company, 1968).

(22) SeeRichard C. Carver, The Middle East: Some Psychological Considerations and U.S. Foreign Policy (Maxwell AFB: Air War College, 1974), for similar considerations.

(23) Berger, Arab World, p. 136.

(24) See Daniel Lerner, The Passing of Traditional Society (Glencoe: The Free Press, 1958); for some 1950's survey material which documents this basic mistrust; Terry E. Prothro and Levon H. Melikian, "Social Distance and Social Change in the Near East," Sociology and Social Research 37 (1952): 3-11.

(25) Michael M. Ripinsky, "Middle Eastern Kinship as an Expression of a Culture - Environment System," Muslim World 58, no. 3 (July 1968): 225-241.

(26) Berger, Arab World, pp. 146-147.

(27) Cf. T.W. Adorno et al., The Authoritarian Personality (New York: Harper and Row, 1950), pp. 759-762.

(28) Nadav Safran, Egypt in Search of Political Community (Cambridge, Massachusetts: Harvard University Press, 1961), pp. 7ff; W.

Montgomery Watt, "Muhammad," in The Cambridge History of Islam, vol. I (Cambridge: Cambridge University Press, 1970), pp. 30-56.

(29) Louis Gardet, "Religion and Culture," in The Cambridge History of Islam, vol. II (Cambridge University Press, 1970), pp. 569-603.

(30) Noel J. Coulson, Conflicts and Tensions in Islamic Jurisprudence (Chicago: The University of Chicago Press, 1969), pp. 3ff.

(31) Abram Kardiner et al., The Psychological Frontiers of Society (New York: Columbia University Press, 1945), pp. 109ff.

(32) Sania Hamady, Temperature and Character of the Arabs (New York: Twayne Publishers, 1960); Jacques Berque, The Arabs: Their History and Future (New York: Praeger, 1964).

(33) Dr. Charles Malik, former Lebanese Ambassador to the UN, for example, once analyzed Middle Eastern political patterns in terms of a conflict model. There are ten dissimilarities, conflicts, or contradictions flowing through the Middle East.

(1) The Western West (the Atlantic world) and the Eastern West (the Soviet world), because the USSR is an integral part of the West.

(2) The three revealed religions - Judaism, Christianity and Islam, in view of the importance of Jerusalem and the Holy Land.

(3) The industrial world and Middle East oil - how the needs of the former are to be coordinated with the material possessions of the latter.

(4) Iran, Turkey, the Arabs and Israel - how, in the long run, these four peoples are to coexist.

(5) The state of being shut in on oneself and the state of being open to the world. There is a great and fundamental distinction between those who are shut in - narrow, timorous and self-sufficient - and those who are seekers - trusting, open to good and the right.

(6) Tradition and renewal - how a heritage is conditioned by science, industrialization and modern ideas - that is, how a heritage is modernized.

(7) Within the framework of renewal: Marxism and democracy.

(8) Israel and the Arabs.

(9) The Israelis and the Palestinians.

(10) Local and regional dissimilarities and rifts between the Arab states and within them. According to Malik, "the equilibrium of the Middle East consists of these ten conflicts, mutually interlocking to different degrees. Nowhere else in the world are there so many and so varied conflicts in such density; each acts to determine the result of the equation...." al-Nahar, September 1, 1974, reproduced in Journal of Palestine Studies 4, no. 1 (Autumn 1974): 162.

(34) Bernard Lewis, The Middle East and the West (New York: Harper & Row, 1966).

(35) Morroe Berger, "The Arabs' Attitude Toward the West", The Yale Review 61, no. 2 (December 1971): 207-225. In this connection, the Soviets occupy an ambivalent position. On the one hand they are perceived as being hostile to the United States and Israel, and thus an ally of the Arabs. On the other hand, they are also seen as being antagonistic toward Islam, and thus a threat to the Arabs. In practice this ambivalence produces a willingness to cooperate with the Soviets in political terms, but a rejection of Communism in cultural terms. Even those Arab states most closely linked to the Soviets, Egypt, Syria, and Iraq, have been hostile to local Communist Parties.

(36) G.E. Von Grunebaum, Medieval Islam (Chicago: The University of Chicago Press, 1953); John S. Badeau, "Islam and the Middle East," Foreign Affairs 38, no. 1 (October 1959): 60-74.

(37) F.S. Vidal, "Religious Brotherhoods in Moroccan Politics," Middle East Journal 4, no. 3 (July 1959): 427-446.

(38) Heikal, Ramadan, pp. 24ff.

(39) See Ibrahim Abu-Lughod, The Arab Rediscovery of Europe (Princeton: The Princeton University Press, 1963).

(40) Malcolm Kerr, "The Arabs and Israelis: Perceptual Dimensions to their Dilemma," in Willard A. Beling, ed. The Middle East: Quest for an American Policy (Albany: The State University of New York Press, 1973), pp. 3-31.

(41) Gamal Abdel Nasser, The Philosophy of the Revolution (Washington, D.C.: Public Affairs Press, 1955), p. 62.

(42) Ibid., p. 87.

(43) Al-Qadhafi has defended his expanded foreign policy by arguing that he is opposing Western (Christian) imperialism everywhere in the world. When specifically asked about his support for the IRA, he replied: "Our stand is clear and we support the struggle for liberation...Our support for the Irish people stems from our belief that they are struggling for independence from Britain..." Interview on BBC broadcast on Voice of the Arab Homeland (Tripoli), May 14, 1976, FBIS, May 18, 1976.

(44) Leonard Binder, The Ideological Revolution in the Middle East (New York: John Wiley & Sons, Inc., 1964), ch. 9.

(45) The intensity of the emotion involved on al-Sadat's part is attested to by the amount of space in his memoirs (Arabic version - the English version contains only scant mention) devoted to attacks on al-Qadhafi. According to al-Sadat's account, he was originally a supporter of al-Qadhafi and his colleagues who had just taken over the government in Libya - al-Sadat refers to the new junta as the

"young men " who needed all the help they could get. But slowly it began to dawn on him that al-Qadhafi's behavior was both odd and uninformed, as for example his unexplained absences: "It was natural that the Presidential council, which consisted of myself, President Hafiz al-Asad and al-Qadhafi should meet....Being the host, I went there (Marsa Matruh) before the appointed date and so did President Hafiz al-Asad. But al-Qadhafi had not arrived....We asked about al-Qadhafi, and we were told that they didn't know his whereabouts but that he would show up soon...They said he was in the desert...It was then said that he was ill and had to have a tooth pulled...It was President Hafiz al-Asad who drew my attention to this strange behavior of al-Qadhafi's. He asked me: 'Don't you see that this is indeed strange? He knew the date of the meeting - the date had been declared to the whole Arab world - and yet he did not come...' I said: 'Perhaps he has his reasons. Maybe he is ill and maybe he is in the desert.' October, April 25, 1977, pp. 19ff. FBIS, April 3, 1977.

This charitable view rapidly changed to one which bordered on contempt: "I am aware that nothing annoys al-Qadhafi more than agreement, unity and solidarity among others. He is a destructive man by nature...All he wants is disunity and division... I had long before noticed his attitude of superiority but, because of my faith in him, I attributed it to the fact that he is an enthusiastic youth who suddenly became rich...He does not know what to do with this money except to satisfy his love for sabotage..." October, May 29, 1977, pp. 11ff. FBIS, June 1, 1977.

Indeed, not only was al-Qadhafi a mischief maker, he also could not be trusted with any secrets (such as the timing of the October attack). For example, al-Sadat's "year of decision" comment was said to have been originally made in private and then spilled to the press by al-Qadhafi: "Had al-Qadhafi been a man to be trusted with a secret, I would have told him about our preparations for the battle, but my experience with him has shown that what goes into his ears comes out of his mouth immediately. I remember upon my return from Moscow, I stopped to see him in Bengazi and told him that 1971 would be the 'year of decision' and that I had agreed with the Soviet Union on this...One day journalist Heikal - al-Qadhafi's advisor - came to me and said that a Lebanese journalist called Fu'ad Matar (sic: generally considered to be an expert on Egyptian politics) had visited him and told him that al-Qadhafi had informed him of all I had said to him...What he (al-Qadhafi) had said was that 1971 would be the year of decision and that by December (Egyptian) forces would have crossed the canal...The newspaper al-Nahar published this report - that 1971 would be the year of decision and so on...." Ibid.

Ultimately, al-Sadat was forced to conclude that there was something wrong with al-Qadhafi: "At noon the following day al-Qadhafi, his wife, children, mother, and brothers left for Libya. They all left by plane except him. I was astonished to hear that he had decided to travel by land. Strange indeed: We were in the beginning of July, it was hot, and the desert road is difficult....It occurred to me that he likes - as he usually does - to be different from other people. If people travel by air, he travels by land; if people are happy, he becomes annoyed; and if people are annoyed, he becomes happy. Thus, he tortures himself and others as well...", ibid.

(46) Binder, Ideological Revolution.

(47) Carleton S. Coon, Caravan: The Story of the Middle East (New York: Holt, Rinehart and Winston, 1958), ch. 10.

(48) Berger, Arab World, pp. 142ff.

(49) Nasser, Philosophy, pp. 34-35.

(50) Hudson, Arab Politics, pp. 1-15.

(51) David E. Apter, The Politics of Modernization (Chicago: University of Chicago Press, 1965), pp. 51ff.

(52) Patai, Arab Mind, pp. 90ff; Berger, Arab World, pp. 135ff.

(53) Berger, Arab World, p. 102.

(54) Peter C. Dodd and Halim Barakat, River Without Bridges: A Study of the Exodus of the 1967 Palestinian Refugees (Beirut: Institute for Palestinian Studies, 1968).

(55) Jervis, Perception and Misperception, pp. 62ff., describes this conflict model as the "spiral model" of escalation. Conflict models of the environment involve, as has been pointed out in connection with Arab cultural themes, certain assumptions about the basic nature of human interaction. The theoretical and perceptual alternative to conflict models are cooperation models. Models which are based on the assumption that the basic datum of human interaction is cooperation, rather than conflict. The utility of either model was at one point the subject of intense debate among social scientists. See Irving Louis Horowitz, Three Worlds of Development: The Theory and Practice of International Stratification (New York: Oxford University Press, 1966), pp. 364-389.

(56) Y. Harkabi, "Basic Factors in the Arab Collapse during the Six-Day War," Orbis 11, no. 3 (Fall 1967): 677-689. Cf. William B. Quandt, Palestinian Nationalism: Its Political and Military Dimensions (Santa Monica: RAND, 1971); John Waterbury, The Commander of the Faithful, (New York: Columbia University Press, 1970), for similar analyses.

Chapter 3

(1) Interestingly, neither Arabs nor Israelis expected the 1967 War to break out. Cf. the comments of FM Ahmad Isma'il: "There is no doubt that the 1967 war was a surprise to the Egyptian armed forces, to the Arab states, and to the entire world." Interview with Fu'ad Matar in al-Nahar, October 6, 1974. "First of all, that we

must be ready for a surprise as we had in the Six Day War, and then
we had in the Yom Kippur War. People forgot that few weeks
before the Six Day War we didn't even speak about the possibility of
war." Chief of Staff Mordekhay Gur interview on ABC, FBIS, June
14, 1977.

(2) Lucian W. Pye, Politics, Personality and Nation Building: Burma's
Search for Identity (New Haven: Yale University Press, 1962), pp.
16-31; Hudson, pp. 18-20; also, Samuel P. Huntington, Political
Order in Changing Societies (New Haven: Yale University Press,
1968), pp. 12ff.

(3) Pye, Politics. See also: Margaret G. Hermann, "Circumstances
Under Which Leader Personality Will Affect Foreign Policy: Some
Propositions," unpublished paper, and ibid., "Leader Personality and
Foreign Policy Behavior," in James N. Rosenau, ed., Comparing
Foreign Policy: Theories, Findings and Methods (Beverly Hills, Ca.:
Sage Publications, 1974), pp. 201-234.

(4) Simmel, Conflict, pp. 76-83; Richard J. Barnet, Intervention and
Revolution (New York: The World Publishing Company, 1968), pp. 3-
46, for the argument that opponents tend to both generate rules
regulating conflicts and also develop mirror image institutional
structures as part of a process of conflict stabilization.

(5) Newsweek, December 11, 1972, p. 60.

(6) Cf: David L. Jones, "Reprisal Israeli Style," Military Review 50,
no. 8 (August 1970): 91-96; Fred J. Khouri, "The Policy of Massive
Retaliation in Arab-Israeli Relations," The Middle East Journal 20,
no. 4 (Autumn 1966): 435-56.

(7) FBIS, September 14, 1973.

(8) FBIS, September 17, 1973.

(9) London Times, December 9, 1973.

(10) Herman Kahn, On Escalation: Metaphors and Scenarios (Baltimore:
Penguin Books, 1965), pp. 284-285.

(11) Ibid. pp. 62ff; Charles W. Yost, "The Arab-Israeli War: How It
Began," Foreign Affairs 46, no. 2 (January 1968): 304-320; John S.
Badeau, "The Arabs, 1967," reprinted in Majdia D. Khadduri, ed., The
Arab-Israeli Impasse (Washington: Robert B. Luce, Inc., 1968), pp.
97-113; Yitzhak Rabin, "Introduction," The Six Day War (Israel: IDF,
1968).

(12) Walter Z. Laqueur, The Road to Jerusalem (New York: The
Macmillan Company, 1968), p. 71.

(13) Don Peretz, The Palestinian Arab Refugee Problem (Santa Monica:
RAND, 1969); Rony E. Gabbay, A Political Study of the Arab Jewish
Conflict, (Paris: Librarie E. Droz, 1959).

(14) Cf. Badeau, "The Arabs,".

(15) Fuad Jabber, The Palestinian Resistance and Inter-Arab Politics (Santa Monica: RAND, 1971); Malcolm Kerr, Regional Arab Politics and the Conflict with Israel (Santa Monica: RAND, 1969).

(16) Cf. Fred J. Khoury, The Arab-Israeli Dilemma (Syracuse: Syracuse University Press, 1968); chaps. 6, 7; J.S. Haupert "Political Geography of the Israeli-Syrain Boundary Dispute, 1949-1967," The Professional Geographer 21, no. 3 (May 1969): 163-171.

(17) Badeau, "Arabs"; Yost, "Arabs-Israeli War"; Brecher, Foreign Policy System, Ch. 12. Barry M. Blechman, "The Impact of Israel's Reprisals on Behavior of Bordering Arab Nations Directed at Israel," The Journal of Conflict Resolution 16, no. 2 (June 1972): 155-181.

(18) Laqueur, Road, p. 71.; On the Jordan waters issue: Y. Nimrod, "The Jordan's Angry Waters," New Outlook 8, no. 5 (July-August 1965): 19-23 and, "Conflict Over the Jordan, New Outlook 8, no. 6 (September 1965): 5-18.

(19) See: Gordon H. Torrey, "Aspects of the Political Elite in Syria," in George Lenczowski, ed., Political Elites in the Middle East (Washington: American Enterprise Institute, 1975), pp. 151-161, especially pp. 155ff.

(20) Michel H. Van Dusen, "Political Integration and Regionalism in Syria," The Middle East Journal 26 no. 2 (Spring 1972): 122-35; Eric Rouleau, "The Syrian Enigma: What Is the Ba'th?" reprinted in Irene L. Gendzier, ed., A Middle East Reader (New York: Pegasus, 1969), pp. 156-171; Moshe Ma'oz, "Attempts at Creating a Modern Political Community in Syria," The Middle East Journal 26, no. 4 (Autumn 1972): 389-404; The Shiloah Center For Middle Eastern and African Studies Tel-Aviv University, Middle East Record, 1967 (Jerusalem: Israel Universities Press, 1971), pp. 489ff; Kamel Abu Jaber, The Arab Ba'th Socialist Party (Syracuse: Syracuse University Press, 1966); Gordon H. Torrey, Syrian Politics and the Military, 1945-1958 (Columbus: Ohio State University Press, 1964); Patrick Seale, The Struggle for Syria (New York: Oxford University Press, 1965); John F. Devlin, The Ba'th Party: A History of Its Origins to 1966 (Stanford: Hoover Institution Press, 1976).

(21) Cf: Clifford Geertz, "The Integrative Revolution," in ibid., ed., Old Societies and New States (New York: The Free Press of Glencoe, 1963), pp. 105-157. Primordial identities are conceptions of the self or community rooted in one or more cultural "givens": race, blood descent, language, religion, locality or life-style. Definitions based on these givens tend to be bound up with notions of honor or shame. Therefore, primordial conflicts are both diffuse in the sense that they involve strife over a wide range of issues, many of them not at all political in the normal usage, and intensely emotional because these issues impinge on ultimate definitions of identity.

(22) New York Times, May 19, 1967; Amos Perlmutter, "From Obscurity to Rule: The Syrian Army and the Ba'th Party," The Western Political Quarterly 32, no. 4 (December 1969): 827-845; "al-Baath

An Uncertain Party in Power", Arab World Weekly, December 14, 1968, pp. 4-9. The U.S. Army Area Handbook for Syria (Washington: Special Operations Research Office, 1965), gives these figures for Syrian religious communities as of 1964, p. 124:

Religious Group	Estimated Number of Adherents	Percent of Group	Percent of Total
Moslem	4,631,000	100.0	84.7
Sunnis	(3,950,000)	(85.3)	(72.2)
Alawites	(600,000)	(13.0)	(11.0)
Ismailis	(56,000)	(1.2)	(1.0)
Other Shiites	(25,000)	(.5)	(.5)
Christian	654,000	100.0	12.0
Greek Orthodox	(246,000)	(37.6)	(4.5)
Armenian Orthodox	(140,000)	(21.4)	(2.5)
Greek Catholics	(80,000)	(12.2)	(1.5)
Syrian Orthodox	(72,000)	(11.0)	(1.3)
Syrian Catholics	(30,000)	(4.6)	(.6)
Maronites	(25,000)	(3.8)	(.5)
Armenian Catholics	(24,000)	(3.7)	(.4)
Nestorians	(15,000)	(2.3)	(.3)
Protestants	(12,000)	(1.8)	(.2)
Roman Catholics	(10,000)	(1.5)	(.2)
Others	184,000		3.3
Druzes	(170,000)		(3.0)
Yazidis	(10,000)		(.2)
Jews	(4,000)		(.1)

See also the data on sectarian representation in Syrian cabinets compiled by Nikolos van Dam, "Sectarian and Regional Factionalism in the Syrian Political Elite," The Middle East Journal 32, no. 2 (Spring 1978): 201-210.

(23) Cf.   Ira M. Lapidus, Muslim Cities in the Later Middle Ages (Cambridge: Harvard University Press, 1967).

(24) George Antonious, The Arab Awakening (New York: Capricorn, 1965), is the classic statement of this Arabist response on the part of religiously marginal Arab populations.; Majid Khadduri, Political Trends in the Arab World: The Role of Ideas and Ideals in Politics (Baltimore: The Johns Hopkins Press, 1970), Ch. 2; C. Ernest Dawn, "The Rise of Arabism in Syria," The Middle East Journal 16, no. 2 (Spring 1962): 145-168.

(25) Sylvia G. Haim, "The Ba'th in Syria," in Michael Curtis, ed., People and Politics in the Middle East (New Brunswick, NJ: Transaction, Inc., 1971), pp. 133ff.

(26) Beside the Ba'th, several other parties have consistently attracted minorities: the Syrian National Socialist Party (SNSP) and local Arab Communist Parties.

(27) Lerner, Passing, pp. 281-82.

(28) Constitution of the Ba'th Party and Michel Aflag, "Nationalism is Love Before All Else," both reprinted in Sylvia G. Haim, ed., Arab Nationalism (Los Angeles: University of California Press, 1964), pp. 233-36; 242-50.

(29) Simmel, Conflict, pp. 97ff: "For this reason, groups, and especially minorities, which live in conflict and persecution, often reject approaches or tolerance from the other side. The closed nature of their opposition without which they cannot fight on would be blurred..."

(30) Coser, Functions, pp. 39ff., for the concept of an institutional safety valve. Coser suggests that the displacement of hostility takes at least three forms: (a) direct expression of hostility against the person or group which is the source of frustration; (b) displacement of hostile feelings onto substitute objects; (c) tension release activity which provides satisfaction in itself. Probably all three were involved in Ba'thist foreign and domestic policies.

(31) Shiloah Center, Middle East Record; Arab World Weekly, March 24, 1967.

(32) Shiloah, Middle East Road.

(33) an-Nahar Arab Report, April 1, 1974; Arab World Weekly, November 8, 1969; ibid., November 21, 1970.

(34) Arab World Weekly, November 21, 1970; an-Nahar Arab Report, April 1, 1974.

(35) Arab World Daily, September 15, 1966; Shiloah Center, Middle East Record.

(36) Shiloah Center, Middle East Record, al-Safa' stated that approximately 4,000 Druze officers in the Syrian military and police force had been dismissed and that Druze contingents had been moved from the Druze area of al-Suwayda in Southern Syria and replaced by 'Alawi contingents.

(37) Ibid., Arab World Daily, September 16, 1966.

(38) Bernard Lewis, "The Consequences of the Defeat," Foreign Affairs 46, no. 2 (January 1968): 321-335.

(39) Shiloah Center, Middle East Record.

(40) Ibid.

(41) London Times, May 9, 1967.

(42) Ibid., Arab World Daily, May 10, 1967.

(43) New York Times, May 12, 1967.

(44) Arab World Daily, May 19, 1967.

(45) Miles Copland, The Game of Nations (New York: Simon & Schuster, 1970), p. 282.

(46) Max Weber, The Theory of Social and Economic Organization, ed. and trans. by A.M. Henderson and Talcott Parsons (New York: The Free Press of Glencoe, 1964), pp. 359-373. See also Arthur Sweitzer, "Theory and Political Charisma," Comparative Studies in Society and History 16, no. 2 (March 1974): 150-181; Leland Bowie, "Charisma, Weber and Nasir," The Middle East Journal 30, no. 2 (Spring 1976): 141-157; R. Hrair Dekmejian, "Marx, Weber and Nasir," ibid., pp. 158-72, for Weber's original statement of the concept, reviews of the literature critiquing it, and comments concerning its utility as applied to the analysis of 'abd al-Nasir's behavior.

(47) R. Hrair Dekmejian, Egypt Under Nasir: A Study in Political Dynamics (Albany: State University of New York Press, 1971), pp. 4-5.

(48) Jacques Berque, Egypt: Imperialism and Revolution (New York: Praeger, 1972), and Hudson, Arab Policies, pp. 127-130.

(49) Erik H. Erikson, Young Man Luther: A Study in Psychoanalysis and History (New York: W.W. Norton & Company, 1958), pp. 14ff.

(50) Nasser, Philosophy, p. 62.

(51) Dekmejian, p. 99.

(52) al-Sadat, Memoirs, al-Ahram, September 26, 1975, FBIS, October 1, 1975.

(53) Jamal 'abd al-Nasir, Philosophy of the Revolution (Cairo: Ministry of National Guidance, n.d.), pp. 26-27.

(54) al-Sadat, Memoirs, al-Ahram, September 28, 1975, FBIS, October 3, 1975.

(55) 'abd al-Nasir, Philosophy (Cairo), p. 22.

(56) Malcolm Kerr, "Coming to Terms With Nasser: Attempts and Failures," International Affairs, 38, no. 1, January 1962; see also Mohamed Haseinein Heikal, The Cairo Documents (New York: Doubleday, 1973).

(57) Patai, Arab Mind, p. 99.

(58) Weber, p. 360.

(59) George Lenczowski, "The Objects and Methods of Nasserism," reprinted in J.H. Thompson and R.D. Reischauer, Modernization of the Arab World (Princeton, N.J.: D. Van Nostrand Company, Inc., 1966), pp. 197-211.

(60) Robert Stephens, Nasser: A Political Biography (New York: Simon and Schuster, 1971), p. 370ff.

(61) Ibid.

(62) Ibid.

(63) Ibid., p. 373.

(64) Leonard Binder, "Political Recruitment and Participation in Egypt," in Joseph LaPalombara and Myron Weiner, eds., Political Parties and Political Development (Princeton, N.J.: Princeton University Press, 1966), pp. 217-240.

(65) James Heaphey, "The Organization of Egypt: Inadequacies of a Non-Political Model for Nation Building," World Politics 28, no. 1 (October 1965): 177-193.

(66) Stephens, Nasser.

(67) Ibid., p. 372.

(68) Anthony Nutting, Nasser (London: Constable, 1972), p. 379.

(69) Laqueur, The Road, pp. 61ff.

(70) Malcolm Kerr, The Arab Cold War, 3rd ed. (New York: Oxford University Press, 1971), ch. I.

(71) Rabin.

(72) Ibid. Arab World Daily, September 13, 1965.

(73) Kerr, Arab Cold War. However, these moves had the reverse effect from that intended. Later al-Sadat recounted the pressures put on 'abd al-Nasir to escalate: "We were in a predicament. If we did not go to Syria's assistance, they (sic: the Russians) would say we abandoned the Syrians when the Israelis struck at them. The Soviets would criticize us in the area. Moreover, we had a joint defense treaty with the Syrians, and Jamal 'abd al-Nasir was a man who kept his word and promise. Thus, there was no escape from fighting..." al-Sadat in al-Siyasa, November 19, 1976.

(74) Rabin; Stephens, Nasser, pp. 449ff.

(75) Note the comments of Saudi Crown Prince Fahd ibn al-'Aziz: "...We know that in 1967 Egypt went to war when disputes between it and Saudi Arabia were most intense over the issue of the Egyptian army's intervention in the Yemen. It was then said that the purpose of the Egyptian army's intervention was the threaten Saudi Arabia directly, something that we do not accept..." Interview in al-Siyasa, April 16, 1977, FBIS, April 21, 1977. And also al-Sadat:"...However, the Yemeni Civil War broke out on September 26, 1962 (the first anniversary of the breakup of unity with Syria), and that was a good opportunity to teach King Saud a lesson. He had financed the breakup of the union with Syria, and led the campaign against Egypt...", Search, p. 162.

(76) Cf. Laqueur, The Road, pp. 62-63.

(77) Arab World Daily, September 3, 1965.

(78) Arab World Daily, September 18, 1969, the figure was given by 'abd al-Nasir during the course of an address to the ASU.

(79) Arab World Daily, September 9, 1965.

(80) Arab World Weekly, April 12, 1969.

(81) Arab World Daily, September 9, 1965.

(82) Ibid.

(83) London Times, September 30, 1965; Arab World Weekly, April 12, 1969; Donald E. Reilly, Urban Guerrillas in Turkey: Causes and Consequences, Carlisle Barracks (Pennsylvania: US Army War College, 1972), ch. III. Vidal.

(84) Arab World Weekly, April 12, 1969.

(85) Arab World Daily, November 25, 1966; also: George H. Quester, "Miscommunication in the Middle East and its Impact on the Outbreak of Wars," in Gabriel Sheffer, ed., Dynamics of a Conflict: A Re-examination of the Arab-Israeli Conflict (Atlantic Highlands, NJ: Humanities Press, 1975),pp. 279-303.

(86) El Sadat, Search, pp. 181ff.

(87) Copeland, pp. 277ff.; Patai, pp. 101ff.; Nutting, pp. 7ff.

(88) Al-Sadat, Search, p. 183. The sources of this suspicious outlook are probably multiple: (a) Ego problems stemming from 'abd al-Nasir's unhappy childhood; (b) Culturally induced attitudes as a byproduct of his rural origins. In this connection, Haykal provides an illustration by arguing that the verbal attacks 'abd al-Nasir made on Western statesmen at the time he nationalized the Suez Canal were partly motivated by a traditional sensitivity to insult: "The way in which Nasser announced the takeover (of the canal), the violence of his speech, and the insults he hurled at Britain and the United States surprised Eden, but there was no reason for his surprise because the insults were deliberately calculated as a reply to the insulting fashion in which Dulles withdrew his offer of help for the Aswan High Dam. President Nasser belonged to the Beni Mor village of upper Egypt. They were the Bitter Ones and they are saiedis (peasants) to whom revenge is sacred..." Heikal, Documents, p. 93.; (c) Instincts developed as a consequence of 'abd al-Nasir's personal experiences as both plotter and leader; (d) Psychological consequences which stemmed from 'abd al-Nasir's physical ailments: diabetes, pains in the nerves and veins of his legs, and a heart condition.

Granting this suspicious nature, one can, in turn, read 'abd al-Nasir's insistence on "serried ranks" as an ideological response to personal insecurity. By creating a social order around him that was totally organized, 'abd al-Nasir could theoretically assure himself of an environment where threat was either eliminated or made organizationally predictable. Cf: Harold D. Lasswell, Psychopathology and Politics, (New York: The Viking Press, 1960); and ibid., Power and Personality, (New York: The Viking Press, 1962), for the argument that political leaders displace their private motives and emotions onto politics and then rationalize their actions in terms of a political ideology.

(89) Pye, pp. 38ff; see also: Sidney Verba, "Assumptions of Rationality and Non-Rationality in Models of the International System," in Rosenau, International Politics, pp. 217-231.

(90) Ibid.

(91) El-Sadat, Search, p. 211.

(92) In addition to Allison, see ibid., "Conceptual Models and the Cuban Missile Crisis," The American Political Science Review 63, no. 3 (September 1969): 689-718, for a shortened version of Allison's three models of decision making. Fred W. Riggs, Thailand: The Modernization of a Bureaucratic Polity (Honolulu: East-West Center Press, 1966), pp. 211-41, points out that clique formation is a characteristic of modernizing elite politics. For the composition of the Egyptian elite see, Dekmejian, pp. 167-224; for a description of bureaucratic politics within this elite, see el-Sadat, Search, pp. 142-80.; Nutting, pp. 304ff.; Stephens, pp. 359ff.; Robert Daniel Springborg, The Ties That Bind: Political Association and Policy Making in Egypt, unpublished PhD dissertation (Sanford University, 1974), pp. 46-50.

(93) El-Sadat, Search, p. 147. He concludes his description of decision making under 'abd al-Nasir by saying: "Such was the political situation I inherited. There was no real Foreign Ministry, no studied or properly planned policy; only the President himself." ibid., p. 212.

(94) Heikel, Documents, pp. 223ff; Badeau,; Nutting, pp. 390ff.; Stephens, p. 470, describes 'abd al-Nasir's outlook as "paranoid."

(95) Nadav Safran, From War to War (New York: Pegasus, 1969), p. 279.

(96) Ibid., p. 280.

(97) A letter purporting to contain the contents of this agreement was published some years later in the Beirut press. For a contemporaneous account see Arab World Daily, October 7, 1966, which contains the original story.

(98) New York Times, May 12, 1967.

(99) al-Ahram, May 26, 1967.

(100) Heikal, Documents, John S. Badeau, "The USA and UAR: A Crisis in Confidence," reprinted in Thompson and Reischauer, pp. 212-228. See also Quandt, p. 38, for the US view.

(101) Heikal, Documents.

(102) Badeau, "The Arabs".

(103) Ibid.

(104) C.O. Huntley, "Arab Versus Jew: The Evolution of Two National Strategies," Naval War College Review 22, no. 3 (November 1969): 69-91.

(105) Harkabi, pp. 376ff.

(106) Nutting.

(107) London Times, May 4, 1967.

(108) FBIS, May 23, 1967.

(109) Harkabi, pp. 447-48.

(110) Ibid., p. 397.

(111) New York Times, May 15, 1967; London Times, May 17, 1967; Quandt, Decisions, p. 38.

(112) New York Times, May 15, 1967.

(113) New York Times, May 17, 1967.

(114) Arab World Daily, May 23, 1967; Laqueur, The Road, pp. 73ff.

(115) New York Times, May 13, 1967.

(116) al-Muharrir, September 21, 1966.

(117) Heikal, Documents, p. 240; Abdullah Schleifer, The Fall of Jerusalem (New York: Monthly Review Press, 1972), pp. 98ff. See Jervis, Perception, pp. 217ff., on decision maker's use of "Lessons" from history.

(118) Walter Laqueur, "The Hand of Russia," The Reporter 36, no. 13 (June 29, 1967): 18-20. Safran notes that even if 'abd al-Nasir did not fully believe any of these reports as to the accuracy of their details, he nevertheless was predisposed to believe that in essence the reports were true: that an Israeli large-scale attack would take place sooner or later. Safran, p. 278. Michael Bar-Zohar, Embassies in Crisis: Diplomats and Demagogues Behind the Six-Day War (Englewood Cliffs, NJ: Prentice-Hall, Inc., n.d.), pp. 12ff., argues that the reasons for this duplication of intelligence reports was because the Russians had given the same information to several Arab intelligence organizations.

(119) New York Times, May 16, 1967.

(120) Badeau, "The Arabs"; Schleifer, pp. 105ff.

(121) FBIS, June 10, 1967.

(122) FBIS, May 23, 1967.

(123) New York Times, May 16, 1967.

(124) Shiloah Center, <u>Middle East Record</u>, p. 185: Amir's Battle Order
no. 1. On May 14, Field Marshal 'abd al-Hakim 'Amir, the Deputy
Commander in Chief of the UAR armed forces, issued Battle Order
No. 1 (not published at the time), in which he stated: "It has
appeared clearly, in the course of the present year and since the
beginning of May 1967, that Israel...urged on by Imperialism...is
trying to direct military blows at the Arab people of Syria.

"In the past few days, reliable reports have disclosed that there are
huge Israeli troop concentrations on the Syrian borders. Their
intention is to intervene on Syrian territory in order to:

1. Overthrow the Arab liberated regime and establish a hired
reactionary regime in Syria.

2. Suppress the movement for the liberation of Palestine.

"This was supported by the aggressive declarations, characterized by
their impudence, which were made by the Israeli PM and CoS of the
Israeli army, and which represent an undisguised provocation of the
Arab liberated forces, at the head of which is the UAR...

"But, after considering all the possibilities, we decided to take a
firm stand against the Israeli military threats and intervene
immediately in case of any aggressive action taken by Israel against
Syria...

"The following orders have been issued:

1. Mobilization of the armed forces;

2. Raising the level of preparedness to full alert for war, beginning
14:30, May 14, 1967;

3. The formations and units indicated by the operation plans will
move from their present stations to their appointed grouping areas;

4. The armed forces will be at full alert to carry out their battle
assignment on the Israeli front according to developments in the
situation..."

(Captured document, published by <u>Ma-'arakhot</u>, June 1968).

(125) <u>London Times</u>, May 16, 1967.

(126) Shiloah Center, <u>Middle East Record</u>, for a summary of these
moves.

(127) Rabin.

(128) Quandt, <u>Decisions</u>, p. 49. See also Steven J. Rosen and Martin
Indyk, "The Temptation to Preempt in a Fifth Arab-Israeli War,"
<u>Orbis</u> 20, no. 2 (Summer 1976): 265-285, and Abraham R. Wagner,
<u>Crisis Decision Making: Israel's Experience in 1967 and 1973</u> (New
York: Praeger, 1974), pp. 50ff, and the literature cited in both for
discussions of Israeli perceptions of the situation which led to the
decision to preempt.

(129) Compare the version cited by Yost, with that cited by Heikal, Documents, p. 241.

(130) Heikal, Documents, C. Ernest Dawn, "The Egyptian Remilitarization of the Sinai," The Journal of Contemporary History 3, no. 3 (July 1968): 201-24; London Times, May 19, 1967.

(131) London Times, May 20, 1967.

(132) Dawn, p. 224.

(133) Laqueur, p. 90, muses on the role of Radio Cairo in the disaster that overtook the Arabs, and also contains a summary of this propaganda; a London Times story out of Cairo noted that the atmosphere was such that compromise seemed doubtful. Egyptian 'ulama' had been ordered to preach the call for jihad. London Times, May 20, 1967; Cf. also FBIS materials from May 15 to June 7, 1967.

(134) Note the comment of the editors of Arab Press Service, July 31, 1978: "....the Arab defeat in June 1967 was not an exclusive victory for Israel. Indeed several Arab parties also benefitted from the outcome of that war. To enumerate but a few examples, King Faisal won the balance of Arab power, as Saudi Arabia, Kuwait and royalist Libya began financing the "steadfastness" of the Confrontation states (Egypt, Jordan and Syria) as well as the then emerging Palestinian Resistance Movement, which also benefitted from the war....If the June war produced a political (as distinct from Arab National) defeat, then subsequent developments proved that that defeat fell almost exclusively on the Nasserist movement and, to a smaller extent, on the Arab leftist movement....Should Israel launch another war....its outcome would have to be in favour of some Arab regimes against other Arab regimes....No matter how and when it should take place, its outcome would be harmful to some of the Arab regimes and beneficial to others. Such is the tragedy of Arab unity so emotionally repeated by its romantic proponents..."

(135) Peter Snow, Hussein (Washington: Robert B. Luce, Inc., 1972), p. 173.

(136) His Majesty King Hussein, Hussein of Jordan: My "War" With Israel (New York: William Morrow and Company, Inc., 1969), p. 48.

(137) Ibid., p. 35.

(138) Ibid., p. 35-36.

(139) Dawn, pp. 217-218, quoting al-Hayat, May 18, 1967.

(140) Ibid., p. 218.

(141) New York Times, May 18, 1967; Shiloah Center, Middle East Record, pp. 192ff; Safran, pp. 292-93.

(142) Shiloah Center ; Safran, pp. 294-95; Quandt, p. 41.

(143) Dawn ; Hussein, p. 49; Badeau ; Yost.

(144) Dawn, al-Anwar, April 17, 1967, carried an extensive comparison of Arab and Israeli arms in an article which reflected popular Arab assessments of their military strength. After pointing out that Arab military strength was superior to that of Israel, the paper cautioned that for this superiority to become effective it was necessary for Arab states to coordinate militarily. It then went on to list the orders of battle of selected Arab countries and Israel:

"UAR. The UAR Army is composed of 4 infantry divisions, and two armoured divisions - all totalling between 100 and 120,000 men. Each infantry division consists of 11,000 men with 200 medium size tanks, supported by artillery of 120 mm., 130 mm., and 152 mm. The armoured divisions consist of 9,000 men each, with a total of 375 tanks.

The main tank force of the UAR consists of the heavy Soviet-made GS-3, T-54, and T-10, and the medium-size, also Soviet-made, T-34-85, for a total of 1,200 tanks, including 32 Centurions.

In the Air Force, the UAR has about 550 war planes, including 30 T-U bombers, 40 Il-28 light bombers, and between 100 to 120 MIG's-21 fighters, plus 80 MIG's-19, and 150 MIG's-17.

In the Navy, the UAR has: 4 Soviet-made destroyers, 6 British-made cruisers, 9 Soviet-made submarines, 44 gun-boats for patrol, 5 small destroyers equipped with "Komar" rockets which have a range of 15 miles, and 6 mine sweepers.

The UAR rockets section consists of: 100 missiles, including the UAR-made "Al Zafer", which has a 175-mile range, and "Al Kaher". The UAR possesses an aerial defense system covering all of its territory, depending on the Soviet-made SAM missiles. Cairo, Alexandria, the Suez Canal and Aswan are fully covered by this system. This system, plus the MIG's-21, can give the UAR full protection in the event of an Israeli attack.

Syria. The Syrian army is composed of 40,000 men now, divided over between 15 and 20 Brigades, equipped with 400 Soviet-made tanks of the T-34 and the T-54 type, plus heavy artillery and radar equipped antiaircraft guns.

The Syrian Air Force is composed of 60 MIG's-17, 20 MIG's-19, 20 MIG's-21, some Il-28 light bombers, and a number of transporter aircraft.

Jordan. The total force of the Jordanian army is 55,000 men, equipped with 200 to 250 tanks, including about 100 American made Patton tanks.

The Jordanian Air Force now consists of 25 Hawker Hunters, 15 Vampires, plus the 36 Starfighters which Jordan is to receive from the United States. Twelve Starfighters have so far been delivered.

Iraq. The Iraqi army's total strength is 70,000 men equipped with 800 tanks and 300 fighter planes. This would have added great strength to the Arab force in fighting Israel, but Iraq is far from the Israeli border and cannot play an effective role in event of war with Israel, unless one of the Arab states bordering Israel allowed Iraqi forces and Air Force to take positions on its territory.

Israel. The Israeli army is composed of 10,000 regulars, but Israel claims it can call up a quarter of a million men and women within 48 hours in case of a general alarm or mobilization. The army is organized in brigades, each formed of 3,500 men. If it mobilized all of its strength, Israel would have 23 brigades, one third of which are armoured brigades, including one brigade of paratroopers. Israel's artillery corps depends on heavy artillery of 155 mm., which has a range of 18 kilometers. Its antiaircraft guns are radar equipped, with a range of about 10,000 meters. Israel possesses about 1,000 tanks, 200 of which are Patton, 400 of the Sherman tanks, also American, 30 British made Centurion, 200 French made MX's, and a number of Israeli made tanks.

The Israeli Air Force has between 350 and 400 military planes -25 of which are light bombers, 48 tactical bombers of the American Sky Hawk types, 72 French made Mirages, 24 French Mysteres, 40 training planes, plus between 30 and 40 transporters.

In the Navy, Israel has two British made destroyers, four submarines, 12 torpedo boats, one landing craft, and a regiment of marines. In 1961, the Israelis launched a two stage rocket with a 50 mile range. But since then, nothing has been heard about the Israeli rocket programme. Furthermore, Israel possesses the US made Hawk ground to air missiles. Israel had said it bought only 72 of these missiles, but it is believed it has more than this."

(145) Shiloah Center. 'Abd al-Nasir was clearly aware of the risks he was running and consequently sought to get as many assessments of the relative capabilities of Egyptian and Israeli armed forces as possible. His efforts, however, ran afoul of both the ongoing pattern of Egyptian bureaucratic politics wherein participants (in this case 'Amir in particular) supplied information designed to further their own career interests and a more general Arab cultural tendency to overstate one's own abilities and understate those of an opponent. This tendency is known in connection with a number of similar traits as the "fahlawi personality," Cf. Sadiq al-'Azm, Self-Criticism After the Defeat (Beirut: Dar al-Tali'a, 1968).

In any event, according to al-Sadat's account, 'Amir repeatedly assured 'abd al-Nasir that Egyptian forces were ready to fight if necessary: "...Nasser convened a meeting of what he called a Supreme Executive Committee toward the end of May 1967...Nasser said: 'Now with our concentrations in the Sinai, the chances of war are fifty-fifty. But if we close the Strait, war will be a one hundred percent certainty.' Then, turning to 'Amir, he asked: 'Are the armed forces ready, Abdel Hakim?' 'Amir pointed to his neck and said: 'On my own head be it, boss! Everything's in tiptop shape....'";

Search, p. 172.

In addition, all Egyptian military commanders attended daily meetings from May 24/25 to June 2 1967 during which the state of Egyptian preparedness was reviewed. At the last meeting, June 2, 'abd al-Nasir announced that the Israelis had formed a coalition cabinet on June 1, and that he now expected them to attack, either on June 3, 4 or 5 at the latest. (The actual Israeli decision to attack was made on June 4.) He then added that, in his opinion, the first Israeli strike would be against the air force. Air Force Commander Sidqi Mahmud replied that: "Your Excellency we have thought of this and the first strike will not cause us more than 10 percent damage." al-Sadat, Interview with Ms. Himmat Mustafa, October 6, 1977, FBIS, October 25, 1977.

(146) Safran.

(147) al-Ahram, October 6, 1967.

(148) Shiloah Center; Safran, p. 300.

(149) Heikal, Documents, p. 244; Safran, p. 300.

(150) Akhbar al-Yawn, November 3, 1973; Safran, pp. 299-300.

(151) According to Quandt, p. 49, the US warned both Israel and Egypt not to preempt. The goal of US policy toward the end of May was to slow down the escalatory process long enough to find some diplomatic formula for preventing war.   To this end, US policy makers secured a promise from the Israelis not to attack before June 11, and secured an Egyptian agreement to have Vice President Zakariya Muhyi al-Din visit the US on June 7 for talks. The failure of these efforts, through no fault of the US, was interpreted by the Egyptians as further proof of Johnson's hostility:

"When he took over, Johnson had already sold out completely to the Zionists. He harassed us in 1965 and told us that he wanted to inspect our armed forces and our atomic progress and learn our strength...Johnson's trickery was part of those things that took place at that time (sic: the escalation of 1967)....Johnson contacted Jamal and it was agreed that one of the vice presidents of the republic should go to the United States on Wednesday, June 7....He (Johnson) contacted Israel and told them: What are you waiting for?....Accordingly, the Israeli plan was submitted to U.S. President Johnson in the presence of American intelligence, the CIA, and leaders of the Pentagon....Johnson asked for their views and they told him that the plan was 100 percent sound. Johnson gave it his blessing and they (sic: Israelis) began their attack on Monday, June 5..." al-Sadat, Interview. Quandt, of course, goes out of his way to refute this thesis.

This pervasive image of Johnson as impacably hostile must have reinforced two other factors that led to the Egyptian charge that US aircraft were taking part in air strikes along with the Israeli air force. These other two factors are: (a) 'Abd al-Nasir's desperate need for a face saving explanation for the Egyptian defeat, a need met in this case by resurrecting the 1956 scenario of major power military intervention on Israel's behalf.   (b) A misreading by Egyptian intelligence of the speed with which the Israeli air force could turn its planes around between strikes, an ability which, when perceived by Egyptians, must have made it appear as though the Israelis had many more aircraft than previously thought.

(152) Dawn, p. 220, quoting al-Nahar, May 23, 26, 1967, al-Hayat, May 28, 1967, Sawt al-'Uruba, May 26, 1967.

(153) Ibid.

(154) FBIS, May 27, 1967, Safran, p. 299.

(155) London Times, May 18, 1967.

(156) al-Ahram, May 26, 1967.

(157) FBIS, June 3, 1967.

(158) Safran, pp. 232ff.

(159) Arab World Daily, June 5, 1967. Al-Sadat, in particular, was moved by the effects of these false reports on Egyptian citizenry: "I grew even more dazed and broken hearted as I watched the crowds flocking in from al-Tahrir Province in big trucks, or filling up the vast Pyramids Road as they marched in 'companies,' chanting, dancing, and applauding the faked up victory reports which our mass media put out hourly....The fact that they were rejoicing in an imaginary victory - rejoicing in what was in effect defeat - made me feel sorry for them, pity them, and deeply hate those who deceived them and Egypt as a whole. Watching those 'victory' processions I wished I could have a heart attack, like the one I had in 1960. I wished I could pass away before these good and kind people woke up to the reality - before they realized that the victory they had been sold was in fact a terrible disaster..." Search, pp. 175-76.

Chapter 4

(1) Brecher, p. 64.

(2) See John W. Amos II, "The Middle East: The Problem of Quarantine," in William Whitson, ed., Foreign Policy and U.S. National Security: Major Postelection Issues (New York: Praeger Publishers, 1976), pp. 76-91.

(3) Cf. Yigal Allon, "Israel: The Case for Defensible Borders," Foreign Affairs 55, no. 1 (October 1976): 38-52; Israel Tal, "Israel's Doctrine of National Security: Background and Dynamics," The Jerusalem Quarterly, no. 4, (Summer 1977), 44-57, for Israeli statements of the "defensible borders" concept. See also Col. Merrill McPeak, "Israel: Borders and Security," Foreign Affairs 54,

no. 3 (April 1976): 426-43, for the American critique of this Israeli doctrine which spurred both Allon and Tal to write the above cited articles in its defense.

(4) On this theme generally, see al-'Azm's comments on the self-delusive qualities of the fahlawi personality, pp. 232-48; also: Halim Barakat, "Alienation and Revolution in Arab Life," Mawaqaf, 1, no. 5 (August 1969): 18-44.

(5) The concern with cultural decline is not new in the Arab world; a body of literature dealing with the problem of coping with the West begins to grow up after the French invasion of Egypt in 1798. On this see Hudson, pp. 107-25. The 1948 War naturally produced a more intense concern for finding some formula to deal with the West. On this literature see: Adnan Mohammed Abu-Ghazaleh, "The Impact of 1948 on Palestinian Arab Writers: The First Decade," Middle East Forum 66, no. 2-3 (1970): 81-92; Musa Alami, "The Lesson of Palestine," The Middle East Journal, 3, no. 4 (October 1949): 373-405: Nissim Rejwan, "Arab Intellectuals and Israel: 1948-1967," New Outlook 15, no. 6 (August 1971): 25-31. Rejwan also summarizes some of the post-1967 literature in, "Impact of the June War on Arab Intellectuals," New Outlook 14, no. 8 (October-November 1971): 25-34. In addition to these summaries, some other works can be mentioned: al-'Azm, of course, is highly critical of existing Arab culture and social structure and argues that only a total revolution can transform both sufficiently to allow the Arabs to cope with the West in general, and Israel in particular. For similar comments see Constantine Zurayq, The Meaning of the Disaster Renewed (Beirut: Dar al-'Ilm lil-Milayin, 1967).

(6) Hudson, pp. 82-106 on the Arab authority crisis in general; and the following: Sa'yd Jumah, The Conspiracy and the Battle of Destiny, (Beirut: Dar al-Kitab al-'Arabi, 1968); Adib Nasur, The Setback and Error: The Intellectual and Ideological Errors Which Led to the Disaster (Beirut: Dar al-Kitab al-'Arabi, 1968). All of these have roughly the same theme: that contemporary Arab leadership was both out of touch with its populace and unable to provide any sort of coherent policy or motivation. Palestinian commentary was much more pointed, and argued flatly that Arab leaders had betrayed their trust: Mehmood Hussain, "The Palestine Liberation Movement and the Arab Regimes: The Great Betrayal," Economic and Political Weekly (Bombay), November 10, 1973, pp. 2023-2028.

(7) Western accounts of this war are agreed that it is an almost textbook perfect demonstration of the use of speed, surprise, and offensive maneuver: "The third Arab-Israeli war is likely to be studied in Staff Colleges for many years to come. Like the campaigns of the younger Napoleon, the performance of the Israeli Defense Force provided a textbook illustration for all the classical principles of war: speed, surprise, concentration, security, information, the offensive - above all, training and morale..." Michael Howard and Robert Hunter, Israel and the Arab World: The Crisis of

<u>1967</u>, Adelphi Papers, no. 41 (London: International Institute for Strategic Studies, 1967), pp. 8ff.

(8) Cf. the comments of John G. Stoessinger, <u>Why Nations Go To War</u> (New York: St. Martin's Press, Inc., 1974), pp. 206ff., on the images generated by the 1967 War. Also, al-Sadat: "Using tactics of psychological warfare and propaganda, Israel inflated the operation to assert the efficiency of its military performance while, in fact, there was no military action in 1967. To be frank, no...(we) withdrew with great bitterness and disappointment and Israel did not fight at all in 1967. Israel did not find anybody to fight because our forces were dispersed....I said (sic: to Kamal Hasan 'Ali, commander of an armored brigade): 'My son, I have been trying to for the past 20 days to determine whether Israel has waged a vicious psychological war. Is this true: Were you surprised by anything? Were you unaware of sophisticated weapons?' He said: 'Not at all.' I asked him: 'Was Israel's performance legendary?' 'Not at all,' he replied. I asked him: 'Were the Israeli tanks superior to yours?' 'Not at all,' he replied. I asked him: 'Was your training not good enough to qualify you for waging a battle?' He said: 'Not at all.' I listened to these answers with astonishment...." <u>Interview</u>, October 25, 1977.

Al-Sadat's remarks quoted above, of course, represent a contemporary, that is to say, a post-1973 interpretation of what happened in 1967. As such, they must be analyzed with some caution. Two interpretations are possible: (a) That Egyptian planners of the October War actually probed sufficiently into the events of 1967 to be able to isolate fact from myth and image. (b) That the history of 1967 has been rewritten by Egyptian spokesmen to confirm and foreshadow the performance of October 1973. In either event, Egyptian concern with the negative image generated by 1967 is clearly evident.

(9) According to Husni Mubarak Commander of the Egyptian Air Force in 1973, now al-Sadat's VP, the Egyptians lost over 90 percent of their aircraft during the first day or so. Husni Mubarak, interview carried in <u>MENA</u>, April 30, 1976, <u>FBIS</u>, May 3, 1976. Egyptian losses were actually much more significant than just numbers of aircraft, because most of these aircraft were destroyed with the pilots in them: in the case of Egypt, pilots were harder to come by than aircraft. As far as total Arab aircraft destroyed, Israeli AF Commander Mordekhay Hod later gave Arab losses as being over 450 aircraft, most of these destroyed in the first day's air strikes, <u>Jerusalem Post</u>, July 2, 1967. The reasons for this success are varied, but among the more important factors were: (a) maximum surprise which allowed Israeli aircraft to hit Arab aircraft while still on the ground; (b) excellent tactical intelligence which permitted location and targeting of Arab aircraft; (c) low level attack patterns which increased bombing accuracy substantially; (d) rapid turnaround of aircraft, permitting one plane to fly a large number of sorties per day. Israeli aircraft flew over 1000 sorties on the first day alone.

In this connection, the accusation of US intervention on the side of Israel seems to have originated in Israeli bombing routes. Israeli aircraft flew out to sea and then turned, coming in on Egyptian targets from the West in order to avoid Egyptian radar based in the Sinai and elsewhere. The net effect, however, to Arab observers was that aircraft were attacking them from the Mediterranean. The report of what appeared to be a carrier based strike seems to have originated from a Jordanian radar station north of Amman which picked up aircraft over the ocean. See Jerusalem Post Weekly, July 24, 1967; Keesing's Research Report, The Arab Israeli Conflict (New York: Charles Scribner's Sons, 1968), pp. 25ff; Gerald Kurland, The Arab-Israeli Conflict (Charlottesville, NC: SamHar Press, 1973), pp. 23ff; IDF, pp. 12ff; Safran, pp. 320ff; Shiloah Center, pp. 214ff.

(10) Stefan Geisenheyner, "The Arab Air Forces: Will They Try Again?," Air Force Magazine 51, no. 7 (July 1968):   44-48; Leo Heiman, "Soviet Air Tactics--No Room for Initiative," Air Force Magazine 51, no. 8 (August 1968):   42-45.

(11) Safran, pp. 333ff; IDF, pp. 34ff; Leo Heiman, "Armored Forces in the Middle East," Military Review 48, no. 11 (November 1968): 11-19; Jac Weller, "Israeli Armor: Lessons from the Six-Day War," Military Review, 51, no. 11 (November 1971): 44-50.

(12) al-Sadat, Interview, FBIS, October 25, 1977.

(13) Shiloah Center, p. 215; Shabtai Teveth, The Tanks of Tammuz (New York: Viking Press, 1968), pp. 121ff.

(14) IDF, pp. 34ff.

(15) Safran, p. 349; New York Times, November 24, 1967: 'Abd al-Nasir is said to have told al-Sadat these losses were so great that no Egyptian forces were left between the Israelis on the Canal and Cairo.   The only reason the Israelis did not cross and move on to Cairo were: (a) The United States-Israeli plan called for the Israelis to stop at the Canal, that being a sufficient defeat to cause 'abd al-Nasir's downfall; and/or (b) The Israelis did not want to move into heavily populated areas and risk becoming embroiled in a local insurgency. Search, pp. 177-178; Interview, October 25, 1977.

(16) Y. Harkabi, "Basic Factors in the Arab Collapse During the Six-Day War," Orbis 11, no. 3 (Fall 1967): 677-91.

(17) Safran, p. 351; Heiman, "Armored Forces".

(18) Shiloah Center, pp. 218, quoting from al-Jumhuriya, June 15, 1968. Al-Sadat insists that 'Amir was personally responsible for the order to retreat.   Not only that, but 'Amir repositioned Egyptian forces which 'abd al-Nasir had ordered to reinforce Egyptian defenses in the Rafah area: 'abd al-Nasir sensed that the Rafah-al-'Arish corridor (now known to UN personnel as "the bowling alley") was weakly defended, told 'Amir and the High Command to add an

additional armored brigade and mechanized infantry unit to the existing defenders. 'Amir, however, later ordered these new units (and apparently some others) withdrawn, leaving only infantry supported by some armor in place. These forces were easily bypassed by Israeli units inside the "fan." al-Sadat, interview in al-Hilal, carried in MENA, September 30, 1976, FBIS, October 1, 1976; Search, pp. 174ff.

(19) Ibid, p. 232, quoting from al-Ahram, June 21, 1968.

(20) Hussein, pp. 54ff; Safran, p. 358.

(21) Safran, p. 358.

(22) Hussein, pp. 106ff.

(23) Shiloah Center, p. 206.

(24) Safran, pp. 375-76.

(25) Heiman, "Armored Forces", Weller, Historical Evaluation and Research Organization (HERO), Target Position Assessment: June 1967 Middle East War, Sinai Front (Dunn Loring, VA: T.N. Dupuy Associates, Inc., 1978); Trevor Dupuy, Elusive Victory: The Arab Israeli Wars, 1947-1974 (New York: Bobbs Merrill, 1977).

(26) Harkabi.

(27) Heiman.

(28) Heikal, Documents, p. 247. Not an especially surprising occurrence given: (a) the preexisting pattern of bureaucratic politics which rested on the various participant's ability to control 'abd al-Nasir's access to information; (b) 'Abd al-Hakim 'Amir's own role in the debacle which would naturally lead him to withhold information about the defeat until the last possible moment. On the evening of the 5th, 'Amir told al-Sadat that Israeli forces had captured al-'Arish (which in al-Sadat's view, meant the end of the war); but al-Sadat himself did not speak to 'abd al-Nasir about the fighting until the 9th. al-Sadat, Interview, FBIS, October 25, 1977.

   Interestingly enough, the Saudis were rather quickly informed of the Israeli air strike, and drew the appropriate conclusion: that the Egyptians had already lost the war. As a consequence, Saudi forces which might otherwise have been sent into battle, were not moved.

(29) Hussein, pp. 60-61; 80.

(30) Arab World Daily, June 5, 1968.

(31) Patai, pp. 96ff.

(32) Berger, Arab World, pp. 300ff: "From one point of view, modern Arab nationalism may be considered an effort to create a new self conception for the Arab, a new identity. For centuries the Near Easterner has seemed to the West to be religious, indolent, patient, grave - a narrow, unambitious person in a narrow, circumscribed

world which was static, while Europe was going through brilliant periods of geographic exploration, scientific discovery, technological progress, and economic prosperity. So pervasive did this image become that it was accepted even by the Arabs themselves. But nationalism now seeks to change both the Arab's self image and the world's conception of him...."

(33) Harkabi, p. 353. The epithets applied by the Arabs to themselves are marked by conspicuous self glorification. Arab spokesmen address their hearers as members of a proud and noble people....Even in official documents, which, in most countries are couched in unemotional terms, we find for example: "our valiant armies and our valiant pilots...."

(34) Shiloah Center, p. 264.

(35) Harkabi, "Basic Factors."

(36) Arab World Daily, June 10, 1967.

(37) Shiloah Center, p. 249, quoting Radio Amman, June 20, 1967.

(38) Arab World Daily, August 18, 1967.

(39) FBIS, April 17, 1973.

(40) Karl W. Deutsch, "Social Mobilization and Political Development," American Political Science Review 55, no. 3 (September 1961): 493-502.

(41) Cf. Lerner ; Hudson, pp. 126-62, for details of these changes.

(42) Anthony McDermott, "Qaddafi and Libya," The World Today 29, no. 9 (September 1973): 398-408.

(43) al-Ahram, December 6, 1968.

(44) New York Times, November 26, 1973; Ali Hillal Dessouki, "Arab Intellectuals and Al-nakba: The Search for Fundamentalism," Middle Eastern Studies 9, no. 2 (May 1973): 187-196, for comments on al-qalaq.

(45) Trevor J. LeGassick, "Some Recent War-Related Arabic Fiction," The Middle East Journal 25, no. 4 (Autumn 1971): 491-505; Nissim Rejwan, "Impact of the June War on Arab Intellectuals," New Outlook 14, no. 8 (October-November 1971): 25-34.

(46) Cf. Michael Sulieman, "An Evaluation of Middle East News Coverage in Seven American Magazines, July-December 1956," Arab Journal 4, no. 2-4 (1967): 63-75; "National Stereotypes and the Arab-Israeli Conflict," Journal of Palestinian Studies 3, no. 3 (Spring 1974): 109-21; Ahmad Baha el-Din, World Media and the Arabs: An Arab Perspective," in Abdeen Jabara and Janice Terry, eds., The Arab World: From Nationalism to Revolution (Wilmette, Ill.: The Medina University Press International, 1971), pp. 77-85; Michael Adams, "European Media and the Arabs," in pp. 86-93; Janice Terry, "A Content Analysis of American Newspapers," in ibid., pp. 94-113;

Cindy Arkelan Lydon, "American Images of the Arabs," Mid East 9, no. 3 (May/June 1969): 3-14.

(47) Arab World Daily, August 18, 1967; A.B. Zahlan, "The Arab Brain Drain," Middle East Studies Association Bulletin 6,no. 3 (October 1, 1977): 1-16; Hudson, pp. 152-53; Yusuf al-Qa'id, "Egyptian Brain Drain Costs Egypt 500 Million Dollars Annually," al-Musawar, April 21, 1978, p. 17ff.

(48) New York Times, November 26, 1978. Arab World Daily, January 3, 1970.

(49) Arab World Daily, July 4, 1967.

(50) Ibid.

(51) Ibid.

(52) Ibid.

(53) Arab World Daily, June 20, 1967.

(54) Arab World Daily, August 29, 1969.

(55) Arab World Daily, February 5-6, 1969; April 26, 1969.

(56) Eliezer Be'eri, "A Note on Coups d'Etat in the Middle East," The Journal of Contemporary History 5, no. 2 (1970): 123-130.

(57) Arab World Weekly, January 29, 1969.

(58) Christian Science Monitor, December 16, 1972.

(59) The Manchester Guardian, May 6, 1972.

(60) Arab World Daily, October 5, 1967.

(61) San Francisco Examiner, August 25, 1969.

(62) Arab World Daily, August 22, 1969.

(63) Time, September 5, 1969, p. 23.

(64) Christian Science Monitor, August 21, 1972.

(65) Michael C. Hudson, "The Palestinian Resistance Movement; Its Significance in the Middle East Crisis," The Middle East Journal 23, no. 3 (Summer 1969): 291-320; ibid, "Developments and Setbacks in the Palestinian Resistance Movement, 1967-1971," Journal of Palestine Studies, 1, no. 3 (Spring 1972): 64-84, analyzes the growth of the movement. For more extended accounts of the Palestinian Resistance Movement see Quandt, Palestinian Nationalism, which treats the Resistance as a nationalist movement; Edger O'Ballance, Arab Guerrilla Power, 1967-1972 (London: Archon Books, 1973), which deals with the military aspects; John K. Cooley, Green March, Black September, (London: Frank Cass, 1973), which treats the cultural aspect of Palestinian nationalism; and Sharabi, Palestine and Israel, for a Palestinian analysis.

(66) Don Peretz, "Arab Palestine: Phoenix or Phantom?", Foreign Affairs 68, no. 2 (January 1970): 322-33.

(67) Abdullah S. Schliefer, "The Emergence of Fatah," Arab World 15, no. 5 (May 1969): 16-20.

(68) Christian Science Monitor, August 4, 1970.

(69) al-Ahram, June 2, 1970; Arab World Daily, June 3, 1970.

(70) Jon Kimche, "Can Israel Contain the Palestine Revolution?," Conflict Studies, no. 13, June 1971.

(71) Quandt, Nationalism, pp. 51ff.

(72) Ibid., p. 57.

(73) Arab World Daily, February 7, 1969.

(74) Arab World Weekly, August 16, 1969.

(75) Ibid.

(76) Halim Barakat, "Social Factors Influencing Attitudes of University Students in Lebanon Towards the Palestinian Resistance Movement," Journal of Palestine Studies 1, no. 1 (Autumn 1971): 87-112.

(77) an-Nahar Arab Report, November 30, 1970.

(78) Arab World Weekly, September 30, 1969.

(79) Ibid.

(80) Arab World Weekly, July 22, 1972.

(81) "Libya's Foreign Adventures," Conflict Studies, no. 41 (December 1973), p. 3.

(82) Arab World Weekly, July 22, 1972.

(83) 'Abd al-Nasir (Cairo edition), pp. 52-52.

(84) McDermott, pp. 398-407.

(85) Ibid., p. 399. Al-Qadhafi's views on this necessity are increasing in popularity.

(86) Conflict Studies.

(87) Arab World Daily, October 17, 1969.

(88) Conflict Studies, p. 4.

(89) McDermott, p. 403.

(90) Conflict Studies, p. 10.

(91) an-Nahar Arab Report, ibid; That al-Qadhafi actually considered himself a worthy successor to 'abd al-Nasir was (and still is) particularly galling to al-Sadat, who was one of 'abd al-Nasir's most loyal lieutenants.

(92) Arab World Daily, July 26, 1968. General Riyad's report was made
      only immediately after the war, but released over a year later.

(93) Hussein, p. 54; Arab World Daily, October 31, 1967. The situation
      was a little more complicated then General Mahmud's negligence
      (although al-Sadat claims that Mahmud had previously demonstrated
      his incompetence in the 1956 War, and that he, al-Sadat, had pressed
      'abd al-Nasir to dismiss Mahmud on several occasions). The key to
      the Israeli air success, aside from the surprise factor, was the
      Egyptian air defenses were ordered not to open fire as long as 'Amir
      and his staff were in the air over the Sinai; in addition, only 'Amir
      himself could countermand this order, Search, p. 174.

(94) Arab World Daily, ibid.

(95) Hussein, pp. 102-103.

(96) San Francisco Examiner, September 19, 1969.

(97) FBIS, May 23, 1967.

(98) al-Ahram, May 26, 1967.

(99) Al-Sadat interview in al-Hilal, carried in MENA, September 30,
      1976, FBIS, October 1, 1976. In addition to the confusion caused by
      lack of planning, al-Sadat argued, this excessive movement wore out
      Egyptian armor: "...We usually see the tanks transported on carriers
      on Cairo streets. Why? In order to save the treads for the battle.
      The armed forces' force and strength depend on its capability to
      transport a tank on a carrier to the nearest point of the battle, in
      order to save the treads for the battle. This applies to all
      armies...This took place here in 1973. I exhausted all the tank
      carriers in the battle and we are now trying to replace them with
      new carriers. This is why our tanks entered the 1973 battle
      valiantly..." In addition to al-Sadat, see the following: Major
      General R.L. Shoemaker, "The Arab-Israeli War," Military Review
      48, no. 8 (August 1968): 57-69; Randolph S. Churchill and Winston
      S. Churchill, The Six Day War (London: Heinemann, 1967), ch. 2;
      William Stevensor, Strike Zion! (New York: Bantam, 1967), pp. 31ff.

(100) al-Sadat, interview in al-Hilal.

(101) Arab World Daily, January 11, 1968; San Francisco Examiner,
      September 19, 1969, Shiloah Center, p. 553.

(102) Cf. Harkabi, "Basic Factors," for a similar conclusion. In this
      case, one that is coupled with the argument that such behavior is an
      Arab cultural trait.

(103) al-Ahram, June 21, 1968.

(104) Ibid.

(105) al-Sadat, Interview, October 25, 1977, the order of some para-
      graphs has been changed slightly.

(106) al-Sadat, interview in al-Hilal, October 1, 1976.

(107) Cf. Shiloah Center, pp. 250-51 for a summary of the Arab press on this point.

(108) Arab World Daily, July 26, 1968.

(109) Cecil A. Hourani, "The Moment of Truth: Toward A Middle East Dialogue," reprinted in Irene L. Gendzier, A Middle East Reader (New York: Pegasus, 1969), pp. 384-405, quote is from p. 386.

(110) Ibid., pp. 389-390.

(111) Ibid., pp. 392-393.

(112) Ibid., p. 306.

(113) Akhbar al-Yawm, November 3, 1973.

(114) Arab World Weekly, September 4, 1971.

(115) Ibid., January 15, 1973.

(116) Mao Tse-tung, Quotations from Chairman Mao Tse-tung (Peking: Foreign Language Press, 1966), p. 88.

(117) Hisham Sharabi, "Palestinian Guerrillas: Their Credibility and Effectiveness," Middle East Forum 46, no. 2-3, pp. 45ff.

(118) Fatah "Political and Armed Struggle," (Beirut: Fatah, 1969); Arab World Weekly, October 26, 1968; Quandt, Nationalism, pp. 79ff; Ehud Ya'ari, "Al-Fatah's Political Thinking," New Outlook 11, no. 9 (November-December, 1968): 24-34.

(119) Life, June 12, 1970, p. 74, Habash interview with Oriana Fallaci.

(120) Fateh 2, no. 9 (May 29, 1970): 4.

(121) "Civil War in Jordan," Mid-East 10, no. 6 (December 1970): 21-24.

(122) Michael Hudson, "Fedayeen are Forcing Lebanon's Hand," Mid-East 10, no. 1 (February 1970): 7-15.

(123) "The Resistance and Jordan and the UAR," al-'Asifa, August 12, 1969, from a partial translation in, The New Middle East, no. 12 (September 1969): 48. In his memoirs, al-Sadat later reproached the Palestinians for these attacks. He pointedly argued that not only had 'abd al-Nasir been a consistent champion of Palestinian rights, but also that it was principally through 'abd al-Nasir's influence that the Palestinian issue was brought into the Arab political arena. Moreover, 'abd al-Nasir was deeply involved in trying to prevent the destruction of the Palestinians in Jordan at the time of his death. Indeed, 'abd al-Nasir's exhaustion at the time of his death was due to his strenuous efforts on behalf of the Palestinians. Search, pp. 200-02.

(124) Shiloah Center, p. 270.

(125) al-Hawadith, January 10, 1969, p. 10.

(126) Arab World Weekly, May 31, 1969, and July 31, 1969. Edger O'Ballance, The Electronic War in the Middle East, 1968-1970

(London: Archon Books, 1974), pp. 131ff, argues that the Egyptians came close to achieving these goals. He gives the relative losses on both sides as follows: Israelis, 346 killed and about 3,000 wounded; Egyptians, about 2,000 killed and 8,000 wounded, plus some 150,000 refugees from the Canal Aone.

(127) al-Jumhurriya, January 7, 1970.

(128) San Francisco Examiner, January 7, 1970.

(129) The Israelis conducted a two-day operation, September 9-10, 1969, against targets in the west coast of the Gulf of Suez. The Israeli force met with Egyptian opposition. Christian Science Monitor, September 11, 1969.

(130) Charles B. McLane, Soviet-Middle East Relations, vol. I, (London: Asian Research Center, 1973): p. 10.

(131) FBIS, July 24, 1970.

(132) Mubarak, May 3, 1976, discusses the problems the Egyptians had, especially in the area of pilot training.

(133) Heikal, Ramadan, claims that the War of Attrition was successful in stimulating Egyptian nationalism, pp. 182-183. In this sense, the War of Attrition was politically successful. In another sense, it was not: One of the unforeseen consequences of the war was to generate a demand among large segments of the Egyptian military for some more aggressive military action. It was this demand that provided one of the major dynamics for the decsion to attack in October 1973. Cf. O'Ballance, Electronic War, pp. 133ff.

(134) Elias Sam'o and Cyrus Elahi, "Cease-fire: Who Needs It?," Arab World 16, no. 11-12 (November-December 1970): 21-22.

(135) Ibid., the quote is from, Hisham Sharabi, "Prelude to War: The Crisis of May-June 1967," The Arab World 14, no. 10-11 (October-November 1968), p. 26.

(136) Arab World Daily, April 11, 1969.

(137) Ibid., Haykal also added that the war should be fought from static positions, wherein the Israeli ability to maneuver would be neutralized, and that the Egyptian forces should be prepared to take as many as 50,000 casualties.

(138) Christian Science Monitor, October .7, 1971; Heikel, Ramadan, p. 182, parallels this view, but O'Ballance, Electronic War, pp. 133-34, claims that the Egyptian Air Force was actually improving and that the Egyptian airwar strategy evolved at this time. In a number of ways the War of Attrition foreshadowed tactics which were later used by the Egyptians: (a) use of massed SAM batteries to deny Egyptian airspace to Israeli aircraft; (b) selective use of the Egyptian Air Force to bomb Israeli positions in the Sinai; (c) extensive use of cross canal commando raids; (d) night repair operations to rebuild Egyptian positions destroyed during the previous day.

Chapter 5

(1) Military Research Organization, In the Memory of the Passing of 2 Years: On the 4th Arab-Israeli Round (Cairo: Military Research Organization, n.d.), p. 11.

(2) Al-Sadat, October, March 27, 1977, pp. 8ff., FBIS, May 10, 1977; Search, pp. 211ff.

(3) Mid-East Report, June 1, 1971; an-Nahar Arab Report, October 5, 12, 26, 1970; November 2, 1970.

(4) Ibid., October 5, 1970.

(5) Time, October 12, 1970, p. 23.

(6) Anwar El Sadat, Revolt on the Nile (New York: The John Day Company, 1957), pp. 60-61. Indeed, a sense of Egypt's greatness pervades many of al-Sadat's later comments: "Egypt today is a civilized country. It has been civilized for 7,000 years. At that time there was a government on the banks of the Nile. The rest of the world lived in caves and in trees." Interview, October 25, 1977.

(7) Ibid., p. 31. This early approval of the Brethren is, not surprisingly, considerably watered-down in al-Sadat's later biography. See Search, pp. 22ff.

(8) Arab World Weekly, October 10, 1970; an-Nahar Arab Report, June 19, 1972.

(9) El Sadat, Revolt , p. 60.

(10) Ibid., p. 14.

(11) Ibid., p. 85.

(12) an-Nahar Arab Report, June 26, 1972; FBIS, August 30, 1974.

(13) Ibid.

(14) Ibid.

(15) Ibid.

(16) Ibid.

(17) Heaphey.

(18) Time, October 29, 1973, p. 34; al-Sadat, Memoirs, October, March 27, 1977, pp. 8ff, FBIS, May 18, 1977, on the "yes, sir" phenomenon. However, al-Sadat takes issue with any interpretation that suggests he was subservient to 'abd al-Nasir: "I was not entirely passive on the matter of my disagreement with 'abd al-Nasir over methods. Throughout 1970 and until his death, I debated and argued with him the necessity to change the course and method which led to the 1967 defeat...", Memoirs, al-Ahram, September 26, 1975, FBIS, October 1, 1975.

(19) an-Nahar Arab Report, June 26, 1972.

(20) <u>Christian Science Monitor</u>, May 18, 1971; This ouster was really
the preemption of an attempted coup by 'Ali Sabri, Sha'rawi Juma'a
and Sami Sharaf, an alliance of two factions which heretofore
(according to al-Sadat) had been at odds. The coup was forestalled
because an officer in the police force, Taha Zaki al-Muli, acci-
dentally listened in on phone conversations between the plotters and
then informed al-Sadat. Currently, al-Muli is al-Sadat's chief of
security. Cf. <u>Search</u>, pp. 221-25, for details on the plot and
counterplot.

(21) <u>Arab World Weekly</u>, January 22, 1972.

(22) Article 2, reprinted in <u>Arab World Weekly</u>, September 18, 1971.

(23) Article 12.

(24) <u>Arab World Weekly</u>, January 22, 1972.

(25) <u>The Manchester Guardian</u>, April 1, 1973.

(26) Ibid.

(27) <u>New York Times</u>, April 30, 1972.

(28) <u>San Francisco Examiner & Chronicle</u>, January 25, 1970.

(29) <u>an-Nahar Arab Report</u>, January 15, 1973.

(30) Ibid., February 5, 1973. About 1000 students were arrested.

(31) Ibid., January 31, 1973.

(32) Ibid., August 6, 1973; Heikal, <u>Ramadan</u>, pp. 188-94, explains and
defends al-Qadhafi's policies in terms of their sincerity. On
intellectual dissatisfaction in general, see P.J. Vatikiotis, "Egypt
Adrift: A Study in Disillusion," <u>New Middle East</u>, no. 54 (March
1973): 5-10.

(33) <u>an-Nahar Arab Report</u>, November 13, 1972.

(34) <u>an-Nahar Arab Report</u>, February 5, 1973; <u>Christian Science
Monitor</u>, December 1, 1972; <u>Newsweek</u>, December 4, 1972, p. 47.
Arab sources reported a rumor going around Cairo to the effect that
Egyptian intelligence had discovered a "secret report" prepared for
Pope Shinuda. In this report there were references to the necessity
of a Coptic struggle against Muslims. It was said that Libya had
financed this propaganda; pamphlets found in Alexandria prior to
religious clashes were supposedly printed in a foreign state - again
rumored to be Libya. Other rumors suggested that the Muslim
Brethren were behind the strife. Still others claimed that a secret
organization headed by ASU Secretary General Mahmud 'Uthman
was responsible. During a mass meeting in Cairo in August 1972,
'Uthman is said to have declared that: "The Egyptian people are
facing three enemies today: the communists, the Christians, and the
Jews. If the first two threats are removed, the third threat will
disappear without difficulty." Whatever the truth of these stories,

they indicate the intensity of religious distrust. <u>an-Nahar Arab Report</u>, November 20, 1972, February 5, 1973.

(35) <u>an-Nahar Arab Report</u>, February 5, 1973.

(36) <u>Christian Science Monitor</u>, October 18, 1972.

(37) Ibid., December 14, 1972.

(38) <u>an-Nahar Arab Report</u>, February 5, 1973.

(39) <u>Arab World Weekly</u>, January 22, 1972.

(40) <u>an-Nahar Arab Report</u>, November 6, 1972.

(41) Ibid.

(42) <u>Newsweek</u>, February 28, 1972, pp. 32-33; <u>an-Nahar Arab Report</u>, November 6, 1972. According to Haykal, Sadiq seems to have had good reason to be anti-Soviet: He had apparently discovered that, in addition to problems associated with arms transfers, Soviet personnel were smuggling large amounts of gold out of Egypt. <u>Ramadan</u>, pp. 162ff. In any event, many Egyptians, including al-Sadat, had become convinced that the Russians were, in no way, interested in helping the Egyptians, but rather were using Egypt for their own interests. See el-Sadat, <u>Search</u>, pp. 227ff; Heikel, <u>Ramadan</u>, pp. 166ff.

(43) <u>an-Nahar Arab Report</u>, November 6, 13, 1972.

(44) al-Sadat, <u>Speech on the Anniversary of Nasir's Death</u>, at ASU Headquarters, September 28, 1975, <u>FBIS</u>, September 29, 1975; <u>Search</u>, pp. 234-36. Cf . Haykal's account, <u>Ramadan</u>, pp. 183-84.

(45) <u>Arab World Weekly</u>, January 22, 1972; <u>an-Nahar Arab Report</u>, November 6, 13, 1972.

(46) <u>an-Nahar Arab Report</u>, February 26, 1973.

(47) Ibid.

(48) <u>FBIS</u>, August 30, 1974.

(49) <u>FBIS</u>, August 27, 1974.

(50) <u>Arab World Weekly</u>, January 22, 1972.

(51) <u>The Manchester Guardian</u>, February 7, 1973.

(52) Ibid., March 5, 1973.

(53) Ibid., February 7, 1973.

(54) <u>an-Nahar Arab Report</u>, October 8, 1973; an earlier <u>MENA</u> dispatch carried the same story, but added that the purported resignation took place in the middle of September, about the time the final plans for the war were coordinated, <u>FBIS</u>, October 1, 1973. Neither Haykal nor al-Sadat mention any sort of disagreement in the Egyptian command (but then of course they naturally would not). Also the timing of the story, i.e. the first week in October, suggests

that it may have been part of a series of stories the Egyptians
floated as part of their disinformation campaign. Nevertheless,
later events, especially the dismissal of Shadhili as Chief of Staff,
indicate that the Egyptian staff was bitterly divided.

(55) Arab World Weekly, December 14, 1968.

(56) From a partial translation in Arab World Daily, October 15, 1968.

(57) Ibid.

(58) Ibid.

(59) Ibid.

(60) Ibid.

(61) Ma'oz.

(62) Arab World Weekly, April 12, 1969.

(63) Ibid.

(64) Ibid.

(65) Evacuation Day Speech of April 16, 1973 in FBIS, April 17, 1973.

(66) Interview with a Yugoslav journalist in FBIS, April 2, 1971.

(67) FBIS, April 17, 1975.

(68) Arab World Weekly, November 21, 1970.

(69) FBIS, April 2, 1971.

(70) Arab World Weekly, January 16, 1971.

(71) Ma'oz. Later al-Asad officially converted to Sunni Islam.

(72) Arab World Weekly, January 16, 1971.

(73) Ibid.

(74) Ibid.

(75) Ibid.

(76) FBIS, April 17, 1973.

(77) FBIS, April 2, 1971.

(78) Arab World Weekly, December 19, 1970.

(79) al-Hayat, February 23, 1973.

(80) Arab World Daily, February 24, 1973.

(81) an-Nahar Arab Report, April 23, 1973.

(82) an-Nahar Arab Report, March 19, 1973.

(83) Ibid; The Middle East Journal 27, no. 3 (Summer 1973): 367; Arab
     Report & Record, April 1-15, 1973.

(84) an-Nahar Arab Report, December 21, 1970.

(85) <u>an-Nahar Arab Report</u>, September 24, 1973.

(86) Cf. Torrey in Lenczowski, ed., <u>Political Elites</u>, for the pattern of military recruitment under al-Asad; and Eliezer Be'eri, <u>Army Officers in Arab Politics and Society</u> (New York: Frederick A. Praeger, Inc., 1969), pp. 331-341, for background.

(87) <u>an-Nahar Arab Report</u>, June 5, 19, 1972.

(88) Summarized in <u>Arab Report & Record</u>, July 1-5, 1973; 42 officers were executed in August, <u>an-Nahar Arab Report</u>, September 10, 1973.

(89) <u>an-Nahar Arab Report</u>, October 1, 1973.

(90) <u>an-Nahar Arab Report</u>, September 24, 1973.

(91) <u>al-Ahram</u>, September 25, 1964.

(92) <u>Arab World Weekly</u>, March 9, 1974, an Arab rendering on the text of <u>Ha'aretz</u>, February 15, 1974.

(93) <u>al-Usbu' al-'Arabi</u>, November 9, 1974.

(94) Ibid.

(95) <u>Arab World Weekly</u>, September 9, 1972; Itamar Rabinovich, "The Limitations of Power: Syria Under al-Asad," <u>New Middle East</u>, no. 54 (March 1973): 36-37.

(96) Summarized in <u>Arab World Weekly</u>, May 31, 1969.

(97) <u>Arab World Daily</u>, March 1969; April 1, 1969.

(98) In this connection, both al-Asad and Talas had apparently been anxious for some time to secure an alternative source of arms. To do this, they needed Arab oil money. Talas is said to have ties with Faysal. On the other hand, Muslim Brethren antiregime activities had, in the eyes of the Syrians, been actively supported by the Saudis. Damascus officials claimed that Muslim Brethren actions had been long planned with the aid of the Saudis, through contacts begun at the time of the pilgrimage and continued in Beirut. Cf. <u>an-Nahar Arab Report</u> March 19, 1973, for a summary of Syrian-Saudi relations.

(99) <u>an-Nahar Arab Report</u>, December 4, 1972.

(100) Syrian casualties were estimated at between 15 and 500. The Mayor of the village of Da'il, near Dar'a, gave this damage report: 75 killed, 45 wounded, 20 houses destroyed and 12 damaged, 200 pregnant women had miscarried, 450 sheep and cattle killed. There were no Palestinians in the village. <u>Arab Report & Record</u>, January 1-15, 1973.

(101) Chaim Hertzog on <u>Israeli Radio</u>, January 13, 1973, in <u>Arab Report & Record</u>, January 1-15, 1973.

(102) <u>Daily Star</u>, January 24, 1973.

(103) al Sadat interview in al Usbu' al 'Arabi, October 7, 1974, in FBIS October 11, 1974.

(104) Talas speech in FBIS, March 12, 1974.

(105) Arab Report & Record, March 1-15, 16-31, 1973.   Ahmad Isma'l was appointed Commander in Chief of Egypt, Syria, and Libya on January 21, 1973.

(106) Arab Report & Record, April 1-15, 1973.

(107) al-Sadat, Interview, October 25, 1977; Newsweek, April 9, 1973, p. 44, commenting on al-Sadat's position, noted that by April 1973, al-Sadat had concluded that the situation was hopeless; that although he might not be able to survive another defeat, he had little to lose by resuming the fighting.   According to his reasoning, such a loss would be similar to the Vietnamese Communist setback during their offensives of 1968 and 1972: a military defeat, but a psychological victory.

(108) Heikal, Ramadan, pp. 1ff; al-Sadat, Interview; Arab Report & Record, May 1-15, 1973.

(109) FBIS, October 11, 1974.

(110) an-Nahar Arab Report, September 3, 1972.

(111) an-Nahar Arab Report, November 12, 1972; August 20, 1973; September 10, 1973.

(112) Ibid.

(113) Ibid.; Cf: The VOP (Cairo) analysis of Husayn's goals: (a) Pardon for his past crimes, (b) An end to Jordan's isolation, (c) Resumption of Arab financial aid, (d) Coexistence with the recognition of the enemy, (e) Arab recognition of the Unified Arab Kingdom, (f) To strike a blow against the Jordanian nationalist movement. Voice of Palestine, September 12, 1973, summarized in FBIS, September 20, 1973.

(114) an-Nahar Arab Report, December 4, 1972.

(115) an-Nahar Arab Report, August 20, 1973.

(116) Ibid.

(117) Arab World Weekly, April 1, 1972.

(118) Ibid.

(119) an-Nahar Arab Report, September 10, 1973.   The Saudis had already sent Husayn a note warning about involvement with Iran. The Voice of Palestine (Cairo) announced on August 20, that units of the Iranian Air Forces had moved into the Mafraq Air Base, Arab Report & Record, August 16-30, 1973.

(120) Arab Report & Record, April 16-30, 1973.

(121) Originally published in L'Orient Le Jour and al-Sharq, excerpted in: Arab Report & Record, May 16-31, 1973.

(122) Summarized in an-Nahar Arab Report, June 11, 1973.

(123) Ibid.

(124) Tehran Journal, March 11, 1973. No doubt the facts of Tal's assassination had something to do with the ominousness of this warning: Tal was shot at point-blank range on November 28, 1971. One of the assassins then leaned down and drank his blood.

(125) an-Nahar Arab Report, July 11, 1972.

(126) an-Nahar Arab Report, July 24, 1973.

(127) al-Hayat, March 31, 1970.

(128) "Abu Da'ud's Confession," Middle East Monitor 3, no. 8 (April 15, 1973): 7-8; see also Christopher Dobson, Black September: Its Short, Violent History (New York: Macmillan Publishing Co., Inc., 1974), originally a series of articles in the Daily and Sunday Telegraph (London).

(129) Abu Da'ud.

(130) an-Nahar Arab Report, February 26, 1973.

(131) an-Nahar Arab Report, January 29, 1973.

(132) an-Nahar Arab Report, October 9, 1972, January 29, 1973.

(133) Ibid.

(134) Ibid.

(135) an-Nahar Arab Report, July 2, 1973.

(136) an-Nahar Arab Report, October 16, 1973.

(137) an-Nahar Arab Report, March 26, 1973.

(138) an-Nahar Arab Report, February 12, 1973.

(139) Ibid.

(140) Summarized in Arab Report & Record, August 1-15, 1973. The plan for stationing commandos in Jordan was apparently worked out by Saudi Arabia. It called for positioning Palestinian forces in a strip of land 50 miles wide and 3 miles deep in Southern Jordan. Saudi Arabian lines of communication and supply would be used; Egypt would supply the air defense. Saudi Troops were already in the area, and could act as a buffer between Palestinian and Jordanian units.

(141) Ibid., 'Arafat had also conferred with the Syrians immediately prior.

(142) Arab World Weekly, September 29, 1973; Arab World Daily, September 10, 1973; al-Yawm, September 24, 1973.

(143) FBIS, October 11, 1974.

(144) an-Nahar Arab Report, November 5, 1973.

(145) Ibid.

(146) FBIS, October 11, 1974.

(147) an-Nahar Arab Report, November 5, 1973.

(148) Africa Confidential 14, no. 21 (October 19, 1973):   7. On the Arab/Israeli confrontation in Africa see   Tareq Y. Ismael, The U.A.R. in Africa: Egypt's Policy Under Nasser, Evanston: North-western University Press, 1971; Bernard Reich, "Israel's Policy in Africa," The Middle East Journal 18, no. 1 (Winter 1964):   14-26; Jake C. Miller, "African-Israeli Relations: Impact on Continental Unity, The Middle East Journal 29, no.4 (Autumn 1975): 393-408.

(149) Africa Research Bulletin 19, no. 9 (October 15, 1973): 2976ff.

(150) Ibid.

(151) Ibid.

(152) FBIS, September 11-19, 1973.

(153) Quoted in Kayhan (Tehran), December 1, 1973.

(154) Ibid.

(155) Ibid.

(156) Christian Science Monitor, March 11, 1971. In addition to this concern to limit external, basically Palestinian, support for Turkish dissidents, Turkish Arab policy rests on two other considerations: (a) getting Arab backing for Turkish goals in Cyprus; (b) securing or maintaining access to Arab oil supplies. A third possible concern, although not nearly as important as the foregoing, has to do with a perceptible movement away from secularism in Turkey. This movement, originally a byproduct of intraelite conflicts over Attaturk's policy of complete secularization, has become especially noticeable since the June 1967 War - as it has elsewhere in the Middle East. Cf. an-Nahar Arab Report, February 26, 1973, for background information.

Apropos the Cyprus crisis see   Dankwart A. Rustow, The Cyprus Crisis and United States Security Interests (Santa Monica: RAND, 1967); J. Boyer Bell, "Violence at a Distance: Greece and the Cyprus Crisis," Orbis, 18, no. 3 (Fall 1974): 791-808; John C. Campbell, "The Mediterranean Crisis," Foreign Affairs 53, no. 4 (July 1975): 605-24. Interestingly enough, the Israelis who originally backed the Turkish position in Cyprus have now come around to backing the Greeks.

(157) Kayhan, June 2, 1973.

(158) FBIS, October 11, 1974.

(159) Ibid.

(160) Arab World Daily, August 18, 1967.

(161) an-Nahar Arab Report, August 6, 1973.

(162) an-Nahar Arab Report, October 1, 1973.

(163) an-Nahar Arab Report, August 6, 1973.

(164) al-Safir, October 25, 1974 carried a story to the effect that opposition within the Saudi military to Faysal's "soft" policy on oil had resulted in an abortive National Guard coup.

(165) Egyptian Gazette, April 13, 1973.

(166) Cf. Time, August 27, 1973, p. 22 for such a desert war story.

(167) an-Nahar Arab Report, October 1, 1973.

(168) Ibid.

(169) an-Nahar Arab Report, July 30, 1973.

(170) Arab World Weekly, July 3, 1971.

(171) Ruz al-Yusuf, September 23, 1974.

(172) an-Nahar Arab Report, October 1, 1973.

(173) Ibid.

(174) an-Nahar Arab Report, September 3, 1973.

(175) Arab Report & Record, August 16-31, 1973. Salih Jawdat, Deputy Chairman of al-Musawwar's editorial board,expressed Egyptian fears for religious strife. Egypt could not follow the Libyan cultural revolution because the circumstances of the two countries were different. All Libyans were Muslims, and the Qur'an could be made the basis of Libya's laws, but, in Egypt, Muslims and Christians formed an indivisible national unity. Al-Qadhafi had a different view: "Drinking and night-life in general are residues of imperialism....How can a drunk make progress in his country? How can a drunk fight in Sinai against the enemy? (A touchy analogy, given in the testimony at the post-1967 court martials in Egypt.) Islam must be the basis of the new state." Summarized with partial translation in Arab Report & Record, June 1-15, 1973.

(176) an-Nahar Arab Report, July 30, 1973.

(177) an-Nahar Arab Report, September 10, 1973.

(178) an-NaharArab Report, September 3, 1973.

(179) Ibid.

(180) Arab World Weekly, July 3, 1971.

(181) Partial translation in Arab Report & Record, August 16-31, 1973. Al-Sadat covered his tracks before going to Saudi Arabia. In a working paper published on the anniversary of the July Revolution, great stress was placed on the twin themes of realism and flexibility, instead of rigid adherence to ideologies. Arabs must

cooperate together to achieve their objectives, in spite of political and social indifferences; they must develop policies of self reliance. The Arab media correctly interpreted this as a rationale for movement toward the Saudis: On the one hand, it disarmed local Egyptian criticism; on the other it alleviated Saudi reservations. Cf. The Manchester Guardian's analysis, August 24, 1973.

(182) Partial translation in Middle East Monitor, no. 18 (October 1, 1973), p. 5-6.

(183) an-Nahar Arab Report, September 10, 1973.

(184) Ibid. This Arab pressure stemmed from an increasing frustration with the status quo situation of Israeli occupation of Arab territories. As a consequence of this, radicalism was increasingly pronounced in the area. In particular, revolutionary movements such as PFLOAG were experiencing an upsurge. This was of great concern to the Saudis.

On a more formal level, a Congress of Arab Trade Unions had convened in May to "mobilize the Arab masses for the battle against Israel." Among the several resolutions of this congress were calls to:

1. Use Arab oil in the battle against Israel and international imperialism.

2. Exploit the energy crisis in the United States.

3. Withdraw Arab deposits from foreign banks and invest them in Arab development projects.

4. Call on those Arab states concerned to rid themselves of British and American military bases.

5. Refuse visits of the 6th Fleet.

6. Employ oil revenues to set up an Arab army for the liberation of Palestine.

7. Boycott American goods and services.

Cf. an-Nahar Arab Report, May 14, 1973, for a summary of these and other moves. In this context, al-Qadhafi's nationalization of four United States oil companies the first week in September, coupled with President Nixon's boycott threat, were very probably the key factors in changing Feisel's mind. Clearly, if Feisel was to remain in control of Arab oil strategy, he had to move to forestall the Libyan. Arab Report & Record, September 1-15, 1973; Newsweek, September 17, 1973, pp. 33ff; Business Week, September 8, 1973, p. 8; The Daily Star (Beirut), September 8, 1973; Middle East Economic Digest 13, no. 9 (September 1973): 1024 ff.

(185) Arab Report & Record, August 16-31, 1973.

(186) an-Nahar Arab Report, September 24, 1973. The terse communi-
       que issued at the end of the meeting stated, "Out of the interest of
       the one nation to which we belong, out of the necessities of the
       confrontation battle of destiny with the enemy, and through the
       contacts that took place some time ago between Cairo, Damascus,
       and Amman, it was agreed to hold a meeting of the heads of states
       of the confrontation. At this meeting, all undecided issues among
       the three countries and all issues and estimations connected with the
       battle of destiny were discussed. It was agreed to continue the
       dialogue and the contacts in order to arrive at ways to implement
       the proposed solutions which are the subject of discussion." FBIS,
       September 13, 1973, an-Nahar Arab Report, October 15, 1973.

(187) Daily Star, September 13, 1973, Egyptian Gazette, September 19,
       1973.

(188) Cf: London Times, December 9, 1973.

(189) al-Yawm, September 24, 1973.

(190) Jerusalem Post, September 18, 1973.

Chapter 6

(1) Al-Sadat, Interview, October 25, 1977.

(2) Ibid.

(3) Ibid.

(4) FBIS, September 30, 1974. For accounts of the Egyptian planning
     process see: an-Nahar Arab Report, October 15, 1973; General
     Chaim Herzog, "The Middle East War 1973," RUSI (Journal of the
     Royal United Services Institute for Defence Studies) Vol. 120:1,
     March 1975, pp. 3-13; Heikel, Ramadan, p. 156. Egyptian planning
     apparently evolved from the original plan to defend the West bank of
     the Canal, Plan 200 which later evolved into the heavily fortified
     embankment and supporting positions built under Ahmad Isma'il's
     aegis, into plans, Liberation 1, 2, and 3 which involved the
     establishment of bridgeheads of various size, into plans Granite 1, 2,
     and 3 which envisioned successively extended operations as far as
     Gaza under a protective missile screen, and finally into Badr. The
     Egyptian part of Badr was roughed out on paper in January 1973; it
     was laid out in a sand model of the Sinai in February; and completed
     by March. Al-Sadat, Interview, October 25, 1977.

(5) Arab World Weekly, November 4, 1972.

(6) Ibid.

(7) An-Nahar Arab Report, November 13, 1972.

(8) His first directive to the armed forces, issued immediately after his appointment, spelled out his conception of military efficiency - planning, training, and execution:

Our objective is clear. It is battle until victory. This makes it imperative that each should know his task well that victory may be ensured. You should know that we are facing an enemy that is beginning to set little store by us, thinking that we are not capable of fighting, which makes his rampage in the region without fear of being repelled or punished.

Along the path of the battle, I urge you to:

--have confidence in your leaders at all levels.
--maintain discipline in all your actions.
--raise the level of training, and do your best in this field.
--raise your combat ability to the maximum.
--preserve your weapons and equipment.
--be serious and sincere in all your actions.
--nothing should occupy your minds except the expulsion of the enemy from our land and his destruction if he refused to withdraw.
--study your enemy well, without exaggerating his ability or underestimating it.
--perform your tasks fully and shoulder your responsibilities completely.
--emphasize to all that our task is to fight and not to draw up policy. May our faith in God, Egypt and our objectives, and our proficiency in doing our jobs be our way to victory. al-Ahram, October 31, 1972.

(9) Al-Ahram, November 18, 1973.

(10) Ibid.

(11) Ibid.

(12) Ibid.

(13) Ibid.

(14) Al-Sadat interview in Ruz al-Yusuf reproduced in FBIS, September 23, 1974.

(15) Riad Ashkar, "The Syrian and Egyptian Campaigns," Journal of Palestine Studies 3:2 (Winter 1974): 19-20.

(16) General Jamal Muhammad 'Ali, Commander of Egyptian Army Engineers in The Manchester Guardian, October 19, 1973; Lawrence Whetten and Michael Johnson, "Military Lessons of the Yom Kippur War," The World Today, vol. 30:3, pp. 101-109; Col. Irving Heymont, USA, Ret., "The Israeli Defense of the Suez Canal," Military Review, vol. 51:1,January 1971, pp. 3-11.

(17) Whetten and Johnson.

(18) Ashkar, al-Asad interview in al-Sayyad, March 7, 1974.

(19) Heymont; Heikel:

The Suez Canal is regarded by military authorities in both the West and the East as one of the most important natural defense lines in the World. Immediately on the East Bank of the waterway, the Israeli's have established their defense line in support of the natural defense line, which is the canal itself. Therefore, the Egyptian army will, in its advance, have to face what other armies had never confronted, namely, a natural barrier in the Suez Canal....al-Ahram, March 12, 1971.

(20) Dawn (Karachi), October 24, 1973; an-Nahar Arab Report, October 15, 1973.

(21) New York Times, October 22, 1973.

(22) FBIS, December 13, 1973.

(23) Arab World Daily, April 23, 1969.

(24) Christian Science Monitor, April 11, 1969.

(25) Shadhili interview in al-Akhbar, November 21, 1973; also reprinted in various versions in: Action, February 25, 1974; Journal of Palestine Studies 3:2 (Winter 1974): 163-168.

(26) Al-Ahram, December 13, 1973; Heikel, Ramadan, p. 186; The Middle East, no.40, February 1978, pp. 49-50. Note that all three senior Egyptian officers spent time in intelligence.

(27) From: Armed Struggle In Facing the Israeli Challenge, excerpted in Arab World Weekly, August 14, 1971.

(28) Ibid.

(29) Ahmad Isma'il interview in al-Nahar, October 7, 1974 in FBIS, October 8, 1974.

(30) Riad Ashkar, "The Syrian and Egyptian Campaigns," Journal of Palestine Studies 3:2 (Winter 1974): 34-45.

(31) Al-Ahram, November 18, 1973.

(32) MENA Military Symposium, December 11, 1973 in FBIS, December 13, 1973.

(33) Al-Ahram, November 18, 1973.

(34) Lawrence Whetten and Michael Johnson, "Military Lessons of the Yom Kippur War," The World Today 30:3 (March 1974): 101-109.

(35) Al-Ahram, November 18, 1973.

(36) The choice of the term "badr" to designate the plan of attack is an example of the sophisticated linguistic possibilities inherent in Arabic. Not only does the noun, "badr," mean a full moon, but the verb from which it is derived, "badara," means "to come unexpectedly," "to surprise."

(37) Cf: Philip K. Hitti, <u>History of the Arabs</u>, 10th ed. (New York: St. Martin's Press, 1970), pp. 116-117, 132.

(38) Cf: Sir William Muir, <u>The Life of Mahomet</u>, 3rd ed. (Smith, Elder, & Co., 1894), pp. 207-243. Ramadan is also known for other battles whose outcome was favorable to the Muslims: "It was the month when an Egyptian Sultan, Muzaffar Sayf al-Din, defeated an invading Mongol army in the 1260s. The name of the battle, 'Ayn Jalut,' was given to the PLA regiment stationed in Egypt. The Mongols called upon the Egyptians to surrender and be spared, but Sayf al-Din instead destroyed the Mongol army, killed their king, and took his son prisoner. This great victory was then celebrated for forty days and nights." al-Jumhurriya, October 8, 1973; cf: Carl Brockelmann, <u>History of the Islamic Peoples</u>,(New York: Capricorn Books, 1960), pp. 250-251.

The relevant passages in the Qur'an are:

> We sent down to Our Servant on the Day of Testing,
> The Day of the meeting
> of the two forces.
> For God hath power
> Over all things
>
> Remember ye were
> On the hither side
> Of the valley, and they
> On the farther side,
> And the caravan
> On lower ground than ye....
>
> But (thus ye met)
> That God might accomplish
> A matter already enacted;
> That those who died might
> Die after a clear Sign
> (had been given) and those who live
> Might live after a Clear Sign
> (Had been given) ....
>
> And remember when ye met,
> He showed them to you
> As few in your eyes,
> And he made you appear
> Contemptible in their eyes:
> That God might accomplish
> A matter already enacted.
> For to God do all questions
> Go back (for Decision).

<u>The Holy Qur'an</u>, trans. Abdullah Yusuf Ali (McGregor & Werner, Inc.,1946), <u>Sura</u> 8:41, 42, 43, pp. 425-426.

(39) Ibid.: Commentary 91, p. 424: "On the Muslim side the few martyrs knew that the victory was theirs and those who survived the battle enjoyed the fruits of the victory. On the pagan side, both those who died and those who lived knew fully the issue joined. Even psychologically both sides went in with full determination to decide the issue...."

(40) David Hirst, one of the few Western writers to grasp the significance of the attack from the Arab perspective, summed up the intensity of Arab emotion and frustration that went into its planning and execution:

"The Canal and the Bar-Lev Line were the symbol of Israeli invincibility. Shattering the myth of invincibility has produced in the Arabs a psychological change which, whatever the outcome of the war, cannot be over emphasized....When Egyptian troops first broke through the Bar-Lev Line, they conquered that inferiority complex from which most Arabs seem to suffer. When the first pictures of Israel (i) captives, barefoot (sic: like Arab prisoners in 1967) or hands on heads, appeared on Arab television screens, apathy, frustration, self disgust - emotions intensified by a haunting sense of a great Arab past, a great military past - swept away....The way in which the crossing was achieved has added to Arab confidence. The use of water hoses to flood Israeli defenses was a genial stroke of imagination of a kind which, in the past, always seemed to be an Israeli monopoly." The Manchester Guardian, October 16, 1973.

(41) Arab World Weekly, October 20, 1973. Compare with this Western source:

(a) Egypt: "The army is organized into three field armies with divisions as the next subordinate echelon, much like the Soviet Combined Arms Army. At the start of the October war, the Egyptian forces were believed to consist of at least five infantry divisions, three mechanized infantry divisions, and two armored divisions. Additional forces were believed to include 2 infantry, 2 paratroop, and 2 separate armored brigades, and up to 26 commando battalions."

(b) Syria: "Major ground forces consist of three infantry divisions and two armored divisions. Additional forces are believed to include three paratroop brigades, two commando brigades, one infantry brigade, one motorized infantry brigade, and three armored brigades." US Army Command and General Staff College, Selected Readings in Tactics: The Middle East War, Fort Leavenworth, Kansas, 1975, p. 2-2.

(42) Al-Sadat Address to Egyptian Air Force units at Aswan, January 26, 1972, partially translated in Arab World Weekly, February 5, 1972.

(43) Al-Sadat Address at Alexandria, April 3, 1974, in Arab World Weekly, April 6, 1974.

(44) Ibid.: This was not the only reason, however, Soviet air defense experts were not allowed to go near the canal: "...anyone who studied my decisions a little could have understood that I intended to enter a battle by ousting the Soviet experts...They would not enter the battle with me. Rather they were banned (sic: by their government) from going near the canal. All of them were here in the interior as experts in arms and other types of training...Our sons were already trained and took over everything....There was no vacuum at all that would have subjected us to a gap in our air defenses..."

(45) An-Nahar Arab Report, May 14, 1973; May 28, 1973; Tehran Journal, October 6, 1973. Also: Aaron S. Klieman, Soviet Russia and the Middle East (Baltimore: Johns Hopkins Press, 1970), especially pp. 78-79 for a discussion of Russian options concerning arms transfers to the Arabs.

(46) An-Nahar Arab Report, May 28, 1973.

(47) FBIS, September 23, 1974.

(48) FBIS, October 11, 1974.

(49) Arab World Weekly, October 20, 1973.

(50) Arab World Weekly, October 13, 1973.

(51) Ibid.

(52) Arab World Weekly, November 9, 1974.

(53) Compare with: The Military Balance, 1973-74 (London: The International Institute for Strategic Studies, 1974); Strategic Survey 1973; Dale R. Tahtinen, The Arab-Israeli Military Balance Since October 1973 (Washington: American Enterprise Institute, 1974).

(54) Ashkar, Ahmad Isma'il in al-Ahram, November 18, 1973. Cf: also General Arik Sharon's comments: "A second thing they (sic: the Israeli General Staff) did not understand, was the objective of the Egyptians was Tel Aviv, or at least the occupation of the Sinai. The Egyptian objective...was to occupy a strip 10-12 kilometers east of the canal and dig in for defense..." Ma'ariv, January 25, 1974, transcribed in Middle East Monitor, February 15, 1974.

(55) Ahmad Isma'il Address at Nasir Stadium, October 6, 1974, in FBIS, October 7, 1974.

(56) Mustafa Talas interview in al-Thawra, October 5, 1975; see also: Ashkar, al-Asad in al-Sayyad, March 7, 1974.

(57) Talas, and the comments of Syrian Information Minister George Saddiqni in al-Nahar, May 28, 1974, FBIS, May 29, 1974. The Egyptians have their own version: "He (Ahmad Isma'il) was surprised when the Syrian officers told him that they would seize the whole of the Golan within 48 hours of the start of the battle...He warned them against overoptimism. He told them that the Golan should be

taken in stages and that the enemy forces should be destroyed in what is known as 'killing areas' during every stage..." al-Sadat, Egyptian Radio, in FBIS, October 29, 1975.

(58) Cf: Philip K. Hitti, History of the Arabs, 10th Ed. (London: MacMillan & Col, Ltd., 1970), p. 647.

(59) Al-Ahram, November 18, 1973. Syrian spokesmen later expressed some bitterness at being forced to attack at the Egyptian's convenience: "Egypt is nationally indebted to Syria. Perhaps other circumstances made it necessary to launch the attack at 1500, because from 1400 to 1500 the artillery and air force were preparing the way for attack, instead of the first hour of daylight - a matter which made our forces break through the enemy's defenses and fortifications in the worst conditions as the sun was about to set in the west and made it difficult for our forces to see..." Talas in al-Thawra, October 5, 1975.

(60) Al-Ahram, November 18, 1973.

(61) FBIS, October 11, 1974. The October timeframe also occurred at the time Soviet fleet units would be augmented. See: Elmo R. Zumwalt, Jr., On Watch (New York: Quadrangle, 1976), p. 437.

(62) FBIS, October 11, 1974.

(63) William R. Polk, "Why the Arabs Went to War," Washington Post, October 14, 1973.

(64) Ibid. Al-Sadat did, in fact, risk a number of gestures in the direction of conciliation:

1. Upon assuming the Presidency, he reaffirmed Egypt's acceptance of UN resolution 242.

2. In February 1971, he offered to sign a formal peace treaty with Israel.

3. In May 1971, he agreed to mediation by the US supposed to lead to an "interim solution" that would open the canal.

4. In July 1972, he expelled USSR advisors.

Cf: U.S. News & World Report, October 22, 1973, p. 33.

(65) Al-Sadat Address at Alexandria University, July 26, 1973, in FBIS, July 27, 1973.

(66) Daily Star, April 8, 1973.

(67) Ibid.

(68) Daily Star, June 28, 1973; Cf also: Moshe Dayan's interview with Francis Ofner in Christian Science Monitor, June 18, 1973.

(69) Kayhan, June 30, 1973.

(70) Arab Report & Record, August 16-31, 1973.

(71) Daily Star, September 9, 1973.

(72) London Times, October 7, 1973.

(73) U.S. News & World Report, October 15, 1973, p. 29.

(74) Arab World Weekly, October 6, 1975.

(75) An-Nahar Arab Report, May 14, 1973.

(76) An-Nahar Arab Report, October 8, 1973. Zuhayr Muhsin officially declared that the "Eagles" were, in fact, part of al-Sa'iqa.

(77) Daily Star, October 4, 1973; October 5, 1973; Arab World Weekly, October 6, 1973.

(78) Arab World Daily, October 4, 1973.

(79) Al-Sadat Address at Alexandria, April 3, 1974, partially translated in Arab World Weekly, April 6, 1974.

(80) Al-Sadat quoted in an-Nahar Arab Report, April 9, 1973.

(81) Al-Sadat Address to People's Assembly, May 16, 1973, text in Arab World Weekly, May 19, 1973.

(82) Al-Sadat address to Egyptian Air Force units at Aswan, January 26, 1972, partial translation in Arab World Weekly, February 5, 1973. In a Radio Cairo broadcast of an interview with Vjesnik (Zagreb) al-Sadat noted: "The United States is Israel's close accomplice, but I administer a certain rebuke also to the Soviet Union...In its assessment of the dangers in this area, and its interests in lessening tension with the United States, the Soviet Union does not consider our analysis as it ought to do..." Radio Cairo, May 28, 1973 excerpted in Arab Report & Record, May 16-31, 1973.

(83) According to an-Nahar Arab Report, July 9, 1973, an Egyptian crowd had attacked the car of the Soviet consul general in Alexandria, and the electricity to a Russian club in Zamalik was suddenly cut off in the middle of a reception - in the darkness, stones were thrown at the club's windows. Because of these and other such incidents, Soviet Ambassador Vladimir Vinogradov was rumored to have drawn up a plan for the evacuation of Soviet civilians.

(84) Polk.

(85) VOP (Algiers), August 25, 1973, in FBIS, August 27, 1973. Dawn, October 14, 1973, summarized these rumors, noting that many of them had their source in comments by Bennett and Senator Fulbright which referred to a contingency plan in which Israel would serve as a United Nations military surrogate, and argued that Arabs could only draw the conclusion that: "...it is not (only) the Jewish vote in the United States that pushes America to support Israel completely, or the West working off its guilt complex towards the Jews or anything like that. It is oil, and having Israel here is a way to control the Arabs..." Dawn's editorial writer went on to comment: "...The idea

that tiny Israel will continue to control its big Arab neighbors through sheer force and intimidation bespeaks a tremendous lack of understanding of the realities and potentialities (sic: of the Arabs)...."

(86) Akhbar al-Yawm, September 1, 1973.

(87) Al-Ahram, September 7, 1973.   Haykal pointed out that the problem, insofar as the Egyptians were concerned, was to escalate the Middle East crisis to a point where it would force itself upon Kissinger's attention.   To do this, it was necessary to strike at United States interests in the area: "We shall not be able to shake the United States from head to toes unless we touch her direct-ly....These United States interests and strategic objectives were domination of the area, continued access to oil, and the maintenance of Israel." To accomplish this, the United States had embarked on a number of policies, designed to:

1. move Russia out of area;

2. oust Russian arms from area;

3. deepen regional conflicts, especially the Palestine issue;

4. harass and exhaust nationalist powers (radicals);

5. control energy sources of area; and

6. control Arab capital.

"And if the foregoing lines of strategy failed, there would always be Israel's thick rod to fall upon any head that would rise...." al-Ahram, September 5, 1973. Cairo Radio echoed these sentiments:

The strangest thing for any Arab to expect in present circum-stances would be for the United States to change its policy on the Middle East or on any other area unless circumstances impose such a change on Washington.   Politics are not steered by emotions or spontaneous encounters but by interests and press circumstances having a material effect and by material force.

United States policy, which was forced to acknowledge the pressure of circumstances in southeast Asia in general, and in Indochina and Vietnam in particular, will remain as it was in 1948, completely partial toward Zionism in the Middle East and against the Arabs' cause unless pressure from within the area is exerted on U.S. policy, and on the interests on which this policy is based. Such pressure can bring about a change in the U.S. policy, its objectives, and its course.   Cairo Radio, September 27, 1973, in FBIS, September 28, 1973.

Cf. al-Sadat's impressions: "Hafiz Isma'il asked (sic: during a presumably secret meeting in Paris, May 20, 1973): 'How can we change it (sic: the status quo)?' Kissinger answered: 'Through a military battle. If the position is not changed militarily, I cannot do anything.   I wish you to convey some advice from me to al-

Sadat....Tell him: Do not try to change the military situation because another defeat of the 1967 type would do away with any hope for a peaceful or any other settlement'..." Interview.

(88) Al-Jumhurriya, October 4, 1973; Christian Science Monitor, October 28, 1973, according to the Monitor, the Kissinger plan (originally reported in the London Times) was said to have called for a partial Israeli pullback in the Sinai and Golan, and Egyptian/Israeli condominium over the Sharm al-Shaykh, a return of the West Bank to Jordan, and Jerusalem to remain in Israeli hands, with Christian and Muslim control over each faith's respective holy places; Cf: also Jim Hoagland, "Arab Fear of Invasion Stirs Anger Toward Us," Washington Post, September 24, 1973.

(89) Cf: Egyptian Gazette, September 14, 1973.

(90) Address at Alexandria University, July 26, 1973, in FBIS, July 27, 1973. Al-Asad made a similar observation in a postwar statement: "The enemy's threats concerning his long arm and strong fist were reiterated time and again.   His insistence on continuing the aggression was firm and did not need further proof. His readiness to impose a fait accompli was before our eyes every day...." Address on Ba'th Revolution Anniversary, March 8, 1974, in FBIS, March 11, 1974.

(91) Ibid; The Manchester Guardian, September 15, 1973:   al-Akhbar opined that the raid was meant to intimidate the Arabs at a time when Egyptian efforts at rallying Arab governments around one strategy seemed to be succeeding; L'Orient Le Jour proclaimed it an "institutionalized, unprovoked, gratuitous aggression...which the enemy deems necessary to administer periodically to the Arabs...." In fact, however, the Syrian Air Force had been carrying out exercises with live ammunition in the days immediately preceding the air battle.

(92) Moshe Dayan, Diary of the Sinai Campaign, (New York: Schocken Books, 1967), p. 203; Cf: Badeau, "The Arabs," for the argument that the same conditions were perceived by the Israelis as being present again in 1967, also see Rosen and Indyk.

(93) Daily Star, January 6, 1974:   the Palestinians claimed to have carried out 1,251 operations in 1973. Although this figure includes the 200 or so wartime attacks, it represents a significant increase from previous years. Moreover, fida'iyin operations had expanded considerably on a global scale. Cf: Arab World Weekly, August 4, 1973 for an analysis of the new fida'iyin tactics. According to it, the shift in emphasis from border raids to attacks on Israeli overseas installations was an outgrowth of the Jordanian civil war, which led to increased restrictions on Palestinian operations by Jordan and Syria, and Israeli success in sealing off border areas.   The advantages of these tactics, insofar as the Palestinians were concerned, was that they were relatively unhampered by Arab governments, they were highly publicized "spectaculars," and they

did not allow for easy Israeli reprisals. These attacks had become mixed up with inter-Arab politics, sponsored by rival Syrian and Iraqi governments.

(94) Al-Thawra, October 4, 1973: A Syrian self-fulfilling prophecy.

(95) Ahmad Isma'il in al-Ahram, November 18, 1973.

(96) Hussein, p. 35.

(97) Cf: al-Quddus in Akhbar al-Yawm, November 3, 1973, who was clearly aware of the fact that the Israelis were in the midst of an election campaign, but preferred not to discount Israeli utterances as campaign rhetoric.

(98) Damascus Radio, October 4, 1973, in FBIS, October 5, 1973. The build up of reports reached a crescendo from October 1 to 6:

Ha'aretz, October 1, 1973: "Tension has been felt recently along the Syrian border with Israel since Syria moved a large number of units from its border with Jordan and from other places to the border with Israel."

Baghdad Radio, October 2, 1973: "The Zionist enemy air force today intermittently violated Lebanese airspace over the southern areas. Arrivals from Lebanon say that the enemy is still massing troops on the Lebanese and Syrian borders, particularly the area facing al-Urqub and the occupied Syrian heights."

Daily Star, October 3, 1973: "Syrian, Jordanian, and Egyptian forces have been alerted following intensified Israeli activity along the ceasefire lines with the three countries. The Israeli build up has sparked fears of another confrontation between the Arabs and Israelis. Despite Israeli denials of any state of emergency, reports received in Beirut, and Sidon affirmed that there was an increase of Israeli concentrations, which had led to the adoption of concerned defensive measures by Jordan and Syria....Reports of concentrations along the border with Lebanon, particularly at settlements opposite Bint Jbail, Ayta Al-Shaab, Ein Ibil, Maroun Al-Ras, and Yaroun. There were also concentrations opposite the town of Yater, three kilometers from the Israeli border, from which the Israelis say a commando of the Vienna train kidnap operation originated. Israeli armored concentrations were also reported opposite Kafr Shouba, Habbariya, Kafr Hamam, Rashaya Al Fukhar, and Shabaa. In Tel Aviv, Israeli military sources denied reports of Israeli troop concentrations along the Suez Canal."

Damascus Radio, October 4, 1973: "Reports from occupied Palestine that Israeli military circles have recently stated that, despite the complete calmness along the ceasefire line with Syria, the Syrians are preparing for certain military operations. These sources said that the Israeli forces were in a state of alert last weekend."

Cairo Press Review, October 5, 1973: "Severe tension on Syrian front threatening to erupt in fighting at any moment. Al-Ahram, October 5, 1973: Israeli military buildup increasing dangerously under cover of continuous air patrols over the whole area/Syrian forces stand poised in readiness to strike at any attack."

Al-Ahram, October 6, 1973: "Tension on all front lines intensifies on Suez Canal front. Israel covers her military movements aimed at escalating the situation by reports about Egyptian military activity along the Suez Canal." Akhbar al-Yawm, October 6, 1973: "Israeli forces massed on all fronts/Israel contemplating a major military operation...."

(99) The decision to act remained the subject of controversy until the last minute. In late September, al-Sadat told a visiting delegation of Lebanese "Nasirites" that Egypt would reopen the war of attrition within three months, indicating some uncertainty as to timing. The strategy as he described it was, at the time, to put two types of pressure on the Israelis. Faysal had agreed to make use of the oil weapon to alter United States policies; the Eastern Front would be revived with the return of Jordan to the resistance; there were reports out of Cairo that the military was split over the advisability of breaking the ceasefire. Rumor had it that Ahmad Isma'il had submitted his resignation in protest over pressure from officers (very probably led by Shadhili) dissatisfied with the state of "phony war." Isma'il apparently considered Egyptian forces to be ill prepared for a new war. Al-Sadat apparently interceded to get the Marshal to postpone his resignation. As an interim measure, (and possibly an alternative to attacking) al-Sadat granted amnesty to all students held in Egyptian prisons, and reinstated journalists who were fired for "activities hostile to the regime." But observers in Cairo reported that neither measure had any appreciable effect, and that the students were determined to begin demonstrations at the beginning of the academic year. An-Nahar Arab Report, October 8, 1973. Again, as noted above, this rumor could have been part of the Egyptian disinformation strategy. Nevertheless, their plausibility seems very great, illustrating the problems of interpreting Arab media.

Later Arab versions of events leading up to the decision to attack tend to give the impression of a rationally thought out, smoothly executed policy. Much of the material already utilized in this study is of the hind-sight variety and its (Arab) authors have naturally made efforts to present their actions in the best possible light. This is only to be expected, since these authors have constituencies to worry about. However, in retrospect, the decision to attack was arrived at only after much hesitation and frequent changes of plan.

As early as December 1971, al-Sadat had ordered an air strike against Israeli installations in the Sinai: Fifty tactical bombers were to hit Israeli installations. Among other things, this was to prove that he meant business when he had declared that 1971 would be a "year of decision." However, the Soviets, who were supposed to have supplied the weaponry for this effort, did not do so (<u>Newsweek</u>, April 9, 1973, p. 43).

The attack, said to be scheduled for December 9, was officially called off because of the Indo-Pak war; a crisis which al-Sadat felt would overshadow events in the Middle East, and therefore nullify any political value such an operation might have (Jon Kimche, "Fall 1973: The Soviet-Arab Scenario," <u>Midstream</u> 19, no. 10 (December 1973): 9-22).

In late July/early August 1972, al-Sadat ordered War Minister Sadiq to drop a parachute brigade into the Sinai and hold a small beachhead for 7 to 10 days. During this operation, the United Nations Security Council was to be called into session; Libya was to cut off oil to Western Europe, and pressure was to be brought on Washington to force an Israeli withdrawal. General Sadiq refused the order on the grounds that the Egyptian army was not ready; that it had sufficient ammunition for only three days intensive fighting; and that the home front was not prepared for any sort of Israeli bombardment (<u>Newsweek</u>, ibid).

Yet another operation was planned for December 1972, but was again called off at the last minute. According to a source close to the Israeli government both United States and Israeli intelligence reported the imminence of the attack. The United States then informed Russia of this and sought a clarification of Russia's position on the matter. Al-Sadat apparently was persuaded by the Soviets once more to postpone action on the strength of Soviet assurances that it would produce a political solution acceptable to Egypt. (Kimche, p. 14). At the end of March, Sadat expelled two opposition ministers from his cabinet and included a new face, Isma'il Fahmi, noted for his critical attitude toward Soviet Middle East policies (<u>An-Nahar Arab Report</u>, April 2, 1973, p. 1), thus, in effect, concentrating Sadat's control for any contingency. This was followed by a series of overt moves designed to put the country in a military posture: dim outs in Cairo, establishment of operations rooms for government ministries, requisition of supplies, and the setting up of citizens militia camps. Speculation in Egypt was to the effect that an attack across the canal might be timed to coincide with Israel's 25th anniversary celebrations (<u>AP</u> from Cairo, April 27, 1973).

Fatah activities triggered an Israeli punitive raid on Beirut on April 10. This in turn triggered a Lebanese/Palestinian mini civil war, a crisis which erupted out of fida'iyin charges that the Lebanese government failed to provide PLO figures with adequate security (<u>Egyptian Gazette</u>, April 12, 1973). The tensions thus generated coincided with one of the dates al-Sadat mentioned as being optimum for a canal crossing. In the third week of April,

Egyptian papers began carrying black-bordered insets giving instructions in civil defense and mobilization procedures to the general
populace; martial music was played on Egyptian radio stations; al-
Sadat dramatically moved to the "war room." Syrian forces were
put on a state of maximum alert on April 27-28.

The attack, however, was called off; partly because of Russian
intervention (Kimche); partly because of Israeli responses. The
Israelis, partially mobilized, maneuvered the Golani birgade, and
warned the Egyptians not to attack. In any event, there were
several important disadvantages to the May target date:

(1) There was no formal military cooperation with Jordan.

(2) The Saudis had not yet committed themselves on the use of
the oil weapon.

(3) There was no element of surprise; the Israelis were partially
mobilized.

The attack was rescheduled for the Fall - August/September -
but again called off, this time presumably because of Western
reaction to the August 5 attack on passengers at the Athens Airport
by a Palestinian group calling itself the followers of the "Martyr Abu
Yusuf." The Arab press was equally hostile, but it was the Egyptian
and Syrian media that were significantly the most outspoken. Al-
Ba'th (Damascus) blamed Israeli agents and al-Ahram claimed that
this action was designed to besmirch the image of the revolution
(An-Nahar Arab Report, August 13, 1973, p. 1).

(100) Ahmad Isma'il quoting al-Sadat in the course of an address to the
People's Assembly, February 19, 1974, in FBIS, February 20, 1974.

(101) Al-Sadat, interview on Beirut Radio, October 8, 1974, in FBIS,
October 9, 1974.

(102) Al-Ahram, November 18, 1973.

(103) Egyptian Gazette, April 12, 1973. The assassinations of
Muhammad Yusuf Najjar, Kamal Nasir, and Kamal 'Udwan, three of
the PLO's top leaders, triggered massive demonstrations, upwards of
100,000 marched in their funeral procession throughout Beirut. Cf.
Action, April 16, 1973 for details. The Fifth of June Society
published a summary of attacks on PLO leaders, "Israel's Silent
War," (Beirut, n.d.); the April 10 raid was duly noted as having taken
place on the 25th anniversary of Dayr Yasin.

(104) Cairo newspapers, in particular, played up a PRAVDA report of
"alien intelligence services" which were said to be helping the
Israelis, and covered a speech by Senator Proxmire criticizing
United States intelligence operations (Egyptian Gazette, April 13,
1973). Other media expanded on this theme and worked it into a
general attack on United States policies in the Middle East. Also
Radio Cairo, April 12, 1973, broadcast these comments: "....It now

follows that the United States has openly entered the anti-Palestinian struggle since the Khartoum incident, that we should take into consideration the prime role of the United States Intelligence Agency and the entire United States espionage machine in the murder and hunting raids undertaken by Israel in the most bloody manner against the Palestinian people..." (FBIS, April 13, 1973).

(105) Baghdad Radio, June 13, 1974, summarized in Arab Report & Record, June 16-30, 1974.

(106) Cf. the comments by Ahmad al-Shuqayri, The Great Defeat: With the Kings and Presidents (Beirut: Dar al-'Awda, 1973), excerpted in Journal of Palestine Studies 3:2 (Winter 1974): 142ff, concerning 'abd al-Nasir's vain attempts to control Arab escalatory moves in 1967: how he sent messages to the Syrians to get them to stop fida'iyin activities in late May, and the subsequent bitterness with which he (and most Egyptians) regarded their erstwhile Arab allies for their role in precipitating the crisis.

(107) Cf. al-Quddus quote in Chapter 4 above and also Schleifer, pp. 150ff concerning the Anderson and Yost missions to Cairo. Schleifer claims that the US warned Husayn that Israel was planning to attack some time around June 5, and that Husayn relayed this warning to 'abd al-Nasir during the course of his May 30 visit. This, says Schleifer, established a certain official United States credibility in Cairo, and set the stage for United States assurances that it would prevent the Israelis from attacking if the Egyptians would likewise hold off. This credibility was then cynically exploited to cause the Arabs to lower their guard at a critical time. To the extent that this version of events is accepted in the Arab world, it would account for a great deal of mistrust Cf. (Al-Sadat's speech to the People's Assembly, October 16, 1973:..."abd al-Nasir had warned against this (sic: air) strike..." al-Ahram, October 17, 1973).

(108) An-Nahar Arab Report, October 15, 1973: "....Sadat was, quite simply, anxious to exclude Kaddafi from his military plans. On the one hand, he had no desire for the colonel's tempestuous presence in the operations room. And on the other, he maintained little faith in Kaddafi's ability to maintain the essential secrecy of the plans. A disastrous leak must have seemed all too possible in view of the Libyan leader's well known outspokenness...."

(109) "Speech on the Anniversary of 'abd al-Nasir's Death", September 28, 1974, in FBIS, September 30, 1974.

(110) Cf: Coral Bell, "Middle East: Crisis Management During Detente," International Affairs, (Oxford University) 50, no. 4 (October 1974): 531-543, for a similar analysis.

(111) FBIS, September 30, 1974.

(112) Comments by Admiral Donald C. Griffin, Ret., during a symposium on, "The Military Balance of Power in the Middle East: An

American View," Journal of Palestine Studies 1:2 (Spring 1972): 10. Arabs themselves were of the same opinion. Haykal, for example, prefaced a question to Ahmad Isma'il 'Ali concerning the surprise that was achieved with these comments: "We used to say that we, for our part, could never keep a secret, while we could not imagine that the enemy, for his part, could ever violate a secret..." (al-Ahram, November 18, 1975).

(113) FBIS, October 11, 1974.

(114) Al-Sadat interview in al-Siyasa published in Akhbar al Yawm, September 14, 1974 in FBIS, September 17, 1974; Interview, October 25, 1977.

(115) An-Nahar Arab Report, October 15, 1973; November 12, 1973; London Times, December 9, 1973. Presumably also, the personal envoys and emissaries of these leaders were brought in: Saudi national security advisor, Kamal Adham (who literally shuttled between Cairo and Riyadh in September), Jordan's 'abd al-Mun'im Rifa'i (also peripatetic), among others. Boumedienne was one of al-Sadat's earliest supporters after 'abd al-Nasir's death. He also was of the firm belief that 'abd al-Nasir had given up too soon in 1967; and of the belief that Third World resources should be used as political weapons against the West to force concessions on the prices of Western goods and technology. Both of these views were accepted to some extent by al-Sadat, first in the use of the oil weapon, and second, in al-Sadat's refusal to give up after the Israelis crossed the canal. For an Algerian spokesman's articulation of Algerian policy see Mohammed Yazid, "Algeria and the Arab-Israeli Conflict," Journal of Palestine Studies 1, no. 2 (Winter 1972): 1-18.

(116) Arab World Daily, November 5, 1973.

(117) Al-Sadat, interview in al-Anwar, March 29, 1974; An-Nahar Arab Report, November 12, 1973.

(118) Abu Iyad, interview in al-Balagh, July 29, 1974.

(119) Tehran Journal, October 8, 1973.

(120) Al-Ahram, May 25, 1974 in FBIS, May 24, 1974. Al-Ahram took the unusual step of publishing heretofore secret exchanges between al-Sadat, and the Libyan RCC, to counter a series of Libyan attacks on the Egyptian handling of the war: "...al-Ahram is of the opinion that the Arab people are entitled to know all the facts now that the Libyan government has disseminated what it termed the statement of account containing figures of what it called aid for the battle together with secret cipher messages on the aid exchanged between the senior officials in the two countries."

(121) Ibid.

(122) Ibid.

(123) Ibid. Al-Sadat's financial problems did not stop there, however. Apparently the Soviets insisted on immediate payment for arms delivered during the course of the war. The Algerians paid for a large percent of the equipment, some $100 million worth. However, this left considerable ill feeling with the Egyptians; ill feeling that was an extension of Egyptian complaints about prewar Soviet arms transfers. For their part, the Soviets may have felt that the Egyptians had squandered immense amounts of expensive military hardware in a war that produced no advantages to Russia; a war that redounded to the benefit of an Egyptian leader the Soviets did not especially trust or support.

(124) In the course of an interview in Le Monde, October 23, 1973, reproduced in Arab Report & Record, October 16-31, 1973, al-Qadhafi had declared his vehement disapproval of everything and everyone connected with the war:

"This war is not my war. Sadat and Asad took their decision and worked out their plan without consulting me, without even informing me. And yet our countries are members of a federation whose constitution clearly states that war or peace could only be decided by a unanimous vote by the three presidents. We also disagreed about the manner of conducting the campaign. I once submitted a strategic plan to them, but their general staffs thought otherwise. I still think my plan is better. Even if Syria and Egypt were to defeat Israel, I cannot lend my name to a comic opera war....Syria alone - whose population is twice that of Israel - ought to be able to beat the Jewish state. Egypt, for her part, has thousands of tanks, and hundreds of aircraft. In these conditions it would be ridiculous to mobilize Arab armies for the pathetic aim of liberating Sinai and the Golan...."

He went on to describe the wartime contributions of Kings Husayn and Faysal. Husayn's efforts were "an odious comedy, a betrayal." As for Faysal, he was accused of "feeding his people with slogans....He proclaims a jihad; he calls his troops to arms (where are they, I wonder?); his radio plays martial music. All this is theater...."

In comparison, however, Libya had succeeded in isolating Israel from the Third World, "We have reduced the Zionist state to the level of Taiwan." The only correct Arab goal was "not to take back from Israel the territories she conquered in 1967, but to free the Palestinians, all the Palestinians, from the Zionist yoke." Any strategy short of that would inevitably fail: "The war will start up again in one year or ten. The Arab regimes who lent their names to such a betrayal would be overthrown. All the military or political defeats in history have been followed by revolution...."

(125) Al-Anwar interview, March 29, 1974. The al-Quadhafi speech apparently referred to was that of October 7, 1973, the Anniversary

of the expulsion of Italians from Libya in 1970, in which he took
initial exception to the Egyptian/Syrian limited war concept: "We
call for the liberation of Palestine and we also call for the transfer
of the battle to the land of Palestine at an early stage according to
a plan quite different from that being carried out...." in Arab
Report & Record, October 1-15, 1973. Al-Sadat later added these
comments on al-Qadhafi's military qualifications:

"I regret to remind you, you of the military (sic: the Libyan RCC),
that the technique of war depends, among other things, on the art of
timing as to when you should attack, when you should strike, and
when you should stop. By all this, you define your political, military,
tactical, and strategic aims....To me, Mu'ammar al-Qadhafi's only
excuse is that he has not practiced war and has not experienced
fighting - the difficult test which Egypt has experienced in four wars
when it sacrificed thousands of martyrs...." FBIS, May 24, 1974.

(126) Al-Ahram, November 18, 1973.

(127) Ibid. Al-Sadat interview in al-Siyasa, in FBIS, September 17, 1974;
       Search, pp. 246ff. Apparently some units did not believe that the
       order to fight was real. Third army units were thrown into confusion
       when they were told that the "exercise" was now real. According to
       Herzog 95% of the Egyptians captured by Israeli forces had learned
       of the attack only on the morning of the 6th. Atonement, p. 39.
       The stress on secrecy was so great that the commanders of the
       Egyptian Red Sea squadron flew to Aden incognito on October 4
       lounged around for two days posing as tourists, and then literally
       rowed out to meet their respective vessels on the morning of the
       6th. Al-Sayyad, April 3, 1974.

(128) Shadhili in al-Akhbar, November 21, 1973.

(129) Al-Ahram, November 18, 1973. In addition, a unit of T-62s which
       was normally stationed in the Cairo area, and which was supposed to
       be the spearhead of any canal crossing, was never moved out of
       position. Field hospitals were established in remote desert loca-
       tions; the clearance of civilian hospitals was avoided. Cf: An-Nahar
       Arab Report, October 15, 1973.

(130) Al-Sadat interview in al-Usbu' al-'Arabi, October 7, 1974, in FBIS,
       October 11, 1974.

(131) Al-Akhbar, December 6, 1973; the London Times, December 9,
       1973; for an Israeli account of the effectiveness of the Arab
       deception plan see London Times, February 3, 1974; in general see
       Shlaim, and the literature on Arab disinformation activities cited
       therein.

(132) Hasan Sabri al-Khuly, Special Representative of President al-
       Sadat, interview in al-Musawar, December 7, 1973. Al-Khuly stated
       that, as a result, the Israelis discounted reports of enormous
       amounts of war materiel being transported to the front; interpreting

it as a muscle flexing parade for the benefit of the Egyptian university opening.

(133) Al-Hayat, September 20, 1973; Search, p. 244.

(134) See Shlaim, and the literature cited therein. On Syrian fears of an Israeli retaliation see David Hirst, "Syria Braced for Meir Retaliation," Manchester Guardian, October 6, 1973, p. 2.

(135) Colin Smith, Carlos: Portrait of a Terrorist (New York: Holt, Rinehart and Winston, 1977), pp. 124ff. On the other hand, Zuhayr Muhsin, head of al-Sa'iqa, was one of the few Syrians to be kept fully informed of the plans for the attack. In fact, Muhsin took his orders directly from al-Asad. An-Nahar Arab Report, December 8, 1975.

(136) Al-Ahram, December 7, 1973. See also Herzog's version, Atonement, pp. 40ff.

(137) Ibid. Arab sources are not clear as to the extent Russia was privy to Egyptian/Syrian planning. In postwar statements, Arab spokesmen have insisted that the decision was "100 percent" Arab. Available Western sources are divided over the Russian role; for contrasting interpretations see Bell, Kimche, Uri Ra'anan, the USSR, and the Middle East: Some Reflections on the Soviet Decision-Making Process," Orbis 17: 2 (Fall, 1973): 946-977; Alvin Z. Rubinstein, "Moscow and Cairo: Currents of Influence," Problems of Communism 23: 4 (July-August 1974): 17-28; Strategic Survey. These sources give a series of dates on which Russia was said to have become knowledgeable about the attack: September 22 (Bell), October 2, (Galia Golan, "Soviet Aims and the Middle East War," Survival 16: no. 3 (May/June 1974): 106-114, October 3/4, (Strategic Survey). Clearly, the Soviets were well aware of Arab intentions to attempt some military action. The persistent dialogue between al-Sadat and Soviet leaders offers ample evidence of this. Moreover, there had been two similar crises in 1973 alone; and a steady stream of Egyptian officials had flown to Moscow seeking more weapons with which to attack. National Security Advisor, Hafiz Isma'il, had visited Russia as late as July 11-14. Hafiz Isma'il was considered to be Egypt's foremost expert on military affairs, and had special experience in negotiating arms deals with the Soviets.

Al-Sadat adds that there was an agreement between himself and al-Asad as to how the Russians were to be informed: al-Sadat was to tell them of the general plan to attack on October 3; al-Asad was to reveal the timing of the attack moments before it occurred on the 6th. Things did not work out as planned. Al-Asad apparently told the Russians of the exact date and time soon after Ahmad Isma'il communicated them to him. (In any event, as al-Sadat points out, there were so many Russians serving with the Syrians that secrecy would have been impossible to maintain.) The Russians, after being officially informed by al-Sadat on the 3rd, came back on the 4th with a request to be allowed to airlift their personnel out of Egypt, which they did on the 5th. (Again there is a problem of interpretation: Were the Russians signaling the possibility of a war by this dramatic move? Or were they trying to dissociate themselves from it?) Cf. al-Sadat, interview in al-Hilal, October 1, 1976.

Alternatively, the Russians could have been informed about the impending attack much earlier. Robert G. Weinland, Superpower Naval Diplomacy in the October 1973 Arab-Israeli War (Arlington, VA: Center for Naval Analysis, 1978), pp. 6ff., argues that the Russians knew as early as mid-September. This time-frame would accord with either the mini-Summit, September 10-12, or the movement on station of Egyptian naval forces on September 16. In any event, the Russians could have been aware for other reasons: Russian vessels moved the Moroccan contingent to Syria. CF: Bradford Dismukes, "Soviet Employment of Naval Power for Political Purposes," in Michael McGwire and John McDonnell, eds. Soviet Naval Influence: Domestic and Foreign Constraints, (New York: Praeger, 1977), pp. 483-509. Clearly, if the Russians were this involved in strengthening the Eastern Front, they were also at least alerted to the possibility of an Arab attack.

However, stories circulated in Beirut, immediately after the outbreak of the war, attributed much of the Arabs' success in surprising the Israelis to the fact that Soviet agents had not been supplying their Israeli counterparts with information on Arab troop movements, an-Nahar Arab Report, November 19, 1973. Both Egyptians and Syrians were of the firm belief that the Soviets had been supplying the Israelis with intelligence for many years. The Manchester Guardian, October 10, 1973; an-Nahar Arab Report, July 9, 1973. The Egyptians reportedly were so incensed with Soviet activities along these lines that they asked for the removal of the Soviet Military Attache; the Syrians restricted the movement of Soviet personnel on September 27, an-Nahar Arab Report, October 1, 1973.

An Arab version of the Russian role suggests that, while the Soviets were opposed to Arab military action, they could not prevent it, especially in view of the rapidly increasing tension during the latter part of September. Another Israeli attack - at a time when Arab forces were fully prepared to go on the offensive - would have meant disaster for the Russian's position in the Middle East, Dawn, October 31, 1973. However, once the war broke out, the Soviets bent every effort to contain and end it; hence the dramatic appearance of the Soviet Ambassador who demanded an audience with al-Sadat within hours after the attack. Cf: al-Sadat interview on Beirut Radio, October 8, 1974, in FBIS, October 9, 1974; al-Sadat interview in al-Anwar, March 29, 1974:

> Six hours after the battle started, at 8 pm, and while I was in the operations room...I was notified of an urgent request for a meeting with the Soviet Ambassador...

(138) Al-Ahram, November 18, 1973; al-Akhbar, November 21, 1973; London Times, December 9, 1973.

(139) Al-Sayyad, March 7, 1974; London Times, December 9, 1973.

(140) Al-Sadat address, January 26, 1972.

(141) Excerpted in Arab World Daily, September 24, 1973.

(142) Aviation Week, December 3, 1973, pp. 18-22; Aviation Week, May 25, 1970.

(143) Manchester Guardian, October 11, 1973.

(144) Ibid.

(145) Aviation Week, December 17, 1973, pp. 14-17.

(146) L'Orient Le Jour, October 10, 1973.

(147) FBIS, October 3, 1974.

(148) Egyptian Gazette, October 31, 1973, quoting a Syrian tank Lieutenant.

(149) Ibid., quoting a Syrian commando Captain.

(150) Arab World Daily, October 24, 1973. Syrian Military Spokesman.

(151) Al-Akhbar, November 21, 1973.

(152) Arab World Weekly, November 10, 1973. Minister of Economy, Dr. Muhammad al-Imadi, comments summarized.

(153) Al-Sayyad, February 9, 1974. Commanding Officer of the Syrian Air Force, Major General Naji Jamil, interview.

(154) Al-Sadat interview in Newsweek, reproduced in FBIS, March 19, 1974.

(155) Al-Thawra (Damascus), in Arab World Daily, September 12, 1973.

(156) Al-Sadat, in FBIS, April 17, 1974.

(157) Al-Sadat quoting 2nd army Commanding Officer, in FBIS, June 7, 1974.

(158) Vice Air Marshal Muhammad Husni Mubarak, in FBIS, February 20, 1974.

(159) Al-Hayat, October 3, 1973; Daily Star, October 3, 1973.

(160) Al-Akhbar, November 21, 1973; al-Ahram, November 18, 1973.

(161) Assistant Commanding Officer of al-Qantara al-Sharqiya Sector, in FBIS, January 2, 1974.

(162) Cf: Ashkar, pp. 24ff.

(163) An-Nahar Arab Report, October 15, 1973; Strategic Survey, Ibid., p. 17.

(164) Al-Asad quoted in Arab World Daily, October 16, 1973; interview in al-Sayyad, March 7, 1974.

(165) Baghdad Radio, June 13, 1974, in Arab Report & Record, June 16-30, 1974.

(166) Al-Sayyad, March 7, 1974.

(167) Three accounts: al-Ahram, November 18, 1973; October 18, 1973.

(168) Al-Akhbar, November 21, 1973; FBIS, January 2, 1974.

(169) Dawn, October 14, 1973; Al-Ahram, December 11, 1973.

The Russians seem to have continuously discouraged any Egyptian attempts to cross the Canal, emphasizing the enormous number of casualties to be expected: 40-60,000 men in the crossing, 30-40 percent of the airforce lost in air battles. Cf: Al-Sadat, "The Russians believed I would embark on such a move. They said my soldiers and I would drown in the Suez Canal..." Interview in October, December 18, 1977, FBIS, December 19, 1977.

(170) Ahmad Isma'il address, April 17, 1974, in FBIS, April 18, 1974.

(171) Mahmud Haddad, text in FBIS, October 19, 1973.

(172) Al-Ahram, October 28, 1973; Daily Star, October 29, 1973.

(173) Al-Akhbar, October 28, 1973; Egyptian Gazette, October 14, 1973:

Military Communique no. 34, October 14, 1973: At 1:05 today (October 13) two hostile reconnaissance aircraft violated our airspace from the north of Port Said and reached Nag Hamady. They returned northwards in the direction of Cairo, turned eastward to the Sinai area, then flew over in the direction of Lebanon and Syria, and then turned in a northwest direction over the Mediterranean Sea. This trio over Egyptian territory took 25 minutes, the two aircraft were flying at an altitude of 25 kilometers, at three times the speed of sound. It is clear that they are of the American SR-71A type.

(174) Haykal.

(175) Ibid.

(176) Ibid.

(177) Daily News (Tanzania), October 27, 1973.

(178) London Times, October 28, 1973; Shadhili, himself, ordered the executions.

(179) Military Communique no. 44, October 16, 1973:....At 2:30 p.m. during the fighting, the enemy made a desperate raid, sneaking seven tanks across the Bitter Lakes in an attempt to raid some positions to the west of the canal. Our military poured intensive fire upon them, destroying three of them. The remaining tanks were scattered and our forces are now in pursuit to destroy them.

(180) <u>Military Communique no. 46</u>, October 18, 1973:... Since Wednesday night, the enemy has been aiming at infiltrating across the Bitter Lakes in a limited area, in an attempt to carry out harassing operations against the forces. Our forces are now besieging him and have ordered him to surrender or face destruction....

(181) <u>Military Communique no. 48</u>, October 19, 1973:... Our troops are continuing their encirclement of the hostile forces which infiltrate at night, so as to neutralize them and foil their aims. Our troops destroyed parts of these forces around the Deversoir area in preparation for liquidating them....

(182) <u>London Times</u>, December 30, 1973.

(183) <u>Al-Ahram</u>, November 18, 1973.

(184) <u>Al-Ahram</u>, October 28, 1973.

(185) <u>MENA</u> Military Editor quoted in <u>Cairo Press Review</u>, October 17, 1973.

(186) <u>Al-Ahram</u>, October 28, 1973.

(187) <u>Al-Anwar</u>, March 29, 1974.

(188) <u>Al-Usbu' al-'Arabi</u>, October 7, 1974, in <u>FBIS</u>, October 11, 1974.
(189) <u>Al-Anwar</u>.

(190) Cf: Kenneth S. Brower, "The Yom Kippur War," <u>Military Review</u> 54: 3 (March 1974): 25-33. But also: <u>Strategic Survey</u>: "The Egyptian Third Army was now surrounded on both east, and west, banks....and nominally the Israeli force was in a position to threaten Cairo itself....This should not, perhaps, be overstressed. The force was still a small one and its communications would have been severely stretched in any further advance; there were reserve troops defending Cairo, the country around the city was close and built up, and the Egyptian army was far from spent...." In fact, there were Egyptian officers who argued that, if the fighting resumed, the Israelis should be allowed to advance further westward, so that their lines would be even more strained. Then Egyptian forces could move in and cut them off, <u>Arab World Weekly</u>, November 30, 1973.

(191) <u>Al-Anwar</u>,: "...Now I will tell you a secret, which is that I had approved the plan to liquidate the Israeli pocket west of the canal, at the rest house at the Barrages, following an eight hour meeting of the Supreme Council of the Armed Forces on December 24, 1973. Nothing remained except for the signal to start the attack..."

(192) Ibid.

Syrian opinion was the same: "The Egyptian forces could have foiled the attempt from the very beginning. As the Egyptian command has said, these forces were made up of an armored division and another mechanized division. We believe that these forces, reinforced by an armored brigade from Algeria, could have destroyed and liquated this breach..." Talas in <u>al-Thawra</u>, October 6, 1975.

In actual fact, Egyptian forces opposite the area of the Israeli cross over were composed of a melange of Egyptian, Algerian, Kuwayti and Palestinian troops known collectively as the "Fourth Army." In addition, the Egyptian First Army guarding Cairo was theoretically available, although it had been stripped of most of its armor and missilery. Nevertheless, after the Egyptians determined the real nature of the Israeli penetration they put tremendous pressure on Israeli bridgeheads with artillery, and later, air strikes.

(193) <u>FBIS</u>, October 11, 1974. Also this exchange between al-Sadat and 3rd army Commanding Officer, Major General Ahmad Badawi Sayyid Ahmad:

Al-Sadat: Orders were sent to you to stand fast? The enemy claimed that he had occupied the town of Suez. Was the town of Suez occupied?

Badawi: The enemy was unable to occupy the town of Suez. All his tanks that tried to enter the town of Suez were destroyed. We clung to the town of Suez. It remained steadfast and the enemy was never able to conquer it.

Al-Sadat: The Badr forces were under your command. They consisted of about 50,000 men with their arms and equipment? Have you preserved the arms and equipment?

Badawi: I have preserved all my equipment and arms and I have fought the enemy and violently repelled all his attacks...

Al-Sadat: At one moment the enemy thought that he had encircled you and cut off your supplies. I gave orders to the Commander in Chief that you should hold on to your positions to the death. Have you preserved my sons, the soldiers and officers?

Badawi: I have preserved the officers and men. We stood fast and the enemy was unable to defeat us...

Al-Sadat: Have my sons, the officers and soldiers, returned to their families on leave?

Badawi: Yes sir, they have returned, almost all of them have taken leave.

Al-Sadat: To the 3rd Army, which was allegedly encircled, to its commander, Ahmad Badawi, whom I promoted during the encircle-ment...to the 3rd Army which stood fast and set the most splendid example of heroism, sacrifice and steadfastness....I express my appreciation...FBIS, February 20, 1974. (In spite of this praise from al-Sadat, officers and men of the 3rd army gathered at Tahrir Square on February 28, to protest al-Sadat's acceptance of the ceasefire.)

(194) Declaration by Syrian Armed Forces Commander in Chief, October 6, 1973, in FBIS, October 9, 1973.

(195) Foreign Ministry Statement, October 6, 1973, in FBIS, October 9, 1973.

(196) Cf. Tahtinen, pp. 27ff.

(197) Cf. Ashkar, p. 29, for comments and criticisms of both Syrian and Egyptian lack of aggressiveness in utilizing their naval forces.

(198) Vice Admiral Ahmad Fu'ad Dhikri's remarks, reported in FBIS, December 13, 1973: "In comparing the naval forces of the two sides, it was obvious that our (sic: Egyptian) forces were superior. The situation of the operation was distinguished by the length of our coasts, which extended some 1,600 kilometers, whereas the enemy coasts, including the occupied territory, extend 400 kilometers.... In view of Israel's political and geographic situation, its maritime lines of communications constitute the main artery of its economy and the supply of military and economic material...."

(199) Ibid.: "...our plan was based on dealing with the enemy on a wide front in the Mediterranean and the Red Seas by using the naval units' maximum efforts during the first days of operations, by exploiting the element of surprise to a maximum degree, and by shattering, and confusing, the enemy's command...."

(200) Ibid.: "The naval forces with all their destroyers, submarines, torpedo and missile boats, coastal artillery, naval shock troops, and frogmen took part in the operations during the first day. The missile boats and artillery fired rockets against the areas of Port Fu'ad, Rummana, and Ras Hirim. The coastal artillery also helped the forces in the Port Said sector. In the Red Sea, Sharm al-Shaykh was shelled with all kinds of rockets. In the Gulf of Suez, the Naval forces attacked the area of Abu al-Duwman on the east coast of the Gulf of Suez. Frogmen groups attacked the oil area in al-Bala'im and destroyed a big drilling rig. They also shelled the Suez-Ras Sidra concentration point with rockets. The coastal artillery opened fire to pave the way for the crossing of the 3rd Army forces....About 50 naval units in addition to special units of the naval forces, took part in the task of the first day. Our forces met with no naval or air resistance on the part of the enemy, which confirms that we achieved the element of complete surprise...."

(201) Arab World Weekly, July 3, 1971.

(202) Ruz al-Yusuf, September 21, 1973.

(203) Ibid.; Davar, June 27, 1969.

(204) Ibid.: The Falasha are a small (est. 20-60,000) group of Agau peoples who live in northern Ethiopia and practice primitive Judaism. Scholars believe that they were converted between the third and fourth centuries A.D. by Jewish missionaries from Yemen

(itself a Jewish kingdom at the time). The Falasha, however, claim much older origins. Some trace themselves to Jews who accompanied Menelik I back to Ethiopia following a visit to his father, King Solomon; others claim descent from migrations from either Egypt or Jerusalem. They are ethnically indistinguishable from the rest of the Ethiopian population; they do not speak Hebrew, and their culture - other than religion - is basically similar to that of other Ethiopians. Cf: Area Handbook for Ethiopia (Washington: GPO, 1970), pp. 33ff, 97, 231.

(205) Daily Nation (Nairobi), December 4, 1973.

(206) An-Nahar Arab Report, September 16, 1974.

(207) Daily Nation, December 4, 1973; Manchester Guardian, November 5, 1973; al-Muharrir, December 10, 1973; FBIS, July 5, 1974.

(208) FBIS, Ibid., an-Nahar Arab Report, December 17, 1973.

(209) Manchester Guardian, October 25, 1973. According to the Guardian a possible clash between United States and Egyptian warships was avoided when French authorities in Djibouti refused to allow the destroyer, Charles Adams, to leave Djibouti to aid the La Salle. It was this incident, the Guardian continued, that may have been the reason for the United States decision to send the carrier, Hancock, and five destroyers into the Indian Ocean, Manchester Guardian, November 16, 1973. The arrival of this flotilla produced considerable comment from South Yemen, Somalia, Tanzania, India, Egypt, and Russia. The general argument adopted was twofold: First, that the introduction of United States forces into the Indian Ocean would bring cold war rivalry into what had heretofore been an area free from such conflict (Cf: Daily News, October 31, 1973, for such an argument). Second, that these United States ships threatened the security of coastal countries and was an attempt to intimidate them (Cf: Egyptian Gazette, December 3, 1973, for a South Yemeni Statement; Ibid, November 3, 1973, for a TASS commentary; India News, March 22, 1974, for the Indian position.

(210) FBIS, October 18, 1973.

(211) An-Nahar Arab Report, December 17, 1973.

(212) Al-Ahram, December 3, 1973.

(213) Manchester Guardian, November 5, 1973.

(214) Ibid., October 25, 1973.

(215) Cairo Press Review, November 4, 1973.

(216) Ibid.

(217) Manchester Guardian, November 10, 1973.

(218) Filistin al-Thawra, November 14, 1973.

(219) Al-Sayyad, October 10, 1973.

(220) Ibid.; Daily Star, October 6, 1973.

(221) Daily Star, October 11, 1973.

(222) Arab World Weekly, October 26, 1968. This doctrine parallels that espoused by Mustafa Talas above.

(223) Al-Sayyad, October 10, 1973.

(224) Daily Star, January 6, 1974; "Arafat revealed that the Egyptians had originally asked for only 50 operations; the fida'iyin had carried out an additional 150 on their own. In so doing, they had utilized Chinese equipment. At this time, our friends, the Chinese, brought us to our military positions, quantities of arms and ammunition as a gift to support our struggle," (Interview with al-Nahar, in Arab World Daily, November 15, 1973).

(225) London Times, October 28, 1973.

(226) Daily Star, January 6, 1974.

(227) Al-Sayyad, October 10, 1973.

(228) Ibid.; Daily Star, January 6, 1974.

(229) Manchester Guardian, October 17, 1973. Al-Sadat was very concerned about the possibility of civilian casualties, possibly as high as 1 million dead; in addition, he was concerned that the Egyptian air defense system could not possibly protect all Egyptian targets: "We counted the vital centers in Egypt which had to be given defense priority. There were 2,000 targets....One of my major concerns was that I had to protect them before I could begin what was to be the battle of October 1973" (Al-Sadat Memoirs in October, June 19, 1977, pp. 14ff., FBIS, June 28, 1977).

(230) FBIS, October 9, 1973.

(231) Arab World Weekly, April 28, 1973. Rugh, describes the result.

(232) In 1967, Israel justified its air strike on the grounds that their radar had picked up waves of attacking Arab aircraft, while at the same time, an Egyptian armored column was moving eastward from al-'Arish. The comparable Arab statements in 1973 were:

Egypt: "At 1330 today the enemy attacked our forces in the areas of al-Za'farana and al-Sukhna in the Suez Gulf using a number of air formations, while a number of enemy naval boats were approaching the western coast of the Gulf. Our forces are now confronting the attacking forces." (General Command Communique, October 6, 1973, in FBIS, October 9, 1973).

Syria: "At 1400 today, the enemy forces began an attack on our advanced positions along the ceasefire line. Our forces are replying to the sources of fire and silencing them. Formations of enemy planes have tried to penetrate our airspace in the northern sector of the front..." (October 6, 1973 in FBIS, October 9, 1973).

(233) London Times, October 14, 1973.

(234) Text in Journal of Palestine Studies 3:2 (Winter 1974): 198-200.

(235) FBIS, October 9, 1973. An early Syrian broadcast reiterated al-Asad's theme:

> RADIO DAMASCUS, October 7, 1973: "We call on you to lay down your arms, and to raise white flags on the battlefront and on housetops. If you do so, you can be sure that no harm will befall you, for the Arab Syrian army is not a vindictive army, but a people's army which arose for the liberation of its occupied land....We are defending ourselves against murders and destruction. We work for peace for our people, and for all peoples"....In Hebrew, Arabic, English, French, Spanish, and German, Cairo Press Review, October 9, 1973; FBIS, October 9, 1973.

(236) Even Arab sources doubted the accuracy of some Syrian claims.

(237) Al-Ahram, November 18, 1973.

(238) Ibid. Isma'il later further defended the veracity of Egyptian military communiques, stating that more conservative versions of events were given when it was not possible to tell the absolute truth: "There were some sharp arguments between me and the commander of the air force and air defenses. He would tell me he had shot down 29 enemy planes and I would say no they were 18. And the communique would come out with 18." al-Ahram, November 26, 1973.

(239) Arab World Daily, October 12, 1973, comparing Israeli propaganda statements such as, "We shall turn your nights into days, and show you the stars at high noon. We shall put your faces in the mud. We shall make the enemy leaders pay heavily for this...." with the Arab treatment of events. Cf: Newsweek, October 22, 1973, which carried the same Israeli statements, and went on to comment:

> "It all seemed backwards and topsy turvy - a sort of looking glass war. There were the dazed prisoners of war, paraded before the television cameras, their uniforms in tatters, their hands clasped submissively behind their heads. But this time the prisoners were Israelis, not Arabs. There were - just as in the Six-Day War of 1967 - the abandoned combat boots, symbols of a hasty retreat before the relentless, grinding advance of the tanks. But this time the boots were left by fleeing Israeli soldiers, not Arabs. And there were the hysterical radio broadcasts, threatening horrible vengeance on their listeners and skirling to embarrassing heights of verbal overkill. But the announcer last week was an Israeli...." p. 60.

> David Hirst of the Guardian offered a similar assessment of the relative merits of Arab and Israeli propaganda efforts early in the war: "It is not only the creditable performance of their armies which has had its effect on Arab morale, it is the improved Arab propaganda. There have been backslidings of course - like reports

that some Israeli pilots' morale had fallen so low that they are chained in their seats (sic: a Syrian broadcast) - but reports from Cairo say the Egyptians now put much more credence in their own side's military communiques than they ever have before....By contrast much of Israel's propaganda has been counterproductive, and its efforts to undermine Arab morale have often been unrealistic. It was foolish on the second day of the war to speak of Damascus under curfew and Syrian troops shooting each other in their flight from the battlefield and it is still premature to describe President Asad as a 'Nero setting alight his country to see the flames.' Arab propaganda has improved. Israeli propaganda seems like old records from the very different war of 1967...." Manchester Guardian, October 16, 1973.

(240) London Times, November 20, 1973; New York Times. November 2, 1973.

(241) Cf. Newsweek, October 22, pp. 60ff, for Western accounts of Arab morale and discipline. The Arabic press naturally gave great prominence to stories of Arab heroics. Al-Akhbar, in particular, was full of eyewitness stories of Egyptian bravery. Typical of the al-Akhbar series was the article by Musa Sabry, "The Meaning of Courage," in which he related examples of Egyptian heroism: "Who could have believed? Who could have imagined the heroism of an Egyptian pilot who, after he raided an Israeli airfield in the Sinai, was told by ground control that he should return to base because his plane had been hit. His voice was heard screaming back on the receivers 'Allahu Akbar,' 'Allahu Akbar,' as he took a death dive to finish off - with his own machine and body - the enemy plane that had escaped his bombs. This is but one in scores and hundreds of chapters in an eternal saga, which some voices have been trying to undercut and which led Israeli intelligence to abnormal and hilarious conclusions...." (Al-Akhbar, December 6, 1973).

Not to be outdone, al-Ahram carried a series of interviews with wounded soldiers: "Soldier Taha: ....our unit destroyed 13 enemy tanks up to the moment I got wounded, in addition to four tanks which collided with one another in disarray....The Israeli soldiers who claim to be such great fighters could have dismounted and tried to disentangle the treads of their tanks. They dismounted alright, but only to flee...." Al-Ahram, October 18, 1973. Cf: Also Dayan in Ha'aretz, for a variety of comments.

(242) San Francisco Examiner, December 17, 1973.

(243) Al-Sayyad, March 7, 1974.

(244) Lecture to the Tel Aviv Engineer's Club, December 28, 1973 in FBIS, January 2, 1974. Cf: Also Dov Bar-Nir's acid commentary on the prewar Israeli outlook which he says rested on two erroneous assumptions:

a) "A feeling of certain and overwhelming military superiority, to the extent that it led them (sic: Israeli hawks) to a military self assurance of the kind that says: "We will tear them to pieces if they dare to raise a finger against us."

b) A sure feeling of political tranquility against a background of Arab impotence, to the extent that they believed that the present situation in the Near East would last forever, and that a 'realistic peace' could be imposed, and even that the United States could be drawn in and brought to act according to Israeli decisions" (Al-Hamishmar, October 29, 1973, excerpted in Journal of Palestine Studies 3, no. 2 (Winter 1974): 154).

(245) London Times, December 9, 1973, on Israeli disorganization.

(246) Cf: Teddy Preuss in Davar, October 25, 1973: "The gap between expectations and what happened this time is the result of a fact that our people had forgotten - namely that the Arab has not been a bad fighter during the past twenty years....There are innumerable examples of this. There was the Faluja pocket in 1949, which can be taken as the archetypal example of encircled Egyptians' power to hold out. Of the Sinai war it is sufficient to recall the way Egyptian forces held out in the Abu Ageila area, where Israeli forces were compelled to fight for three days to get past. There were similar manifestations in the Six-Day War: at the Rafah crossroads there was a fierce battle between Israeli forces and the Egyptian army which several times closed the gap made by the Israeli force....But these facts have been forgotten, as have the psychological examinations of Egyptian prisoners of war captured in 1967. The results of these were far from showing that the Egyptian soldier should be underestimated. It was found that the Egyptian soldier has a great power of endurance, good physical capacity and an aggressive spirit...." excerpted in Journal of Palestine Studies 3:2 (Winter 1974): 160.

(247) Norman Daniel, Islam, Europe and Empire (Edinburgh: The Edinburgh University Press, 1966), especially chps. 1, "The Developing Image," 17, "The Imperial Point of View," and 18, "A Summing Up," for documentation concerning this imagery.

(248) Daniel, Islam and the West: The Making of an Image (Edinburgh: The Edinburgh University Press, 1966), for the impact of Christian dogma in producing a derogatory image of Muslims, and Robert Schwoebel, The Shadow of the Crescent: The Renaissance Image of the Turk (New York: St. Martin's Press, 1969), especially chaps. 1, "The Scourge of God," 2, "The Enemy of the Cross," 3, "The Perfidious Infidel."

(249) Time, June 16,1967, pp. 16ff contains a number of comments and jokes dwelling on purported Arab cowardice. Arab armies were described as "papyrus tigers," and in an inset captioned, "Blintz-krieg," a series of jokes were reproduced: "Early in the week, the fastest thing in the world was an Israeli in a kayak in the Aqaba Gulf; by week's end, it was an Arab with his shoes off." "Jealous of Moshe Dayan's stunningly quick victory, South Viet Nam's Premier

Key asked him how he did it. 'Well, to start with,' said the Israeli Defense Minister, 'it helps if you can arrange to fight against Arabs!'" As might be expected, these characterizations were especially offensive to the Arabs, and were resurrected bitterly even after the October War. Cf: Said Ibrahim, "American Domestic Forces and The October War," Journal of Palestine Studies 4, no. 1 (Autumn 1974): 55-81, especially pp. 70-71.

(250) Ahmad Isma'il in al-Ahram, November 18, 1973.

(251) Ibid.

(252) Be'eri, pp. 322ff., on the values and self image of the Egyptian officer class.

(253) Cf. Henry Habib Ayrout, The Egyptian Peasant (Boston: Beacon Press, 1963). Although dated (published originally in 1938), Ayrout's account of the fellahin is still by and large accurate.

(254) Ahmad Isma'il interview in al-Nahar, October 7, 1974.

(255) See S.N. Eisenstadt, The Absorption of Immigrants (London: Routeledge and Kegan Paul, 1954); Judith Shaval, Immigrants on the Threshold (New York: Atherton Press, 1963), for descriptions of these institutions.

(256) Ahmad Isma'il in al-Ahram, November 18, 1973.

(257) See Malcolm H. Kerr, "Egypt," in James S. Coleman, ed., Education and Political Development (Princeton, New Jersey: Princeton University Press, 1965), pp. 169-194; Edward William Lane, Manners and Customs of the Modern Egyptians (London: Alexander Gardner, 1895), pp. 217-231; TaHa Hussein, The Stream of Days (London: Longmans, 1948), for descriptions of Egyptian educational techniques.

(258) Shadhili, Address to Arab Chiefs of Staff Conference, November 1971.

(259) Ahmad Isma'il, Directive to the Egyptian Armed Forces.

(260) Interview in al-Siyasa in FBIS, September 17, 1974.

(261) General Abu Sa'ada quoted in A.J. Barker, The Yom Kippur War, (New York: Random House, 1974), p. 91.

(262) Shadhili in al-Akhbar, November 21, 1973. Syrian troops, it is said, joined the battle shouting their determination to conquer or die for Hafiz al-Asad. Jordanian forces also utilized the cry of "Allahu Akbar," but they added a more traditionally Bedouin cry, the zaghrata, a shrill, trilling cry designed to produce the same psychological effect as the rebel.

(263) Ibid.; Insight Team, Yom Kippur War, p. 147.

(264) Al-Ahram, November 18, 1973.

(265) Al-Ahram, December 7, 1973.

(266) Al-Sayyad, March 7, 1974.

(267) Cf: Strategic Survey, p. 16, for a similar analysis.

(268) Arab World Weekly, October 27, 1973; Manchester Guardian, October 19, 1973; November 19, 1973.

(269) Text is summarized in Arab World Weekly, December 9, 1972.

(270) Robert E. Hunter, The Energy "Crisis" and US Foreign Policy, Foreign Policy Association: Headline Series, no. 16, June 1973, p. 50; James Akins, "The Oil Crisis: This Time the Wolf Is Here," Foreign Affairs 51, no. 3 (April 1973): 462-490.

(271) Daily Star, October 13, 1973; Dawn, October 14, 1973; Arab World Weekly, October 27, 1973.

(272) Dawn, October 25, 1973.

(273) Arab World Weekly, October 27, 1973; Fuad Itayin, "Arab Oil - The Political Dimension," Journal of Palestine Studies 3, no. 2 (Winter 1974): 84-97.

(274) Ibid.

(275) Ibid.; Strategic Survey.

(276) In addition, Faysal declared a jihad: "At the instructions of King Feisal, the interior minister appeals to the sons of our dear homeland...as the jihad is a duty of all Moslems...every citizen is called upon to back the freedom fighting brothers..." Daily Star, October 21, 1973.

(277) Itayin; ibid.

(278) Ibid.

(279) George Lenczowski, Middle East Oil in a Revolutionary Age (Washington: American Enterprise Institute, 1976), summarizes the course of the embargo.

(280) An-Nahar Arab Report, March 18, 1974.

(281) Al-Sadat interview in Der Spiegel, reproduced in FBIS, October 16, 1974.

(282) Haykal, al-Ahram, October 26, 1973, added international opinion.

(283) Al-Sadat in al-Anwar, March 29, 1974.

(284) Al-Asad in al-Sayyad, March 7, 1974. The Egyptians ridiculed this assertion, but the Syrians had a different view of their proposed counterattack: "On the southern front...our forces established their positions along the ceasefire line after enemy attacks failed to cause any wedge. In the central sector, all enemy attempts to penetrate our lines failed. In the northern sector, where a division commander and a brigade commander were martyred in battles for honor and manhood, the enemy succeeded in penetrating along a narrow strip. After violent battles...it was obvious to the enemy

that he was involved in a salient not more than 10 kilometers deep. Four enemy brigades were encircled by one infantry and two armored divisions. This in addition to a reconnaissance group and Jordanian armored brigades which arrived on October 21, 1973. Orders were given to be prepared for a counteroffensive to cut off, capture or destroy the enemy force..." Talas in al-Thawra, October 5, 1975.

(285) Reproduced in Arab Report & Record, October 16-31, 1973.

(286) Barker, p. 136.

(287) Military Communique no. 55.

(288) Quandt, Decisions, pp. 197-198.

(289) Ibid., p. 196; New York Times, April 10, 1974.

(290) Quandt, Decisions, pp. 197-98; Aviation Week, October 22, 1973; November 5, 1973. See also William B. Quandt, Soviet Policy in the October 1973 War (Santa Monica: RAND, 1976), for an extended analysis of these moves. See also the Insight team's comments on the Aviation Week story, Yom Kippur War, pp. 411ff. The matter is perhaps even more complicated, however. According to Time, April 12, 1976, pp. 39-40, the Israelis had activated a number of nuclear weapons; therefore, the alleged Russian injection of nuclear warheads might very well have been a response to Israeli moves.

(291) Cf: Admiral Elmo R. Zumwalt's account of the crisis: Washington Post, July 28, 1975, and Denver Post, February 15, 1975. "If we had to go to war with the Soviets in the Eastern Mediterranean we would have been defeated..."

(292) Cairo Press Review, December 13, 1973.

(293) FBIS, January 7, 1974; An-Nahar Arab Report, December 22, 1973.

Originally al-Sadat gave the fact that Shadhili had suffered a nervous breakdown over the events of the Israeli crossing (a story remarkably similar to one circulating in Israel about a breakdown on the part of Dayan). Later this was changed to a story that Ahmad Isma'il and Shadhili had been personal enemies since the time of the Congo crisis in 1960, al-Sadat, Memoirs in October, July 10, 1977, pp. 19ff., FBIS, July 15, 1977; Heikal, Ramadan, pp. 185-186.

However, in addition to some very practical political considerations there were two military factors: (a) Shadhili refused to work within the framework of the conservative military strategy laid down by al-Sadat; and much more importantly, (b) Shadhili appears to have been responsible for an order stripping Egyptian missile sites of their ground defenses, in order to use these extra ground forces in the Egyptian attacks of the 14th. The consequence was that when the Israelis crossed the Canal, these sites which ordinarily would have been defended against attack were left with no defenses.

Shadhili was given the post of Ambassador to Great Britain and later shifted to Ambassador to Portugal. However, he continued to criticize Egyptian military conduct of the October War: (a) the war should have been continued because the original strategy called for a long war of attrition, the "longer the war continued, the enemy would be forced to go on its knees"; (b) the Soviets did play a major role, "We won the battle with Soviet weapons. The weapons in our hands were 100 percent Soviet"; (c) "al-Sadat made a major mistake in alienating the Soviets, 'Since you say that the Soviet Union cannot be dispensed with, where is the logic in the Egyptian campaigns against the Soviet Union?' Shadhili replied, 'The logic is with Kissinger'..." (Interview in al-Safir, August 22, 1974).

PARTIAL CHRONOLOGY

October 6:   Large scale fighting breaks out between Egypt in the Sinai, Syria in the Golan Heights, and Israel at 1:30 P.M. Each side accuses the other of beginning the war. Naval, ground, air battles take place. Egypt crosses the Suez Canal; Egyptian communique says Egypt destroyed 27 Israeli planes, 60 tanks, 15 fortified positions, and took several prisoners; it said Egypt lost 15 planes and some helicopters. Syria says it has pierced through the Golan Heights ceasefire line; claims to have destroyed 10 planes, 6 vessels; says Mount Hermon is taken. King Husayn holds emergency meeting, puts forces on alert; Iraq says it has 12 aircraft stationed in Egypt; Moroccan forces fighting alongside Syrians; Algeria promises resources and support; Lebanon says armed forces have orders to repel aggression; Palestinians say forces have joined Syrians.

October 7:   Egyptian troops continue pouring into the Sinai over Suez bridges; 30 Israeli planes said shot down, 32 tanks destroyed. Syrian ground forces still engaged in fierce fighting; 43 Israeli planes said shot down, 9 pilots captured. Jordan said to be under great Arab pressure to join battle. Iraq calls up reservists, nationalizes two United States oil companies as start of "oil war," invites Iran to resume diplomatic relations. Algeria says forces have arrived in Egypt. Tunis, Bourguiba says, sending forces to front. Morocco, Hasan says, will send reinforcements to Syria. Commandos say they are engaging enemy on all fronts. Libya says they will send money, other Arab governments send messages of support.

October 8:   Israeli massive air strikes on Syria; Syrians say
                 attempts to shell air bases foiled; Syrians say 35 planes
                 shot down, 6 pilots captured; says forces are advancing
                 to al-Qunaytira in Golan; Russian added to languages
                 used in addressing messages to Israeli military and
                 civilian personnel asking them to surrender. Naval,
                 land and air battles in the Sinai; Cairo carries
                 interviews on TV with prisoners of war; Egypt captures
                 towns of al-Kantara, al-Sharqiya, sets fire to Bala' oil
                 fields. Israel claims to have destroyed all Egyptian
                 bridges on Suez; raids civilian targets in Port Said;
                 claims to have driven Syrians back in Golan. Jordan
                 shoots down two Israeli planes which violated airspace.
                 Iraq pleased with Iran favorable reply. Saudi forces
                 placed on alert; Faysal sends messages to al-Sadat, al-
                 Asad, Husayn. UN meets for two hours, adjourns
                 without setting date for future meeting. Nixon holds
                 contacts with Brezhnev.

October 9:   Egypt captures Bar-Lev line, destroys Israeli tank
                 brigade no. 190, captures commander. Damascus
                 attacked by Israeli planes, civilian targets hit, hun-
                 dreds of casualties including diplomats, Soviet Cultural
                 Center hit. Homs also attacked. Syrians say they shot
                 down 23 planes, captured 5 pilots; say forces have
                 encircled al-Qunaytira.   Baruk radar station in
                 Lebanon destroyed by Israelis; Israelis claim to have
                 recovered all of Golan. Iraqi forces said to have
                 arrived in Syria. Saudi Arabia calls back officers and
                 soldiers on leave. Kuwayt places armed forces under
                 Syrian-Egyptian command, calls for meeting of oil
                 producers to discuss role of Arab oil in war. Brezhnev
                 says rest of Arab states should not leave Egypt and
                 Syria alone.

October 10:   Homs, Tartus and Latakia attacked by Israeli aircraft;
                 in naval battle Syria says 8 Israeli boats sunk. Israel
                 said to be concentrating on Syria, Syria says 43 Israeli
                 planes shot down; says that newsmen are being barred
                 by Israel from visiting the front. In Sinai, Egypt said
                 to be consolidating positions, says they have captured
                 Israeli prisoners, tanks.   Large scale tank battle
                 begins. Libya agrees to Kuwayti call for Arab oil
                 producers meeting. Jordan: Royal decree orders full
                 mobilization, calls reservists. Iraq says they made 80
                 sorties against Israeli planes on both Syrian and
                 Egyptian fronts in past 2 days. United States, Meir
                 accuse Soviet Union of airlifting weapons to Egypt,
                 Syria. United States accused of same by Arabs.

October 11:   Massive air raids on Syria by Israel, Syria reports as
                many as 93 enemy planes shot down. Syria says
                checked enemy counteroffensive in north of front,
                destroyed 61 tanks. Naval battle goes on. Large scale
                tank battle in Sinai continues. Egypt says it has won
                and completely destroyed enemy tanks - 25 tanks and
                half-tracks. Egyptian planes attack Israeli positions in
                the Sinai. Israeli planes attack Egyptian positions in
                front and interior, but Egypt says attempt foiled.
                Shadhili says that half Israeli tank force in Sinai has
                been destroyed. Cairo says that United States
                Phantoms from aircraft carrier in Mediterrannean
                strafed Egyptian positions. Arabs boycott Israel.
                Office warns foreign airlines against carrying foreign
                soldiers, military experts, and airmen to Israel,
                threatens boycott. Waldheim issues appeal to end
                Middle East hostilities. Abba Eban says Israel willing
                to accept ceasefire based on pre-October 6 positions.
                Faysal said to have sent urgent message to Nixon.

October 12:   Syria says it has checked Israeli advance into its
                territory. Israel announces that their troops clashed
                with Iraqi forces, and widening breakthrough against
                Syria on road to Damascus. Egypt says shot down 12
                jets, 3 helicopters in Israeli raids on Port Said.
                Commandos say destroyed Israeli heliport on the Huleh
                plain.

October 13:   Jordan takes part in fighting by sending troops to
                Syria. Israel claims to be moving towards Damascus;
                Syria says forces mounted counterattack and forced
                Israelis back. Last Israeli stronghold north of Gulf of
                Suez surrenders to Egypt. Faysal said to have offered
                $1 billion to help Syria in war effort, said to have sent
                message to Nixon threatening to break off diplomatic
                relations and discontinue flow of oil. Egypt lodges
                formal complaint with United States over 2 reconnais-
                sance planes flying over Egypt. Meir says Israel will
                be ready for ceasefire if offered.

October 14:   Main burden of war switches to Sinai as Egypt mounts
                a large scale offensive along the whole front to
                remove pressure off Syria; Egypt says destroyed 150
                enemy tanks, shot down 44 planes. Dayan claims that
                Syrian armed forces defeated and licking wounds, but
                Syrians report that repulsed an Israeli attack in north,
                and counterattacked in north, central, and southern
                part of front. Saudi Arabia says sending forces to
                Syrian front. Tunis, Algeria say they are resuming
                diplomatic relations with Jordan after Husayn decided
                to send troops to Syrian front. Israel says only 655

killed since war; Brigadier-General Abraham Mendler, Commander of Israeli armored corps in Sinai, killed.

October 15:
Syria says they pushed Israeli troops back, and shelling Israeli positions in Huleh and Tiberias valley. Egypt said consolidating positions, striking at Israeli rear position on Mediterrannean. Iraq, Iran resume diplomatic relations. United States intervenes, admits airlifting supplies to Israel; Nixon said United States will not allow Israel's security to be jeopardized; sharp Arab reaction, but feeling dominates that neither new arms or threats will stop Arabs from fighting. Soviet Union assures Arabs at visit in Moscow by Boumedienne that it is determined to help in liberation of Arab territory occupied by Israel in 1967.

October 16:
Syria, Iraq launch offensive in the northern sector of front, report having destroyed 80 tanks. Egypt reports heavy fighting on East side of Canal. Israel says commando task force has landed on West side of Canal, and attacking military bases; Egypt said task force consisted of seven tanks, three of which were destroyed, and others dispersed. Sadat speech: outlines five point peace plan on basis of complete Israeli withdrawal from occupied lands in 1967, then international peace conference at United Nations. Meir speech: will not accept ceasefire before Arab armies broken. Gulf states raise oil prices by 17 percent at meeting in Kuwayt after inconclusive meeting in Vienna between companies and producers.

October 17:
Weight of war shifts to Suez front as tanks and armored troops fight in central sector of front; Egypt says inflicted heavy losses; Israel says destroyed 100 Egyptian tanks. Arab oil ministers meeting in Kuwayt decide to cut oil production by 5 percent on a monthly basis until Israel withdraws from occupied territories, and rights of Palestinians are insured. Four Arab foreign ministers - Saudi Arabia, Kuwayt, Algeria, Morocco - meet Nixon and Kissinger; said to have told United States President about expected reaction in Arab world on United States supplies to Israel. Israelis blow up Lebanese communications, damaging marine cable between Beirut and Marseilles.

October 18:
Fierce tank battle rages in central sector of Sinai front; Israelis push forces to West side of Canal to reinforce task force sent Tuesday. Egypt says its forces have encircled "infiltrating forces" and destroyed them. Dayan says task force will remain till end of war. Syrians say knocked out 30 tanks, 2 missile sites and several armored vehicles during

fighting. Syrians said to have pushed Israelis back several miles. Kosygin visits Egypt, said to be on peace mission. Saudi Arabia cuts production by 10 percent, Abu Dhabi discontinues oil shipments to US.

October 19:   Egypt engages Israeli task force on West Bank of Suez Canal; Syrian forces hit Israeli positions in Golan. Libya cuts oil supplies to United States, doubles oil prices.

October 20:   Kissinger leaves for Moscow for talks on how to establish ceasefire. Egypt fights Israeli task force on West Bank; Egypt says has destroyed 85 tanks, 56 halftracks, 15 planes in central sector of Suez front. Syria raids oil refinery in Haifa; fierce fighting on front but no advances mentioned. Saudi Arabia announces suspension of oil exports to United States; Algeria cuts oil supplies to United States, Holland, for support of Israel.

October 21:   Security Council issues resolution 338 calling for immediate ceasefire, implementation of UN 242 resolution and negotiations between Israel, Arabs. Israel accepts on conditions that ceasefire apply to all forces involved, freedom of navigation ensured, and exchange of prisoners. Egypt and Syria do not reply. Egyptian front: fierce fighting; Egypt says it has checked Israeli thrust on West Bank; Israel said to be holding three bridgeheads. Syrian front: fierce fighting; Israel tries to recapture outpost on Mount Hermon which Syrians occupied in first week of war; hand to hand fighting in progress. Kuwayt, Bahrayn cut oil supplies to United States, completing number of Arab oil producing states to do so. Arab states cutting oil to United States at this time are: Saudi Arabia, Iraq, Algeria, Qatar, Kuwayt, Bahrayn, Abu Dhabi, Dubai. Iraq seizes Dutch assets in Basra Petroleum Company in protest against support for Israel. Arab League calls for boycott of Holland.

October 22:   Egypt accepts ceasefire, Syria considering it; Arab reaction: disappointment, rejection of ceasefire. Jordan accepts ceasefire; Iraq, Libya, Palestinian commandos reject. Syrian front: continued fierce fighting to control tops of Mount Hermon. Egyptian front: ceasefire goes into effect at 1552 GMT, Egypt denies Israeli allegations of ceasefire violations. Sadat sends envoys to Arab countries to explain position, said received assurances from Brezhnev. Kosygin said to be in Cairo for talks. Kissinger in Israel for talks. Arab Chambers of Commerce meet, support measures

	taken by Arab states against United States, Holland, suggest gradual boycott of United States goods.

October 23:   Syria still considering ceasefire, United Nations resolution. First ceasefire breaks down on Egyptian front; Security Council repeats call for ceasefire. Israel, Egypt, accuse each other of breaking ceasefire. Fierce fighting on west bank of canal as Egypt says reacting to Israel's attempt to move further in. Egypt mobilizes popular resistance forces. Fierce fighting on Syrian front as Syrians intercept 60 Israeli aircraft over Damascus, intercept Israeli boats attacking Latakia, Banias. Israel blames Lebanon for commando action across Lebanese border. Ethiopia breaks ties with Israel.

October 24:   Egypt accuses Israel of continuing to violate ceasefire, trying to storm town of Suez; Israel claims to have encircled Egyptian Third Army.. Sadat asks for dispatch of United States–Soviet troops to Middle East to ensure ceasefire; United States refuses, hopes Russia will do same; Russia not too enthusiastic about suggestion. Morocco rejects ceasefire; Syria accepts it.

October 25:   United States places bases all over world in state of alert after reported moves by Soviet forces and after Russia allegedly said it will intervene to ensure ceasefire. Non-aligned nations draft resolution endorsed by United Nations Security Council; United Nations to send emergency force to Middle East to enforce ceasefire. Cairo welcomes decision; Meir says Israel has been "saved" from serious Soviet threat. Israel said to have repeated violations of ceasefire and efforts to move further in west bank and to bring in reinforcements. Egypt says Israel has cut road between Suez and Cairo and refuses to allow United Nations observers to be stationed there. More Arab criticism of ceasefire.

Source: Arab World Weekly, October 13, 1973; October 20, 1973; October 27, 1973.

Chapter 7

(1) For a series of discussions on how to cope with this problem, including a specific application of forecasting methodology to Middle Eastern conflicts, see: Richards J. Heuer, Jr., ed., Quantitative Approaches to Political Intelligence: The CIA Experience (Boulder, Colo.: Westview Press, 1978).

(2) Patai, pp. 96ff.

(3) Blechman, Benjamin Beit-Hallami, "Some Psychosocial and Cultural Factors in the Arab-Israeli Conflict: A Review of the Literature," pp. 269-280: An Arab intellectual quoted in Time, October 29, 1973, p. 29, described the Arab reaction to these Israeli raids: "No Westerner can fully understand the sense of peril we felt after 1967...."

(4) Dawn, October 23, 1973.

(5) Speech to People's Assembly, October 16, 1973, al-Ahram, October 17, 1973; compare with the Time, October 29, 1973, p. 29, version. The Egyptians set up a war trophies exhibit in al-Jazira amid much fanfare. Both Egypt and Syria have produced official battle films, and the Egyptians have come forth with a romanticized version, The Bullet is Still in My Pocket, which is said to be financially, if not artistically, successful. At one point in his memoirs al-Sadat muses on the artistic necessity for making a large scale film of the canal crossing: something on the order of The Longest Day, with Omar Sharif in one of the title roles.

(6) Al-Ahram, November 18, 1973.

(7) Faysal's message to the Egyptian people, Radio Cairo, August 7, 1974, in FBIS, August 8, 1974.

(8) Al-Ahram, November 18, 1974.

(9) A Syrian tank commander quoted in the Egyptian Gazette, October 31, 1973.

(10) FBIS, September 17, 1974.

(11) Al-Ahram, November 18, 1973.

(12) His comments are summarized in FBIS, August 22, 1974.

(13) FBIS, October 11, 1974. Other Egyptian officials have suggested that the United States involvement was more direct than resupply of materiel. Egyptian pilots, for example, claim that they were engaging better pilots during the last days of the war: "These Phantom pilots we met after October 17, had a much different style to their combat tactics that we never encountered with the Israelis....Whether they were volunteer reservists or regular United States military pilots we don't know, but they certainly were not Israelis...." (Aviation Week, June 30, 1975, p. 15). Arab media carried some stories to the effect that the Israelis were advertising for foreign volunteers; and there was some play given to a story that the Israelis went out of their way to recover one particular pilot, to the extent of sending in an airborne commando team, plus some supporting units. Cf: Aviation Week, July 7, 1975, p. 20, for comments. The Egyptians averred that this pilot was an American; but he could have been equally a high ranking Israeli officer.

(14) <u>FBIS</u>, August 30, 1974.

(15) <u>FBIS</u>, September 30, 1974.

(16) Kamal abu al-Majd in <u>FBIS</u>, September 24, 1974.

(17) Cf. <u>Aviation Week</u>, July 31, 1975, pp. 49-53.

(18) Ghassan Tueni, "After October: Military Conflict and Political Change in the Middle East," <u>Journal of Palestine Studies</u> 3, no. 4 (Summer 1974): 127.

(19) Ahmad Isma'il in <u>al-Ahram</u>, November 18, 1973.

(20) Ashkar.

(21) Al-Sadat <u>Speech to the ASU</u> on September 28, 1974, in <u>FBIS</u>, September 30, 1974; interview in the <u>London Times</u>, June 4, 1976, for same comments.

(22) Ashkar.

(23) Ibid.

(24) <u>Al-Ahram</u>, November 18, 1973.

(25) Cf: Rosen and Indyk, on the determinants of Arab decisions preempt; de Rivera, pp. 65ff, on projection of future situations and the generation of forced consensus by the pressure of events: the events of 1973, especially toward the end of the summar appeared to have generated such a forced consensus. Cf. Heikel, <u>Ramadan</u>, pp. 24ff, toward the last Arab decision makers operated in a near panic that the Israelis were going to preempt them.

(26) <u>FBIS</u>, September 12, 1973.

(27) <u>Christian Science Monitor</u>, October 10, 1973.

(28) <u>FBIS</u>, October 11, 1974.

(29) Ibid.

(30) de Rivera.

(31) J.C. Hurewitz, <u>Middle Eastern Politics: The Military Dimension</u> (New York: Praeger, 1969), pp. 28-46, makes this argument most persuasively.

(32) Al-Sadat interview in <u>al-Hawadith</u>, April 26, 1974.

(33) Al-Sadat interview in <u>Ruz al-Yusuf</u>, translated in <u>FBIS</u>, September 23, 1974.

(34) Richard L. Crump, "The October War: A Postwar Reassessment," <u>Military Review</u> 54, 8 (August 1974): 12-26.

(35) Geoffrey Kemp, <u>Arms and Security: The Egypt-Israel Case</u>, Adelphi Papers, no. 52 (London: International Institute for Strategic Studies, 1968), p. 14.

(36) Cf. United States Army Command and General Staff College, for details.

(37) The equipment used by the Egyptians in the attack was standard Soviet river crossing equipment, with some Egyptian modifications. See Eugene D. Betit, "River Crossing: Key to Soviet Offense," Military Review 51, no. 10 (October 1971): 88-96, for a description.

(38) The use of high-pressure water hoses to clear embankments was developed in the course of constructing the Aswan Dam.

(38) See: Reinhard Bendix, Nation Building and Citizenship: Studies of Our Changing Social Order (New York: John Wiley and Sons, Inc., 1964), for this argument in terms of political acculturation; also: Bronislaw Malinowski, The Dynamics of Culture Change (New Haven: Yale University Press, 1961), for an anthropolotical perspective.

(40) See T.N. Dupuy, "The War of Ramadan: An Arab Perspective of the October War," Army 25: .3 (March 1975): 13-23; S.L.A. Marshall, "Tank Warrior in the Golan," Military Review 56: 1 (January 1976): 3-12; Charles Wakebridge, "The Syrian Side of the Hill," Military Review 56: 2 (February 1976): 20-30, for Western accounts of how well Arab troops performed.

(41) Aviation Week, June 30, 1975, on the Egyptian Air Force.

(42) Aviation Week, December 10, 1973; Martin J. Miller, Jr., "The Israeli Navy: 26 Years of Non-peace," U.S. Naval Institute Proceedings 101: 2 (February 1975): 48-54, on the naval war.

(43) There is of course a considerable literature on guerrilla warfare: J. Boyer Bell, The Myth of the Guerrilla: Revolutionary Theory and Malpractice, (New York: Alfred A. Knopf, 1971); Frantz Fanon, The Wretched of the Earth (New York: Grove Press, 1968); Vo Nguyen Giap, People's War, People's Army (New York: Praeger, 1962); Mao Tse-tung, On Guerrilla Warefare (New York: Frederick A. Praeger, 1966); Andrew R. Molnar, Undergrounds in Insurgent, Revolutionary and Resistance Warfare (Washington: The American University, 1963); Franklin Mark Osanka, Modern Guerrilla Warfare (Glencoe: The Free Press of Glencoe, 1962).

(44) For a Western assessment of the advantages and disadvantages of Egyptian tactics see: Charles Wakebridge, "A Tank Myth or a Missile Mirage?," Military Review 56: 8 (August 1976): 3-11.

(45) Ahmad Isma'il in al-Ahram.

(46) See the comments of Edward Luttwak and Dan Horowitz, The Israeli Army (New York: Harper & Row, Publishers, 1975), pp. 287-89; 359-69.

(47) Ahmad Isma'il.

(48) FBIS, October 11, 1974.

(49) Chief of Staff Gur was especially sensitive to the necessity of keeping Israeli military technology sufficiently far ahead of Arab technology to avoid the Arab numbers strategy:

"Of course a certain grasp of balance of forces can turn into a concept, and we must guard against this exactly as we must be on our guard against any concept. The State of Israel was indeed for many years cast in the mold of 3 to 1 but, objectively, it was not always 3 to 1 and quite often it was better - in our favor. Secondly, there is importance in an absolute number too. If in all the Arab countries together - the confrontation countries with the second-line countries (such as Libya or Saudi Arabia) - there are close to 9,000 tanks, this is an enormous absolute number.

So it is clear that we have to check the absolute numbers, their quality, the speed of their introduction into the battle and the territory on which all these systems will be expressed. That is, we are not satisfied with mechanical checking of numbers, but of the whole system of forces and so there is a very serious influence on the comprehensive grasp of the balance of forces.

...What, in my view, will be our advantages? We will have sophisticated people with sophisticated weapons systems, while the enemy will have sophisticated systems but people who are less sophisticated. In this way our quality will be kept above that of the enemy and this is of prime significance..."

In this context, Arab strategists have been quite concerned to create a wholly Arab technological base from which to generate sophisticated weaponry. An Arab Organization for War Industries has been created. Its membership consists of representatives from Egypt, Saudi Arabia, Qatar and the United Arab Emirates (UAE). The goals of this organization are to "produce sophisticated weapons which the war factories of the four member-countries are not yet producing." Whether this effort will be successful or not is uncertain; but the fact that an effort is being made is of considerable importance.

(50) Cf. Robert J. Pranger and Dale R. Tahtinen, Implications of the 1976 Arab-Israeli Military Status (Washington: American Enterprise Institute, 1976), for an overview of this strategy. See also Anthony H. Cordesman, "How Much is Too Much?" Armed Forces Journal, December 1977, pp. 17-21, arguing that Arab governments have closed the technological gap also Irvine J. Cohen, "Israeli Defense Capability," National Defense, January-February 1976, pp. 271-73; "Can the Arabs Go to War?" The Middle East, March 1977, pp. 23-25.

But Israeli analysts are equally aware that the Arabs are capable of developing a long-range bombardment capability. Lack of this capability, i.e., the absence of long range missiles other than a few Scuds and Frogs, and the relatively short range of available aircraft,

effectively prevented much bombardment in the October War. For
Israeli concerns about this possibility see Uri Bailer, "Thinking the
Unthinkable: The Possibilities of Strategic Bombing Against Israel,"
RUSI 122, no. 4 (December 1977): 65-71, and the comments of Chief
of Staff Gurr, interview in YEDI'OT AHARONOT, October 4, 1975,
supplement, pp. 1ff., FBIS, October 8, 1975; "There are very many
targets which ground to ground missiles can reach without
endangering people....It depends upon the kind of war and on its total
scope. In the Yom Kippur War, for example, the Syrians tried to hit
the Ramat David airfield, with Frog missiles and they hit civilian
settlements....Our operational assumption is that they (sic: the
Arabs) will attempt to hit any sensitive targets with missiles...."

(51) Israeli nuclear capabilities have been the subject of some debate
within and without the Middle East. See: Fuad Jabber, "Israel's
Nuclear Options," Journal of Palestine Studies 1, 1 (Autumn 1971):
21-38; J. Boyer Bell, "Israel's Nuclear Option," The Middle East
Journal 26: 4 (Autumn, 1972): 379-88; Shlomo Aronson, "Nucleariza-
tion of the Middle East," The Jerusalem Quarterly, no. 2, (Winter
1977), pp. 27-46; Cordesman, on the number of nuclear weapons said
to be in Israeli hands; and Robert Pranger and Dale R. Tahtinen,
Nuclear Threat in the Middle East (Washington: American
Enterprise Institute, 1975). See also: Robert W. Tucker, "Israel and
the United States: From Dependence to Nuclear Weapons,"
Commentary 60, no. 5 (November 1975): 29-43, for the argument
that the Israelis should openly deploy nuclear weapons; Nadav
Safran, "Israel's American Connection," The Jerusalem Quarterly,
no. 4, (Summer 1977), pp. 3-30, for the rejoinder that this would
destabilize the Middle East; and Robert E. Harkavy, Spectre of a
Middle Eastern Holocaust: The Strategic and Diplomatic Implications of the Israeli Nuclear Weapons Program (Denver: University of
Denver Monograph Series, 1977), for an especially gloomy projection
of nuclear scenarios.   Al-Jamasi stated that if Israel acquired
nuclear weapons, the Egyptians would make every effort to do so
also (Interview in al-Madina, December 7, 1976, FBIS, December 7,
1976).   Al-Sadat underscored this warning with one of his own,
asserting that if the Israelis employed nuclear weapons against
Egyptian targets, the Egyptians would hit the heavily populated
areas in the Tel Aviv, Jerusalem, Haifa triangle (Daily Telegraph,
July 13, 1977). Al-Asad visited India in April 1978 amid speculation
that he was asking for Indian aid in developing nuclear weapons.

(52) Cf: Heikal, "Egyptian Foreign Policy," Foreign Affairs, 56, no. 4,
(July 1978): 714-27, for an analysis of Egyptian strategies in the
context of linkage between Western defensive systems and intra-
Arab politics.

(53) Cf: Saad E. Ibrahim, "Arab Images of the United States and Soviet
Union Before and After the June War," Journal of Conflict
Resolution 16:2, (June 1972): 227-40.

(54) Cf: George Lenczowski, Soviet Advances in the Middle East (American Enterprise Institute, 1971); Winfred Joshua, Soviet Penetration into the Middle East, National Strategy Information Center, no. 4, 1971; Robert E. Hunter, The Soviet Dilemma in the Middle East, part I: Problems of Commitment; part II: Oil and the Persian Gulf, Adelphi Papers, nos. 59-60, September-October 1969.

(55) Arab World Weekly, December 4, 1967.

(56) McLane, pp. 8ff.

(57) Tueyni, p. 118.

(58) William B. Quandt, United States Policy in the Middle East: Constraints and Choices (Santa Monica: RAND, 1970), pp. 45ff.

(59) An-Nahar Arab Report, August 3, 1970.

(60) See: Quandt, Decisions, pp. 271ff., for a summary of these negotiations, and the reactions to the arms package.

(61) Arab World Weekly, February 26, 1972.

(62) Tom Little, "The New Arab Extremists: A View From the Arab World, Conflict Studies, no. 4, May 1970, p. 19.

(63) A.S. Becker and A.L. Horelick, Soviet Policy in the Middle East, (Santa Monica: RAND, 1970), pp. 63-64.

(64) Ibid., pp. 65-66.

(65) Ibid., pp. 79-80.

(66) Ibid., p. 82.

(67) Ibid., Arab World Weekly, July 29, 1974 has a similar analysis of the differences between Russia and the Arabs: Strategic disagreements over how far Russia should go in supporting its Arab clients; ideological differences between Scientific Socialism and Arab nationalisms.

(68) Little, "New Arab Extremists."

(69) An-Nahar Arab Report, October 1, 1973.

(70) An-Nahar Arab Report, January 28, 1974. A conference of national liberation movements was held in Baghdad at the PLO HQ in early 1974, the list of delegations gives some clue to Russian designs:

--The Palestinian Revolutionary Committee
--The Iranian National Front
--The Popular Front for the Liberation of Ahvaz (Iran)
--The Front for the Liberation of Chad (FROLINAT)
--The United Front for the Liberation of Western Somalia
--The Front for the Liberation of Eritrea (ELF)
--The Kurdistan Democratic Party in Iran
--The Popular Front for the Liberation of Baluchistan

For overviews of insurgent activities, Cf.: Mordechai Abir, "Red Sea Politics," in Conflicts in Africa, Adelphi Papers, No. 93, December 1972, pp. 25-41; Christopher Clapham, "Ethiopia and Somalia," in ibid., pp. 1-74; J. Boyer Bell, "South Arabia; Violence and Revolt," Conflict Studies, No. 40, November 1973. Iraqi sponsorship of insurgents in the Gulf of Iran is of considerable concern to the Iranians.

By 1978, the Iraqi sponsorship of terrorist groups foreshadowed by this meeting had come to fruition. According to a German source, European counter-terror agents had discovered documentary proof that many of the organizations which used to operate in Beirut were moving their headquarters to Baghdad, foremost among these, the PFLP General Command, and the remnants of Wadi' Haddad's group. In addition, Baghdad had been the headquarters for Black June, a BSO/Fatah splinter and the Arab Liberation Front. Further a number of non-Arab terrorists, Germans, Dutch, Japanese and South Americans also found refuge in Iraq. Iraqi support of these individuals and organizations was apparently varied and extensive: ranging from training them in scattered camps, to direct financial aid, to providing them with forged documents. Deutsche Zeitung, June 16, 1978, JPRS, July 27, 1978.

(71) An-Nahar Arab Report, October 7, 1974. Russia has apparently replaced China as the major power supporter of PFLOAG (now known as PFLO: Popular Front for the Liberation of Oman).

(72) An-Nahar Arab Report, July 29, 1974.

(73) An-Nahar Arab Report, August 12, 1974.

(74) The presence of large quantities of Soviet arms in Libya was one of the reasons which led to the July 1977 war. According to al-Sadat, Russia was "piling sophisticated weapons in Libya in order to export problems to the neighboring countries. I do not underestimate Libyan leader al-Qadhafi, because a snake no matter how small it may be is still dangerous. The role which al-Qadhafi is playing is bigger than him." October, September 11, 1977, excerpted in Arab Press Service, September 14, 1977.

(75) The same analysis is contained in an-Nahar Arab Report, June 16, 1976. These arms have been apparently used in Lebanon, Angola, the Sudan and Ethiopia. Soviet arms which went to Algeria similarly have been used in the western Sahara. Arab sources also claim that arms are being stockpiled in South Yemen, for use against Arabian peninsula states (Arab Press Service, August 7, 1978). According to Akhir Sa'a, July 5, 1978, there are about 1500 Cubans in Aden, Libya, and Algeria; some 200 in Palestinian camps in Lebanon, and 250 in Syria. Avigdor Haselkorn is one of the more vigorous Western exponents of the theory that the Soviets are building up an arms infrastructure which will give them a capability of deploying force anywhere in Africa and the Middle East. See his comments in U.S.

Senate Committee on Foreign Relations, Subcommittee on Near Eastern and South Asian Affairs, Central Influences and Pressures at Work in Middle East Area, Washington: GPO, 1977, and The Evolution of Soviet Security Strategy, 1965-1975, National Strategy Information Center, Inc. (New York: Crane, Russak & Company, Inc., 1978).

(76) An-Nahar Arab Report, July 15, 1974; August 12, 1974.

(77) An-Nahar Arab Report, September 23, 1974.

(78) Al-Anba' (Kuwayt) gave the figures for Soviets, East Germans and Cubans in the PDRY as about 6,000 total (Al-Anba', June 28, 1978, FBIS, June 28, 1978). See also: Peter Vanneman and Martin James, "Soviet Thrust into the Horn of Africa: The Next Targets," Strategic Review 6: 2 (Spring 1978):   33-40, and the literature therein cited. Vanneman and James argue that the Soviet position in Ethiopia gives them a bridgehead from which to put pressure on Saudi Arabia, Kenya and to threaten Western shipping through the Red Sea.

(79) Al-Ahram, June 28, 1978, FBIS, June 28, 1978, claimed that Rubayyi' 'Ali found out about the assassination and attempted to warn al-Ghashmi. Al-Anba', June 28, 1978, reported that another 500 Cubans were sent to the PDRY to reinforce forces already adjoining the leftists. See also An-Nahar Arab Report and Memo, July 17, 1978 and David Hirst, "Moscow's Foothold in the Sand," The Guardian. September 10, 1978.

The situation in North Yemen is not less unstable than that in South Yemen.   Al-Ghashmi himself had taken over following the assassination of Ibrahim al-Hamdi in October 1977. Al-Hamdi had led a 1974 coup that installed a relatively conservative, and pro-Saudi, military government.   Both al-Hamdi and al-Ghashmi had adopted a policy of close relations with Saudi Arabia and one of rapprochement with conservative Arab governments.   The regime, however, was (and is) engaged in a struggle to pacify separatist northern tribes who reject any attempts to extend the authority of the San'a government.

(80) About 3,000 of the estimated 17,000 Cubans in Ethiopia transited via South Yemen (Vannaman and James).

(81) An-Nahar Arab Report, September 23, 1974.

(82) Vanneman and James. According to Iraqi sources, Siddam Husayn Takriti warned the Soviets in 1977 that their attempt to keep both Somalia and Ethiopia as clients would lead to their expulsion from one or possibly both (Al-Thawra, August 16, 1977, FBIS, August 17, 1977).

(83) See The New York Times, November 14, 1977. Western sources initially saw this ouster as costing the Soviets a major foothold in the Red Sea/India Ocean, especially the naval facilities at Berbera

and Kismayu. However, the Arab and Israeli observers saw things differently. According to Israeli analysts the Soviet strategy in the Horn was not really set back by the expulsion from Somalia. The Soviet's began to actively back the Ethiopian drive to clear Somali forces from the Ogaden desert; and intensify relations with the PDRY. Here the port of Aden was apparently to replace the Somali port of Berbera as the center of Soviet naval operations. In spite of the loss of Somalia, Soviet ability to project power into Eastern Africa remained relatively undiminished. Middle-East Intelligence Survey, February 16-28, 1978.

(84) See Middle-East Intelligence Survey, September 16-30, 1977, for and analysis of the problems facing Somalia.

(85) An-Nahar Arab Report, February 25, 1974. There is considerable debate in U.S. circles as to the meaning of these Soviet moves in specific, and the strategic importance of the Horn of Africa in general. In addition to Vanneman and James, see J. Boyer Bell, The Horn of Africa: Strategic Magnet in the Seventies (New York: Crane, Russak & Company, Inc., 1973), who argues for the Horn's strategic importance. This argument is opposed by Tom Farrar, who feels that the Horn's importance has been overplayed. See Farrar's remarks in U.S. Senate, Committee on Foreign Affairs, Ethiopia and the Horn of Africa (Washington, GPO, 1976). In addition, the problem of Soviet intentions and influence is taken up in U.S. Senate, Committee on Foreign Relations, Angola (Washington: GPO, 1976).

(86) An-Nahar Arab Report, February 25, 1974.

(87) An-Nahar Arab Report, May 13, 1974; September 2, 1974.

(88) An-Nahar Arab Report, July 15, 1974.

(89) Ibid.: "Considerable postwar unrest has been manifest in Egypt: student demonstrations, working class riots, scuffles and fights at soccer matches and even at bus stops. Such domestic discontent could open the way for the pro-Moscow segment of the Egyptian left to act. In this connection, the Egyptian military is ideologically closer to the left than it is to the conservatives around al-Sadat. By withholding economic aid, Russia places al-Sadat in a position where he would be forced to either move toward socialist policies favored by the military and Russia and risk a rightwing coup, or continue with his 'liberalization' policies, thus retaining conservative support but risking a leftwing coup."

(90) An-Nahar Arab Report, September 9, 1974; according to an-Nahar, the matter of the Egyptian army's weapons' supply takes on increasingly important dimensions the closer Egypt gets to a possible settlement. "In the last few weeks of August/September, the pressure from the army has considerably increased. This has particularly been the case since the recent Israeli maneuvers in the Sinai desert and the practice mobilization carried out a fortnight

ago. Meetings of senior officers have been reported taking place outside the normal course of duty, while President Sadat, learning of such activities, seems to have preferred not to react. The declarations made by the ex-chief-of-staff and current ambassador to London, General Saaludin Shazli, have appeared in the Arabic press and caused a marked stir among army officers."

(91) An-Nahar Arab Report, October 7, 1974; September 9, 1974: "President Sadat has for some time envisaged Western Europe as a new source of weapons. Negotiations are even now in progress with the French for the purchase of fighter aircraft. But such a diversification of arms' supply poses two major problems. In the first place, since the Egyptian army has been traditionally - and almost exclusively - equipped with Soviet material, the purchase of arms from any other source implies retraining and adaptation. This will obviously take more time than the army things it has got."

(92) An-Nahar Arab Report, July 29, 1974.

(93) An-Nahar Arab Report, February 18, 1974: "The Shah himself considers that the Soviet Union is responsible for the potentially hostile encirclement of his country, by supporting India, hastening the scission of Pakistan, and extending aid to the new, pro-Moscow regime in Afghanistan. He feels that his eastern borders are so insecure as to warrant a permanent state of alert, and the presence of Iraq to the west is scarcely a comfort. The Iranians claim that a Soviet airbase has been set up in northern Iraq, and have complained on several occasions of overflights by Soviet MIG-25 aircraft. The April 27, 1978 coup in Afghanistan, of course, intensified this fear; and it has been one of the main reasons for Iranian cooperation with the Saudis and Egyptians." On the Shah's problems see: Patrick Sealey's comments in An-Nahar Arab Report and Memo, August 21, 1978, pp. 3-4.

Iranian/Arab cooperation took place on several levels. Diplomatically, Iran backed al-Sadat's peace initiative. In addition, the Iranians have supported Saudi efforts to organize an Islamic bloc (basically on the theory that such a bloc would counter the spread of radical nationalism in the Gulf). Militarily, Iranian forces have been operating against PFLO in Oman (and doing so in conjunction with Saudi, Egyptian and Jordanian contingents of varying sizes). The Iranians were also said to have concluded an agreement with the Egyptians whereby Iran would get naval facilities at Port Said. Arab Press Service, February 18, 1978.

Further, the Iranians are said to have offered to supply the Somalis with armor, personnel carriers, artillery, air defense equipment, aircraft and some patrol boats, as well as financing some of the costs of the war with Ethiopia (this in conjunction with the Saudis). Arab Press Service, November 28, 1977.

(94) Subcommittee on the Near East and South Asia, Means of Measuring Naval Power with Special Reference to U.S. and Soviet

Activities in the Indian Ocean (Washington, D.C.: U.S. Government Printing Office, 1974), Cf.: George Lenczowski, ed., United States Interests, pp. 97ff., for a more extended list of U.S. interests:

    (a) Security pledges; voluntary legal and political commitments to a variety of countries of the area.

    (b) Preservation of military presence: NATO, CENTO, Saudi Arabia, Bahrain, and the 6th Fleet.

    (c) Preservation of friendly regimes.

    (d) Prevention of the establishment of USSR satellites.

    (e) Protection of access to oil.

    (f) Continued access to air/sea routes in the area.

    (g) Preservation of cultural/educational interests.

(95) Huntley; Cf: also the comments made by an American Friends team after a two year fact finding mission in the area:

"At bottom, each side is filled with what seems to be absolute distrust of the other. The Israelis fear that the Arabs do not accept their existence, will not make peace with Israel, and could not be trusted to keep the peace if one were signed. The Arabs fear that the Israelis will not return any of the Arab lands now occupied and will, in time, demand more."

Search for Peace in the Middle East (Philadelphia, American Friends Service Committee, 1970), p. 70ff.

(96) During the course of the Jordanian civil war of September 1970, when Syrian armor and troops began a massive intervention into northern Jordan, both the U.S. and Israel were prepared to intervene. See: Hudson, Decade, pp. 115-123. In Lebanon, the Israelis were prepared to move when the Syrians began large-scale intervention in June 1976. In this case, the United States operated as an intermediary between the Israelis and Syrians to forestall a larger confrontation.

(97) Al-Asad himself was among those Syrian officers who engineered the breakup of the UAR in 1961.

(98) Al-Jamasi, for example, was quite blunt in asserting that Egypt would go to war if Israel attacked Syria. Interview in al-Madina, December 7, 1976, FBIS, December 8, 1976.

(99) See: Elie Kedourie, In the Anglo-Arab Labyrinth (Cambridge: Cambridge University Press, 1976) and Briton Cooper Busch, Britain, India and the Arabs, 1914-1921 (Berkeley: University of California Press, 1971), for details.

(100) The original statement of this thesis is in Antonious.

(101) Al-Akhbar, November 3, 1973.

(102) Excerpted in Arab World Weekly, April 6, 1974.

(103) The arms sale to Egypt and Saudi Arabia assumed a symbolic significance out of proportion to the actual numbers of aircraft involved: King Khalid himself made a personal appeal to President Carter (Washington Post, May 14, 1978).

(104) Cf. John C. Campbell, "The Mediterranean Crisis," Foreign Affairs 53: 4 (July 1975): 605-24, for this argument.

(105) MENA summary of al-Sadat's interview on Italian TV on June 21, 1978, July 24, 1978, FBIS, June 26, 1978.

(106) Al-Sadat interview in October, December 11, 1977, FBIS, December 13, 1977.

(107) Al-Sadat interview in al-Anwar excerpted in Arab World Weekly, April 6, 1974.

(108) Tueyni.

(109) An-Nahar Arab Report, October 8, 1973; Air Force Commanding Officer Naji Jamil was also considered part of the Saudi connection.

(110) Al-Sadat in FBIS, August 30, 1974.

(111) Al-Sadat in FBIS, October 11, 1974.

(112) Prisoner's dilemma is a two person non zero sum game. The situation is conceptually this: Two prisoners are accused of a variety of crimes; they are separated and therefore cannot communicate with one another. If they coordinate their alibis, they can go free; if one "sells out" the other, he goes free and his cohort serves a long sentence; if both confess, both serve intermediate sentences. The issue raised is whether a player can trust his cohort or not; and the most prudent strategy (although not the most optimal) is to go it alone, and sell out the cohort. See Rapoport, pp. 48-57, for a description. In terms of actual international relations situations, this means that leaders cannot opt for strategies which require some measure of trust, especially in situations characterized by latent or actual conflict; intra-Arab and Arab/Israeli relations are, of course, archetypal examples of this situation.

(113) Harkabi, Arab Attitudes, p. 459.

(114) Of course, the dramatic gesture is itself part of the Arab political style. See Harkabi's comments cited above.

(115) MENA summary, June 24, 1978, FBIS, June 26, 1978.

(116) Interview in October, December 11, 1977, FBIS, December 13, 1977.

(117) Ibid.

(118) MENA summary, June 24, 1978, FBIS, June 26, 1978.

(119) October, December 11, 1977, FBIS, December 13, 1977.

(120) MENA, June 24, 1978; FBIS, June 26, 1978.   On al-Sadat's combination of charisma and surprise see: A.I. Dawisha, Egypt in the Arab World: The Elements of Foreign Policy (New York: John Wiley and Sons, 1976), pp. 181ff.

(121) Binder.

(122) The concept of linkages is contained in James N. Rosenau, Linkage Politics: Essays on the Convergence of National and International Systems (New York: The Free Press, 1969). Formal linkage theory attempts to conceptualize and categorize patterns of interpenetration between variously defined systems of action.

(123) Susannah Tarbush, "Beirut: Syrian-Rightist Showdown," Arab Report and Record, July 1-15, 1978, pp. 478-480; Phalangist sources claim that their regular membership runs between 80 and 100,000, with their militia at between 10 and 25,000.   Sham'un's NLP is considerably smaller, but its militia, al-Numur (the Tigers) of between 3 and 6,000 is perhaps the best equipped of all Lebanese paramilitary organizations.   The late Tony Franjiya had set up a counter organization, the Zaghurta Liberation Army, which also fought under the name "Marada (Giants) Brigade."   See also: "Review of Militias in Lebanon," The Arab World Weekly, January 18, 1975.

(124) Tarbush, "Beirut."

(125) The Lebanese civil war is an evolution of preexisting primordial conflicts. These have their origin in French policies aimed at divide and rule in the 1920s. The tactic used was to carve up Syria into a number of autonomous regions, each region based on the geographical distribution of primordial groups; these could then be governed independently of each other, and the likelihood of some cross-boundary nationalist movement would be reduced.

This expanded territory included a number of primordial groups, Sunni and Shi'a Muslims, and various Christian sects   whose families   included   both   Muslims   and   Christians   and cross-cut   otherwise   unbridgeable   primordial   cleavages. A   system   of   patron-client   relationships   was grafted onto this family structure; and the net effect was to produce a politics of familialism and relative pragmatism. In 1943, these familial patterns were incorporated in the National Pact, which formally divided all Lebanese political offices among these groups, according to a numerical ratio based on the 1936 census.

Primordial tensions, however, began to increase in the 1940s and 1050s as a consequence of differential patterns of social mobilization: the Christian community became more westernized, while the Muslim community remained more traditional. In addition, Christian birthrate remained more or less static, while that of the Muslims climbed. Nevertheless, the division of offices and other benefits remained fixed. Tensions arising out of this increasingly unequal division led to the civil war of 1958.

The present (1975/78) conflict is both an outgrowth of these tensions and a consequence of the impact of Palestinian operations in Southern Lebanon. As a corollary to the Palestinian theory of using Arab countries surrounding Israel as bases, the Palestinians set up extensive fortifications in Southern Lebanon, especially in the al-'Arqub area. Attacks from these bases led to Israeli reprisals, which in turn led to a movement of Shi'a populations from the south into the area around Beirut. These added to already deteriorating relations between Christians and Muslims.

By 1975, Lebanon was rocked by a series of kidnappings carried out in a traditional manner, with each side selecting personages from the other side who were equal in status to the person originally kidnapped. This sort of warfare was socially and territorially confined to zones between primordial enclaves. By the middle of 1975, however, the tactics changed. No longer were selected persons kidnapped; instead random killing of opposing personnel became the tactic; later even this restraint was abandoned. A series of Christian and Muslim private armies were organized and a multi-sided fighting developed. By December 1975, Palestinian forces had become engaged, in what was now a full-fledged civil war, on the side of the Muslims. See Enver M. Koury, The Crisis in the Lebanese System (Washington: American Enterprise Institute, 1976); Michael C. Hudson, "The Lebanese Crisis: The Limits of Consociational Democracy," Journal of Palestine Studies, V:3-4 (Spring/Summer 1976), 109-122; and Paul H.B. Godwin and Lewis B. Ware, Linkage Politics and Coercive Diplomacy: A Comparative Analysis of the Two Lebanese Crises (Maxwell AFB: Air University, 1976), and the literature therein cited for details.

(126) Al-Asad clearly set forth Syrian aims in Lebanon on a number of occasions. In a delivery on April 12, 1976, he made it clear that Syria considered itself duty bound to interfere in the Lebanese fighting (excerpted in an-Nahar Arab Report, May 10, 1976). Following the invasion, al-Asad again reiterated Syrian aims:

In my opinion, if we ask them today, perhaps they will repeat the same words. At this point a person may ask: Why confuse Syria? How is Syria connected with events taking place in Lebanon?.... First, one of the objectives of the plot is to strike at an issue which is the issue of every citizen in this country. If the conspiracy has the aims I spoke about, including striking at the Palestinian resistance and partitioning Lebanon, how can Syria stand by as a spectator to a plot aimed at achieving these objectives?...

Secondly, through history, Syria and Lebanon have been one country and one people. The people in Syria and Lebanon have been one through history. Genuine joint interests ensued.... Close kinship between the people in the two countries also ensued. Many thousands of families in Syria have relatives in Lebanon. Many thousands of families in Lebanon have relatives in Syria....

The third result: A decisive military action in this way would open doors to every foreign intervention, particularly Israel's intervention. Let us all visualize the magnitude of the tragedy which might ensue if Israel were to intervene and save some Arabs from other Arabs. (Speech to Provincial Councils, July 20, 1976, FBIS, July 21, 1976).

(127) Cf. An interview with Syrian Ambassador to Great Britain, Adnan 'Umran, in Arab Report and Record, July 1-15, 1978, p. 480-481, for the Syrian argument that the Phalangists were planning to take over all of Lebanon.

(128) See Saul Friedlander and Raymond Cohen, "The Personality Correlate of Belligerence in International Conflict," Comparative Politics 7, 2 (June 1975): 155-86. Friedlander and Cohen's findings that Western decision makers who were notably belligerent in their foreign policies were characterized as having either authoritarian personalities or indulging in "compensatory masculinity" seems to accord with Arab decision making behavior.

(129) For theories of the international system which stress elite insecurity as one of the major factors in any escalatory process, see: Richard N. Rosecrance, Action and Reaction in World Politics: International Systems in Perspective (Boston: Little, Brown and Company, 1963); Raymond Aron, Peace and War: A Theory of International Relations (New York: Frederick A. Praeger, Publishers, 1967); Ernst B. Haas and Alan S. Whiting, Dynamics of International Relations (New York: McGraw-Hill, 1956); Quincy Wright, A Study of War (Chicago: University of Chicago Press, 1942); Jonathan Wilkenfeld, ed., Conflict Behavior and Linkage Politics (New York: David McKay Company, 1973); and Rudolph J. Rummel, Understanding Conflict and War, 2 vols., (New York: John Wiley and Sons, 1975/6), summarize the literature on international conflict.

(130) Harold D. Lasswell, World Politics and Personal Insecurity, reprinted in A Study of Power (Glencoe, Ill: The Free Press, 1950), p. 54.

(131) Entente membership currently consists of Egypt, Saudi Arabia, Jordan, Kuwayt, Sudan, North Yemen, Somalia, Morocco and Mauritania.

(132) Steadfastness Front members currently are Syria, Iraq, Libya, Algeria, the PLO, and South Yemen.

(133) See Bernard Lewis, "The Return of Islam," Commentary 61, 1 (January 1976): 39-49.

(134) In addition to taking part in antiregime rioting, most notably in January 1977, the Brethren and/or their offshoots have been involved in a number of acts of assassination and sabotage: one group, Jama'at al-Takfir al-Hijra (the Group for the Infidelization and the Emigration) was especially active and, among other acts, killed the Minister for Waqfs (religious endowments), Shaykh

Muhammad Husayn al-Dhahabi. Al-Ahram, November 23, 1976, FBIS, November 24, 1976. Another group, the Jihad Organization, emerged in 1977, al-Ahram, August 30, 1977.

(135) In February 1977, rioting broke out in Najaf and Karbala and then spread to other cities including Mosul. Iraqi sources claimed that Syrian agents were responsible.

(136) Seale, Struggle. In addition to existing tensions between Shi'a populations and their respective governments, the disappearance of Shi'a Imam Musa al-Sadr in September 1978, while enroute from Tripoli, Libya to Rome, and under mysterious circumstances, further inflamed shi'a sensibilities.

(137) Cf. An-Nahar Arab Report, February 24, 1975; March 10, 1975, and May 5, 1975, for background details. In addition to the more overt confrontation between Syrian and Iraqi forces and agents, the conflict also involved Kurdish populations. In this case because the Syrians purportedly began to supply Kurdish insurgents in Northern Iraq with arms.

(138) Cf. Arab Press Service, August 8, 1978. Black June is led by Sabri al-Banna (Abu Nidal) who was ejected from Fatah in 1974 after it was discovered that he had planned to kill a number of Fatah leaders. Black June operates out of Baghdad and has been responsible for a number of hijackings and, lately, assassinations. See: An-Nahar Arab Report, December 2, 1974, for details on Abu Nidal's split with Fatah.

(139) Cf. Arab Report and Record, July 16-31, 1977, for details.

(140) Cf. Arab Report and Record, July 1-15, 1978 and Arab Press Service, August 7, 1978, for details.

(141) Huntington, pp. 55ff.

(142) Al-Sadat in FBIS, August 30, 1974:

After the October 6 war, we received 300 million dollars, which saved our economy and breathed new life into us, and ever since then we have been drawing up a short-range plan which begins as of now and will last until 1975. This plan represents the second crossing, from economic bankruptcy and the exhaustion of all our utilities, to the second stage, during which we will begin developing our economy and utilities....

(143) Middle-East Intelligence Survey, January 16-31, 1977; Arab Report and Record, January 16-31, 1977.

(144) Janet Stevens, "Political Repression in Egypt," MERIP Reports, no. 66, pp. 18-20; The Manchester Guardian, January 21, 1977.

(145) An-Nahar Arab Report, July 29, 1974.

(146) Cf. the comments in the Syrian press: "Lt. General al-Shadhili explained in a categorical way the extent of the al-Sadat regime's

deviation from Egypt's domestic and foreign policy and its domestic and pan-Arab commitments. He likened al-Sadat's regime to the dictatorial regimes of Salazar and Franco..." (al-Bath, June 20, 1978, FBIS, June 20, 1978).

(147) Al-Dustur (London), August 7, 1978, FBIS, August 7, 1978.

(148) Al-Ra'y al-'Amm, October 7, 1978, FBIS, October 11, 1978. In addition, the new Minister of Defense, Kamal Hasan 'Ali, was significantly enough head of Egyptian internal security prior to his appointment.

(149) Cf. Arab Report and Record, September 16-30, 1977; and the comments of David Hirst in the Manchester Guardian, September 22, 1977.

(150) Middle-East Intelligence Survey, August 16-31, 1978. Jamil's brother was implicated in the abortive attempt on al-Asad's life in 1973. Additional conflict was added because of a Syrian film version of the October War: The film gave a prominent role to the Defense Brigades commanded by Rif'at. Violent objection to this portrayal was taken by a number of high ranking officers; as a consequence, the film was withdrawn from circulation (An-Nahar Arab Report, June 17, 1974).

(151) Middle-East Intelligence Survey.

(152) There were also reports of extensive arrests.

(153) Stories of splits in the Royal Family began circulating in November 1974 when there were reports of a revolt of National Guard officers (Middle East Monitor, November 15, 1974). See also the extensive analysis, "Saudi Arabia: A Super-Power in Many, But Not Military, Terms," Arab Press Service, June 26, 1978; Middle-East Intelligence Survey, August 16-31, 1978.

(154) Susannah Tarbush, "The Divided Front," Arab Report and Record, August 16-31, 1978, pp. 614-617.

(155) Arab Press Service, April 25, 1978. The most spectacular incident of intra-Palestinian violence was the blowing up of an apartment building housing the headquarters of the Palestine Liberation Front (PLF), a pro-Iraqi group. (Action, August 21, 1978).

(156) See Bernard Lewis, The Assassins: A Radical Sect in Islam (London: Weidenfeld and Nicolson, 1967).

(157) King Hussein I, Uneasy Lies the Head (New York: Bernard Geis Associates, 1961), p. 246.

(158) Africa Confidential, June 14, 1974, pp. 4-6.

(159) An-Nahar Arab Report, April 7, 1975.

(160) Arab Report and Record, March 16-31, 1977.

(161) Arab Press Service, September 14, 1977.

(162) Egyptian media carried stories about assassin training bases in Ethiopia and Aden, Akhir Sa'a, July 5, 1978. In addition there were stories about extensive plots to kill Palestinian leaders, Akhir Sa'a, June 21, 1978 - these in the context of a battle between PLO and Iraqi agents which resulted in shoot outs and attacks in major European cities, as well as murders in the Arab world.

(163) In terms of the extension of conflict, the contemporary Middle East resembles Stanley Hoffman's notion of a "revolutionary system." In this international system, the legal limitations on conflict largely disappear because the legal boundaries of the actors themselves are not defined. The consequence is a system where "the power and policies of states are directly involved in almost every aspect of international activity." The State of War: Essays on the Theory and Practice of International Politics (New York, 1965), p. 98.

(164) An Arab analysis of why the Israelis would want to hang onto the Sinai is offered by Elias Shoufani, "The Sinai Wedge," Journal of Palestine Studies 1, no. 3 (Spring 1972): 85-94. Shoufani stresses the reasons: (a) continued Israeli access to Sinai oil; (b) maintenance of an Israeli land buffer, splitting Egypt geographically from the rest of the Arab world.

(165) Text of the joint Syrian/Jordanian Agreement is in an-Nahar Arab Report, August 25 and September 1, 1975. Similarly, the Syrian extension of air defense missile systems into areas of Lebanon in the summer and fall of 1978 was an attempt to block an Israeli "left hook" against Syrian targets.

(166) Ibid.

(167) Both moves, of course, strengthened Syrian willingness to risk escalation. This is denied by the Libyans, but otherwise well documented. In addition to the sources already cited see: Heshayahu Ben-Porat, Eitan Haber and Zeev Schiff, Entebbe Rescue (New York: Dell Publishing Co., Inc., 1977); Brian M. Jenkins, International Terrorism: A Chronology, 1968-1974 (Santa Monica: RAND, 1975); Colin Smith, Carlos: Portrait of a Terrorist (New York: Holt, Rinehart and Winston, 1977); Peter Snow and David Phillips, The Arab Hijack War (New York, 1970); William Stevenson, 90 Minutes at Entebbe (New York: Bantam Books, 1976); Tom Weber, "The Strange Capital of World Terrorism," San Francisco Chronicle, October 9, 10, 11, 1978.

(168) See: Fuad Ajami, "Stress in the Arab Triangle," Foreign Policy, no. 29, Winter 1977-78, pp. 90-108.

(169) Pranger and Tahtinen, p. 2; also Rosen and Indyk.

(170) Ibid., pp. 4ff. In this connection, al-Jamasi has commented on the possibility of surprise: "Surprise can be realized a second, and even a third time, provided that we benefit from our previous experience. This time, we should take into our calculations that the enemy will

be more cautious and alert" (Interview in al-Musawar, January 10, 1975.

(171) Pranger and Tahtinen, pp. 11ff.

(172) For details see New York Times, March 12, 1978; Middle-East Intelligence Survey, March 16-31, 1978.

(173) PFLP Leader George Habash in an interview on U.S. television is quoted as saying: "(We) will do all we can to make America's present leadership pay the price for what it is doing at the present moment, against our national aims, our national rights..." (excerpted in the Baltimore Sun, September 22, 1978). To forestall possible Palestinian (and other) attempts on al-Sadat's life, the Israelis have detailed a special section of Israeli Intelligence to uncover assassination plots (San Francisco Examiner, October 3, 1978).

(174) An-Nahar Arab Report, October 7, 1974.

(175) Al-Nahar, September 11, 1974, FBIS, September 11, 1974; an-Nahar Arab Report, November 25, 1974.

(176) Chief of Staff Gur, interview in YEDI'OT AHARONOT, October 4, 1975, FBIS, October 8, 1975.

(177) Cf. Rowland Evans and Robert Novak, "Egypt: Rhetoric vs. Reality," Washington Post, February 22, 1975, p. 25; George Ball, "The Looming War in the Middle East and How to Avert It," The Atlantic Monthly, no. 235, January 1975, pp. 6-11.

(178) Cf. Robert W. Tucker, "Oil: The Issue of American Intervention," Commentary, 59:1 (January 1975): 21-31; Miles Ignotus, "Seizing Arab Oil," Harper's, March 1975, pp. 45-62; US House Committee on International Relations, Oil Fields As Military Objectives: A Feasibility Study (Washington: GPO, 1975).

(179) See Charles W. Cordry, "Israelis Consider Reprisal on Libya," Baltimore Sun, August 15, 1976, p. 1.

(180) Among others, see: "Fears for Safety of Arab Oil Reservoir," Arab Press Service, October 31, 1977, pp. 2-5; Jim Hoagland, "Israeli War Plan Readied if New Peace Effort Fails," Washington Post, October 26, 1977, and reprinted in The Link 10: 5 (Winter 1977-78).

(181) The "Qeniq Plan" said to have been written by Yisra'el Qenig, an Interior Ministry official, was published by Al Hamishmar, September 7, 1976, FBIS, September14, 1976. Its publication roused a storm of protest both among Israelis and Arabs.

(182) Arab media immediately began debating the likelihood of an Israeli preemptive strike.

(183) Al-Sadat, Address to People's Assembly, November 26, 1977; FBIS, November 28, 1977.

(184) See Middle-East Intelligence Survey, September 16-30, 1978, for the same analysis in the context of the Camp David Accords; also,

Arnaud de Borchgrave's report of additional secret agreements concerning: a) strategic redeployment of Egyptian forces from the Sinai to the Libyan border; b) expansion of cooperation between Israeli and Egyptian intelligence; c) strengthening of the Egyptian army to meet threats from Russia and its clients in the Arab world (summarized in Arab Press Service, October 17, 1978).

(185) Ibid.; but see also the extremely perceptive analysis of Ze'ev Shif, "War is the Last Option," Ha'aretz, January 1, 1978; JPRS, March 23, 1978: "On the eve of the Yom Kippur War Egypt estimated that its situation could not be worse and that a military action would help it in any event....Today the situation is the opposite. Sadat and egypt have much to lose if they wage a war prematurely with an army that is not properly prepared...The gains of October are the apple of the Egyptian nation's eye.... It is no wonder that the first goal dictated to the Egyptian army since that time has been 'preserving the achievements of the October War.'... Sadat was also afraid that a war might break out by mistake, owing to the sensitivity of Israel...or because the new Israeli government that dame to power in June would take advantage of the situation in order to take revenge on Egypt (sic: note the revenge motive, projected from Arab cultural values) and to restore Israel's gains. Before his visit to Jerusalem...Begin seemed to them (sic: the Egyptians) the most extreme and aspiring to expansion.... Such a situation obliged Sadat to take quick and unusual action...."

(186) MENA, June 24, 1978 summary of al-Sadat's interview on Italian TV, June 21, 1978, FBIS, June 26, 1978. Unlike some of his earlier diplomatic initiatives, al-Sadat was careful to size Begin up before making any conciliatory gesture. The actual decision to act was made after a number of contacts. According to Time, August 14, 1978, pp. 21-22, one key factor was an Israeli intelligence warning to al-Sadat in July 1977 that he along with leaders of the Sudan and Saudi Arabia was a target of projected Libyan sponsored coups. This warning says Time gave Arab leaders the feeling that Begin might have the stature to make significant concessions in peace negotiations (a stature that Rabin lacked). Further Arab/Israeli contacts followed, with King Hasan II of Morocco functioning as an intermediary.

Al-Sadat says that the key figure was President Ceausescu of Romania: "Before thinking of the initiative or its form or anything else, I made a trip to Romania (sic: in late October 1977) to meet Ceausescu and ask him two questions. The first question was: Does Mr. Begin really want peace? I knew that Begin was his (sic: Ceausescu's) friend and had visited him...The second question was: If Mr. Begin really wants peace, is he strong enough to be able to go along with me to achieve peace? ... When I asked Ceausescu these two questions, his reply to the first was that Begin really wanted peace. As for the second, he told me that he had come to the conclusion that Begin really wanted peace and could ratify peace and present it to the Israeli people and the Knesset....After meeting with Ceausescu, I left for Iran. On the way from Romania to Iran – while flying over Turkey to be exact - I started having the first notions about the initiative..." MENA, summary of interview on Italian TV, June 24, 1978, FBIS, June 26, 1978.

(187) The "Begin Plan" was first released in the Israeli press on December 15, 1977 (see The Jerusalem Post, December 15, 1977; it was presented to the Knesset on December 28, 1977; and instantly raised a storm of protest concerning perceived (and real) Israeli plans to fill the West Bank with settlers. This settlement policy remains one of the most touchy issues in the peace negotiations. See: SWASIA, May 21, 1976; US Senate Committee on the Judiciary, The Colonization of the West Bank Territories By Israel (Washington: GPO, 1978); David G. Nes, "The US and Israeli Settlements," Middle East International, no. 82, April 1978, pp. 11-12; Sarah Graham Brown, "Settlements: Israel's Political Dilemma," Arab Report and Record, August 1-15, 1978, pp. 579-582.

(188) Time, August 14, 1978, p. 20.

(189) Chief of Staff Eytan interview on Israeli Radio, May 11, 1978, FBIS, May 12, 1978: "The state of Israel occupies an area. It is not located in the air or in the sea. The territories are supremely important and the state of Israel will not be able to survive without territories....We had better stop being naive. Despite the modern means of war, the IDF will not be able to defend the state and maintain it as an independent state without Judea and Samaria, without the Golan Heights...."

(190) Excerpted in Arab Press Service, May 29, 1978.

(191) This renewal of threats was promptly commented on in the Israeli press, adding to the cycle of threat and counterthreat.

(192) On one hand, this was incredibly bad timing; but on the other hand, the Syrians appeared to be escalating their activities in Lebanon - an escalation which, in connection with the extension of Syrian air defenses into Lebanon, could have been the prelude to an attempt to break up the Camp David talks by setting up a Syrian/Israeli confrontation in Lebanon.

(193) Arab Press Service, September 4, 1978.

(194) Ibid.

(195) Kerr in Berlino, p 31. For Israeli perceptions see Wagner, Brecher, especially pp. 229-250; Amos Perlmutter, "Begin's Strategy and Dayan's Tactics: The Conduct of Israeli Foreign Policy," Foreign Affairs, 56: 2 (January 1978): 357-72.

(196) Texts of the Camp David accords are available in a variety of sources. See The Camp David Summit, Department of State Publication 8954 (Near East and South Asian Series 88) (Washington: Office of Public Communication, Bureau of Public Affairs, September 1978) for a full text of the agreements plus other material.

(197) Al-Asad's comments were made in the course of an address to the leaders of the Steadfastness Front meeting in Damascus, excerpted in the San Francisco Chronicle, September 21, 1978.

(198) In this connection, al-Nahar, November 20, 1973, claimed that Saudi Arabia would not have used the oil weapon if Arab forces had scored a decisive victory.

(199) An-Nahar Arab Report, October 7, 1974. Other factors influencing an Israeli decision to preempt would be:

1. Declining military situation to the point where Israeli military superiority is seriously jeopardized as a consequence of Russian arms shipments to Arab states (or Arab purchase of significant quantities of Western arms).

2. Declining international situation; especially Western recognition of the PLO; coupled with increasingly anti-Israeli United Nations moves.

3. Increased terrorist activities within Israel, coupled with West Bank unrest.

4. A feeling that the United States was about to shift its Middle East policies and force unacceptable concessions on Israel.

Once this escalatory process reaches the state where threats and counterthreats start reinforcing each other, the chances for either the United States or Russia to successfully intervene to prevent war become next to nil. In fact, such intervention would probably be counterproductive: Both sides are exceptionally suspicious of super power intentions. The Arabs, as noted, are still bitter over United States and Soviet activities in 1967; a bitterness which was reinforced in 1973. The Israelis initially appeared to think that the October attack was, in part, the outcome of United States/ Russian collusion.

For the Syrians to move with any chance of success, they would have to garner both Egyptian and Jordanian support. At present, this does not seem forthcoming: The Egyptians have not received sufficient Soviet arms to permit successful operations; the Jordanians have not solved their lack of air defense; nor have they really anything to gain by joining in the fighting.

The patterns of escalation would be different, depending on which side proposed to attack. For the Arabs, a situation of no warning, no propaganda build up is critical. This would permit larger Arab forces in being to engage smaller Israeli units, recreating the 1973 scenario. For the Israelis, some dramatic escalation is necessary so that they can justify mobilizing reserves, thus recreating the 1967 scenario. See: Steven J. Rosen, What a Fifth Arab-Israeli War Might Look Like: An Exercise in Crisis Forecasting (Los Angeles: Center for Arms Control and International Security, 1977).

Index

About the Author

JOHN W. AMOS holds a Ph.D. in political science from the University of California at Berkeley and a J.D. from the Monterey College of Law. He teaches Middle Eastern politics at the Naval Postgraduate School in Monterey, California. In addition, he has spent time in the Middle East, including residence at the American University of Cairo, studying Arabic. Dr. Amos has written and lectured extensively on Middle East politics.

Pergamon Policy Studies